Students' Basic
Grammar of Spanish

W9-BBN-913

Students' Basic Grammar of Spanish

Rosario Alonso Raya
Alejandro Castañeda Castro
Pablo Martínez Gila
Lourdes Miquel López
Jenaro Ortega Olivares
José Plácido Ruiz Campillo

First edition: august 2009

© Los autores y Difusión.
Centro de investigaciones
y publicaciones de idiomas, S.L.
c/Trafalgar, 10, entlo. 1ª
08010 Barcelona
Tel. (+34) 93 268 03 00 / Fax (+34) 93 310 33 40
editorial@difusion.com
www.difusion.com

Authors: Rosario Alonso Raya
Alejandro Castañeda Castro
Pablo Martínez Gila
Lourdes Miquel López
Jenaro Ortega Olivares
José Plácido Ruiz Campillo

English edition: Bob Flory, Brian Brennan

Coordination and design: Jordi Sadurní i Ventura
Educational consultant: Agustín Garmendia
Documentation: Olga Mias

Illustrations: David Revilla

Photographs: Pág. 36, 102, 106, 116, 140,
146, 153, 217, 234, 237: autores y familiares.
Pág. 44: 1: Rasmus Evensen, Didvision, 2: John
Pring (john@johnpringphotography.com), 3: Franco
Giovanella (franco@revistanossa.com.br), 4: San San
(san@loungefrog.com). Pág. 110: João Estevão A.
de Freitas (jefras@netmadeira.com). Pág. 193: Real
Ibérico, Consorcio para la Promoción del Jamón
Ibérico Español.

Printed by Novoprint

ISBN: 978-84-8443-635-5
Depósito legal: B-31720-09

Queda prohibida cualquier forma de reproducción,
distribución, comunicación pública y transformación
de esta obra sin contar con autorización de los titulares
de la propiedad intelectual. La infracción de los derechos
mencionados puede ser constitutiva de delito contra
la propiedad intelectual (arts. 270 y ss. Código Penal).

difusión
Centro de
Investigación y
Publicaciones
de Idiomas, S. L.

Acknowledgements

People who search for grammar books are looking for a map to an unknown land. They are pirates, astronauts, crazy adventurers bent on discovering an entire universe. There is nothing more daring nor more generous than learning a language. It is an endless undertaking, overwhelming and worthy of heroes. Like Adam in the Garden of Eden, you start to name the world afresh. If you have got this far and are holding this grammar book in your hands, you are already one of us. Thank you.

Thanks also to our students of the Centro de Lenguas Modernas of the University of Granada, of the Escuela Oficial de Idiomas-2 in Barcelona and of the Instituto Cervantes in Istanbul, all expedition members on the Safari of learning, for it is really they who have shown us where the sinking sands, the oases, the caves and volcanoes, the wild watercourses and the cool pools of crystal-clear waters are. For it is they who have guided and corrected the lines on this map with the lucid testimony of their grammatical adventures. For it is not they who have learned from this grammar book: it is this grammar book that has learned from them.

Thank you to the inventive genius of David Revilla our artist; thank you for the support, patience and help of Agustín Garmendia and the Difusión production team, thank you for the sensitivity, involvement, understanding and enthusiasm of Jordi Sadurní.

And, above all, we thank our long-suffering families and our temporarily abandoned friends for having put up with our long absences in imaginary countries.

From our long stays in the region of the pronouns, in the jungle of the subjunctive, and on the planet of qué, quién, cuál or in the castle of ser and estar, we returned worse off than we had set out, more aware of the bottomless chasms and on the verge of being seduced by the dark side of the force. Adoración, Alicia, Ángela, Antonio, Arnau, Carlota, Carmen, Carmen, Francisca, Gloria, Héctor, Inma, Juani, Jesús, Lucía, Lucía, Lucía, Luis, Mari, Mopa, Plácido, Puchi, Rosario, Samuel, Teo, Xavier, your contributions are priceless.

The map makers

Index

SECTION 5   Prepositions

Introduction

What is the SBGS?

The *Students' Basic Grammar of Spanish* (SBGS) is a grammar book for students of Spanish at elementary and intermediate level (A1-B1 in the Common European Framework of Reference) who are looking for clear, useful and practical descriptions of how the Spanish language works.

The key features of the SBGS are:

- It explains the grammatical system of Spanish bearing in mind – both in the grammatical explanations and in the exercises – the meaning and real life use of the various resources.
- It uses a series of design elements (drawings, colours and other graphic conventions) in a consistent way to support and facilitate the understanding of grammatical features.
- It presents a thorough, workable and reliable description of the grammar features: the student will be able to apply the rules given in a meaningful and systematic way, as well as to limit possible mistakes.

Structure of the SBGS

The book is organised into seven sections that cover the main aspects of the grammatical system of Spanish: NOUNS AND ADJECTIVES; DETERMINERS; PERSONAL PRONOUNS; VERBS; PREPOSITIONS; SENTENCES, AND SPELLING.

These sections contain various units that alternate between grammar feature explanation files (accompanied by numerous examples and illustrations) and high-impact exercises (that allow the student to practise and check their assimilation of the previous explanation). The different units are linked together by thorough cross-referencing.

The SBGS also provides an answer key, conjugated verb tables (where you will find the conjugations of regular verbs and an alphabetical list of the most common irregular verbs), and a thematic index to make it easier to use and check up on the different grammatical features.

Grammar instructions and language examples

The grammar instructions (with few technical terms and a vocabulary adapted to the level), the diagrams, the language examples that accompany the explanations and the drawings have all been devised with the students' perspective in mind. We have taken into account their need to learn grammar in a way that bears in mind the systematic nature of the language, as well as the communicative value of the elements dealt with.

Exercises

The SBGS offers a wide range of exercises involving repetition, interpretation and production, as well as correction of the mistakes common to students' interlanguage, which have been designed and organised in such a way as to make the work interesting, enjoyable and meaning-focused. The exercises present the language in real and credible contexts and in this way, aid a better comprehension of the way the grammar works. The exercises have closed answers, so that the student can control their own learning by checking the answer key in the back of the book.

Educational contexts

As the SBGS is so easy to use and consult, it is an efficient tool for self-study for students at levels A1-B1. However, the SBGS is also useful for students with a more advanced level of Spanish, thanks to the fresh way in which the most common and frequently occurring problems in Spanish have been formulated, and for the reliability and usefulness of the rules provided.

Furthermore, the SBGS can be used regularly in class both to present and to go more deeply into the various grammatical areas and practise them in the classroom context focusing on group correction, which can encourage thoughtful grammatical study.

How the SBGS is organised

■ The SBGS is divided into seven SECTIONS which cover the main aspects of the grammatical system of Spanish. Each SECTIONS and the **units** it consists of are colour coded:

■ The units are organised in **subsections**, where you will find **explanations** and **exercises**:

Number and **name** of the unit. The **colour** shows you which section it belongs to.

Each **subsection** is indicated by a letter (**A, B, C**...) and provides **explanations** with **examples** and **exercises**. The subsections are listed in the index.

The **explanations** with **examples** are presented in boxes with a cream-coloured background.

Following each explanation, there are **exercises** (transformations, comprehension and production) so you can start to use the features that you are studying. You can check your own answers by looking in the **answer key**.

In the **exercises**, the language forms are connected to the **meaning**: you should pay particular attention to the context and meaning of the sentences and texts.

11

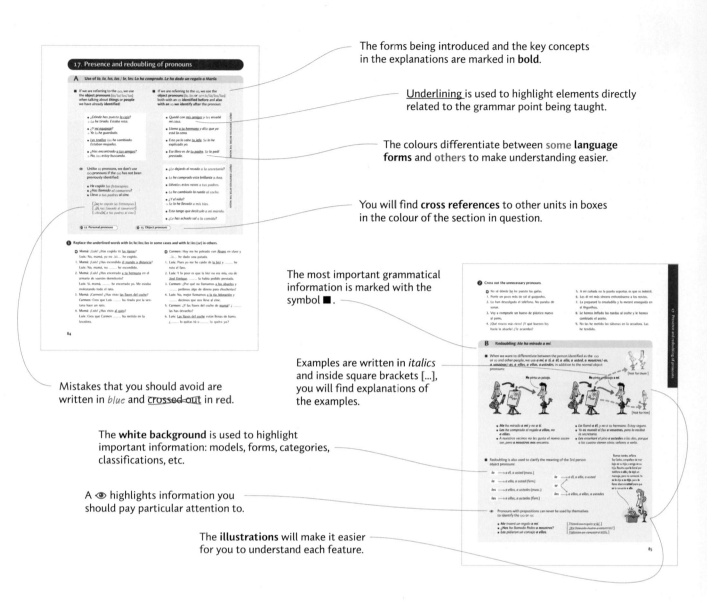

The forms being introduced and the key concepts in the explanations are marked in **bold**.

<u>Underlining</u> is used to highlight elements directly related to the grammar point being taught.

The colours differentiate between some **language forms** and others to make understanding easier.

You will find **cross references** to other units in boxes in the colour of the section in question.

The most important grammatical information is marked with the symbol ■.

Examples are written in *italics* and inside square brackets [...], you will find explanations of the examples.

Mistakes that you should avoid are written in *blue* and ~~crossed out~~ in red.

The **white background** is used to highlight important information: models, forms, categories, classifications, etc.

A ⊚ highlights information you should pay particular attention to.

The **illustrations** will make it easier for you to understand each feature.

■ In addition to the units, this grammar book also provides you with **conjugated verb tables**, an **answer key** and a complete **thematic index**:

The **conjugated verb tables** show conjugation models for regular verbs and the most common irregular ones. The stressed syllable is <u>underlined</u>. Irregularities are shown in **green**.

With the page, unit and exercise numbers you can look up the answers in the exercise **answer key**.

The **thematic index** will help you to easily find any feature dealt with in this grammar book.

Nouns and Adjectives

¡Camarero!
¡Hay un mosca en mi sopa!

No es **un** mosca, es **una** mosca.

¡Caramba, qué vista tiene usted!

1. Noun. The gender of things

In Spanish, **all nouns always have a gender**, which can be **masculine** or **feminine** (there are no neuter nouns). It is very important to know if a noun is masculine or feminine, as all the elements that refer to it (articles, adjectives, demonstratives...) have to take the same gender:

- *Éste es el <u>edificio</u> más alto de esta ciudad.*
- *Toma otra <u>taza</u>, porque ésa está rota.*

A General rule: *el edificio*, *la casa*...

■ Nouns that refer to things (physical objects, ideas, feelings, etc.) **have only one gender**: some are always masculine and others are always feminine. Generally, the masculine ends in *-o*, and the feminine ends in *-a*:

MASCULINE IN -*o*:	*el bolígraf**o**, el diner**o**, el edifici**o**, el florer**o**, el pañuel**o**, el vas**o**...*
FEMININE IN -*a*:	*la car**a**, la cas**a**, la mes**a**, la palabr**a**, la plaz**a**, la taz**a**, la ventan**a**...*

1 Connect each sentence to the object it refers to.

➲ Tengo dos así, rojos, muy parecidos a éstos. ———

1. Tienes que lavarlo, porque está un poco sucio.
2. No están mal, son bonitas, pero me parecen un poco caras.
3. La mía es más grande que la suya.
4. Éstos son muy baratos.

- casa
- pañuelos
- gafas
- vaso
- floreros

2 Write in the noun endings. They all follow the general rule.

➲ Carmela tiene el pel**o** muy negro y la car**a** muy blanca.

1. Nunca escribo con bolígraf.... azul o negro. Escribo con una plum.... de mi abuela que me gusta mucho.
2. Nuestro pis.... es bastante pequeñito, pero tenemos una cas.... en Asturias que es bastante grande y muy bonita.
3. ¿Quién es el marid.... más simpático del mundo? ¿Quién me va a hacer un regal.... precioso?
4. Los Martín son una famili.... muy numerosa. Son ocho hermanos, creo.

B Special rules: *el problema*, *la mano*...

■ There are a few **masculine nouns ending in -*a*** that don't follow the general rule (of these, the majority end in -*ema*):

MASCULINE IN -*a*:	*el clima, el día, el idioma, el mapa, el planeta, el programa, el sofá...*
	el esquema, el poema, el problema, el sistema, el tema...
	(PERO: *la crema*)

■ There are also a few **feminine nouns that end in -*o***:

FEMININE IN -*o*:	*la foto (fotografía), la mano, la moto (motocicleta), la radio...*

■ Nouns ending in *-aje* and *-or* are generally **masculine**:

-aje: el mas**aje**, el gar**aje**, el pais**aje**, el pas**aje**, el pe**aje**, el pot**aje**...	*-or*: el am**or**, el dol**or**, el err**or**, el ol**or**, el sab**or**, el terr**or**... (PERO: *una flor*)

■ Nouns ending in *-ción*, *-sión*, *-dad* and *-tad* are **feminine**:

-ción: la can**ción**, la rela**ción**, la traduc**ción**...	*-dad*: la bon**dad**, la ciu**dad**, la ver**dad**...
-sión: la expre**sión**, la pri**sión**, la televi**sión**...	*-tad*: la amis**tad**, la leal**tad**, la liber**tad**...

■ In all other cases, the gender cannot be told from the form of the word. Remember, however, that a dictionary will always tell you the gender of each noun:

nave. (Del lat. *navis.*) f. Emba
neral, barco. ‖ 2. Embarcac

MASCULINE

el café, el coche, el champú, el esquí, el hambre, el jersey, el pie, el sobre, el tabú, el taxi...

el árbol, el lápiz, el lavavajillas, el metal, el móvil (*teléfono móvil*), el microondas (*horno microondas*), el país, el papel, el paraguas, el salón, el sillón, el sol...

FEMININE

la clase, la carne, la fiebre, la frente, la gente, la llave, la muerte, la nave, la noche, la nube, la parte, la suerte, la tarde...

la cárcel, la cicatriz, la col, la crisis, la hipótesis, la imagen, la nariz, la sal, la sed, la síntesis, la tesis...

3 Which one is the odd one out?

➲ día, pentagrama, clima, plaza, idioma.   *(plaza is feminine and the other words are masculine.)*
1. mano, foto, brazo, moto, radio.
2. mapa, impresora, planeta, idioma, sofá.
3. problema, esquema, poema, crema, tema.
4. color, monedero, canción, sabor, paisaje.
5. garaje, libertad, prisión, expresión, ciudad.

4 Masculine or feminine? Put these nouns in the right box.

noche ✓ champú ✓ salón crisis luna sobre tesis taxi clase microondas
café tarde sal pie leche nariz árbol carne sol lavavajillas

Masculine

El champú,

Feminine

La noche,

5 Mark the correct form of the article.

I

Mariano:

He dejado el/la coche en el/la garaje
y he cogido el/la ordenador portátil.
Llego tarde al/a la clase de las siete.
Un beso.

II

Pepa:
Tienes el/la potaje en el/la microondas.
Compra el/la champú para el perro
y coge el/la paraguas, que llueve mucho.
¡Ah! Tienes que poner el/la jersey verde
en la secadora.
Gracias, cariño

III

José:
Tenemos un/una problema
con el/la moto.
Y, además, no encuentro los/las llaves.

IV

Ana:
Hay un/una error en
el/la traducción del señor Weiss.
¿Puedes corregirlo?, por favor.

V

Raquel:
¿Hablamos mañana del/de la tema
de la reunión? ¿Me llamas tú?
Dime algo pronto.

VI

Jacinto:
¿Puedes ir tú a Yanokea a recoger
el/la sillón? Tenemos un/una reunión
que me ocupará un/una parte
del/de la tarde.
Llámame al/a la móvil.

6 The singer-songwriter Joan Ismael Lumbago has written this song. Finish it with the articles *el/la*.

Vendo una canción

➜ Compra ..*el*.. lápiz de labios;
1. compra .... móvil,
2. compra .... crema antiarrugas,
3. compra .... paraguas para la lluvia.
4. Pero nunca podrás comprar ....
   poema que no te escribí,
5. ni .... amor que nunca sentí,
6. ni .... olor
7. de .... flor que nunca te di.
8. Compra .... champú,
9. compra .... jersey,
10. compra .... sal,
11. compra .... papel.
12. Pero nunca podrás comprar .... beso
13. en .... frente al empezar .... día,

14. ni .... sabor
15. de .... noche del verano que termina.
16. Compra .... café;
17. compra .... reloj,
18. compra .... leche,
19. compra .... col.
20. Pero nunca podrás comprar .... tarde
    en que nos conocimos,
21. ni .... paisaje,
22. ni .... planeta en que tú y yo vivimos.
23. Si no amas .... libertad,
24. .... vida,
25. .... canción que te canto,
26. .... nube al pasar...,
    ¿qué podrás amar?

2. Nouns. The gender of people and animals

A General rule: *doctor, doctora*...

- Nouns that designate people or animals generally have **two forms**: one **masculine** and another **feminine**. The masculine is the basic form (the form that appears in the dictionary).

- Generally, if the masculine ends in the vowel -*o*, the feminine is made by **changing** this vowel for an -*a*; if the masculine ends in a **consonant**, the feminine is made by **adding** an -*a*:

MASCULINE IN -*o*	FEMININE IN -*a*
el chico, un gato	*la chica, una gata*

MASCULINE IN **CONSONANT**	FEMININE IN **CONSONANT** + -*a*
un doctor, un león	*una doctora, una leona*

- 👁 With some nouns ending in -*e* the feminine is also made by changing this vowel for an -*a*: *el jefe/la jefa; el nene/la nena; un presidente/una presidenta*. (BUT: *el/la paciente, el/la teniente, el/la vidente*...).

---

1 Link the sentences and underline the gender markers that help you to decide. Look at the example.

➲ La president<u>a</u>
de la comunidad de vecinos... ——
1. Mi peluquera...
2. Mi psicólogo...
3. Mi ginecóloga...
4. Mi jefe...
5. Mi vidente...
6. Mi profesora de español...
7. Mi panadero...

a. es muy comprensivo, pero habla poco con sus empleados.
b. es expert<u>a</u> en energías alternativas y, por eso, tenemos energía solar en el edificio.
c. es extraordinario. Con él me ha tocado dos veces la lotería.
d. es muy nervioso. En la terapia, él habla más que yo.
e. es un artista. Hace unos bollos integrales riquísimos.
f. está loca. Ayer vino a clase vestida de gitana.
g. es muy moderna. Peina muy bien.
h. es fantástica y trata muy bien a las pacientes.

2 Complete as in the example.

➲ El marido de mi hermana es mi cuñado y la mujer de mi hermano es mi cuñad*a*... .

1. Mi abuelo paterno se fue a Cuba con mi abuel...... . Y allí se casaron.

2. Tengo muchos primos: diez primos y siete prim...... .

3. La verdad es que tengo más amigas que amig...... .

4. Mi padre tiene dos hermanas y dos herman...... . Así que, por su parte, tengo cuatro tíos.

5. No, mi madre no tiene hermanos. Sólo tiene herman...... . Tres, sólo mujeres.

6. Tengo dos hijos gemelos. La parejita: un niño y una niñ...... .

B Special rules for the gender of people: *marido, mujer*...

■ In some cases there is a different word for each sex:

> un **hombre**/una **mujer**   el **padre**/la **madre**

👁 Some words have a special ending for the feminine:

> el actor/la ac**triz**   el emperador/la empera**triz**   el alcalde/la alcald**esa**

■ In other cases there are nouns that have **a single form for both sexes** (like those ending in -*ante* or -*ista*), and the words that refer to them (articles, adjectives etc.) are used in the masculine or feminine, depending on the gender of the person:

> **el/la** amante/cant**ante**/estudi**ante**...
> art**ista**/social**ista**...
> cónyuge/mártir/testigo...

- • *Paca Nela es una <u>artista</u> muy conocida.*
- ○ *Sí, pero Camilo Décimo también es **un** <u>artista</u> muy conocido, ¿o no?*   [*Un artista*]   *a*

---

3 Complete the sentences with words from the box. In some cases you will have to repeat words. There may be several correct answers.

> | hombre | mujer | marido | padre | madre | hermano | hermana | hijo | hija |

➡ El ...*hombre*... con el que estoy casada es mi ...*marido*... .

1. El .... de mi .... es mi abuelo.
2. La .... de mi .... es mi abuela.
3. La .... con la que estoy casado es mi ....
4. La .... de mi .... es mi tía.
5. Mi .... es la nieta de mis padres.

6. El .... de mi .... es mi tío.
7. El .... de mi .... es mi suegro.
8. La .... de mi .... es mi suegra.
9. Mi .... es el nieto de mis padres.
10. Mi mujer es la madre de mi única ....
11. Mi marido es el padre de mi único ....

4 The children of the Escuela Futurible already know what they want to be when they grow up, but they don't know the names of the jobs. Why not help them out as in the example? Bear in mind that there are both boys and girls.

> | pintor ✓ | cantante | profesor | periodista | taxista |
> | pianista (x2) | actor (x2) | policía | veterinario | futbolista |

➡ Adela quiere pintar cuadros. Quiere ser ..*pintora*..... .

1. Pablo quiere tocar el piano y dar conciertos. Quiere ser ....
2. Irene también quiere tocar el piano y dar conciertos por todo el mundo. Quiere ser ....
3. Javier quiere meter a los ladrones en la cárcel. Quiere ser ....
4. Elvira quiere conducir coches por la ciudad. Quiere ser ....
5. Carmen quiere dar clases. Quiere ser ....
6. Miguel quiere escribir en los periódicos. Quiere ser ....
7. Arturo quiere cantar. Quiere ser ....
8. Elena quiere actuar en el teatro. Quiere ser ....
9. David quiere ser como Antonio Banderas. Quiere ser ....
10. Mateo quiere curar animales. Quiere ser ....
11. Encarnita quiere jugar al fútbol. Quiere ser ....

¿Y tú qué quieres ser de mayor?

C Special rules for the gender of animals: *toro, vaca*...

■ In the same way as with nouns that refer to people, in some cases there is a different word for each gender:

> el *caballo*/la *yegua*   el *toro*/la *vaca*

👁 There are some words with special endings for the feminine:

> el *gallo*/la *gallina*   el *tigre*/la *tigresa*

■ Many words for animals have **a single form**, for the masculine and feminine:

el *buitre, calamar, caracol, cocodrilo, dinosaurio, jabalí, mejillón, pulpo...*

la *almeja, cigüeña, codorniz, gamba, hormiga, jirafa, mosca, tortuga...*

👁 **el** *cocodrilo hembra* [✗ *cocodrilo*]
la *jirafa macho* [✗ *jirafa*]

---

5 Classify these animal names according to their gender. Look up the ones you don't know in a dictionary.

> jirafa   perro ✓   mosca ✓   tortuga   tigre   gato   pulpo ✓   cerda   vaca ✓
> cocodrilo   perra ✓   gallina   cerdo   toro ✓   dinosaurio   caballo   calamar
> yegua   tigresa   gata   hormiga   caracol   mejillón   gamba   gallo

Male/female marker: (-o/-a or other endings)	A different word for each gender	Unchanging feminine	Unchanging masculine
		mosca	*pulpo*
perro / perra	*toro / vaca*		

---

6 In the Zoo Penco there are too many animals. Males and females should not be together, so two new keepers have to classify the animals. Complete as in the example.

➔ Ayudante 1: ¿Esto qué es?, ¿ *un oso o una osa* ?

Ayudante 2: Ni idea. ¿Y esto qué es?, ¿ *un pingüino macho o un pingüino hembra* ?

1. Ayudante 1: ¡Qué difícil!, ¿esto es .... ?

2. Ayudante 2: Y yo qué sé. Y esto, ¿es .... ?

3. Ayudante 1: Anda que esto, ¿qué será?, ¿ .... ?

4. Ayudante 2: Esto parece más fácil, pero no lo sé. ¿Qué es?, ¿ .... ?

5. Ayudante 1: Esto sí que es verdaderamente imposible. ¿Es .... ?

6. Ayudante 2: Este trabajo es una locura. ¿Qué será esto?, ¿ .... ?

3. Noun. Number

In Spanish, apart from gender (masculine and feminine), nouns also have number (singular or plural). The number indicates the **quantity** of objects that the noun refers to. The **singular** is the basic form (the form that appears in the dictionary), whereas the **plural** is always indicated by at least a final -s.

- ● ¿Has traído el coche?
  [*Coche* is singular: it refers to **just one** thing.]

- ● ¿Cuántos coches tienes?
  [*Coches* is plural: it refers to **several** things.]

A   Forming the plural: *mapa*, *mapas*; *país*, *países*...

■ When the **singular ends in a vowel**, the plural is formed by adding a final -*s*:

SINGULAR IN -*a, -e, -i, -o, -u*:	mapa	sofá	clase	café	bici	israelí	moto	tabú
PLURAL IN -*s*:	mapas	sofás	clases	cafés	bicis	israelís	motos	tabús

■ When the **singular ends in a consonant**, the plural is formed by adding -*es*:

SINGULAR IN -*d, -j, -l, -n, -r, -s, -z*:	pared	reloj	árbol	cajón	botón	motor	país	pez
PLURAL IN -*es*:	paredes	relojes	árboles	cajones	botones	motores	países	peces

👁 Words ending in an accented -*í* and -*ú* can also form the plural by adding -*es*:

> israelí → israelís/israelíes
> tabú → tabús/tabúes

👁 If the singular ends in an unstressed vowel (with no accent) + -*s*, the plural does not change (note that the accent falls on the underlined vowels):

> *el/los*: abrebot<u>e</u>llas, abrel<u>a</u>tas, cumple<u>a</u>ños, ju<u>e</u>ves, lavavaj<u>i</u>llas, micro<u>o</u>ndas, par<u>a</u>guas, sacac<u>o</u>rchos...

> *la/las*: cr<u>i</u>sis, t<u>e</u>sis ...

■ When the **singular ends in -*y***, the plural is formed with an -*s* in words of foreign origin (the -*y* is treated as an -*i*). For Spanish words ending in -*y* (very few), the plural is formed with -*es*:

> jersey → jerséis
> penalti (penalty) → penaltis...

> rey → reyes
> ley → leyes...

1 **How many are there?**

➲ Tres flor.*es.*

1. Dos pe.....

2. Dos so.....

3. Dos rel.....

4. Cinco bot.....

5. Dos jer.....

2 **Here is a page from the diary of a six-year-old girl. Complete the plurals of the words in the text.**

Mis padres no me dejan pintar las ➲ pared*es*, ni escribir en sus (1) papel....., ni coger las (2) sarten...., ni los (3) tenedor...., ni apagar y encender las (4) luc.... cuando yo quiero. Además, sólo puedo usar (5) lápic....: los (6) bolígrafo.... y los (7) rotulador.... están prohibidos. Tampoco me dejan subir a los (8) árbol...... ¿Cuándo comprenderán que los niños de seis años ya no somos unos (9) bebé....?

3 **Bea and Miguel have just got married and have been given lots of presents. However, some of them are duplicated so they have decided to pass them on to other friends. Which present does each friend get?**

➲ Alejandro necesita una máquina para lavar los platos: un *lavavajillas* .

1. A Rafa le hace falta una cosa para no mojarse cuando llueve: un ....
2. Adoración quiere un electrodoméstico para lavar la ropa: una ....
3. Iñaqui necesita algo para abrir botellas: un ....
4. Joaquín quiere un mueble para sentarse a ver la tele: un ....
5. Julia quiere alguna cosa para adornar las paredes de la casa: un ....
6. Lola necesita un aparato para preparar café: una ....
7. Lucía necesita algo para abrir las latas: un ....
8. María quiere algo para calentar rápidamente la comida: un ....

2 lavavajillas ✓
4 abrelatas
2 lavadoras
2 sofás
6 abrebotellas
3 cafeteras
6 cuadros
2 microondas
4 paraguas

B   **Special cases: *la gente, las gafas.***

■ **Uncountable** nouns (referring to things you cannot count) are used in the **singular** to talk about the **thing in general** or an **unspecified amount**.
When the plural is used it is to talk about **different types** or **various units** of the same thing:

> *agua, arroz, carne, luz, madera, música, pan, papel, pescado, plástico, té, vino...*

SINGULAR	• ¿Tú tomas **vino** en las comidas?	[Wine, a type of drink.]
PLURAL	• Aquí hay muchos **vinos** de calidad.	[Different types of wine.]
	• Si me tomo tres **vinos**, me mareo.	[Several glasses of wine.]

■ Some nouns in the singular refer to groups with various members, but their concordance is singular:

> *la familia, la gente, el público...*

● En España **la** <u>gente</u> come mucho, ¿no?
  [*La gente come* ✗ *mucho.*]

■ Other nouns are normally used in the plural:

> **las** gafas, **las** tijeras, **los** zapatos...
> **unos** pantalones, **unas** pinzas,
> **unos** prismáticos...

● *Esas* <u>gafas</u> *de sol* **son** *nuevas, ¿verdad?*
● *¿Le gustan estos* <u>pantalones</u>? **Son** *italianos.*

4 **Singular or plural? Choose the most appropriate form.**

↪ Me gusta España porque tiene mucha luz / ~~muchas luces~~. Es un país fantástico.

1. ¿Has visto la luz / las luces de ese árbol de Navidad? Sí, allí, mira.

2. Esta sopa necesita más agua / aguas. Está muy espesa.

3. Nunca más voy a comer carne / carnes. A partir de ahora seré vegetariana.

4. Una mancha de vino / vinos es muy difícil de quitar. Siempre queda un poco.

5. ¿Qué tipo de té / tes compramos? ¿O prefieres manzanilla?

5 **Was the singer José Plácido Domingo a success or a failure? Identify the reaction of each group and underline what has helped you find it.**

↪ <u>La</u> gente... ——————— a. estab<u>a</u>, en general, encantad<u>a</u>.

1. Sus amigos...   b. esperaba atenta el final del concierto.

2. Sus seguidoras...   c. estaban muy interesadas.

3. El público...   d. salió muy contento.

4. La policía...   e. aplaudieron entusiasmados.

6 **Rosa had an awful morning, when everything went wrong. Read about what happened and complete as in the example.**

↪ El gato le ha roto dos jarrones. Sólo le queda un
  .*jarrón* .

1. Ha quemado dos pasteles de queso. Sólo le queda un .... para el postre.

2. Sin darse cuenta, ha tirado tres peces por el desagüe. Ya sólo le queda el .... azul.

3. Ha quemado dos jerséis con la plancha. Afortunadamente tiene otro ....

4. Ha estropeado casi todas las luces de la casa. Únicamente funciona la .... del pasillo.

5. Tenía hambre y se ha comido diecinueve canapés. Sólo le queda un .... para la cena.

7 **Maxitim department store is running a special two-for-the-price-of-one offer.**

¡¡GRAN OFERTA!!   ¡¡REGALAMOS EL DOBLE!!   ¡¡GRAN OFERTA!!

POR LA COMPRA DE:	LE DAMOS:	POR LA COMPRA DE:	LE DAMOS:
↪ Un kilo de arroz...	*Dos kilos de arroz* .	3. Unas cortinas de baño...	....
1. Un reloj de pared...	....	4. Unas bragas de algodón...	....
2. Un abrelatas...	....	5. Un paraguas...	....

4. Adjective

Adjectives are used to talk about the qualities of the objects we name when we use nouns:

un <u>chico</u> **guapo**   una <u>gata</u> **cariñosa**   una <u>casa</u> **grande**   una <u>idea</u> **interesante**

A   Gender: *guapo, guapa; interesante...*

Cambian

■ Some adjectives have **one form for the masculine and another for the feminine**. The masculine is the basic form (the form that appears in the dictionary).
If the masculine ends in *-o*, the feminine is formed by **changing** this *-o* for an *-a*.
If the masculine ends in *-or*, or in a *stressed vowel* (a vowel that is accented) + *n*, an *-a* is added.

-o		**-o̶ -a**	
guapo	● ¿Verdad que mi <u>novio</u> es guapo?	guapa	● ¿Verdad que mi <u>novia</u> es guapa?
italiano	● Ese <u>señor</u> parece italiano.	italiana	● Esa <u>señora</u> parece italiana.
largo	● A mí me gusta más el <u>pañuelo</u> largo.	larga	● A mí me gusta más la <u>chaqueta</u> larga.

-or		**+ -a**	
hablad**or**	● <u>Pepe</u> no es muy hablad**or**, ¿verdad?	hablad**ora**	● <u>Pepa</u> no es muy hablad**ora**, ¿verdad?
trabajad**or**	● Pues <u>Javier</u> es muy trabajad**or**.	trabajad**ora**	● Pues <u>Lucía</u> es muy trabajad**ora**.

-stressed vowel + n		**+ -a**	
catal**án**	● <u>Josep</u> es catal**án**.	catalana	● <u>Montserrat</u> es catalana.
holgaz**án**	● <u>Luis</u> es muy holgaz**án**. No hace nada.	holgazana	● <u>Ana</u> es muy holgazana. No hace nada.
llor**ón**	● El <u>niño</u> no es llor**ón** y duerme mucho.	llorona	● La <u>niña</u> no es llorona y duerme mucho.

👁 The adjectives *mayor, menor, mejor, peor, superior, inferior*... never change gender:

● Éste es mi <u>hermano</u> **mayor** y ésta mi <u>hermana</u> **menor**.   ● Mira, esa <u>cafetería</u> es **mejor** que aquélla.

No cambian

■ Other adjectives, however, *have a single form for both masculine and feminine*. These adjectives may end in:

-a, -e, -i, -u, -ista or *consonante* (*-l, -n, -r, -s, -z*)

belga, hipócrita, lila, malva, persa...	● <u>Ella</u> es belga y <u>él</u> es canadiense, ¿no? ○ No, al revés: <u>ella</u> es canadiense y él es belga.
amable, estadounidense, fuerte, pobre, verde...	● La <u>situación</u> de la economía es muy preocupante, pero el <u>paro</u> es aun más preocupante.
cursi, iraní, marroquí, hindú, zulú...	● Tengo alumnos de muchos sitios. Hay una <u>chica</u> marroquí, <u>otra</u> hindú y un <u>chico</u> iraní.
pacifista, progresista, socialista...	● Raúl es un <u>hombre</u> muy pesimista. Su <u>novia</u>, sin embargo, es bastante optimista.
azul, principal, joven, familiar, cortés, gris, feliz...	● Siempre va vestida del mismo color. Hoy lleva una <u>falda</u> azul y un <u>jersey</u> también azul.

👁 Adjectives of **nationality or origin that end in a consonant** form the feminine by adding an -*a* to the masculine:

-l:	*español → española*
-n:	*alemán → alemana*
-s:	*francés → francesa, inglés → inglesa, japonés → japonesa, portugués → portuguesa*
-z:	*andaluz → andaluza*

1 Pablo, his friend Lourdes and his cousin Javier are looking for a boyfriend or girlfriend who is just like them. What should their partners be like?

Pablo es...	Ella debe ser...	Lourdes es...	Él debe ser...	Javier es...	Ella debe ser...
➲ hablador	..*habladora*.....	6. ecologista	....	12. nervioso	....
1. cariñoso	....	7. tímida	....	13. fuerte	....
2. vago	....	8. alegre	....	14. optimista	....
3. guapo	....	9. trabajadora	....	15. inteligente	....
4. superficial	....	10. independiente	....	16. feo	....
5. dormilón	....	11. frágil	....	17. pedante	....

2 Think about the way the adjective is formed: which is the odd one out?

➲ inglés, francés, español, alemán, <u>estadounidense</u>   *(Es el único adjetivo de género invariable.)*

1. iraní, italiano, israelí, iraquí, marroquí
2. feliz, alegre, impaciente, contento, amable
3. optimista, pesimista, ecologista, socialista, lista
4. azul, joven, hermosa, débil, feliz
5. alemán, charlatán, llorón, joven, dormilón

B Number: *guapos, guapas, interesantes...*

■ Adjectives form the plural by following the same rules as nouns:

SINGULAR ENDING IN ***vowel*** + -*s*	*habladora → habladoras* *importante → importantes* *simpático → simpáticos*
SINGULAR ENDING IN ***consonant*** + -*es*	*azul → azules* *hablador → habladores* *feliz → felices*

⤷ 3. Noun. Number

👁 The -*z* becomes a -*c*

3 Mineral water makes Casimiro feel bad. It makes him see double. What does he see in the following cases?

Cuando...	Casimiro ve...
➲ hay un coche verde...	.*dos coches verdes*....
1. hay una niña cursi...	....
2. hay una persona feliz...	....
3. hay un niño llorón...	....
4. hay una camisa gris...	....
5. hay un hombre hablador...	....
6. hay una mujer interesante...	....

C   Concordance: *Unos amigos griegos*.

■ The adjective has to have the same gender and number as the noun that it refers to. The form of the adjective can show which noun we are talking about:

- *Mañana vienen a casa unos <u>amigos</u> griegos.*
- ¿*Aquéllos tan simpáticos de la fiesta de Inés?*

- *Esa <u>película</u> es muy buena pero un poco larga.*
- *Sí, larga, lenta y pesada...*
- *Pero interesante.*

- *Bueno, mira: ahí hay chaquetas y <u>vestidos</u>. ¿Te decides por algo?*
- *El amarillo no está mal.*

[we know that *amarillo* is referring to a <u>vestido</u> (masculine) because the adjective is in the masculine.]

■ When we are talking about **masculine** and **feminine**, nouns at the same time, the plural takes the **masculino**:

- *Mira ese <u>jersey</u> y esa <u>chaqueta</u>. Me encantan, pero son carísimos.*

- *Rafael tiene cuatro hermanos: tres <u>chicas</u> y un <u>chico</u>. Los cuatro son muy simpáticos.*

4 Where are your things from? Pay attention to the gender and number.

| alemán ✓ | español | francés | escocés | finlandés | senegalés | japonés |
| colombiano | cubano | italiano | chino | turco | suizo | estadounidense |

➲ Si tu coche es de Alemania, es ...*alemán*......

1. Si tu ordenador es de EEUU, es ....
2. Si tus pizzas son de Italia, son ....
3. Si tu café es de Colombia, es ....
4. Si tu alfombras son de Turquía, son ....
5. Si tu puros son de Cuba, son ....
6. Si tu cámara de fotos es de Japón, es ....

7. Si tu whisky es de Escocia, es ....
8. Si tu cacao es de Senegal, es ....
9. Si tus relojes son de Suiza, son ....
10. Si tu sauna es de Finlandia, es ....
11. Si tus vinos son de España, son ....
12. Si tus perfumes son de Francia, son ....
13. Si tu porcelana es de China, es ....

5 José is poor and Alejandro is rich. Who will the beautiful Claudia marry? Help her to look at the consequences of each choice.

➲ Con José tendrá que llevar ropa...
1. Con Alejandro podrá llevar ropa...

- a. elegante
- b. caras
- c. barata
- d. viejo

4. Con José tendrá un coche...
5. Con Alejandro podrá tener un coche...

- a. grande y rápido
- b. vieja y fea
- c. lujosos y bonitos
- d. lento e inseguro

2. Con José vivirá en una casa...
3. Con Alejandro vivirá en una casa...

- a. pequeña y ruidosa
- b. amplia y luminosa
- c. grande y cómodo
- d. pequeñas y oscuras

6. Con José tendrá que ir a hoteles...
7. Con Alejandro podrá ir a hoteles...

- a. impresionantes
- b. incómodos
- c. sucia
- d. estupendas

6 Choose an appropriate ending for each sentence and complete with the correct gender and number markers.

➲ El gazpacho y la ensalada de pasta...
1. Mi padre y mi madre...
2. La ciudad y los alrededores...
3. La radio y la prensa...
4. La moto y la bicicleta...
5. El tabaco y el alcohol...
6. Ten cuidado, el suelo y la bañera....

son más ecológic..... . Los coches contaminan mucho.
están buenísim.*os*. . Pruébalos.
están mojad..... y te puedes caer.
son medios más objetiv..... que la televisión.
son asturian..... , pero yo nací en Madrid.
son muy mal..... para la salud.
son maravillos..... , aunque hace mucho frío.

D   Adjective after noun: *¿Vino tinto o vino blanco?*

■ In Spanish adjectives can come **before** or **after** the noun.

■ **After** the noun, adjectives are normally used to differentiate between the object we are talking about and other objects:

- Al final, ¿vas a comprarte la <u>mesa</u> **cuadrada** o la **redonda**?
- Su <u>oficina</u> está en un <u>edificio</u> **alto**, **vanguardista**, realmente **precioso**.
- Entonces, ¿qué prefiere?, ¿la casa, el <u>apartamento</u> **grande** o el <u>apartamento</u> **pequeño**?
- Es una <u>chica</u> **inteligente**, **comprensiva** y **educada**. No como su hermana.

Some types of adjective will usually **only come after** the noun, such as those that express:

Colour:	un <u>coche</u> **azul** (negro, rojo, blanco, verde...)
Form:	un <u>objeto</u> **cuadrado** (redondo, alargado, rectangular, ovalado...)
State:	una <u>caja</u> **abierta** (cerrada, llena, rota, vacía...)
Type, origin:	un <u>tema</u> **español** (familiar, internacional, socialista, portátil...)

7 Put the words into the right order in the following sentences.

➔ [un/sueco/Tengo/novio] *Tengo un novio sueco* .... y, por eso, este verano me voy a Estocolmo.

1. [abierto/un/Hay/grifo] .... Se oye el agua.

2. [el/Ponte/naranja/jersey] .... Te queda muy bien.

3. [cenicero/vacío/Dame/un] .... Éste está lleno de colillas.

4. [la/sucia/Trae/ropa] .... Voy a poner una lavadora.

5. [botella/llena/Mete/la] .... en el frigorífico y saca la vacía, por favor.

6. [coche/familiar/un/Es] .... Caben por lo menos ocho personas.

7. [universitaria/Vivo/una/en/residencia] .... , pero el año próximo quiero ir a un piso.

8. [vuelos/Los/internacionales] .... salen de la terminal B.

9. [un/sobre/Está/en/cerrado] .... porque es confidencial.

E   Adjective before noun: *Mi apartamento pequeño / Mi pequeño apartamento*

■ **Before** the noun, adjectives are normally used to **highlight a quality** of the object, but not to differentiate it from others:

Mira, Alicia, la <u>ballena</u> **grande** es la mamá y la <u>ballena</u> **pequeña**, el hijo.

Sorprendentemente, la **gran** <u>ballena</u> se alimenta de las **pequeñas** <u>criaturas</u> del plancton.

Ballena

Mamífero
Vive en el mar
Color oscuro
Grande (hasta 30 metros)

Before the noun you can use adjectives like: *largo-corto, frío-caliente, pequeño-grande, fuerte-débil, lejano-cercano, ligero-pesado, rápido-lento, ancho-estrecho, claro-oscuro, viejo-joven, alegre-triste, blando-duro, áspero-suave, bonito-feo*, etc. All of these have a relative meaning: something is *big* or *small*, *fast* or *slow*, etc., depending on what we compare it with.

8 Decide whether in these sentences, the adjective is highlighting a quality of the object or being used to differentiate the object from others of the same type.

	Distingue	Destaca
⮕ La **vieja radio** todavía funciona.	....	........√.........
⮕ Dame las **zapatillas viejas**, por favor.	........√.........	....

1. Mire, verá, tengo una **pequeña duda** sobre el precio del hotel.
2. Pásame el **destornillador pequeño**, por favor, éste no me sirve.
3. Nos ha tocado el **camarero lento** y hemos tardado tres horas.
4. Amelia dio un **lento paseo** por la ciudad y se fue al hotel.
5. Desde la puerta se veía un **ancho pasillo** que llegaba a la terraza.
6. Es mejor que entres por el **pasillo ancho**, así no te pierdes.
7. Un plato de **frías lentejas** le esperaba en la mesa.
8. Tráete las **cervezas frías** a la mesa, por favor.

■ With adjectives of relative meaning (*largo/corto, oscuro/claro*, etc.), the position before the noun is an option that depends on the **style of writing** (journalistic, literary, etc.). Adjectives whose meaning is not relative (colour, shape, state, etc.) are only used before the noun in **poetic style**:

EVERYDAY LANGUAGE	FORMAL LANGUAGE	POETIC LANGUAGE
• *La niña de los ojos azules estaba al fondo de una habitación oscura.*	• *La niña de los ojos azules se hallaba en una **oscura** habitación.*	• *Al fondo de una **oscura** habitación brillaban los **azules** ojos de la niña.*

---

9 This newspaper article has mistakes: there are adjectives (the example and five more) that should come after the noun. Cross them out and write the correct version.

El presidente de Gililandia ha emprendido un largo viaje diplomático por lejanos países, acompañado de su ministro de ~~exteriores~~ asuntos y su joven esposa. Durante los últimos días se han producido ya numerosas anécdotas. En la inauguración de un industrial edificio, por ejemplo, alguien entregó a la esposa del presidente un redondo objeto que resultó ser un japonés reloj de pared. Pero también ha habido malos momentos. Cuando iban en el oficial coche a la inauguración de un nuevo edificio por una estrecha carretera de montaña, el coche del presidente sufrió un pequeño accidente y choco contra una vacía casa.

asuntos exteriores ....

....

....

....

....

....

■ Adjectives that indicate the order of a series (*primero, segundo, último, siguiente, próximo, futuro, nuevo, antiguo*, etc.) normally go *before* the noun:

- *Ana fue mi **primera** novia.*
- *Todo esto lo veremos en la **siguiente** reunión.*
- *Sólo te pido una **segunda** oportunidad.*
- *Esto son cosas del **antiguo** régimen.*

But when we are talking about the floors of a building or the chapters of a book, these adjectives are also used **after** the noun:

- ***Segunda** planta / Planta **segunda***
- ***Primer** capítulo / Capítulo **primero***

They are always used **after** when we are talking about kings, popes, etc.:

Juan Carlos I [primero]   *Pablo VI* [sexto]   *Isabel II* [segunda]

10 This is the story of Catalina Jiménez de Hurtado's loves and losses. Put the adjectives from the boxes in the right places.

➡ Mi .._primer_... marido .... era arquitecto. Construía .... chalés .._adosados_.. . Se cayó de un décimo piso. (1) Mi .... marido .... era marinero. Se ahogó frente a (2) las .... costas ....(3) Mi .... marido .... era piloto. Se estrelló en (4) una .... carretera .... (5) Mi .... marido .... era bombero. Murió apagando (6) una .... barbacoa .... (7) Mi .... marido .... será (8) el .... presidente .... del gobierno. No sé qué ocurrirá. Por el momento ha abierto varias cuentas a mi nombre en (9) un .... banco .... Últimamente dice que no se encuentra muy bien.

| cuarto |
| próximo |
| primer ✓ |
| segundo |
| futuro |
| tercer |

| adosados ✓ |
| secundaria |
| familiar |
| caribeñas |
| suizo |

F *Un gran problema / Un problema grande*

■ The adjectives *grande*, *bueno*, *malo*, *primero* and *tercero* have another form –a shortened form– when they come before and are referring to a singular noun:

CHANGE IN BOTH MASCULINE AND FEMININE

| **Grande**: | *un coche* **grande** / *un* **gran** *coche* | *una casa* **grande** / *una* **gran** *casa* |

CHANGE ONLY IN MASCULINE

Bueno:	*un amigo* **bueno** / *un* **buen** *amigo*	(*una amiga buena / una buena amiga*)
Malo:	*un día* **malo** / *un* **mal** *día*	(*una noche mala / una mala noche*)
Primero:	*el capítulo* **primero** / *el* **primer** *capítulo*	(*la sección primera / la primera sección*)
Tercero:	*el piso* **tercero** / *el* **tercer** *piso*	(*la planta tercera / la tercera planta*)

DO NOT CHANGE WITH PLURAL NOUNS

Las **grandes** *casas, los* **grandes** *coches, las* **buenas** *amigas, las* **malas** *noches, los* **primeros** *capítulos...*

11 Correct the underlined words in the text below.

Sé que es una ➡ b̶u̶e̶n̶ ..buena.. chica, y la quiero, pero tengo miedo. Mi (1) primer .... novia se marchó a las Bahamas el día de la boda. De la segunda prefiero no hablar, por su culpa pasé (2) muy mal .... momentos. Ésta es mi (3) tercer .... novia y no quiero volver a pasar una (4) mal .... experiencia. El otro día me dio un (5) bueno .... susto. Me dijo: "Quiero casarme ya: estoy segura de que serás un (6) grande .... padre." Yo le dije: "Para mis padres será una (7) grande .... alegría porque tienen muchas ganas de tener nietos", pero la verdad es que estaba un poco asustado. Al final cambió de opinión y, por ahora, seguimos siendo una (8) buen .... pareja de novios. Novios que están buscando un (9) bueno .... piso con un (10) bueno .... precio...

Determiners

5. Articles: *un, el, ø...*

A   Forms

■ Articles are classified as indefinite or definite. The forms of each group change according to the gender and number of the noun:

	INDEFINITE		DEFINITE	
	MASCULINE	FEMININE	MASCULINE	FEMININE
SINGULAR	**un** amigo	**una** amiga	**el** gato	**la** gata
PLURAL	**unos** niños	**unas** niñas	**los** chicos	**las** chicas

👁 When the noun is not mentioned, *un* becomes **uno**:
¿Tienen helados? ¿Me da un de fresa?
                             uno

■ After the prepositions *a* and *de*, the article *el* joins together with them to form one word:

> *a + el = **al***
> *de + el = **del***

● *¿Puedes bajar un momento **al** supermercado, por favor?*
● *¿Vas a ir al concierto **del** viernes?*

👁 **With proper nouns (names)**, the article and the preposition **do not join together**:

● *Mañana me voy **a El** Cairo.*
● *Esta noticia es **de** El País. Un periódico muy serio, ¿no?*

■ When we have to use the article with a **feminine singular noun** that starts with a **stressed *a*-** we use ***el/un*** if there are no other words between the article and the noun:

> *el agua, un águila, el ala, el alma, un arma, el área, el arte, un aula, un ave, el hada, el hambre...*

But these nouns are feminine and therefore, in all other cases the concordance is feminine:

With adjectives and other determiners:	With singular articles separated from the noun:
El agua fresca, un hambre tremenda, esa águila, algunas armas...	*La última águila, **la** misma arma, una gran aula...*
With plural articles:	
*Las águilas, **las** artes, **unas** aulas...*	

---

1 The detective Rodrigo Trigo reaches the scene of a crime and notices many suspicious things. He goes to fetch the police and when he returns, all that is left are some objects on the floor. Help him complete his report.

Cuando entré en la habitación, vi a:

➔ ...*Un*..... profesor de español lleno de sangre, en el suelo.

1. .... alumnas que parecían muy nerviosas, escondiendo .... papeles.

2. .... hombre joven que llevaba .... tijeras en la mano.

3. .... mujer con .... vestido rojo, muy tranquila.

4. .... niño llorando delante de .... caja llena de regalos.

Cuando volví, sólo encontré:

➔ ..*La*.. sangre *del*.. profesor.

5. .... papeles de .... alumnas.

6. .... tijeras de .... hombre joven.

7. .... vestido rojo de .... mujer.

8. .... caja que pertenecía a .... niño.

2 **Complete with the correct forms of the article. If necessary, also complete the gender and number of the adjective.**

➲ Vamos a buscar ..*un*.. aula libre para hacer el examen.

1. Tengo .... hambre que me muero.

2. Mira en .... últim.... aula en la que has estado a ver si encuentras el bolígrafo.

3. Papá, ¿ .... hadas existen?

4. En la puerta de su chalé hay .... águila horroros.... , de piedra y de madera. No he visto una cosa más fea en mi vida.

5. .... hada buena convirtió a la rana fea en un príncipe guapo.

6. .... aguas de este balneario son excelentes para el riñón.

7. Mató al policía con .... mism..... arma que había utilizado para matar a su novio.

8. Mamá, ¿dónde está .... alma?

9. Coge la olla por .... dos asas. Si no, se te va a caer.

B Uses: *Toma una carta / Toma la carta*

■ We use *un*, *una*, *unos*, *unas* to refer to something that is not particularly easy for the listener to identify among other objects of that type because, for example:

I. There are various people or things of the same type.
- *Éste es Pedro, un hermano de María.*
  [We say *un hermano* because María has several brothers.]
- *Necesito un móvil. Es para un regalo.*
  [We are not looking for a particular mobile phone. There are many that would do.]

■ We use *el*, *la*, *los*, *las* to indicate that we are referring to something that is identifiable to the listener among all other objects because, for example:

I. There are no other people or things the same.
- *Éste es Pedro, el hermano de María.*
  [We say *hermano* because María has only one brother.]
- *Tengo el móvil roto. ¿Ustedes arreglan?*
  [The person is talking about their own mobile phone.]

Hay **una** carta para ti.

...**una** carta

La carta es para ti.

...**la** carta

II. We are talking about this person or thing for the first time.
- *También vienen unos amigos de Ana: Pedro y Juan.*
  [They are specific friends, but they are not identifiable because we have not spoken about them before.]

II. We have talked about the person or thing before.
- *Entonces, no cabemos en mi coche: Rosa, Jesús, Cati, tú, los amigos de Ana y yo. Somos muchos.*
  [We are talking about some friends we have already identified because we have spoken about them before.]

...**una** carta y un paquete...

He recibido **una** carta y un paquete.

La carta es de mi prima.

...**la** carta

3 Carmen and Lucía have to do an assignment for class. Do you know what are they talking about? Read the sentences and link each one to the corresponding explanation.

➲ a. **Carmen:** Un amigo de Julia nos puede ayudar.   a. Lucía y Carmen ya han hablado del amigo de Julia.

b. **Carmen:** El amigo de Julia nos puede ayudar.   b. Lucía y Carmen no han hablado antes de ese chico.

1. a. **Lucía:** He traído unos libros que había en casa.   a. Carmen ya sabe de qué libros habla Lucía.

b. **Lucía:** He traído los libros que había en casa.   b. Carmen no sabe de qué libros habla Lucía.

2. a. **Carmen:** Tenemos que entregar un trabajo el martes.   a. Hablan del trabajo que están haciendo.

b. **Carmen:** Tenemos que entregar el trabajo el martes.   b. Hablan de otro trabajo distinto.

3. a. **Lucía:** Un profesor de Filosofía me ha dejado esta revista.   a. Hablan de otro profesor de Filosofía.

b. **Lucía:** El profesor de Filosofía me ha dejado esta revista.   b. Hablan de su profesor de Filosofía.

4. a. **Carmen:** ¿Me dejas el bolígrafo?   a. Lucía tiene sólo un bolígrafo.

b. **Carmen:** ¿Me dejas un bolígrafo?   b. Lucía tiene tres bolígrafos.

5. a. **Lucía:** Ha llamado Luis, un chico de Barcelona.   a. Lucía y Carmen han hablado muchas veces de Luis.

b. **Lucía:** Ha llamado Luis, el chico de Barcelona.   b. Carmen no conoce a Luis.

4 Look carefully at the context and write in the appropriate article.

➲ En el salón de casa de Lucía hay sólo un cuadro en la pared.

Carmen: Me gusta mucho _el_.... cuadro del salón. Siempre he querido tener _una_.. pintura como ésa.

1. Carmen y Lucía han terminado su trabajo de Historia.

Lucía: ¿Puedo llevarme .... trabajo a casa para leerlo otra vez? Si quieres, puedo hacer .... copia.

2. Carmen llega con una tarta muy grande. Lucía no sabía nada.

Carmen: Mira, mi madre ha hecho .... tarta. ¿Te apetece .... trozo?

3. Carmen ha cortado la tarta. Hay un trozo grande y otro pequeño.

Lucía: A mí dame .... trozo pequeño.

4. Las dos chicas conocen a toda la familia de Julia.

Lucía: Voy a ir al cine con .... amigos. Bueno, tú los conoces, son Paco y Pepe, ... hermanos de Julia, ¿te acuerdas?

5. Carmen tiene un reloj, como todas sus compañeras de piso.

Carmen: ¿Sabes qué? Pues que he perdido .... reloj.

Lucía: Bueno, yo he visto .... reloj pequeño encima de la cama, no sé si es .... tuyo.

5 Read the start of this story and mark whether the statements that follow are correct.

Leopoldo Luis II, un rey de Gantea (➲), salió el sábado de paseo en un caballo de la reina (1). En la puerta un soldado lo despidió. Al llegar a un río (2), cruzó por un puente y se encontró con los duendes del agua (3) y éstos le dijeron: Va a venir un príncipe (4) del país vecino (5), se va a enamorar de tu mujer y va a huir con ella. El rey no creyó nada de las palabras de los duendes, cruzó el puente (6) y volvió a palacio. Pero en la puerta estaba el soldado (7) que, muy nervioso, le dijo: Majestad, la reina se ha ido.

➲. En Gantea sólo hay y ha habido un rey.   Sí (No)

1. La reina tiene varios caballos.   Sí   No

2. Leopoldo probablemente iba a ese río todos los días.   Sí   No

3. Seguramente Leopoldo no había oído hablar de esos duendes.   Sí   No

4. Este príncipe viene mucho a Gantea.   Sí   No

5. Gantea tiene frontera con cinco países.   Sí   No

6. El mismo puente de antes.   Sí   No

7. Es el mismo soldado que lo había despedido.   Sí   No

C   ¿*Un* or *el* or *ø*?: *Tenemos teléfono. Suena un teléfono. He roto el teléfono.*

■ When we use a noun **without an article** (*article Ø*), we are not referring to any particular object:

■ When we use a noun **with an article** (*un...* or *el...*), we are referring to individual objects: indefinite (*un...*) or definite (*el...*):

¡Tenemos **Ø** teléfono!

¡Suena **un** teléfono!

Suena **el** teléfono.

[They are not talking about a particular object, but about a means of communication.]

[They are talking about a particular but indefinite telephone: it cannot be identified.]

[They are talking about a particular and definite telephone: it can be identified.]

- *La forma más rápida y sana de ir es en <u>bicicleta</u>.*
- *Están recibiendo clases de <u>guitarra</u>.*
- *He hecho un avión de <u>papel</u>.*
- *En ese restaurante hay que llevar <u>traje</u> y <u>corbata</u>.*

- *Voy a comprarme **una** <u>bicicleta</u> para hacer ejercicio.*
- *He visto **una** <u>guitarra</u> ideal para ti.*
- *Apunta esto en **un** <u>papel</u>.*
- *Voy a comprarme **un** <u>traje</u> y **una** <u>corbata</u> en las rebajas.*

- *Antes de salir tengo que arreglar **la** <u>bicicleta</u>.*
- *Acuérdate de guardar **la** <u>guitarra</u> en su sitio.*
- *Éste es **el** <u>papel</u> que decía.*
- *Me he manchado **el** <u>traje</u> y **la** <u>corbata</u> con salsa de tomate.*

■ When we are talking about an indefinite amount of something and we don't need to specify or identify any concrete object, we use the noun without an article (**Ø**):

COUNTABLE NOUNS (in the plural)	UNCOUNTABLE NOUNS (in the singular)
• *¿Venden ustedes **alfombras**?* • *Mi vecino arregla **ordenadores**.*	• *Si vas al súper, compra **aceite** y **café**.* • *No, no tengo **dinero**. Lo siento.*

6 **Cross out the incorrect option and match.**

➔ ¿Me pasas Ø/**un** tomate, por favor? ——————— a. Voy a hacer una ensalada.

1. ¿Le has echado sal a Ø/**el** tomate?

2. ¿No te gusta la salsa de Ø/**un** tomate?

3. Máximo, no puedes recibir a los invitados en Ø/**un** pijama.

4. Máximo, echa Ø/**el** pijama a la lavadora.

5. Máximo, voy a comprarte Ø/**un** pijama.

6. Me duele Ø/**el** pie derecho.

7. Está cerca: vamos a Ø/**el** pie.

8. He visto Ø/**un** apartamento precioso.

9. He perdido la llave de Ø/**el** apartamento.

10. He conocido a mi profesor de Ø/**un** piano.

11. Cierra Ø/**el** piano con cuidado.

b. Ahora hay rebajas.

c. Ponte unos pantalones y una camisa.

d. Está muy soso.

e. Hace quince días que no te lo quitas.

f. Es casera. La he hecho con aceite de oliva.

g. Me he dado un golpe jugando al fútbol.

h. Puedes hacerte daño en los dedos.

i. No puedo entrar. ¿Puedo quedarme en tu casa?

j. Creo que voy a alquilarlo.

k. Me gusta. Tiene mucha paciencia.

l. Así hacemos ejercicio.

7 **Complete with the words in the box. Some need to be made plural.**

| pila | dinero | tomate ✓ | aspirina | agua | huevo | café |

Cariño, tienes que hacer tú la compra. Acuérdate de traer ➡ ...*tomates*....... para el gazpacho, que no hay, y también compra (1) .... para la tortilla. Necesitamos (2) .... mineral y (3) .... descafeinado. La linterna no tiene (4) .... , así que trae también. Y tienes que ir a la farmacia. Hacen falta (5) .... Por cierto, saca (6) .... del banco. Yo no tengo.

D Generalising: *A los españoles les gusta el café...*

■ When we are referring to a whole class of people or things we use *el, la, los, las*:

COUNTABLE	UNCOUNTABLE
Singular (the class in general)	**Singular**
Plural (all members of the class)	

- *El <u>perro</u> es el mejor amigo **del** <u>hombre</u>.*
  [Dog and man as classes of living beings.]
- *Los <u>niños</u> siempre dicen la verdad excepto cuando mienten.* [All children, in general.]
- *Las <u>mujeres</u> todavía no tienen las mismas oportunidades que **los** <u>hombres</u>.*
  [All women and all men, in general.]

- *Aquí **la** <u>gente</u> va mucho al cine.*
  [Everybody, in general.]
- *No me gusta **el** <u>café</u>, me pone nerviosa.*
  [Coffee, in general.]

■ When we are talking about an object as a representative of its class, in other words, any object of a particular class, we use *un, una* (and *unos, unas* for nouns that do not take the singular):

- *¿Qué es **un** <u>flexo</u>?*
- ***Un** <u>flexo</u> es **una** <u>lámpara</u> de mesa para leer.*

- ***Unos** <u>prismáticos</u> permiten ver de lejos.*
- ***Un** <u>médico</u> tiene que saber tratar a los pacientes.*

El hombre **es** un mamífero.

👁 In Spanish, when we generalize, the **subject** of the sentence must have **an article**:

- ***Un** <u>niño</u> necesita espacio para jugar.* [N~~iño~~ necesita espacio para jugar.]
- ***La** <u>naranja</u> tiene vitamina C.* [~~Naranja~~ tiene vitamina C.]
- *Me encanta **el** <u>café</u>.* [Me encanta ~~café~~.]
- ***Los** <u>delfines</u> son muy inteligentes.* [~~Delfines~~ son muy inteligentes.]

8 Look carefully at the underlined words and classify the sentences into type I, II or III.

I. Toda una clase de objetos o personas.	II. Cualquier objeto o persona de una clase.	III. Una cantidad indeterminada de objetos o personas.

➦ a. <u>Los colchones</u> de agua son muy relajantes ..!...

   b. Evidentemente, prefiero dormir en <u>un colchón</u> a dormir en el suelo. ..!!...

   c. Tenemos <u>colchones</u> de látex, de algodón y de muelles. .!!!.

1. a. Se venden y alquilan <u>apartamentos</u>. Razón: 031676742. .....

   b. <u>Los pisos</u> en este barrio son muy caros. .....

   c. <u>Un apartamento</u> suele ser más pequeño que un piso. .....

2. a. <u>Los dentistas</u> ganan mucho dinero. .....

   b. Lo conocí en un congreso de <u>dentistas</u>. .....

   c. <u>Un dentista</u> no debe comer ajo antes de la consulta. .....

3. a. Linus sólo bebe <u>vino tinto</u>. .....

   b. A estas horas, <u>un vino tinto</u> es mejor que un refresco. .....

   c. Perdona, pero <u>el vino tinto</u> es mucho mejor que el blanco. .....

4. a. ¿Tú sabías que <u>los murciélagos</u> son ciegos? .....

   b. ¿Has comido <u>murciélagos</u> alguna vez? Están buenísimos. .....

   c. Ese perro es más feo que <u>un murciélago</u>. .....

5. a. No tengo <u>hijos</u> pero tengo sobrinos. Sobrinas, en realidad, porque son todas chicas .....

   b. <u>Los hijos</u> dan muchos disgustos. .....

   c. Tener <u>un hijo</u> es lo mejor que te puede pasar en esta vida. .....

9 Complete with the words from the box using the appropriate article when necessary.

kioscos ✓   agua   helados   carrito   hormigas   abanico   cajeros   ratón   té   café   mostaza

➦ ..*Los kioscos*.... son tiendas en las que se venden periódicos y revistas.

1. En España, ... es algo muy típico en verano. Además es perfecto para el calor.

2. .... automáticos son máquinas para sacar dinero con tarjeta.

3. ¿Esas albóndigas llevan .... ?

4. Me encantan .... tanto en verano como en invierno. La pena es que engordan mucho.

5. .... van siempre en fila unas detrás de otras.

6. .... es tan excitante como ....

7. Se lo aseguro: .... inalámbrico no da problemas. Es más caro, pero funciona mucho mejor.

8. Pues .... es una cesta con ruedas para hacer la compra en los supermercados.

9. No te puedes duchar. No hay ....

10 Jerónimo and Alablanca sometimes forget to use the articles in Spanish. Correct what they say by adding *el, la, los, las,* where necessary.

➦ Cuando hojas caen, indios cazan y recogen muchos frutos. Ahora árboles están tristes porque hace frío.
las hojas caen...; los indios cazan...;
los árboles están...

1. Después de cazar bisontes, nos duelen mucho piernas, pero gran jefe Halcón Maltés nos da zumo de uvas y aspirinas. ....
....

2. Indios quieren ser como oso y águila y respetan a seres vivos. Sólo cazan animales para comer. ....
....

3. A indios les gusta fumar hierba seca con anciano más viejo de tribu. ....
....

4. Para indios amor es sentimiento más hermoso. Indios aman naturaleza y también a hombre blanco.
....
....

5. Indios hacen fuego y bailan danza de lluvia cuando llega primavera. ....
....

6. Todas primaveras osos bajan de montañas a río para pescar salmones. Indios aprenden mucho de ellos. ....

7. Hombres indios se pintan para guerra. Mujeres indias nunca se pintan. Les gusta paz. ....

E   *Uno alto, el de Soria, el que te dije...*

■ When it is clear what we are talking about, ***uno, una, unos, unas***
can be used without mentioning the noun to which they refer:

- *Pásame un* <u>boli</u>. ***Uno*** *de ésos.* ***Uno*** *rojo vale.*
- *Necesito* <u>tomates</u>. *Tráeme* ***unos*** *que hay en el frigo.*
- *¿Has visto mis* <u>cintas</u>? *Son* ***unas*** *con canciones de Prins.*
- *Estas* <u>camisas</u> *no están nada mal. Cómprate* ***una***.
- *Tengo varios* <u>amigos</u>, *pero sólo salgo con* ***uno***.

👁 The forms ***unos, unas*** are used by themselves only when they
refer to nouns that are not normally used in the singular (*unas
gafas, unos pantalones, unos prismáticos, unas tijeras...*):

- *Yo tengo varias* <u>tijeras</u>. *¿Te dejo* ***unas***?
- *No tiene* <u>prismáticos</u>. *Regálale* ***unos***.

■ The articles ***el, la, los, las*** can also be used without mentioning
the noun to which they refer, but only when they are followed by an
ADJECTIVE / ***de*** + NOUN / ***que*** + SENTENCE:

	ADJECTIVE	
El, la, los, las +	***de*** + NOUN	
	que + SENTENCE	

- *Sólo me está bien un* <u>traje</u>: *el negro.*
- *Esa* <u>mesa</u> *no está mal, pero me gusta más* ***la de*** *cristal.*
- *¿Quieres una* <u>tapa</u>? ***Las que*** *ponen aquí son muy buenas.*

11 Cross out the noun when it is not necessary and change *un* for *uno* as required.

➡ • Prueba un canapé.

    ○ Gracias, ya me he comido un~~o~~ ~~canapé~~.

1. ¡Qué horror! Se me han roto las medias. ¿Me prestas unas medias?

2. Estos sobres son pequeños. Mejor usamos los sobres amarillos, los sobres que están ahí.

3. • ¿Quieres una cerveza?

    ○ No, gracias, acabo de tomarme una cerveza.

4. • Me han regalado un reloj con alarma.

    ○ Pues yo tengo un reloj que tiene cronómetro.

5. • ¿Cuál de esas chicas es tu hermana?

    ○ La chica de las gafas, la chica alta, la chica que está de pie.

6. • Han venido unos amigos preguntando por ti.

    ○ Sí, ya lo sé. Son unos amigos que conocí en la discoteca.

7. • ¿Me pasas ese libro, por favor?

    ○ ¿Cuál? ¿El libro gordo? ¿El libro de física?

8. • ¿Ustedes han pedido un café?

    ○ Dos: yo un café sólo y él un café con leche.

12 These characters are the authors of this grammar book. Complete the sentences to find out who is who.

➡ Los que *llevan gafas* son Jenaro, Alex y Pablo.

1. El que .... es Jenaro.

2. La de los .... es Rosa.

3. El de la .... es Alex.

4. El .... es José Plácido.

5. El del .... es Pablo.

6. La que .... es Lourdes.

7. Las .... son Lourdes y Rosa.

llevan gafas ✓
guapísimas
delgado
lleva peluca
guantes largos
pistola
pañuelo de lunares
está cantando

6. Demonstratives: *este, ese, aquel... esto, eso, aquello...*

A   *Este libro*; *ese libro*; *aquel libro*.

■ Demonstratives can be feminine, masculine or neutral:

	SINGULAR			PLURAL		
MASCULINE	*este* libro	*ese* niño	*aquel* edificio	*estos* libros	*esos* niños	*aquellos* edificios
FEMININE	*esta* mesa	*esa* niña	*aquella* tienda	*estas* libretas	*esas* niñas	*aquellas* tiendas
NEUTRAL	*esto*	*eso*	*aquello*			

  👁 The **masculine** and **feminine** forms **agree with the noun they refer to in gender and number.**

■ Demonstratives are used to indicate things or people and identify them in terms of three different ideas of proximity:

Este indicates that the thing is in **the same space as the person speaking** (*yo, nosotros, nosotras*).

Ese indicates that the thing is in **a different but nearby space to the person speaking.**

Aquel indicates that the thing is in a **space that is different to and distant from the person speaking.**

Este gato

AQUÍ

Ese gato

AHÍ

Aquel gato

ALLÍ

- *¿Qué regalo quieres?: ¿**esta** pelota?, ¿**ese** cochecito?, ¿**aquella** muñeca?*

  [by saying *esta* we indicate a ball that is **here** (next to the person speaking); by saying *ese* we indicate a toy car that is **nearby**, not next to the person speaking, but not far away either) and by saying *aquella* we indicate a doll that is **over there** (a long way away from the person speaking).]

Esa camiseta te sienta estupendamente.

She says *esa* because she is talking about the T shirt of the person being spoken to.

■ To talk about **things that are in the personal space of the person we are talking to** (*tú, usted, ustedes, vosotros y vosotras*) we use *ese/-a/-os/-as* because we are talking about a space that is different to that occupied by the person speaking, but not far away:

- *Este bolígrafo no funciona, ¿me dejas ese rotulador?*

  [We say *este* because we are talking about the ballpoint we are using; and say *ese* to indicate the felt-tip that is near to the person being spoken to.]

1 Mª José is at a Japanese restaurant and she is very hungry. Complete what she says.

¡Qué rico está ➜ *este* .... atún y qué buenas están (1) .... gambas! ¡(2) .... tallarines están exquisitos y (3) .... salsa de soja es fantástica!

Y póngame también (4) .... salmón, (5) .... trucha, (6) .... sardinas y (7) .... mejillones.

Y, por favor, de postre, me trae (8) .... tarta, (9) .... bombones, (10) .... natillas, y (11) .... flan.

2 Write the number of the dialogue by the right picture.

➜ María: **Este** jersey es muy bonito.
Ana: Sí, y **estos** zapatos tampoco están mal.

1. María: Mira, **ese** jersey es precioso.
Ana: Un poco caro, ¿no? Mejor te compras **esos** zapatos.
María: Sí, o **esa** chaqueta marrón.

2. Ana: **Este** jersey es precioso, pero es carísimo.
María: Y **aquellas** chaquetas, ¿qué te parecen?
Ana: ¿Cuáles? ¿Las del fondo?

3. Ana: **Estos** zapatos son bonitos, ¿verdad?
María: Sí, están bien pero los jerséis me gustan más.
Ana: ¿**Esos** jerséis? A ver cuánto cuestan.

A ➜ ......

B ......

C ......

D ......

3 Look carefully at the context in which the sentences are spoken and underline the appropriate demonstrative.

➜ (Luis está leyendo un libro.)	Luis: <u>Este</u>/ese/aquel libro es fantástico. ¿Lo conoces?
1. (Luis y Pedro están en la cocina comiendo pasteles.)	Luis: ¿**Estos/esos/aquellos** pasteles los ha hecho tu madre? Están buenísimos.
2. (Pedro saca unas cervezas de la nevera. Luis está sentado en la mesa.)	Luis: No sé si **estas/esas/aquellas** cervezas estarán muy frías.
3. (Luis y Pedro están de excursión. Muy a lo lejos hay un pequeño bosque.)	Luis: ¿Qué tal si nos acercamos a **este/ese/aquel** bosque de pinos?
4. (Luis va con Pedro y señala a una chica que ven a mucha distancia.)	Luis: Mira, Pedro, **esta/esa/aquella** chica es Carmen, la que ha tenido trillizos.
5. (Pedro tiene unos discos en la mano.)	Luis: Si te gustan **estos/esos/aquellos** discos, puedes llevártelos.

B   Uses connected with time: *Este mes. Ese día. Aquel fin de semana.*

■ Demonstratives are also used to situate something in connection with time.

Este, esta, estos, estas are used to refer to the present as well as
the most immediate past and future:

  ● *Este* verano *ha sido un desastre;* **este** mes *está siendo
    espantoso, pero* **estas** Navidades *me voy a Cuba.*

Ese, esa, esos, esas can refer to the **future** or the **past**:

  ● *Del 1 al 8 de julio no trabajo. Y* **esa** semana
    me voy de vacaciones.   [The future week that has been identified.]
  ● *Ese* día *estaba muy cansado, por eso no te llamé.*   [That day in the past that we have spoken about.]

Aquel, aquella, aquellos, aquellas refer to a **distant past**:

  ● *Aquella* semana *fue la más feliz de mi vida.*   [That week, in the distant past, that we have spoken about.]
  ● *Aquel* novio *que tenías antes no me gustaba mucho.*   [A boyfriend I had in the past.]

4 Link each sentence to its other half.

  ⮕ Hace diez años vendí el Volvo 240.   a. Ese día tienes que estar aquí.
  1. Podemos ir pasado mañana si quieres.   b. Ese día supe que mi mujer estaba embarazada.
  2. Nos conocimos la Semana Santa del 87.   c. Me acuerdo porque aquellos días hizo
  3. Me caso el 15 de febrero.   un calor espantoso.
  4. Mi antiguo profesor de español   d. Esta semana no tengo mucho trabajo.
     era mucho mejor que el que tenemos ahora.   e. Aquel coche era fantástico, de verdad.
  5. Volví a casa el día de Navidad, después   f. Me encantaban aquellos estupendos
     de dos años trabajando en el barco.   ejemplos que ponía.

C   *Éste, ése, aquél...*

■ Demonstratives can be used **without mentioning the noun** to which they
refer, when it is clear what we are talking about. When this happens, we write
them with an accent (*tilde*) to show that they are pronouns:

  ● *Son preciosas* **estas** lámparas. *Me llevo* **ésta**,
    ésa, *y* **aquélla** *roja.*

  ● *Este* vaso *está limpio,*   ● *¿Cuál es tu* clase*?*
    pero **ése** *no.*   ○ **Ésa** *de la derecha.*

  ● *¿Te acuerdas de Raquel, la antigua* novia *de Rafa?*
  ○ *Sí, claro,* **aquélla** *sí que era guapa.*

5 What do the following demonstratives refer to?

⮕ Aquéllas me gustan más.	~~chaqueta~~	gafas	~~pantalones~~	~~caramelos~~
1. ¿Son éstos?	amigo	personas	chica	hombres
2. Déjame ésa.	hoja	libros	bolígrafo	plástico
3. Aquél era mucho más interesante.	película	novelas	discos	chico
4. Con éste es suficiente, gracias.	libreta	tijeras	papel	papeles
5. Ésos para ti, y éstos para mí.	reloj	silla	pendientes	monedas

D Neutral demonstratives: *¿Dónde pongo esto? No me digas eso. ¿Qué es aquello?*

■ Neutral demonstratives are always singular and are never used with a noun because there are no neuter nouns in Spanish:

	SINGULAR			PLURAL		
MASCULINE	*éste*	*ése*	*aquél*	*éstos*	*ésos*	*aquéllos*
FEMININE	*ésta*	*ésa*	*aquélla*	*éstas*	*ésas*	*aquéllas*
NEUTRAL	**esto**	**eso**	**aquello**			

■ The **neutral forms** of the demonstratives are used when we want to refer to something in relation to the ideas of proximity *aquí*, *ahí* and *allí* but we **do not know its name, its name is not important** , or **we are not talking about a physical object** (for example an event, a situation, what somebody said, etc.):

WE DO NOT KNOW
THE OBJECT'S NAME

¿Qué es **eso**?

● *¿Quieres un... ashtray? ¿Cómo se dice **eso** en español?*

[The speaker does not know the object's name.]

● *¿Has visto **eso**? Parece un ratón, ¿no?*

[The speaker doesn't know exactly what the thing is.]

[The speaker does not know what is inside a box covered in wrapping paper and so cannot refer to it with a noun.]

THE OBJECT'S NAME
IS NOT IMPORTANT

Toma, **esto**
es para ti.

● *Tengo que irme ya. ¿Puedes tú recoger todo **esto**?*

[All the things that have to be tidied up.]

● *Mira, **esto** lo pones encima del armario, **eso** dentro y **aquello** en la otra habitación.*

[Three things we identify by pointing a finger at them.]

IT IS NOT A PHYSICAL
OBJECT

¡Qué sorpresa!
Esto no lo esperaba.

● *No lo entiendo. Le he pedido perdón y sigue sin hablarme.*
○ *Es que **eso** no es suficiente.*

[The fact of saying sorry.]

● *Estábamos durmiendo y, de repente, oímos un ruido muy raro... **Aquello** no me gustaba nada...*

[The situation he is telling us about.]

● *Creo que voy a dejar este trabajo.*
○ *¿Por qué dices **eso**?*

[The words the other person has said.]

👁 **We do not use** these neutral forms to talk about **people** but use the masculine or feminine forms instead:

● *¿Quién es **ése**?* [*¿Quién es eso?*]
○ *Es mi padre.*

6 Victor has lost his memory and has great difficulty remembering the objects around him. Help him get it back by completing the spaces with demonstrative.

Están AQUÍ

- ¿Qué es ➡ ..*esto*..?
- ○ Son servilletas.
- ¿Y (1) .... tan raro?
- ○ Son tenedores y cuchillos y
  (2) .... que está aquí son
  cucharas. ¿No te acuerdas?

Están AHÍ

- ¿Qué es (3) .... que se
  mueve ahí?
- ○ No te preocupes. Son las cortinas.
- ¿Y (4) .... con tanto pelo
  que está ahí?
- ○ Es una alfombra. Y (5) ....
  de ahí debajo, también. Las compramos hace años.

Están ALLÍ

- Oye, ¿y (6) .... ? Parecen
  monstruos.
- ○ ¿Monstruos? Son las sombras de
  las plantas del jardín.
- ¿Y (7) .... tan peludo allí,
  al fondo? ¿Son alfombras?
- ○ No, Víctor, no. Son tus perros, Caín
  y Abel...

7 A tourist has just arrived in Spain. Complete the conversation between him (T) and a Spaniard (S) with the information in the box.

➡ T: (*Tiene una fruta en la mano que no conoce.*)

E: Granada. Es una fruta de otoño.

1. T: (*Señala un monumento que está bastante lejos.*)

   E: Es la Puerta de Alcalá. Es del siglo XVIII.

2. T: (*Está en una discoteca. Le gusta el ambiente,
   la música, la gente...*)

   E: Sí, está muy bien. Es el local de moda.

3. E: ¿Qué vas a tomar?

   T: (*Señala una comida que toman unas personas.*)

4. T: Yo no estoy acostumbrado a acostarme tan tarde.

   E: (*Comenta algo sobre esa costumbre en España.*)

5. T: (*Le da un regalo a su acompañante.*)

   E: Muchas gracias. Pero no tenías que regalarme nada.

6. T: Tengo 30 euros.

   E: (*Explica para qué puede servir ese dinero.*)

a. ¿Cómo se llama esto?

b. Pues eso, aquí, es bastante
   normal.

c. Esto es fantástico.

d. Toma, esto es para ti.

e. Con eso puedes pagar el taxi
   y poco más.

f. ¿Qué es aquello de allí?

g. Me apetece aquello que comen
   aquellos señores.

Classify the answers. Which of the following possibilities is the most likely in each case?

No sabe el nombre ....

....

No importa el nombre ....

....

No es un objeto ....

....

8 Juan and Jorge have just moved to a new house. The whole place is a mess. They do not know what anything is but they are trying to establish a bit of order. Complete the dialogues.

● ¿Dónde pongo   ○ (1) .... ponlo en la cocina.
➜ ..esto.. ?   Me parece que es la batidora.

● ¿Y (2) ....   ○ (3) .... puedes
que está ahí?   dejarlo en el dormitorio.

○ ¿Y dónde ponemos
(4) .... del fondo?

● A ver... Huy, me parece que es la lámpara que nos regaló tu madre.

○ Cielos. Es horrible. ¿La ponemos en el desván?

○ Oye, ¿y (5) ....
que está ahí qué es?

● Ni idea. Déjalo de momento.

9 Underline the most appropriate option. Sometimes both are possible.

➜ ● ¿Quién es <u>ese chico</u> / eso?
○ El novio de Maite.

1. ● ¿Qué es **aquel pájaro** / **aquello**?
○ No sé, parece un pájaro.

2. ● Lucía dice que no te quiere.
○ **Esa chica** / **eso** me da igual.

3. ● ¿Por qué no enviaste **esa carta** / **eso**?
○ Porque no la pude terminar.

4. ● ¿Quieres manzanas?
○ Sí, pero sólo una; dame **ésa** / **eso**.

5. ● ¿A qué se dedica **ese señor** / **eso**?
○ Me han dicho que es profesor de instituto.

6. ● ¿En qué piensas?
○ En **aquella chica** / **aquello** que vino ayer.

7. ● ¿En qué piensas?
○ En **aquella chica** / **aquello** que ocurrió ayer.

8. ● ¿Dónde puedo poner **este mueble** / **esto**?
○ En el pasillo, aquí molesta.

9. ● ¿**Ése** / **eso** de la barba es tu hermano?
○ No, mi hermano es el de la gorra.

7. Possessives: *mi, tu, su... mío, tuyo, suyo...*

A   Possessives before the noun: *mi amigo, mi amiga...*

	SINGULAR	PLURAL
yo	**mi** *amigo/amiga*	**mi**s *amigos/amigas*
tú	**tu** *libro/revista*	**tu**s *libros/revistas*
él/ella/usted	**su** *hermano/hermana*	**su**s *hermanos/hermanas*
nosotros/as	**nuestro** *primo* **nuestra** *vecina*	**nuestro**s *primos* **nuestra**s *vecinas*
vosotros/as	**vuestro** *gato* **vuestra** *gata*	**vuestro**s *amigos* **vuestra**s *amigas*
ellos/ellas/ustedes	**su** *tío/tía*	**su**s *discos/películas*

Ésta es **mi** <u>cama</u> y éstos son **mis** <u>amigos</u>.

Ésta es **nuestra** <u>casa</u> y éstos son **nuestros** <u>vecinos</u>.

👁 In Spanish, the possessives do **not** agree with the corresponding grammatical person: they **agree with the object being talked about**. *Mi, tu* and *su* agree with the object being talked about **only in number**. *Nuestro* and *vuestro* agree in **gender** and **number**:

- *Mirad, esta foto es del día de **mi** <u>boda</u>. Éstos son **mis** <u>padres</u>, **vuestros** <u>abuelos</u>; éste, **mi** <u>hermano</u> Javier, **vuestro** <u>tío</u>. Esta chica del sombrero, **mi** <u>hermana</u> pequeña, **vuestra** <u>tía</u> Alicia. Y éstas son **vuestras** <u>primas</u> Ángela y Lucía, **mis** <u>sobrinas</u>.*

👁 *Su* (talking about a single object) and *sus* (talking about various objects) mean:

DE USTED/USTEDES

- *¿Y usted? Vendrá a la boda, ¿verdad?*
- ○ *Sí, claro, muchas gracias.*
- *¿Y **su** <u>mujer</u> y **sus** <u>hijas</u>?*
- ○ *Sí, también. Están encantadas.*
- *Por el hotel no se preocupen ustedes, porque ya tengo **su** <u>reserva</u>.*

DE ÉL/ELLA/ELLOS/ELLAS

- *¿A quién más has invitado a la boda?*
- ○ *Al jefe, con **su** <u>mujer</u> y **sus** tres <u>hijas</u>; a la tía Ana, con **su** <u>novio</u> y **sus** <u>amigas</u>; a los tíos de Almería, con **su** <u>hijo</u>, **su** <u>nuera</u> y **sus** dos <u>nietos</u>; y a las hermanas López, con **su** <u>madre</u> y **sus** <u>novios</u>.*

1 Here you have a selection of summer holiday offers. Complete them with the right possessives.

1

¡Viaje con nosotros y disfrute de nuestros maravillosos HOTELES, de .... estupenda COCINA TRADICIONAL, de .... fantásticas EXCURSIONES y de .... inmejorables PRECIOS!

Agencia Odisea

2

Academia de baile

RítmicA

Baila y disfruta con .... música favorita. En nuestras clases de salsa, merengue, tango o rumba aprenderás todo lo necesario para sorprender a .... novio o a .... novia, a .... amigos y a .... amigas.

Especial para ti.

3

El chef en casa

El cocinero para sus fiestas

Disfrute de:

.... delicioso arroz con pimientos.

.... especialidades en cocina tropical.

.... postres de chocolate.

.... experiencia en restaurantes de lujo y .... estudios en las mejores escuelas me permiten ofrecerle el mejor servicio de la ciudad.

Llámeme al 017 65 43 21

4

Queridas familias:

¿Qué vais a hacer con vuestras plantas este verano?

¿Quién va a cuidar .... jardín?

¿Quién va a regar .... macetas?

¿Quién va a podar .... rosas?

Hogar Botánico

¡Llamadnos! Tel. 013 45 67 89

A la vuelta lo veréis todo VERDE.

5

◁▷ **BÚNKER** ◁▷

Empresa de seguridad y servicios

¿Preocupado por la seguridad de .... vivienda durante el verano?

¡ **R E L Á J E S E !**

Nosotros vigilamos .... apartamento o casa y recogemos .... correo.

Además, por un precio adicional, llenamos .... frigorífico justo a tiempo y avisamos a .... proveedores habituales (lechero, panadero, ...).

Somos .... ángeles de la guarda.

2 Bea and Miguel are getting separated and are dividing up their things. Read and complete the conversation with the appropriate possessives.

Bea: Te puedes quedar con el equipo de música, pero yo me llevo ➜ _mis_ cedés y (1) .... libros, por supuesto.

Miguel: Perfecto, quédate con (2) .... cedés y con (3) .... libros, pero el microondas es mío.

Bea: ¡Ah, no! Perdona, pero éste es (4) .... microondas. El tuyo lo tiene María, ¿no te acuerdas?

Miguel: Pues el lavavajillas sí es mío, y la lavadora, también.

Bea: Mira, me da igual, quédate con (5) .... lavavajillas y (6) .... lavadora; pero (7) .... cuadros y (8) .... sofá no vas a tocarlos.

Miguel: Muy bien, muy bien. Llévate (9) .... sofá y esos cuadros horribles. Ah, y llévate también el abrebotellas de (10) .... madre y el paraguas de (11) .... prima Jacinta y yo me quedo con todo lo demás.

B Possessives after the noun: *un amigo mío*, *una amiga mía*...

	SINGULAR		PLURAL	
	MASCULINE	FEMININE	MASCULINE	FEMININE
yo	un amigo **mío**	una amiga **mía**	unos amigos **míos**	unas amigas **mías**
tú	ese libro **tuyo**	aquella casa **tuya**	esos libros **tuyos**	aquellas casas **tuyas**
él/ella/usted	otro coche **suyo**	otra casa **suya**	otros coches **suyos**	otras casas **suyas**
nosotros/as	otro gato **nuestro**	otra gata **nuestra**	otros gatos **nuestros**	otras gatas **nuestras**
vosotros/as	ese primo **vuestro**	esa prima **vuestra**	esos primos **vuestros**	esas primas **vuestras**
ellos/ellas/ustedes	un disco **suyo**	una mesa **suya**	unos discos **suyos**	unas mesas **suyas**

■ These possessives are adjectives and, like all adjectives, must agree in gender and number with the noun, in the same way as articles, demonstratives, quantifiers and indefinite pronouns:

- He traído <u>muchos discos</u> **míos**.
- En mi mesa hay <u>varios libros</u> **vuestros**.
- <u>Esta calculadora</u> **tuya** no tiene pilas, ¿sabes?
- Javier es <u>un amigo</u> **suyo** de la universidad, ¿no?

👁 un amigo ~~de mí~~, un amigo ~~de ti~~, un amigo ~~de vosotros~~...
     mío   tuyo   vuestro

➲ 4. Adjective

3 Link the sentences and complete with the appropriate possessive adjectives.

➲ Estoy saliendo con un chico guapísimo. ——————
1. A tu marido le gusta mucho Elvis, ¿verdad?
2. Pues nosotros tenemos un amigo que sabe mucho de ordenadores.
3. A Aurelio se le olvida devolver las cosas.
4. ¿Qué os regaló Francisco por vuestra boda?
5. En casa organizamos en Navidad una comida para más de veinte personas.

a. ¡No me digas!, ¿y tienes alguna foto _suya_..?
b. ¿Y eran todos amigos .... ?
c. Ya lo sé, todavía tiene algunos libros .... que le presté el año pasado.
d. Varios cuadros .... Son increíbles.
e. ¡Ah!, ¿sí?, pues ¿por qué no le decís a ese amigo .... que si puede venir a ayudarnos?
f. Sí, tiene un montón de discos ....

4 Your Spanish teacher has asked you to correct this exercise done by a classmate.

➲ Estoy supercontento. Han colgado un cuadro ⟨de mi⟩ en el Guggenheim de Bilbao.

1. Ha sido un éxito tremendo. Al final, miles de fans gritaban: "Queremos un hijo de ti".

2. ¿Ése es profesor de vosotros? Increíble, pero sí es jovencísimo.

3. ¿Se puede saber qué hace un zapato de ti en el coche de Fernando?

4. Imagina la ilusión que nos hace tener un libro de nosotros en las librerías.

➲ ...... un cuadro mío ......
1. ....
2. ....
3. ....
4. ....

45

C *Un amigo mío / Mi amigo*

■ With *mío*, *tuyo*, *suyo*... in the same way as with other adjectives (*familiar*, *español*, etc.), we indicate that a single thing (or various) forms a part of a larger unit of things connected to something or someone:

- *Ester es vecina nuestra.*
  [She is one of the group of our neighbours.]

- *He encontrado fotografías vuestras.*
  [An unspecified number of photos that are either of you or that you have taken. There may be more of them.]

- *Tres profesores míos hablan chino.*
  [Three of the teachers I have. I may have more.]

- *Una novela suya ha ganado el premio.*
  [One of the novels that he or she wrote. There may be more.]

■ With *mi*, *tu*, *su*... we are talking about things that can be identified amongst all the others because of their connection with something or somebody. There are no more or they are the only ones we have talked about:

- *Ester es nuestra vecina.*
  [She is the only person identified as our neighbour.]

- *He encontrado vuestras fotografías.*
  [The photos that are of you or which you have taken. The only ones we have talked about...]

- *Mis tres profesores hablan chino.*
  [The three teachers I have or the three that I have talked about...]

- *Su novela ganó el premio.*
  [The only one he or she has written. The one that was entered for the prize...]

Mañana viene Lena Mercadal, **una** amiga **mía** de Menorca.

Mira, ésta es Lena Mercadal.

Ah, sí, **tu** amiga de Menorca. Encantado.

[We have not talked about her before]

Ésta es Paula, **mi** amiga.

¿Amiga especial?, ¿novia?, ¿amante?, ¿sólo tiene una amiga?...

[We have talked about her before.]

[We have not talked about Paula before. She is unique for some reason...]

■ Possessives **before the noun** are noun determiners and are never combined with articles or demonstratives:

- *Su tío ha llamado. / Un tío suyo ha llamado.*   [Un su tío ha llamado.]
- *Ese teléfono está sonando. / Nuestro teléfono está sonando.*   [Ese nuestro teléfono está sonando.]
- *¿Fuiste con tu coche? / ¿Fuiste con el coche?*   [¿Fuiste con el tu coche?]

■ Possessive **after the noun** are not determiners. They can be combined with articles or demonstratives:

- *El ordenador suyo del otro despacho es más rápido.*
- *El otro día nos llamó un compañero nuestro del instituto.*
- *No soporto esa manía tuya de gritarme.*

➲ 5. Articles

➲ 6. Demonstratives

5 Complete the sentences as in the example.

➜ Vinieron todos ...*sus hermanos*............ .
  a. hermanos suyos
  b. sus hermanos *(circled)*

1. .... vive en Nueva York
   y la otra en Dublín.
   a. Una hermana mía
   b. Mi hermana

2. Me gustan mucho ....
   Tienen un color precioso.
   a. ojos tuyos
   b. tus ojos

3. Estará ....
   He visto luces encendidas en tu casa.
   a. compañero de piso tuyo
   b. tu compañero de piso

4. Todos tuvimos que decirle ....
   para poder pasar.
   a. nombres nuestros
   b. nuestros nombres

5. Es director de cine, ¿verdad?
   Me gustaría ver ....
   a. su película
   b. alguna película suya

6. Yo no estoy de acuerdo, pero es ....
   Tú decides.
   a. vida tuya
   b. tu vida

7. Aquí tienes .... que estaban en
   mi casa. Hay más, pero no podía traértelos todos.
   a. estos libros tuyos
   b. tus libros

6 There has been a robbery on the Occident Express. Complete the text below by putting the possessives into the right places.

Marquesa de Montefosco: ¡Qué desgracia! Esto es terrible. Se han llevado ➜ ...*mis*.... joyas .... , (1) todos .... camisones de seda .... y (2) .... dentadura postiza ....

El Duque y la Duquesa de Aguasturbias: Pues nosotros hemos perdido todo el equipaje: (3) .... dieciocho maletas .... , (4) .... seis abrigos de pieles .... y (5) .... gorros de dormir .... Estamos desolados.

La Marquesa: Querido Duque, ¿y (6) .... magnífica colección de pipas de marfil .... ? ¿Está a salvo?

El Duque: ¡Qué va! También ha desaparecido. Y el anillo de diamantes que le regalé a (7) .... esposa .... con motivo de (8) .... último cumpleaños ....

La Duquesa: Guillermo, te olvidas de (9) .... ordenador portátil .... y de (10) .... doce palos de golf preferidos ....

Hércules Jolms: Cálmense. Parece que se han encontrado algunos (11) .... objetos .... en la Estación de

Albacete: Señor Duque, ha aparecido (12) .... ordenador ...., con documentos bastante comprometidos, por cierto.

El Duque: No sé a qué se refiere.

Hércules Jolms: Hay varios (13) .... poemas .... dedicados a la Marquesa de Montefosco. También hemos encontrado algunas (14) .... joyas ...., Señora Marquesa, junto con (15) .... anillo .... , Señora Duquesa. Dos (16) .... pipas .... , y (17) .... doce palos de golf .... estaban en los servicios de la estación, señor Duque.

Hay otro asunto delicado: dos (18) .... camisones .... , Señora Marquesa, estaban en una (19) .... maleta .... , Señor Duque.

La Duquesa: Ahora lo comprendo todo: Querida Marquesa, aquí tiene (20) .... dentadura postiza .... La encontré en el bolsillo de (21) .... pijama .... , Guillermo.

D   Without noun: *Tu casa es bonita pero la mía es más grande.*

■ We use *el mío, el tuyo, el suyo,* when it is not necessary to use the noun with the possessive, because we already know which one we are referring to:

- *¿Con qué lavas tus sábanas? Están más limpias que **las mías**.* [my sheets]
- *Mi sillón es más cómodo que **el tuyo**.* [your armchair]
- *Le he prestado la moto a mi hermano, **la suya** no funciona.* [your motorbike]
- *Vosotros vais en vuestro coche y nosotros en **el nuestro**, ¿vale?* [our car]

7 **Change the following sentences to avoid repeating the noun.**

➲ Tu hija se lo pasa muy bien con mi hija. Se divierten mucho juntas.

   Tu hija se lo pasa muy bien con la mía...

1. Me gusta más su dentista que <u>nuestro dentista</u>. Hace menos daño.

   ....

2. Mi móvil se ha quedado sin batería. ¿Me dejas <u>tu móvil</u>?

   ....

3. Éstas son mis toallas. <u>Tus toallas</u> están en el armario.

   ....

4. El barrio donde vivo no está mal, pero <u>su barrio</u> es más tranquilo.

   ....

5. Mi sueldo es más alto que <u>vuestro sueldo</u>. Y eso que yo trabajo bastante menos...

   ....

6. Yo tengo una letra muy difícil de leer, pero <u>tu letra</u> no se entiende nada.

   ....

7. Entre la bicicleta de David y <u>nuestra bicicleta</u>, prefiero la de David.

   ....

8. Tenemos el mismo coche, pero <u>su coche</u> tiene aire acondicionado.

   ....

9. Nunca te lo había dicho, pero prefiero su café a <u>tu café</u>.

   ....

E   **¿De quién es? Es nuestro**: *mío, tuyo y de Pepe.*

■ Possessive adjectives are used with the verb *ser* to express ownership:

- **¿De quién** <u>es</u> esta revista?
  ○ Es **mía**.

- **¿De quiénes** <u>son</u> estas copas?
  ○ Son **nuestras**.

- ¿Ese sombrero rojo <u>es</u> el **tuyo**?
  ○ Sí, ¿te gusta?

- **¿De quién** <u>son</u> estas gafas?
  ¿<u>Son</u> las **tuyas**?

- **¿De quiénes** <u>son</u> estos abrigos?
  ¿<u>Son</u> **suyos**, señores Núñez?

- ¿Este cuadro <u>es</u> **de tu abuela**?
  ○ Sí, **suyo**.

---

8 **Carmen and her boyfriend Alberto have gone shopping with Inma. After paying, they find that their things and those of another man have got mixed up and have to be separated. Look at their shopping lists and fill the gaps in the exercise on the next page with possessives.**

Inma:

leche
café
naranjas

Carmen y Alberto:

yogures
queso
naranjas
tomates
pasta
sandía

El señor:

Patatas

Sandía

Inma: ¿El pan es ➡ ..*nuestro*..?

Carmen: No, no es (1) ....
¿El pan es (2) .... , señor?

Señor: No, (3) .... tampoco.
Alguien lo ha olvidado.

Carmen: Las patatas sí son (4) ....
.... , ¿verdad, señor?

Señor: Sí, son (5) ....
Muchas gracias.

Carmen: ¿De quién es la leche?

Inma: (6) ....

Carmen: ¿Y el café?

Inma: También es (7) .... ,
¿me lo pasas?

Señor: Señora, ¿esa sandía de ahí es
(8) .... ?

Carmen: No, la (9) .... es
aquella que es más grande.

Señor: Entonces es la (10) ....
¿Me la pasa?

Carmen: ¿De quién son las naranjas?

Alberto: (11) .... , cariño.

Inma: No, éstas son (12) .... ;
las (13) .... son aquéllas.

Inma: Y, ¿de quién son los yogures?

Carmen: Los yogures son (14) ....
....

Inma: ¿Y el queso?

Carmen: También (15) es ....

Inma: Toma, Alberto, los tomates
son (16) ....

Alberto: Gracias, la pasta también es
(17) .... , ¿me la das?

F Special cases: *Tengo el pelo mojado*.

■ In Spanish, possessives are not normally used to talk about the parts of the
body, clothes or other things we have on us; in these cases we use the articles
el, *la*, *los*, *las*:

- *¿Vas a salir con **el** pelo mojado? ¡Vas a resfriarte!*   [¿Vas a salir con ~~tu~~ pelo mojado?]
- *Llevas una mancha de aceite en **la** camisa.*   [Llevas una mancha de aceite en ~~tu~~ camisa.]
- *Mejor, no voy. Me duele **la** cabeza.*   [Me duele ~~mi~~ cabeza.]
- *¿Os habéis lavado **las** manos?*   [¿Os habéis lavado ~~vuestras~~ manos?]

Te llamo luego.
Estoy lavándome **los** dientes.

➡ **18. Reflexive and opinion-expressing constructions**

---

9 Complete the conversations and link them as in the example.

A. Venga, a dormir. ¿Os habéis puesto ➡ ..*el*.. pijama?
¿Os habéis lavado ➡ *los*. dientes? ¿Sí? Pues, a la cama.

B. Oye, pues al principio muy bien, pero luego, un horror,
Borja, un horror. Me rompí (1) .... brazo izquierdo por
dos sitios, (2) .... dos piernas, (3) .... nariz y
(4) .... cadera. Creo que esto de esquiar no es para mí.

C. No, de verdad que no puedo. El sábado tengo una boda
y quiero cortarme (5) .... pelo, depilarme (6) ....
piernas y pintarme (7) ...... uñas de (8) .... pies
y de (9) .... manos. Imposible, chica.

D. Mire, es que realmente me encuentro fatal. Me parece
que es la gripe. Me duele (10) .... cabeza,
(11) ...... garganta, (12) .... estómago y tengo
muchísima fiebre. De verdad, lo siento.

➡ Un padre habla con sus hijos. ..*A*....

1. Dos amigas charlan por teléfono. ....

2. Un empleado llama al trabajo
para disculparse por su ausencia. ....

3. Un amigo le cuenta a otro
sus vacaciones en Sierra Nevada. ....

8. Indefinite articles: *todos, algunos, alguien, nada, otros...*

A   *Algún estudiante*, *ninguna casa*, *todos los días...*

■ These indefinite articles are used to talk about **things that we select from a group**. They always refer to a noun that expresses the **type** of person or thing we are talking about:

Alguno/-a /-os/-as	*Ninguno/-a/-os/-as*	*Todos/-as*
Alguno: One or more things from a group, without specifying which or how many.	**Ninguno**: Nothing (ø) from a group.	**Todos**: The whole group.

Alguno/-a /-os/-as

Alguno: One or more things from a group, without specifying which or how many.

- *Se han comido **algún** <u>bombón</u>.*
- *Han dejado **algunos**.*

Ninguno/-a/-os/-as

Ninguno: Nothing (ø) from a group.

- *No se han comido **ningún** <u>bombón</u>.*
- *No han abierto **ninguno**.*

Todos/-as

Todos: The whole group.

- *Se han comido **todos** <u>los bombones</u>.*
- *Han abierto **todos**.*

  👁 Before a noun, the masculine singular forms *alguno* and *ninguno* are shortened to **algún** and **ningún**:

     Algún lápiz [~~Alguno lápiz~~]   ***Ningún lápiz*** [~~Ninguno lápiz~~]

■ These forms agree with the noun they refer to in both gender and number:

Algún** chico / **alguno	***Ningún** chico / **ninguno***	***Todos** los chicos*
***Alguna** chica*	***Ninguna** chica*	***Todas** las chicas*
***Algunos** chicos*	***Ningunos** pantalones*	
***Algunas** chicas*	***Ningunas** tijeras*	

  👁 *Ningunos/-as* are only used with nouns that are not normally used in the singular: *pantalones, tijeras, prismáticos, gafas,* etc. With nouns that have a singular (*chico*) and a plural (*chicos*) we use ***ninguno/-a***.

■ We can use these forms **with the noun** they refer to or without the noun when we already know which noun we are talking about:

- *¿Tenéis **alguna** <u>pregunta</u>?*
  ○ *No, **ninguna**. Está todo clarísimo.*
- *Jesús tiene un montón de <u>discos</u> de los años ochenta.*
  ***Algunos** son muy buenos.*
- *Sólo tengo cuatro <u>amigos</u>, pero **todos** son estupendos.*

Alguno/-a/-os/-as and *ninguno/-a* are used without a noun and with the preposition *de* when we mention the group that we are selecting things from:

- ***Algunas** <u>de las preguntas</u> que nos hizo eran muy difíciles.*
- ***Ninguno** <u>de esos discos</u> es de los Rolin Estón.*

1 Look at the example and guess the answers of these three competitors in a television memory game. Pay careful attention to the gender and number.

¿Recuerda usted...

NORMA CORRIENTE 354 · OLVIDO MAYOR 7 · PEPE RECUERDA 1997

➲ ... las películas que vio de pequeño?   Sí, _algunas_ .   No, _ninguna_ .   Sí, _todas_ .

➲ ... los nombres de sus vecinos?   _Algunos_ .   No, _ninguno_ .   _Todos_ .

1. ... sus primeras palabras?   Sí, _algunas_ .   No, _ninguna_   Casi _todas_ .

2. ... las gafas de sol que ha tenido hasta ahora?   Sólo _algunas_ .   Mmm, _ningunas_   _todas_ .

3. ... a sus compañeros de clase de la escuela?   A _algunos_ sí .   No, a _ningunos_   Sí, a _todos_

4. ... a sus profesores de la escuela primaria?   Sí, a _algunas_   _ninguno_ A _..._ , me temo.   Claro, a _todos_ .

5. ... las marcas de vino que ha probado?   _algunas_ .   Casi _ninguna_   Casi _todas_

6. ... los discos que le han regalado?   Bueno, _algunos_ .   ¿Discos? _ninguno_   _todos_ , creo.

7. ... los títulos de los libros que ha leído?   Sólo _algunos_ .   Pues no, _ninguno_   _todos_

8. ... las canciones de éxito de la década de los 90?   _algunas_ .   Esto... No, _ninguna_   _todas_ .

2 Chose and complete with the correct form.

alguna	algunas	algunos	algún ✓	algún	algún	ningún	ningún	ninguno	todas	todos

➲ ¿Tienes _algún_ día libre la semana que viene?

1. No entiendo _algunas_ cosas de este libro. ¿Puedes ayudarme?

2. _algunos_ jóvenes son muy responsables, pero son pocos.

3. Te puedes llevar _todos_ los diccionarios. No necesito _ninguno_ .

4. No me gustan los caramelos ni los pasteles. _ningún_ dulce me gusta.

5. ¿Qué te pasa? ¿Tienes _alguna_ problema?

6. Ten cuidado con el horno. En _ningún_ caso debes tocar el cristal. Quema.

7. A Jaime le gustan _todas_ las películas de Rigoberto de Nilo.

8. Si necesitas _alguna_ chaqueta, yo te puedo prestar una.

9. El perro se escapó y no ocurrió nada al final, pero en _algún_ momento pasamos muchísimo miedo.

3 Fátima Gómez has been to a school reunion.
Complete with *todos, todas, algunos, algunas, ninguno, ninguna*.

➲ _Todos_ , sin excepción, estamos más viejos. ¡Cómo pasa el tiempo! (1) _algunos_ se han quedado completamente calvos, aunque Fernando Dávila sigue con su impresionante mata de pelo; (2) _algunas_ están bastante más gorditas —Maite Céspedes y Conchi Moreno siguen pesando cincuenta kilos, ¿cómo lo harán?-, pero (3) _ninguna_ se ha operado nada —al menos eso dicen ellas. ¡Hasta hay (4) _algunas_ embarazadas! En general , la verdad es que (5) _todas_ las chicas seguimos estando muy guapas. (6) _algunas_ ya se han divorciado, creo que José Miguel Lombardo y Paco Goikoetxea, y vinieron a la fiesta con sus segundas parejas. Es curioso, pero (7) _todos_ _ningunos_ de ellos vive en el extranjero, (8) _todos_ se han quedado en España. Sólo yo vivo fuera. (9) _todas_ las chicas, sin excepción, trabajamos. Es una suerte. Sin embargo, no (10) _todos_ los chicos tienen trabajo. (11) _algunos_ están en paro.

B — *Alguien*, *nadie*; *algo*, *nada*; *todo*.

■ These indefinite articles are used as nouns and are used to talk about **people** (*alguien, nadie*) or **things** (*algo, nada, todo*) **without specifying which type of person or thing we are talking about:**

Alguien [somebody]	**Nadie** [nobody]	**Algo** [something]	**Nada** [nothing]	**Todo** [everything]

*Veo a **alguien**.* *No veo a **nadie**.* *Veo **algo**.* *No veo **nada**.* *Lo veo **todo**.*

■ *Alguien*, *nadie*, *algo*, *nada* and *todo* never change their form and they **always agree with the masculine singular:**

- *¡Hola! ¿Hay **alguien** despiert**o**?*

  [We could be talking about: a man, a woman, several men, several women...]

- *Tenía **algo** roj**o** en la mano.*

  [We could be talking about: a toy, a ball, several pencils several cherries...]

- *Me gusta este libro. **Todo** está muy clar**o**.*

  [We could be be talking about: the text, the layout, the examples...]

---

④ This is a fragment of the script of a detective film. Complete with the words *alguien*, *nadie*, *algo*, *nada* or *todo*.

➲ ..*Alguien*.. pone, con mucho cuidado, (1) *algo* en el bolso de la agente del 069, Laura Ladrón. (2) *nadie* se da cuenta: ni su compañero, el agente Cortés, ni su ayudante. Cuando la agente abre el bolso, ve que dentro hay (3) *algo* muy extraño, pero no dice (4) *nada*, porque Cortés siempre quiere saber (5) *todo* lo que ella hace. La agente cierra el bolso y va a su coche. Allí abre el bolso, pero ya no hay (6) *nada*. El paquete ha desaparecido. Laura se pone muy nerviosa y, de repente, ve que en el asiento de atrás hay (7) *alguien*. Es el conocido Manazas, un ayudante del mafioso Gil.

● ¿Buscas (8) *algo*, muñeca?

○ No, no busco (9) *nada*.

● Tengo un mensaje de mi jefe para ti. Me ha dicho que tiene (10) *algo* que decirte. Tienes que ir a su casa esta tarde, pero sola; (11) *nadie* puede acompañarte.

○ ¿Y por qué tengo que ir a verlo? Gil es un mafioso y no tengo (12) *nada* que decirle.

● Pero Gil te interesa mucho. Tiene información sobre (13) *alguien* sobre una persona que estás buscando. A las cinco y media en su casa, sola, sin (14) *nadie*. ¿Lo has entendido (15) *todo*?

○ Sí.

● Toma, tengo (16) *algo* para ti.

Laura ve que Manazas le da (17) *algo*. Es el paquete que antes estaba en su bolso.

---

⑤ Complete with the most suitable adjective in the appropriate gender.

➲ Es verdad que no eres guapísima, pero nadie es ..*perfecto*.. .

1. Una persona *perezosa* es alguien que no quiere trabajar mucho.

2. Algo que es tan *barato* no puede ser de buena calidad.

3. Si miras las cosas con pesimismo, **todo** lo verás *oscuro*.

4. Para atraer la atención de un toro necesitas una tela roja o algo *rojo*.

5. Nada es más *oscura* *rápido* que la velocidad de la luz.

rápido/-a
rojo/-a
barato/-a ✔
perezoso/-a ✔
perfecto/-a ✔
oscuro/-a ✔

6 Complete with the correct form.

alguien	nadie	algo	nada	algún/-o (-a, -os, -as)	ningún/-o (-a, -os, -as)

➔ ● Necesito otro pañuelo.
¿Tienes *alguno* más?
○ Lo siento. Ya no me queda
ninguno .
● Si quieres una servilleta de
papel...
○ Bueno, *algo* es *algo* .

1. ● .... sabe lo
nuestro, Ernestina, tengo miedo.
○ No, hombre, tranquilo, no lo
sabe .... , sólo nuestros
amigos íntimos.
● Bueno, es que ....
de ellos puede decir
.... , ¿no crees?

2. ● ¿Tienes .... para el
dolor?
○ Pues me parece que no tengo
.... Espera, sí,
tengo aspirinas.
● ¿Sólo aspirinas?
○ Pues sí, mejor es ....

que .... , ¿no?

3. ● ¿Tienes .... para
picar?   ¿Aceitunas, por
ejemplo?
○ Aceitunas sí, creo que tengo
.... en el frigorífico.

4. ● ¿Quedan .... galletas? Estaban muy ricas.
○ Pues creo que no. He mirado
hace un momento y no quedaba
....

5. ● ¿Ha llamado .... ?
○ Sí.
● ¿Quién era?
○ No me lo ha dicho.
.... amigo tuyo,
supongo.

6. ● Esta sopa necesita ....
más. ¿Hay tomates?
○ Pues la verdad es que no
queda .... tomate.
● ¿En serio? ¿ .... ?

¿Y cebolla?
○ Ni tomates ni cebolla. No
queda ....

7. ● Buenas. Estaba buscando ......
.... bonito para una fiesta.
○ Muy bien. Tenemos unos
conjuntos muy modernos y
unos vestidos preciosos.
● ¿Puede enseñarme ....
barato?
○ ¿ .... vestido o
.... conjunto?

8. ● ¿Crees realmente que tus
compañeros de trabajo te
odian?
○ .... , sí.
Sobre todo el gerente.
● Pero, ¿tú les has hecho
.... malo?
○ ¿Yo? No, ...
Bueno, a .... de ellos
sí, ... vez.

C   Double negative: *No hay ninguno*; *no hay nadie*; *no hay nada*.

■ The negative forms *nadie*, *nada* or *ningún/-o (-a, -os, -as)* can go **before**
or **after the verb**. If they go **after**, it is also necessary to express negation before the verb:

Ningún problema es grave.	BUT:	*No existe ningún problema grave.*
Nada le parece bien.		*No le parece bien nada.*
Nadie me comprende.		*No me comprende nadie.*

[Existe ningún problema grave.]
[Le parece bien nada.]
[Me comprende nadie.]

■ In Spanish, the negation must always come before the verb. To do this
we use *no* together with **other forms that convey negative meaning**:

No, ni, tampoco...	● *No me ha llamado ningún amigo. Tampoco me han hecho ningún regalo.* ● *Ni me ha llamado nadie ni me han regalado nada.*
Nunca, jamás...	● *Nunca / Jamás he tenido ningún problema con esta chica.* ● *Nunca / Jamás he hecho nada malo ni he ofendido a nadie.*
Nadie, nada...	● *Nadie ha dicho nada malo de ti.* ● *Había mucha comida, pero nada le ha gustado a nadie.*
Ningún/-o (-a, -os, -as)	● *Ningún empleado ha observado ninguna cosa extraña.* ● *En ningún caso debes dejar ninguna ventana abierta.* ● *Yo creo que en ningún momento he dicho nada en contra de ella, ¿no?* ● *De ningún modo va a entrar nadie en esta casa.*

7 Identify the four sentences that need a double negative and correct them as in the example.

➲ Yo esperaba una visita, pero ha venido **nadie**.

..no.ha.venido.nadie................

Si no lo dices, **ninguno** de ellos lo sabrá.

............✓............

1. A **nadie** le importan mis problemas.

....

2. Bueno, yo esperaba tu ayuda, pero si no puedes, pasa **nada**. ....

3. Llamé a Berta, a Julia y a Paco, pero **nadie** contestaba al teléfono. ....

4. Dicen que Rosa y aquel chico se besaron, pero yo vi **nada**. ....

5. Tiene cuatro gatos, pero quiere regalarme **ninguno**. ....

6. No lo dudo, será tu hijo, pero se parece en **nada** a ti. ....

D Otro, otra, otros, otras.

■ *Otro/-a /-os/-as* refers to one or more different objects of the same type:

¡Un billete! ¡Otro billete! ¡Anda! ¡Otros dos! ¡Y otro!

- *¿Sabe si hay **otra** gasolinera en este pueblo? En ésta no hay gasolina para motos.*
  [The person is asking for a different petrol station to the one they are in.]

- *¿Has cambiado de perfume? Creo que me gustaba más el **otro**.*
  [The previous perfume, different from the one being worn now.]

■ These forms agree in gender and number with the noun they refer to:

- *Tengo que buscar **otro** trabajo mejor.*
- *¡Qué cola! ¿No hay **otros** cajeros automáticos cerca?*
- *Si quieres a Andrés, dale **otra** oportunidad.*
- *¿No tienen **otras** gafas más baratas?*

■ When it is clear what the noun is, it is not necessary to repeat it:

- *Ya no vivo en ese piso. Ahora vivo en **otro**.*
- *Los Hidalgo tienen una casa en la costa y **otra** en la montaña.*

■ *Otro/-a /-os/-as* can also be combined with other determiners (demonstratives, possessives, definite articles, etc.) but they never combine with *un/-a /-os/-as*:

- *Hoy te han llamado **otras** dos chicas.*
- *Hay dos posibilidades: una, quedarnos en casa y la **otra**, salir.*
- *Es bonito, pero prefiero ese **otro**.*
- *El hijo mayor es muy simpático, pero sus **otros** hijos, no.*

- *Dame **otro** café.* [Dame un otro café.]
- *Tienes que venir **otra** vez.* [Tienes que venir una otra vez.]

👁 Cardinal numbers (*dos, tres*...) go **after** otros, otras, not before:

[Tengo dos otros trabajos para ti.]
      otros dos

8 Isabel Préslez is a very demanding shopper. Link and complete the sentences with *otro, otra, otros, otras*. Underline the noun that they refer to.

⮑ Estas <u>chaquetas</u> son muy bonitas, pero ——— ⮑ ¿no tiene _otras_ más baratas? No quiero gastar mucho.

1. Oh, qué jersey más mono, pero es un poco caro,   a. ¿no tiene .... más grande y más sofisticada?

2. Me gusta muchísimo esta pulsera de plata, pero   b. ¿no tiene .... más barato? Es para ir muy deportiva.

3. Estas botas son estupendas, pero   c. ¿no tiene .... un poco más anchos y más oscuros?

4. ¡Qué pantalones más divinos! Pero   d. ¿no tiene .... con el tacón alto? Son para una fiesta.

9 Mercatoma department store has its Sale on: for everything you buy they give you several extra, as indicated in the brackets. Complete the advertisement with the missing words.

⮑ Si se lleva un perfume de señora, le regalamos (I) _otro_ y si se lleva dos perfumes de caballero, le regalamos (III) _otros tres_ .

1. Si se lleva unas medias, le regalamos (I) ....

2. Si se lleva tres cedés, le regalamos (III) ....

3. Si se lleva un juego de cama, le regalamos (I) ....

4. Si se lleva dos colchas, le regalamos (II) ....

5. Si se lleva una maquinilla de afeitar, le regalamos (I) ....

6. Y si se lleva una calculadora, le regalamos (II) .... Así podrá descubrir todo lo que se ha ahorrado.

10 Vicenta is writing to his brother Manolo to tell him about what is going on in the village. Put the words in brackets into the right order and cross out any elements that cannot be used in combination with *otro/-a/-os/-as*.

Marmolejo, 29 de diciembre de 1970

Querido Manolo:

Te escribo (~~una~~, vez, otra) (⮑) _otra vez_ para contarte las últimas novedades en Marmolejo. Papá y yo nos hemos mudado a (una, casa, otra) (1) .... más pequeña en (otra, la, parte) (2) .... del pueblo. El tío Agapito ya no vive con su hijo Paco sino con (otra, su, hija) (3) ...., Elvira. Tu prima Felisa ha tenido (hijos, otros, dos) (4) .... y están todos muy bien. La vaca

también ha parido (ternero, un, otro) (5) .... Tu hermano Aureliano ha comprado (tres, casas, otras) (6) .... y quiere hacer un hotel y un restaurante para traer turistas a Marmolejo. Y yo ya no salgo con Rogelio, sino con (chico, otro, aquel) (7) .... de Madrid que conociste en verano. Ya ves que hay muchos cambios en el pueblo. ¿Cuándo piensas venir a vernos? Un beso de tu hermana,

Vicenta

11 Jerónimo and Alablanca sometimes have relationship problems, as well as difficulties with *otro, otra, otros* and *otras*. Find and correct the four mistakes, apart from the example.

⮑ Jerónimo: En las fiestas miras a <u>unos otros chicos</u>. _otros chicos_ .

1. Alablanca: Estás celoso, mi único sol. Miro a otros, sí, pero no miro a nadie en especial. A mí los otros no me interesan ....

2. Jerónimo: ¿Por qué te fijas en unos otros si me tienes a mí? ....

3. Alablanca: Jerónimo, yo no miro unos otros ojos, no miro una otra boca, no miro otras manos. Yo sólo te miro a ti. ....

4. Jerónimo: Eso deseo yo, Alablanca. Porque tú eres mi única luna y no hay en todo el mundo ninguna otra. Nunca podrá haber una otra. Sólo te quiero a ti ....

9. Cardinal numbers: *uno, dos, tres...*

Cardinal numbers are used to express quantities: *un globo*, *dos globos*, *tres globos*.
They always refer to a noun, but may also be used alone when it is clear what we are
talking about:

- ● *Tengo **dos** <u>entradas</u> para el concierto, ¿y tú?*
- ○ *Yo tengo **tres**.*

A From 0 to 15

0	cero	**4**	cuatro	**8**	ocho	**12**	doce
1	uno	**5**	cinco	**9**	nueve	**13**	trece
2	dos	**6**	seis	**10**	diez	**14**	catorce
3	tres	**7**	siete	**11**	once	**15**	quince

■ ***Uno**, **una*** have gender, and agree with the noun:

- ● *¿Qué van a tomar?*
- ○ ***Una** <u>cerveza</u> y dos vinos, por favor.*

- ● *¿Cuántos <u>bocadillos</u> quieren?*
- ○ ***Uno**.*

👁 ***Uno*** changes to ***un*** before the noun: ***Un** <u>té</u> y tres cafés, por favor.*

❶ Claudio always wants to outdo his friend Julio, and whatever Julio wants, Claudio wants double.
Compete by writing the numbers in word form.

➲ Si Julio se come dos bocadillos, él se come ..*cuatro*.. bocadillos.

1. Si Julio se bebe cinco cafés, él se bebe .... cafés.

2. Si Julio se toma una cerveza, él se bebe .... cervezas.

3. Si Julio tiene tres novias, él tiene .... novias.

4. Si Julio invita a seis amigos, él invita a .... amigos.

5. Si Julio se come siete pasteles, él se come .... pasteles.

6. Si Julio compra cuatro botellas de vino, él compra .... botellas de vino.

7. Si Julio alquila cinco vídeos, él alquila .... vídeos.

8. Si Julio se come tres platos de pasta, él se come .... platos de pasta.

9. Si Julio se cae una vez, él se cae .... veces.

❷ The following conversation is heard in Carlota's bar between the waiters and the customers.
Write the numbers and be careful with *un, uno, una*.

➲ ● Buenas tardes, quería **2** ..*dos*.. cafés y **1** ...*un*. té con limón, por favor.

1. ○ ¿**2** .... tes?
   ● No, **1** ....

2. ● ¿Cuántas cervezas me ha dicho?
   ○ Sólo **1** .... , y **3** .... vinos de Rioja.

3. ● **1** .... cerveza, por favor.
   ○ ¡Marchando!
   ● ¿Me pones también **1** .... vaso de agua?

4. ● ¿Qué van a tomar?
   ○ **1** .... bocadillo de queso y **1** .... limonada.

5. ● ¿Cuántos cafés?
   ○ **3** .... : **2** .... solos y **1** .... con leche.

6. ● ¿Cuánto es todo?
   ○ **2** .... bocadillos, **1** .... botella de vino y **1** .... carajillo. Espera, ahora te lo digo.

3 **Help Jaime to do his arithmetic.**

dos + uno = ...*tres*..........   seis + tres = ...   diez + cuatro = ...

quince - ocho = ...   dos + nueve = ...   doce + tres = ...

nueve + cuatro = ...   trece - siete = ...   siete + cinco = ...

B   From 16 to 99

■ From **16** to **29**, the numbers are written as **a single word**:

16	*dieciséis*		20	*veinte*	25	*veinticinco*
17	*diecisiete*		21	*veintiuno*	26	*veintiséis*
18	*dieciocho*		22	*veintidós*	27	*veintisiete*
19	*diecinueve*		23	*veintitrés*	28	*veintiocho*
			24	*veinticuatro*	29	*veintinueve*

- ¿Cuántos años tienes?
- **Diecisiete**. ¿Y tú?
- **Veintitrés**.

- ¿Qué día es hoy?
- **Diecinueve** de febrero.

- ¿Cuánto cuestan esos calendarios?
- Los grandes **veinticinco** euros y los pequeños **dieciocho**.

■ From **31** to **99**, the numbers are written are written as two words joined together by *y*:

30	*treinta*			*uno/a*
40	*cuarenta*			*dos*
50	*cincuenta*			*tres*
60	*sesenta*	*y*		*cuatro*
70	*setenta*			*cinco*
80	*ochenta*			*seis*
90	*noventa*			*siete*
				ocho
				nueve

- *Mi abuela Lupe tiene **ochenta y tres** años y mi abuelo **noventa**. La tía Amalia tiene unos **sesenta y cinco** años y su marido, el tío Paco, **setenta** o **setenta y dos**. Mi madre tiene **sesenta y siete** años. Mi hermana Blanca tiene **treinta y nueve** y Carlos, su ex-marido, **treinta y dos**. Mi prima Eloísa, que está a la derecha, es la más joven del grupo: tiene **treinta años**.*

👁 Remember that when numbers end in *uno/una* they agree in gender with the noun. *Uno* changes to *un* before the noun:

- *Te has comido **treinta y una** <u>galletas</u> saladas. Te vas a poner malo.*
- *Carla cumple pasado mañana **veintiún** <u>años</u>.*

4 **All the following people were born on 24 March. Today, 24 March 2015, is everybody's birthday, but how old are they all?**

➲ Carmen: 24-03-1975: ....*cuarenta*......... años.

1. Pepe: 24-03-1976: .... años.

2. Celia: 24-03-1984: .... años.

3. Clara: 24-03-1988: .... años.

4. Marina: 24-03-1996: .... años.

5. Juan José: 24-03-1992: .... años.

6. Beatriz: 24-03-1990: .... años.

7. Pablo: 24-03-1999: .... años.

5 Carla is moving house and is making a list of all the things to pack into boxes. Help her. Be careful with *un/una*.

➲ cuadros: 30 ..*treinta cuadros*...............

1. novelas: 71 ....

2. libros de arte: 63 ....

3. discos de jazz: 84 ....

4. discos de pop: 3 ....

5. botellas de vino: 9 ....

6. cubiertos: 52 ....

7. plantas: 5 ....

8. candelabros: 2 ....

6 Antoñito is learning to write numbers, but is not finding it easy. Can you help him?

➲ ~~veinte y dos~~: ..*veintidós*............

1. diez y siete: ....

2. sietenta y nueve: ....

3. nueventa y seis: ....

4. treintaytrés: ....

5. vientiuno: ....

6. cuarentacinco: ....

7. seisenta y uno: ....

8. ochoenta y dos: ....

9. cincuentaséis: ....

C   From 100 to 999

■ We only use *cien* when we are talking about the number **100** exactly:

- *Doña Pura tiene cien años, ni uno más ni uno menos.*

■ We use *ciento* in all other cases:

- *Ese reloj cuesta ciento dos euros.* [102]
- *De Granada a Córdoba hay ciento ochenta y cinco km.* [185]
- *El noventa por ciento de la población está en contra de la decisión.* [90%]

👁 When we are talking about approximate numbers we use *cientos*:

- *Había cientos de tortugas en la playa.*

■ The numbers from **200** to **999** agree with the noun to which they refer:

- *Póngame trescientos gramos de jamón.*
- *Necesito seiscientas cincuenta copias de este documento.*

👁 The hundreds (groups of 100 things) and the tens (groups of 10 things) are not joined together by *y*:

450 *cuatrocientos cincuenta*
[cuatrocientos✕cincuenta]

583 *quinientos ochenta y tres*
[quinientos✕ochenta y tres]

100	*cien; ciento...*
200	*doscientos/as*
300	*trescientos/as*
400	*cuatrocientos/as*
500	*quinientos/as*
600	*seiscientos/as*
700	*setecientos/as*
800	*ochocientos/as*
900	*novecientos/as*

7 Ana and Julie are saving for a journey (one in Euros and the other in Pounds) and making a note of the amounts saved in their notebooks. Help them by writing the following numbers into the right notebook with the digits next to it.

Ana's notebook:

Euros:

Julie's notebook:

Libras esterlinas:
trescientas veintiuna (321)

Trescientas veintiuna ✓
Doscientos cincuenta
Seiscientas doce
Ochocientos
Setecientos dos
Quinientas treinta y una
Novecientos veintidós
Setecientas
Cuatrocientas cincuenta

8 Help! It's the end of the month and there are lots of bills to pay. Complete these cheques with the amounts in words.

Alquiler: 999 euros ...*novecientos noventa y nueve*....

Teléfono: 411 euros ....

Electricidad: 281 euros ....

Agua: 576 euros ....

Móvil: 789 euros ....

Droguería: 125 euros ....

D From 1,000 to 999,999

■ The word *mil* does not change when talking about round numbers:

1.000	2.000	3.000	10.000	100.000	500.000
Mil	Dos mil	Tres mil	Diez mil	Cien mil	Quinientos/as mil

1.635 $ *mil seiscientos treinta y cinco <u>dólares</u>.*
38.751 m²   *treinta y ocho mil setecientos cincuenta y un <u>metros</u> cuadrados.*
912.182 £   *novecientas doce mil ciento ochenta y dos <u>libras</u>.*

👁   When we are talking about approximate numbers we use *miles*:

     ● *Había **miles** de personas en el concierto.*

👁 In Spanish, thousands and high numbers are written with points and decimals with commas, exactly the opposite of the convention in English.

9 Write the following numbers in reverse.

➡ (2.321) dos mil trescientos veintiuno ...*(1.232) mil doscientos treinta y dos*...........................

1. (9.714) nueve mil setecientos catorce ....

2. (76.159) setenta y seis mil ciento cincuenta y nueve ....

3. (1.205) mil doscientos cinco ....

4. (48.118) cuarenta y ocho mil ciento dieciocho ....

5. (10.913) diez mil novecientos trece ....

6. (23.472) veintitrés mil cuatrocientos setenta y dos ....

Mil trescientos veintiuno.   Mil doscientos treinta y dos.

E *Millón, millones...*

■ The word *millón* is only used in the singular when talking about *1 millón*.
To talk about more than one million we use the plural: *millones*.

1.000.000	2.000.000	10.000.000	100.000.000	200.000.000	1.000.000.000
Un millón	Dos millones	Diez millones	Cien millones	Doscientos millones	Mil millones

👁   *Millón* is a masculine noun and therefore the hundreds (doscientos, cuatrocientos...) that precede it will always be in the masculine:

     *200.340.000 personas: doscien**tos** <u>millones</u> trescien**tas** cuarenta mil <u>personas</u>.*
     *700.278.000 palabras: setecien**tos** <u>millones</u> doscien**tas** setenta y ocho mil <u>palabras</u>.*

■ When the words *millón* or *millones* are immediately followed by a noun, they take the preposition *de*:

     ● *Más de cuatrocientos **millones** de <u>personas</u> hablan español.*
     ● ***Un millón** de <u>turistas</u> han visitado Mallorca este año.*

👁 *Un millón **cien mil** <u>turistas</u> han visitado Mallorca este año.*

■ In Spanish, a *billón* (1.000.000.000.000) is a million million, and is therefore written with 12 zeros.

10 You are working on the *Gran Enciclopedia Panhispánica.* You have the population data for these countries and have to write them in words.

➡ Argentina = 38.812.817 *Treinta y ocho millones ochocientos doce mil ochocientos diecisiete habitantes.*

1. México = 104.200.165 ....

2. Venezuela = 25.287.670 ....

3. Ecuador = 14.447.494 ....

4. Paraguay = 6.084.491 ....

5. Guatemala = 14.314.079 ....

6. España = 41.077.100 ....

7. Chile = 16.498.930 ....

F How to say numbers in Spanish.

■ 345 € = *trescientos cuarenta y cinco euros*.
579 personas = *quinientas setenta y nueve personas*.

■ When talking about thousands, you say the number in two halves:
96.345 € = *noventa y seis **mil** // trescientos cuarenta y cinco euros*.
269.579 personas = *doscientas sesenta y nueve **mil** // quinientas setenta y nueve personas*.

■ When talking about millions, you pause after *millón/-es* and again after *mil/miles*:
204.796.345 € = *doscientos cuatro millones // setecientos noventa y seis **mil** // trescientos cuarenta y cinco euros*.

> You only use **y** to connect the tens and the units.

| 325. | 456. | 815 |

Trescientos veinticinco millones cuatrocientos/as cincuenta y seis mil ochocientos/as quince

> The hundreds of millions are always masculine (*-os*) because they agree with the word *millones*.

> In the plural, the hundreds of thousands and the hundreds agree with the noun (*-os/-as*).

---

11 Mark has a problem when writing numbers: he does not know when to write the *y*. Help him by crossing the *y* out when it isn't necessary. Then write the number in digits.

➡ Trescientos ~~y~~ veinte mil seiscientos ~~y~~ treinta y siete
320.637

1. Cuarenta y dos mil ciento y cinco ....

2. Tres millones y ochenta y ocho mil trescientos y cuarenta y seis ....

3. Cuatrocientos y cinco mil sesenta y uno ....

4. Cincuenta y nueve mil y once ....

5. Noventa y dos mil trescientos y quince ....

6. Ochocientos y cinco mil quinientos y ochenta ....

7. Trescientos y veintiséis ....

8. Setecientos y setenta mil ....

---

12 Read the following text about the island of Golandia and complete the half-written numbers with the ones from the box.

Golandia tiene una superficie de ...*seiscientos*.... quince ...*mil*...... km² y un total de dos millones .... habitantes. La capital, Gola City, está situada al norte del país y tiene .... trescientos habitantes; la segunda ciudad importante de Golandia es Rúcola, con .... siete .... habitantes. El monte principal de la isla es El Golón con una altura de .... y ocho metros, y tiene dos ríos principales: el Gologolo, de .... setenta .... kilómetros y el Golín, de doscientos .... kilómetros.

4.058
615.000
849.300
235
307.000
2.565.000
479

10. Ordinal numbers: *primero, segundo, tercero...*

A   Meaning and forms

■ Cardinal numbers express the **order** of a series:

- La **primera** novela de Clemente Bernad me gustó mucho más que la **segunda**.
- De los seis hijos del doctor Muñiz sólo el **segundo** y la **cuarta** han estudiado Medicina.

■ These are the most commonly used cardinal numbers in Spanish:

1º	primero/a	6º	sexto/a
2º	segundo/a	7º	séptimo/a
3º	tercero/a	8º	octavo/a
4º	cuarto/a	9º	noveno/a
5º	quinto/a	10º	décimo/a

The masculine forms are written with a floating **º** symbol after the number: 1º, 5º, 10º, ... The feminine forms have a floating **ª** symbol: 2ª, 4ª, 7ª...

👁 Before a masculine noun, **primero** and **tercero** use a shortened form: **primer** and **tercer**.

- Mira, éste es mi **primer** <u>trabajo</u> con el ordenador.
- Éste es el **tercer** <u>año</u> que vivimos en el extranjero.

The feminine forms, **primera** and **tercera**, do not change:

- Vivís en la **primera** <u>puerta</u> de la **tercera** <u>planta</u>, ¿verdad?

➲ 4. Adjective

■ In spoken language, cardinal numbers are generally used up to **10º**. For higher cardinal numbers, the corresponding ordinal numbers are used:

➲ 9. Cardinal numbers

- La oficina donde trabajo está en el **primer** piso.
- La **cuarta** sinfonía de Mahler.
- Ha batido el récord en el **tercer** intento.

BUT:
- Vivimos en el piso **quince** de ese edificio.
- La sinfonía **cuarenta** de Mozart.
- Ganó la edición **treinta y dos** del Festival de la TOTI.

---

1 The Alonso Blanco family has lots of children. Look at their ages and put them in order.

Carlos tiene 25 años, María 18 y Juan 15. Francisco, no me acuerdo, pero es mayor que María y menor que Carlos. Laurita tiene 27, y Ana, la mayor, un año más. El más pequeño es Ricardo, que tiene 12 años.

Ana fue la ➲ ..*primera*.......... en nacer; Carlos es el .... ; .... ; María es la .... ; Juan es el .... , Francisco es el .... ; Laura es la .... y Ricardo es el ....

2 The *What's On* section of the newspaper gives information on the following events. Write the ordinal numbers in words. Take care with the agreements.

➲ 7º ..*Séptimo*......... Premio de Novela Histórica "Marqués de Lozoya"

1. 2º .... Certamen de Pintura al aire libre ciudad de Pedraza

2. 9º .... Festival de la Canción Popular "Agapito Marazuela"

3. 8º .... Concurso de Cocina "Mesón de Cándido"

4. 3º .... Concurso de guitarra flamenca "Fuente y caudal"

5. 1ª .... Muestra de Trajes Regionales Españoles de la ciudad de Sepúlveda

6. 3ª .... Exhibición de gaita asturiana del Concejo de Escampero

7. 1º .... Congreso Nacional de las Caras de Bélmez de la Moraleda

PREMIOS

1er Premio de Novela "Marqués de Lozoya" Convocado por la revista *Blasón*, podrán optar a él suscriptores. Las obras pr... han de ser inéditas y escrita... tellano. Su extensión no de... sar los 200 folios mecanogra... doble espacio. El tema de los... co. Se otorgará un primer pr... 10.000 eur...

3 Write the corresponding ordinal or cardinal number for the following kings and queens.

➔ Juan Carlos I: *Juan Carlos Primero* .... [1]

1. Carlos III: .... [3]

2. Luis XV: .... [15]

3. Alfonso X: .... [10]

4. Isabel II: .... [2]

5. Alfonso XIII: .... [13]

B How they work

■ They agree with the noun in gender and number:

- *Vivo en el **cuarto** <u>piso</u>, **segunda** <u>puerta</u>.*
- *Las **primeras** <u>gafas</u> que llevé eran cuadradas.*

■ They are used with determiners:

- *<u>Mi</u> **primera** sobrina se llama Carlota y <u>el</u> **segundo** sobrino, Arnau.*

■ When used with nouns, they generally go before:

- *¡Bien! Hoy es el **primer** <u>día</u> de las vacaciones...*   (➔ 4. Adjective)

■ It is not necessary to use the noun when it is clear what we are talking about:

- *Ésta es la **primera** <u>casa</u> construida por Gaudí en Barcelona.*
  *Y ésta, la **segunda**.*

---

4 Look at this week's concert programme of the *Orquesta Filarmónica de Cañadahonda* and complete the text that follows. Take care with the agreements.

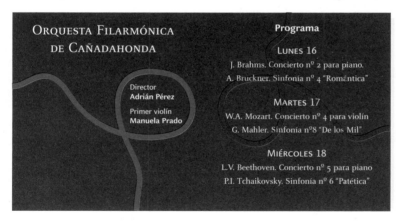

ORQUESTA FILARMÓNICA
DE CAÑADAHONDA

Director
Adrián Pérez

Primer violín
Manuela Prado

Programa

LUNES 16
J. Brahms. Concierto nº 2 para piano.
A. Bruckner. Sinfonía nº 4 "Romántica"

MARTES 17
W.A. Mozart. Concierto nº 4 para violín
G. Mahler. Sinfonía nº8 "De los Mil"

MIÉRCOLES 18
L.V. Beethoven. Concierto nº 5 para piano
P.I. Tchaikovsky. Sinfonía nº 6 "Patética"

El ➔ *primer* .... día, la orquesta va a tocar el .... concierto para piano de Brahms y la .... sinfonía de Bruckner. El .... día, el .... concierto de violín de Mozart y la .... sinfonía de Mahler. Y el .... día va a tocar el .... concierto para piano de Beethoven y la .... sinfonía de Tchaikovsky.

C Uses

■ Ordinal numbers are used to indicate the order of things in a sequence (in space and time):

¿Dónde están los servicios?

La **segunda** <u>puerta</u> a la derecha.

Me enamoré de ti la **primera** <u>vez</u> que te vi.

👁 To talk about the days of the month, Spanish uses cardinals **not** ordinals:

- *¿Cuándo es el cumpleaños de Lourdes?*
- *El <u>tres</u> de enero.*   [El ~~tercera~~ de enero]

■ We can use *primero, segundo, tercero* to order the points in a text:

- ¿Cómo preparas el daiquiri?
- **Primero**, pico cuatro cubitos de hielo y los meto en la coctelera; **segundo**, echo una cucharada de azúcar, un vasito de ron blanco y un poco de zumo de lima y lo agito bien; **tercero**, lo cuelo todo y, al final, lo pongo en copas de martini.

[First of all...]
[Next...]
[Then...]

5 This recipe for bread with tomato and *jamón* (cured ham) is not right. Put the instructions in the right order.

.... se echa
sal y aceite de oliva.

.Primero........ se corta
una rebanada de pan.

.... se unta
con tomate.

.... se cubre
con lonchas finas de jamón.

D   Ordinals from 10th upwards

■ In formal language, ordinal numbers are used from *10º* upwards to talk about:

Events
- *Duodécima (12º) Asamblea de Micología.*
- *Vigésimo cuarto (24º) Encuentro Nacional de Libreros.*

Anniversaries
- *Trigésimo (30º) aniversario de la muerte del poeta Alberto Mori.*
- *Undécimo (11º) aniversario de la Sociedad Bonaerense de Peletería.*

Position in a series
- *España asciende al vigésimo (20º) puesto de los países desarrollados.*
- *Décimo octavo (18º) día de guerra en Aquinostán.*
- *El corredor español llegó en el puesto trigésimo tercero (33º).*

11º	*undécimo/a*
12º	*duodécimo/a*
13º	*décimo tercero/a*
14º	*décimo cuarto/a*
15º	*décimo quinto/a*
	...
20º	*vigésimo/a*
30º	*trigésimo/a*
40º	*cuadragésimo/a*
50º	*quincuagésimo/a*
60º	*sexagésimo/a*
70º	*septuagésimo/a*
80º	*octogésimo/a*
90º	*nonagésimo/a*

6 Write the corresponding number next to the following ordinals.

➲ Vigésimo séptimo: ...27º...

1. Sexagésimo noveno: ....
2. Cuadragésimo sexto: ....
3. Nonagésimo primero: ....

4. Décimo octavo: ....
5. Undécimo: ....
6. Octogésimo segundo: ....
7. Septuagésimo sexto: ....

8. Trigésimo cuarto: ....
9. Quincuagésimo: ....
10. Duodécimo: ....
11. Nonagésimo noveno: ....

7 Write the missing ordinals in the following newspaper headlines.
Take care with the masculine and feminine nouns.

➲ Un corredor bengalí gana la (22ª) vigésimo segunda carrera popular de Vallecas.

1. Se reúne la comisión para la celebración del (45º) .... aniversario del descubrimiento de la isla de Tacri.

2. El (26º) .... Congreso de

Medicina Natural tendrá lugar en Berlín, en marzo.

3. La novelista Alameda Robles gana la (19ª) ....
.... edición del premio Ciudad de Murcia.

4. El motorista Nito Fons sufre un accidente y llega a la meta en la (31ª) .... posición.

11. Quantifiers: *demasiado, mucho, bastante...*

Quantifiers are used **to modify the intensity or the quantity** of the meaning of a noun, an adjective, a verb or some adverbs.

A   With nouns: *mucho chocolate / muchas galletas*

UNCOUNTABLE NOUNS

Demasiado chocolate   **Mucho** chocolate   **Bastante** chocolate [enough]   **Poco** chocolate [not enough]   Nada de chocolate

COUNTABLE NOUNS

Demasiadas galletas   **Muchas** galletas   **Bastantes** galletas [enough]   **Pocas** galletas [not enough]   Ninguna galleta Ningún plato

- With nouns, quantifiers –with the exception of **nada de**– behave like adjectives: **demasiado**, **mucho**, **poco** and **ningún** agree in gender and number, but **bastante** only agrees in number.
  These forms may be used without a noun when it is clear what we are talking about.

➔ 8. Indefinite articles

- ¿Tenemos **bastantes** <u>cervezas</u> para todos?
- ○ Sí, en la nevera hay **muchas**.
- Yo pensaba que había **pocas**.

- Date prisa. Tenemos **poco** <u>tiempo</u>.
- ○ Tenemos **bastante**. Todavía nos queda una hora.
- Sí, pero hay **mucho** <u>tráfico</u>.

---

1 Describe the drawings using the quantifiers *nada de / ningún, poco, bastante, mucho* and *demasiado* in that order. Take care with the agreements.

➔ Hay poca agua y
   muchos cubitos.

mucho
1. hay bastante
   agua y pocos
   cubitos

2. hay bastante
   agua y bastante
   cubitos

3. hay nada de agua
   y demasiados cubitos

4. hay demasiado
   agua y nada de
   ninguna
   cubitos

2 Complete with *ningún*, *ninguna* or *nada de*. Check carefully whether the noun is countable or not.

➔ No hay ...*nada de*... agua y tampoco queda
...*ningún*... vaso.

1. Puedes tomarlo. No lleva *nada de* cafeína.

2. No puedo comprarlo. No tengo *ningún* dinero.

3. Ya no queda *ninguna* botella de aceite.

4. Todavía no ha entrado *ningún* cliente.

5. Sabe mejor así, sin *nada de* azúcar.

6. Al final no ha hecho *ningún* comentario.

B   *Poco/un poco de* + uncountable nouns: *Hay un poco de comida pero hay poca bebida.*

■ Used with uncountable nouns, **poco** and **un poco de** express small quantity, but with **poco** we are focusing on the negative –what there isn't, and with **un poco de** we are focusing on the positive– what there is:

No hay mucha
limonada pero **hay**.

Hay **un poco de** limonada.
Podemos probarla.

Hay **poca** limonada.
No hay para los dos.

Hay limonada, pero
no suficiente.

👁 *Poco/a/os/as* agree with the noun. *Un poco de* does not take agreements:

● Queda *poca* leche.

● Dame un poco de leche. [Dame ~~una poca~~ de leche]

---

3 The Jiménez family finds it very difficult to make a shopping list. Bonifacio, the husband, always sees what they have, whereas his wife always sees what is missing. Complete the missing words.

Hay un poco de tortilla de patatas en la nevera.
➔ ...*Bonifacio*...

Nos queda un poco de leche.
1. *Bonifacio*

Hay poco vinagre.
2. *Wife*

Hay muy poco tomate frito.
3. *Wife*

Queda un poco de jamón serrano.
4. *Bonifacio*

Hay un poco de fruta.
5. *Bonifacio*

Tenemos poco atún.
6. *Wife*

Hay poca sal.
7. *Wife*

---

4 Complete with *un poco de* or con *poco, poca, pocos, pocas*.

➔ No veo casi nada. Hay ...*poca*... luz.

1. Todavía puedo leer. Hay *un poco de* luz.

2. La sopa está sosa. Creo que tiene ...*poca*... sal.

3. La sopa está sosa. Ponle *un poco de* sal.

4. Queda ...*poca*... arroz. Tenemos que comprar más.

5. Queda *un poco de* arroz. Puedes probarlo.

6. Tenemos ...*poco*... dinero. Voy al banco.

7. Tenemos *un poco de* dinero. Podemos tomar algo.

8. Hace *un poco de* frío. ¿Enciendo la calefacción?

9. Hace ...*poco*... frío. ¿Vamos a dar un paseo?

C With adjectives, adverbs and verbs: *Corre mucho*; *es muy rápido*; *está muy lejos*.

■ When the quantifiers are referring to an adjective, adverb or verb, they **do not change**:

- *Mis vecinos son **muy** <u>agradables</u>.*
- *Ya estamos **bastante** <u>cerca</u> de mi pueblo.*
- *Las novelas policíacas me <u>gustan</u> **mucho**.*

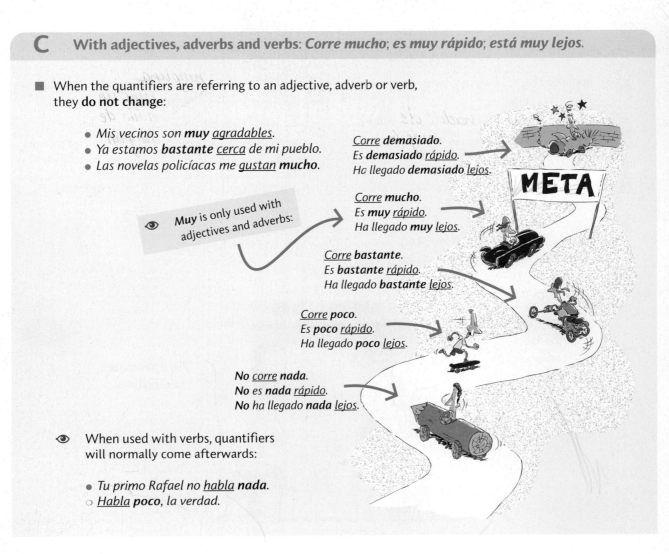

👁 *Muy* is only used with adjectives and adverbs:

*Corre **demasiado**.*
*Es **demasiado** <u>rápido</u>.*
*Ha llegado **demasiado** <u>lejos</u>.*

*Corre **mucho**.*
*Es **muy** <u>rápido</u>.*
*Ha llegado **muy** <u>lejos</u>.*

*Corre **bastante**.*
*Es **bastante** <u>rápido</u>.*
*Ha llegado **bastante** <u>lejos</u>.*

*Corre **poco**.*
*Es **poco** <u>rápido</u>.*
*Ha llegado **poco** <u>lejos</u>.*

*No <u>corre</u> **nada**.*
*No es **nada** <u>rápido</u>.*
*No ha llegado **nada** <u>lejos</u>.*

👁 When used with verbs, quantifiers will normally come afterwards:

- *Tu primo Rafael no <u>habla</u> **nada**.*
- *<u>Habla</u> **poco**, la verdad.*

---

5 Complete the examples with a quantifier that expresses a greater degree than the previous one. To get the form right, check whether the quantifier refers to a noun or not.

➲ ● Hace **bastante** calor, ¿verdad?
  ○ Sí, _mucho_ .

1. ● ¿Has recibido **muchas** cartas?
   ○ _demasiadas_ no he podido leerlas.

2. ● Esta chica habla **poco**.
   ○ Pues conmigo sí habla _bastante_ .

3. ● Han venido **muchos** invitados.
   ○ _demasiados_ ; ya no cabemos.

4. ● ¿Tu hermano es un chico **bastante** alto?
   ○ Sí, _muy_ alto: mide dos metros.

5. ● ¿Come usted **muchos** dulces?
   ○ Como _demasiado_ , pero dulces, no.

6. ● Últimamente trabajas **mucho**.
   ○ _demasiado_ .Voy a buscar otro trabajo.

7. ● Este niño no come **nada**.
   ○ Es cierto. Come _poco_ .
   ¿Lo llevamos al médico?

8. ● Casi no nos vemos. Vivimos **muy** lejos.
   ○ _demasiado_ : dos horas en avión.

9. ● Es **bastante** temprano, ¿verdad?
   ○ _muy_ temprano; todavía no ha salido el sol.

10. ● Yo viajo **poco**, pero no me gusta viajar.
    ○ Pues yo por mi trabajo viajo _bastante_ .

---

6 Complete with *poco, bastante* or *demasiado*. Take care with the agreements.

➲ Este barco puede llevar 2000 personas y hoy lleva 2500. Es _demasiado_ peso.

1. Corres _demasiado_ . El límite de velocidad es 120 Km. por hora y tú vas a 150.

2. Son dos personas y cada uno toma 2 litros de agua al día. Con 4 litros tienen _bastante_ agua para hoy.

3. Estudia _poco_ . Seguro que no pasa el examen.

4. Estoy engordando. Como _demasiados_ dulces y hago _poco_ deporte.

5. Todas las naranjas no caben en esta bolsa. Son _demasiadas_

Personal pronouns

Pero, Antonia, ¿a mí me gustan los caracoles?

12. Personal pronouns. Introduction.

To use personal pronouns well you need to be able to identify the subject and the different types of objects a verb can have.

➲ 13. Subject pronouns

➲ 15. Object pronouns

A   Subject, direct object and indirect object

■ In some cases we only need to say the **subject** and the **verb** that agrees with it:

- *Laura pinta*.

SUBJECT

> We are only talking about one subject (Laura) who is carrying out an activity (painting).

➲ 19. Conjugation. The basic building blocks

■ In other cases you also have to talk about another element, different from the subject, which is **directly related to the verb**. This other element is the **direct object** (DO) or accusative:

- *Laura pinta paisajes*.

SUBJECT — DO

- *Laura pinta a sus hijos*.

SUBJECT — DO

> We say that Laura paints and that Laura paints: landscapes, her children...

👁 **The DO can refer to people or things**. When it refers to people, we use the preposition **a**:

- *Desde la ventana veo mi coche*.
- *Desde la ventana veo a mi hijo*.

■ In other cases, the verb can have another object that normally refers to the receiver of the action of the verb. This new element is called the **indirect object** (IO) or dative, and may be combined with the DO:

- *Laura les pinta paisajes a sus hijos*.

SUBJECT — DO — IO

- *Laura les pinta hojas a los árboles*.

SUBJECT — DO — IO

> We are also able to indicate who receives the things that Laura paints.

👁 **The IO can refer to people or things**, and is always preceded by the preposition a:

- *Les he comprado unos juguetes a mis sobrinos*.
- *Le he quitado la mancha a la camisa*.

1 The Gómez family has lots of children, and each of them, except the baby, helps with the housework.

Paco, el padre, hace la compra.

Dolores les prepara el desayuno a sus hermanos pequeños.

Eduardo pone la ropa en la lavadora.

Leonor les echa agua a las plantas cada día.

María, la madre, les hace la comida y la cena a todos.

Elisabeth lleva a los pequeños al cole.

Felipa, la asistenta, limpia la casa y cuida al bebé.

Así, la casa siempre funciona bien.

Now answer these questions. Your answers will show you the subject of each sentence.

➲ ¿Quién limpia la casa y cuida al bebé? ➲ *Felipa*

1. ¿Quién les echa agua a las plantas? 1. ....
2. ¿Quién hace la compra? 2. ....
3. ¿Quién prepara el desayuno? 3. ....
4. ¿Quién lleva a los pequeños al cole? 4. ....
5. ¿Quién pone la ropa en la lavadora? 5. ....
6. ¿Quién hace la comida? 6. ....
7. ¿Qué funciona bien? 7. ....

Now answer these questions. Your answers will tell you the DO (accusative) of each sentence.

➲ ¿Qué limpia Felipa? ➲ *La casa*

8. ¿Qué les echa Leonor a las plantas? 8. ....
9. ¿Qué prepara Dolores? 9. ....
10. ¿Qué hace el padre? 10. ....
11. ¿A quién lleva Elizabeth al cole? 11. ....
12. ¿Qué pone Eduardo en la lavadora? 12. ....
13. ¿A quién cuida Felipa? 13. ....
14. ¿Qué hace la madre? 14. ....

Now answer these questions. Your answers will tell you the IO (dative) of each sentence.

➲ ¿A quién le hace María la comida? ➲ *A todos*

15. ¿A qué le echa agua Leonor? 15. ....
16. ¿A quién le prepara Dolores el desayuno? 16. ....
17. ¿A quién le hace María la cena? 17. ....

2 Link the sentences with their other halves, as in the example. Decide if the words in the column on the right are DO or IO.

➲ Andrés riega cada dos días... a. a sus amigos que están de viaje *IO*

Andrés les riega las plantas... b. el jardín *DO*

1. El secretario anota siempre... a. todas las citas ....

El secretario le anota sus citas... b. a la directora ....

2. El profesor les enseña música jugando... a. las matemáticas ....

El profesor enseña con juegos... b. a los niños ....

3. El hijo les lava y les plancha la ropa... a. a sus padres ....

La lavadora lava y seca en dos horas... b. las camisas ....

4. Paco pone en la mesa... a. la comida ....

Paco le pone la comida... b. a Marta ....

B   Reflexive constructions: *Ella se pinta*.

■ With the reflexive forms (*acostarse*, *lavarse*, *vestirse*...), the object
(direct or indirect) and the subject refer to the same person or thing:

- *Laura <u>se</u> pinta en sus cuadros.*
  SUBJECT = DO

- *Laura <u>se</u> pinta los labios.*
  SUBJECT = IO

❸ **Link as in the example and indicate which of the sentences on the left are reflexive.**

➔ a. Raúl se ata los zapatos. *Reflx.* ⎯⎯ a. Son pequeños y tiene que ayudarles.

   b. Raúl les ata los zapatos. .... ⎯⎯ b. Es ya mayor y puede hacerlo solo.

1. a. Tú siempre me pones la comida primero. ......   a. Eres muy amable conmigo.

   b. Tú siempre te pones la comida primero. ......   b. Eres un maleducado.

2. a. Me he cortado el pelo. ......   a. Con mi nueva máquina no necesito a nadie.

   b. Me han cortado el pelo. ......   b. Mis peluqueros son muy buenos.

3. a. Nos hemos despertado pronto esta mañana. ......   a. Nos hemos enfadado mucho con ellos.

   b. Nos han despertado pronto esta mañana. ......   b. Pusimos el despertador a las 6:30 para salir temprano.

C   Constructions that express opinions: *A Jaime le gustan las motos*.

■ With verbs like *apetecer*, *doler*, *encantar*, *gustar*, *molestar*, *preocupar*, etc.,
the subject is something that produces an effect (sensation, feeling, emotion
or reaction) in someone, and the indirect object (IO) refers to the receiver, the
person who feels this effect:

- *A Alfredo le gusta<u>n</u> <u>los cuadros</u> de Laura.*
   IO   SUBJECT

➲ 18. Reflexive and opinion-expressing constructions

❹ **Underline the subject of the following sentences.**

➔ a. <u>Eduardo</u> tiene muchas plantas.

   b. A Eduardo le gustan <u>las plantas</u>.

1. a. Esta mañana me duele la cabeza.

   b. Alicia tiene la cabeza muy pequeña, ¿verdad?

2. a. A los niños les apetecen unos helados.

   b. Los niños han pedido unos helados.

3. a. A nosotros ese problema no nos preocupa.

   b. Nosotros resolveremos ese problema.

4. a. ¿Tu madre ha llamado a los niños?

   b. A Rocío le encantan los niños.

5. a. ¿Les molesta a ustedes el ruido?

   b. Los niños hacen mucho ruido.

6. a. Las chicas prefieren la música disco.

   b. A las chicas les encanta la música disco.

7. a. La tele le molesta a tu madre.

   b. Tu madre no quiere ver la tele.

13. Subject pronouns: *yo, tú, él...*

A   Forms: *yo, tú, él...*

■ The Personal pronouns that are used as the subject of the sentence and therefore agree with the verb are:

	SINGULAR	PLURAL
1st PERSON	*yo*	*nosotros, nosotras*
2nd PERSON	*tú*	*vosotros, vosotras*
3rd PERSON	*él, ella*	*ellos, ellas*

➔ 14. Pronouns with prepositions

■ In mainland Spanish (unlike the Spanish of the Canary Islands) *tú* and *vosotros/vosotras* are used in less formal relationships or between friends. *Usted* and *ustedes* are used in more formal or hierarchical relationships:

¿Vosotros queréis algo más?

¿Ustedes quieren algo más?

INFORMAL	FORMAL
tú	*usted*
vosotros/vosotras	*ustedes*

👁 *Usted, ustedes* always take verbs in the 3rd person:

MÉDICO: *Se <u>encuentra</u> usted estupendamente.*
PACIENTE: *¿<u>Está</u> usted seguro, don Dimas?*

> Doctor and patient have a formal relationship. *Encuentra* and *está* are third person singular forms.

MANUEL: *¿Te <u>encuentras</u> bien?*
PACO: *Yo, estupendamente; ¿y tú?, ¿cómo <u>estás</u>?*

> Manuel and Paco have an informal relationship. *Encuentras* and *estás* are 2nd person singular forms.

---

1 **Claudia is talking to her friend Marta. Which pronoun does she use to talk about...?**

➔ Claudia .... *Yo* ....   5. el ex-novio de Claudia ....

1. Claudia y Marta ....   6. una amiga de Marta ....

2. Claudia y el novio de Claudia ....   7. las hermanas de Marta ....

3. unos amigos de Claudia ....   8. Marta y el novio de Marta ....

4. Marta ....   9. Marta y su hermana ....

yo ✓   nosotras   ellos   vosotros   vosotras   nosotros   tú   él   ellas   ella

2 *Tú* **or** *usted***? Link and indicate which form is used to talk to each of these people.**

➔ Con una dependienta de una tienda. ...*usted*...   a. ¿Sabe cómo se sale hacia Madrid?

1. Con la novia de un amigo. ....   b. ¿Y vas a venir mañana a clase?

2. Con un compañero de la universidad. ....   c. ¿No me puede hacer una rebaja?

3. Con una vecina de setenta años. ....   d. ¿Necesita ayuda, doña Reme?

4. Con un policía de tráfico. ....   e. Por favor, ¿nos trae la cuenta?

5. Con un vecino de dieciocho años. ....   f. Te vas a caer. Ten cuidado.

6. Con un camarero en un restaurante. ....   g. Aquí tienes el aceite que me ha pedido tu madre.

7. Con un niño pequeño. ....   h. Eres la persona perfecta para Pepe, de verdad.

B With and without the pronoun: *¿Cómo te llamas?*/*¿Tú cómo te llamas?*

■ Unlike other languages, in Spanish the subject pronoun **is not always used** with the verb. Its use is **necessary** when we want to highlight or contrast the person or people identified as the subject as opposed to other people:

Hola, soy Pepe. Llámame.

Hola, **Yo** soy Pepe y **él** es Javier.

[There are no people to contrast Pepe with, only him.]

[There is a contrast of people. *Yo/él.*]

PACO: *Alicia y yo vamos a cenar fuera, ¿os venís?*
SONIA: *Es que **nosotras** habíamos pensado ir al concierto de Gamberries.*

[Sonia says *nosotras* to contrast the plans she and her friend have with those suggested by Paco.]

👁 The forms *usted*/*ustedes* cannot always be used to create a contrast. They are also used to make the formal mode of address clear:

- *Adelante, pase **usted**, pase. Siéntese **usted**.*
- *¿Vendrán **ustedes** a la inauguración?*

- *¿Han reservado **ustedes** mesa?*
- *Debe traer **usted** el pasaporte.*

3 Complete with the best option.

➲ a. yo voy después
   b. voy después

- La próxima semana voy a París y, si tengo tiempo, ...*voy después*... a Bruselas.
- ○ ¿Ah sí? Qué suerte.

- ■ La próxima semana Carlos se va unos días a París.
- ❑ Sí, ya lo sé. *Yo voy después* , del diez al veinte de mayo.

1. a. **nosotras** no queremos
   b. no queremos

- El jefe ha propuesto venir a trabajar los sábados; y algunos en la oficina han dicho que sí, pero ....
- ○ ¿Y si venís el sábado también tenéis que trabajar el lunes?

- ■ ¿Tenemos que venir el sábado a trabajar? ¿Es obligatorio?
- ❑ Bueno, obligatorio no. Si .... , podemos quedarnos el lunes hasta las nueve.

2. a. sabe cocinar
   b. **ella** sabe cocinar

- Lucía es fantástica: trabaja muy bien, ... , y, además, baila.
- ○ Tú también bailas muy bien.

- ■ Yo no tengo ni idea de cocina, y tú tampoco. ¿ .... ?
- ❑ Espero que sí. Esta cena es importante para nosotras.

3. a. **él** no se levanta
   b. no se levanta

- Carlos dice que si quieres ir tú a pescar a las seis, que muy bien, pero que .... tan temprano un domingo.
- Carlos últimamente está muy raro: .... hasta las once, fuma sin parar, no me habla... No sé, chica, muy raro.

4. a. **ellas** no vinieron
   b. no vinieron

- Marina y Antonia me dijeron que iban a venir, pero al final ....
- Avisamos a las chicas y a los chicos, pero .... Sólo los chicos.

5. a. lo has roto **tú**
   b. lo has roto

- No le eches la culpa al perro. El jarrón .... Sólo quiero saber por qué ....

14. Pronouns with prepositions: *a mí, para ti, con él...*

A Formas

■ When personal pronouns are used after a preposition, we use the subject
forms, except *yo* and *tú*:

PREPOSITION	PRONOUN
a	*mí*
de	*ti*
en	*él, ella*
para	*usted*
por	*nosotros/-as*
sin	*vosotros/-as*
contra	*ellos, ellas*
desde	*ustedes*
...	

👁 [a ~~yo~~ a mí]
[para ~~tú~~ para ti]

➲ 13. Subject pronouns

¿Son para mí?

No, no son para ti.

- *Estoy segura de que mi novio piensa mucho **en mí**.*
- *Me han hablado muy bien **de ti**.*
- *¿Puedo hacer algo **por usted**?*
- *No sé qué van a hacer **sin nosotros**.*
- *Esto me lo han dado en la fotocopiadora **para vosotras**.*
- *Ellos no están **contra usted** están **contra mí**.*
- ***A mí** me han regalado un bolígrafo, ¿y **a vosotros**?*
- *Si te pones delante **de ella**, no va a ver nada. Eres muy alto.*

👁 The prepositions *entre*, *hasta* (when it means "even") and *según* are used
with the forms *yo* and *tú* rather than the *mí and ti*:

- ***Entre tú** y **yo** no hay nada.*
- *Eso, **hasta yo** lo entiendo.*
- ***Según tú**, ¿quién ganará las elecciones?*

---

1 Complete with the appropriate pronouns. Then link each sentence from the first column
with the correct response from the second.

vosotras vosotros tú ti ✓ mí usted ustedes

yo ✓ mí nosotros nosotras ti vosotros

➲ • Mira, he comprado estos pasteles pensando en
ti...... , que te gustan tanto.

1. • Mirad, me he acordado de .... y he
traído la tarta que os gusta tanto a las dos.

2. • Señora Cuevas, le he traído rosas porque sé que
a .... le encantan.

3. • Me he comprado esos dulces que ....
compras siempre, a ver qué tal están.

4. • Dime la verdad, ¿hay algo entre .... dos?
Porque todo el mundo dice que sois novios.

5. • Para .... es muy importante: tienen que
venir a mi boda. No sería igual sin ....

a. ○ Ah, ¿son para .... ? Muchas gracias, es
verdad que son preciosas.

b. ○ Muchas gracias. ¿Te quedarás a comerla con
.... verdad?

c. ○ *Yo....* también te he comprado una cosa: mira.

d. ○ Entre .... no hay absolutamente nada. Te lo
prometo. Somos simplemente amigos.

e. ○ Muchas gracias. Nosotros ya no salimos nunca.
Pero iremos por .... Os queremos
mucho a los dos.

f. ○ Te van a encantar, son buenísimos. ¿Y son
todos para .... o me dejarás comer
uno?

B   *Conmigo, contigo, con él...*

conmigo   👁 [con mí]
contigo   [con ti]
con él, ella
con usted
con nosotros/-as
con vosotros/-as
con ellos/-as
con ustedes

*Ni contigo ni sin ti
tienen mis males remedio.
Contigo porque me matas,
sin ti porque yo me muero.*

- *Clara va a venir **conmigo** al ginecólogo. Menos mal, porque no quiero ir sola.*
- *Voy a ir **con ella** al ginecólogo, porque no quiere ir sola.*

- *No pienso irme a vivir **contigo**. Eres un desastre.*
- *No me voy a vivir **con él** porque es un desastre.*

- *Stephan no quiere salir ni **contigo** ni **conmigo**.*
- *Stephan no quiere salir **con nosotras**. ¿Estará enfadado?*

2 Read Ana and Montse's letter to their brother Daniel, and complete it by writing in the correct option from the box below.

Querido Daniel:

➔ *Sin ..ti.. ya nada es igual en casa. Desde que te fuiste con esa chica sueca, la tía Berta no para de hablar (1) de .... Dice que (2) para .... eres el más simpático de la familia, el más inteligente. (3) A .... casi ni nos habla y a tía Rita sólo le grita. Tú sabes que (4) con .... siempre ha tenido una relación difícil, pero ahora es insoportable. El abuelo dice que tenemos que hablar en serio (5) con .... , y que si no dejas a la sueca, toda la herencia, al final, será (6) para .... y tú te quedarás sin nada. Pero no te preocupes porque no es mucho y ya sabes que el abuelo siempre piensa que todos estamos (7) contra .... , y cambia de opinión con frecuencia. Mamá insiste en que sólo podemos confiar (8) en .... porque es la única que puede poner orden en esta casa, pero sigue yendo al bingo todas las tardes.*

Un abrazo de tus hermanas y recuerdos a Inge,

Ana + Montse

➔ tú / (ti) / te   5. tú / ___tigo / ti
1. te / ti / tú   6. nosotras / nos
2. la / ella / le   7. lo / él / le
3. nosotras / nos   8. ella / la / le
4. ella / la / le

3 Write the preposition with the appropriate form of the pronoun, as in the example, and then put them in the appropriate sentence.

Preposición + Pronombre		
para	+ yo ✓	*para mí*......
a	+ tú	....
con	+ yo	....
sin	+ nosotras	....
entre	+ tú y yo	....
con	+ tú	....
según	+ tú	....
de	+ tú	....
hasta	+ yo	....
sobre	+ tú	....
de	+ yo	....
por	+ yo	....
para	+ ellos	....

➔ ¿El regalo es *para mí*........... ? ¡Muchísimas gracias!
1. ¿Quieres venir .... al cine esta tarde?
2. No puedo salir .... esta noche. Lo siento.
3. Los espárragos que hay en la nevera son ....
4. Gracias .... ahora soy una mujer feliz.
5. Este secreto debe quedar ....
6. Nuestros maridos no podrían vivir ....
7. Cada día te siento más lejos ....
8. Estos ejercicios son muy fáciles, ... los hago bien.
9. Cuidado, tienes un camión detrás ....
10. ¿Y, ... , cuál es la mejor solución al problema?
11. Venga, por favor, apúntate a la excursión. Hazlo ....
12. Mira, mira, en el periódico de hoy hay un artículo ....

A — First and second person: *me, te, nos, os.*

■ When the objects of a sentence refer to the persons *yo, tú, nosotros/-as, vosotros/-as,* we use **the same form** of the pronoun for both the direct object (DO) and indirect object (IO):

GRAMMATICAL PERSON	yo	tú	nosotros/-as	vosotros/-as
FORMS OF DO AND IO	*me*	*te*	*nos*	*os*

→ 12. Personal pronouns

→ 16. Position and combination

→ 17. Presence and redoubling

Me pinta.

Me pinta un paisaje.

- • ¿*Me* han llamado?
- ○ Sí, *te* han llamado tres clientes.

- • Renata *nos* ha invitado a su casa. *Os* recojo a las nueve, ¿vale?

- • ¿*Me* das las señas de Enrique?
- ○ *Te* doy el móvil y la dirección de casa.

- • Los ladrones *nos* dieron un susto tremendo.
- ○ ¿Y *os* robaron algo?

---

1 Earth is visited by some extraterrestrials. Complete the sentences with *me, te, nos, os.*

→ ¿ ..Me.. has llamado tú a mi antena telepática?

1. Sí, he sido yo. ¿ .... prestas tu pistola de rayos?

2. ¿ .... lleváis a los dos a vuestro planeta? Queremos conocerlo.

3. ¿ .... enseñáis vuestro platillo volante a mi hermano y a mí?

4. ¿Vosotros coméis comida como la nuestra? ¿......... preparo algo?

5. ¿ .... controlan mucho tus jefes?, ¿y tu mujer?

6. ¿......... enseño una foto de mi hijo? ¿Vosotros también tenéis hijos como los humanos?

7. Los terrícolas .... hacen preguntas muy raras. Creemos que tienen miedo.

8. Queridos terrícolas: .... invadiremos en el año 2040 y .... quitaremos la Tierra para siempre.

B   Third person: *lo*, *la*, *los*, *las* / *le*, *les*.

■ When the object of a sentence refers to a third person or persons (*él*, *ella*, *ellos*, *ellas*) or to the *usted*, *ustedes*, polite forms, we use **different pronoun forms** for the **direct object** (DO) and **indirect object** (IO):

GRAMMATICAL PERSON	DO FORMS		IO FORMS
	MASCULINE	FEMININE	MASCULINE AND FEMININE
Él, ella, usted	*lo*	*la*	*le*
Ellos, ellas, ustedes	*los*	*las*	*les*

Lo pinta.

Le pinta un paisaje.

■ We use the pronouns to refer to <u>a person</u> or <u>a thing</u> we have talked about before, or that has been clearly identified

DO

lo
- ¿Has recibido <u>mi e-mail</u>?
- ○ Sí, *lo* he leído. Es muy interesante.

- ¿Y <u>Juan</u>? No *lo* encuentro.

la
- ¿Llevas <u>la cartera</u>?
- ○ Sí, *la* llevo en el bolso.

- ¿Ha venido <u>Elisa</u>? Todavía no *la* he visto.
- ○ Ha venido, pero *la* han llamado y se ha tenido que ir.

- ¿*La* acompaño en coche, <u>señora Cueto</u>?

los
- ¿Y <u>los documentos</u>? ¿*Los* habéis visto?

- He quedado con <u>tus primos</u>. *Los* he invitado a comer.

- ¿Qué tal <u>Ángela y Alfredo</u>?
- ○ Pues ayer *los* llamé y están muy bien.

las
- ¿<u>Estas gafas</u> son tuyas? *Las* he encontrado en el coche.

- ¿Sabes algo de <u>las hermanas de Sofía</u>?
- ○ Ayer *las* vi. Fuimos a dar una vuelta.

IO

le
- ¿Y <u>el coche</u>?
- ○ *Le* están cambiando el aceite.

- ¿Has hablado con <u>tu hermano</u>?
- ○ No, *le* he escrito un e-mail.

- ¿Ya has hecho <u>la ensalada</u>? ¿*Le* has echado sal?

- Hoy es el cumpleaños de <u>Julia</u>. Y no *le* he comprado nada.

- ¿Quiere que *le* traiga un café, <u>señor Pérez</u>?

les
- Aquí tienes <u>los sobres</u>. ¿*Les* pones el sello?

- Ayer quedé con <u>mis amigos</u> y *les* devolví las llaves del piso.

- ¿Has avisado <u>a sus padres</u>?
- ○ Sí, *les* he dejado un mensaje.

- ¿Has regado ya <u>las plantas</u>?
- ○ No, *les* estoy quitando los bichos.

- <u>Las chicas</u> están muy contentas. *Les* han dado un premio.

2 Victoria's grandmother is a bit deaf. Complete as in the example.

➔ **Victoria:** Víctor baila la rumba con mucho estilo.
Abuela: ¿Qué? ¿Que ...*la*.... baila vestido?

1. **Victoria:** Víctor plancha las camisas mejor que mi madre.
Abuela: ¿Qué? ¿Que .... plancha con vinagre?

2. **Victoria:** Víctor corta el pelo como un profesional.
Abuela: ¿Qué? ¿Que .... corta en un funeral?

3. **Victoria:** Víctor ayuda a las ancianitas a ir a la iglesia.
Abuela: ¿Qué? ¿Que .... ayuda con la anestesia?

4. **Víctor:** Conocí a Victoria en un gimnasio.
Abuela: ¿Qué? ¿Que .... conociste en un armario?

5. **Víctor:** Victoria cuida a sus sobrinos todas las noches.
Abuela: ¿Qué? ¿Que .... lleva en coche?

6. **Víctor:** Victoria lleva a su madre a jugar al mus.
Abuela: ¿Qué? ¿Que .... lleva en autobús?

7. **Víctor:** Victoria prepara los macarrones como nadie.
Abuela: ¿Qué? ¿Que .... prepara con alguien?

3 Complete the following conversations with the appropriate pronouns.

➔ **Víctor:** ¿Y mi pijama? No lo veo.
Victoria: Está secándose. ...*Le*.... he quitado las manchas.

1. **Víctor:** ¿Vas a ver a tus sobrinos este fin de semana?
Victoria: Claro, ¿no te acuerdas? .... doy clases de natación todos los sábados.

2. **Victoria:** ¿No te parece que la sopa está un poco sosa?
Víctor: Es que .... he echado poca sal. Es más sano.

3. **Victoria:** ¿Cómo están tus tíos?
Víctor: No lo sé. Esta semana no .... he llevado el correo y no los he visto.

4. **Víctor:** Ha llamado un tal Javier preguntando por ti.
Victoria: ¡Anda, se me había olvidado! .... pedí unos libros prestados y no se los he devuelto.

5. **Victoria:** El perro está muy nervioso.
Víctor: No pasa nada. Ahora .... pongo la correa y salimos a dar una vuelta.

4 Complete the following sentences with *lo, la, los, las, le, les*.

Nuestro robot C3PO hace cosas extrañas:

➔ Ha aprendido a preparar natillas. ...*Las*.... hace muy ricas.

1. Se enfadó y .... rompió la antena a mi coche.
2. Alquiló un vídeo y .... metió en el microondas.
3. .... dio un susto tremendo a mi tía Eugenia.
4. Se ha comido mi radio y .... ha vomitado.
5. .... ha regalado una cama de agua a mis padres.
6. .... ha echado aceite lubricante a las plantas de mi abuela.
7. Sacó a pasear a los niños y .... llevó al bingo.
8. Discutió con el abuelo y .... encerró en el armario.
9. Se ha enamorado de mi hermana Fernanda. Esta noche .... ha invitado a cenar.
10. Ha cogido los discos de Julio Iglesias de mi padre y .... ha tirado por la ventana.
11. No soporta a las amigas de mi madre. El otro día .... echó a la calle.

C Neutral *lo: Yo eso no lo entiendo. Parece fácil, pero no lo es.*

■ The direct object DO pronoun *lo* can refer to things that we name with masculine singular nouns, but it may also refer to things that we talk about without naming them (neither masculine nor feminine):

- *No puedo entender <u>su libro</u>.*   *No puedo entenderlo.*   *Lo* = <u>*su libro*</u> (masculino)
- *No puedo entender <u>a ese hombre</u>.*   *No puedo entenderlo.*   *Lo* = <u>*ese hombre*</u> (masculino)
- *No puedo entender <u>por qué no vienes</u>.*   *No puedo entenderlo.*   *Lo* = <u>*por qué no vienes*</u> = *eso* (neutro)

■ We use the **neutral *lo*** DO pronoun when referring to objects that we don't identify as either masculine or feminine, because:

WE DON'T KNOW THE NAME OF THE OBJECT/THING.	• *¿Qué ha sido <u>eso</u>?, ¿**lo** has visto?*	• *¿Me das <u>esto</u>? **Lo** necesito.*
THE NAME OF THE OBJECT/THING IN NOT IMPORTANT.	• *¿Puedes tú recoger <u>todo eso</u>?* ○ *Sí, ya **lo** recojo yo mañana.*	• *¿Me acercas <u>aquello</u> de allí?* ○ *Sí, ahora mismo te **lo** doy.*
IT IS NOT A CONCRETE OBJECT/THING (facts, situations, things we say, think, know, feel, etc.).	• *¿Sabes qué? Al final, <u>Carlos se ha casado</u>.* ○ *No **lo** puedo creer. ¿Con quién? No me **lo** digas... ¡Con Adelina!*	• *¿Qué pasó el sábado en la piscina?* ○ *No **lo** sé. ¿Por qué **lo** dices?*

■ We also use *lo* when referring to the objects of the verbs **ser, estar** and **parecer**:

- *Es <u>muy rico</u>, pero no **lo** parece.*
- *Mira, tu jefe está <u>completamente loco</u>.* ○ *No, no **lo** está.*
- *Ya no eres <u>cariñoso conmigo</u>.* ○ *Sí que **lo** soy, pero tú no te das cuenta.*

5 The actress Margarita Bosque has been murdered. The police are questioning her lover, Amadeo Sanjosé. Indicate what *lo* refers to in each case and mark whether it is neutral (N) or masculine (M).

A= Amadeo   P= el policía

➲ P: ¿Cuándo durmió en su chalet por última vez?
    A: No **lo** recuerdo. Hace poco. (.N.)
       a. su chalet
       b. el último día que durmió en su chalet ✓

1. P: ¿Había otro hombre en la vida de Margarita Bosque?
    A: **Lo** siento. No tengo esa información. (....)
       a. el hecho de tener Margarita otro amante
       b. el hecho de no tener esa información

2. P: El cadáver tenía esto en un bolsillo. ¿Sabe qué es?
    A: No **lo** he visto en mi vida. (....)
       a. el cadáver
       b. el objeto encontrado en el bolsillo

3. P: ¿Y entiende eso que hay apuntado en su diario?
    A: ¿Cómo se atreve a tocar**lo**? (....)
       a. el diario
       b. las cosas escritas en el diario

4. P: ¿A usted este asesinato le parece sorprendente?
    A: Claro que me **lo** parece. (....)
       a. el asesinato
       b. sorprendente

5. P: Yo creo que este crimen no es un asesinato profesional.
    A: Pues, yo creo que sí **lo** es. (....)
       a. este crimen
       b. un asesinato profesional

6. P: Le aseguro que muy pronto vamos a detener al culpable.
    A: Así **lo** espero. (....)
       a. al culpable
       b. el hecho de detener al culpable

7. A: ¿Puedo llamar a mi abogado?
    P: Si **lo** tiene, está en su derecho. (....)
       a. el abogado
       b. el hecho de llamar al abogado

16. Position and combination of object pronouns

A One pronoun: *Te he visto. Os he visto.*

■ Object pronouns go **before the verb**, except when the verb is in
the affirmative imperative:

➜ 17. Presence and redoubling

DO + VERB

- ¿Me _llevas_ a la estación?
- Te _he visto_ en El Corting Less.
- No nos _llames_ tan tarde.
- Os _necesito_ ahora.

- Tú abres el frigorífico pero no lo _cierras_.
- La ensalada está muy rica. ¿La _has hecho_ tú?
- Los niños están con mi madre. ¿Los _recojo_ yo?
- Las camisas están ahí, pero no las _he planchado_.
- Se _ducha_ tres veces al año.

IO + VERB

- ¿Me _haces_ un favor?
- Te _he mandado_ un e-mail.
- Nos _regaló_ una mesa horrorosa.
- ¿Os _leo_ un cuento?

- Ayer quedé con Paco y le _devolví_ su libro.
- Hoy es el santo de Pepa. ¿Le _envio_ un sms?
- Si ves a los vecinos, no les _digas_ nada.
- Llamé a tus tías y les _di_ el móvil del pintor.
- A José María le _encantan_ los caracoles.

1 Put the words in each sentence in the right order and then match them to the correct picture.

 A ...... B ...... C ...... D ......

I

➜ ¿compro-le-entradas-para la ópera?

¿Le compro entradas para la ópera?

1. ¿en su restaurante de siempre-reservo-mesa-le?

....

2. ¿a alguna parte-llevo-lo?

....

3. ¿un baño caliente-preparo-le?

....

II

4. ¿a la peluquería-llevo-te?

....

5. ¿música-pongo-te?

....

6. ¿enciendo-te-el aire acondicionado?

....

7. ¿el cinturón de seguridad-abrocho-te?

....

III

8. ¿laváis-los dientes-os?

....

9. ¿acostáis-temprano-os?

....

10. ¿llevan-os-al médico?

....

11. ¿os-hacen regalos-en Navidad?

....

IV

12. han aplaudido-nos-durante veinte minutos

....

13. han tirado-ropa interior-al escenario-me

....

14. muchos autógrafos-han pedido-nos

....

15. han hecho-me-miles de fotos

....

B Combination of two pronouns: *Te lo compro. Os lo compro.*

- When we need to use **two pronouns** (one DO and the other IO) the order is:

IO	+	DO	+	VERB
Te		*lo*		*compro*

me/te/nos/os   lo/la/los/las

➡ 12. Personal pronouns

➡ 15. Object pronouns

- Oye, me gusta mucho esa <u>camisa</u> tuya. ¿*Me la dejas*?

- Necesitamos tu <u>ordenador</u>. ¿*Nos lo prestas*?

- He recibido unas <u>fotos</u> preciosas de José. ¿*Te las mando*?

- Sé dos <u>chistes</u> nuevos. ¿*Os los cuento*?

2 Ana and Andrés are about to have a baby daughter. Andrés is very nervous and wants to make sure everything is ready. Complete the responses.

En casa

➲ Andrés: ¿Has preparado la ropa de la niña?
Ana: Sí, ya *la* he preparado.

1. Andrés: ¿Llevas todos los documentos?
Ana: Sí, ... llevo todos: el informe médico, la ecografía, todo.

2. Andrés: ¿Has cogido la cámara de vídeo?
Ana: No, no .... he cogido. ¿Dónde está?

3. Andrés: ¿Llevas el osito de peluche?
Ana: Claro que .... llevo.

En el hospital

4. Andrés: ¿Te ha traído el agua la enfermera?
Ana: Sí, ... ha traído, pero está muy fría.

5. Ana: ¿Nos van a devolver los documentos?
Enfermera: Sí, no os preocupéis. El médico .... devolverá enseguida.

6. Andrés: ¿Os han traído el café?
Abuelos: Sí, ... han traído, no te preocupes.

7. Ana: ¿Me puedes abrir la ventana?
Andrés: Ahora mismo .... abro.

C Combination of two pronouns: *Se lo compro. Se la compro.*

- When the IO pronoun refers to a third person (*él, ella, ellos, ellas*) or the second person polite form (*usted, ustedes*), and it is combined with a DO pronoun (*lo/la/los/las*), the CI pronoun always takes the form *se*:

IO (3ʳᵈ PERSON)	+	DO	+	VERB
~~Le/Les~~ (Se)		*lo*		*compro*

lo/la/los/las

Se ... ⟨ a él / a ella / a ellos / a ellas / a usted / a ustedes ¿?

Se los he dado...

¿Qué has hecho con los exámenes, Jaimito?

¿A quién?

- ¿*Le* mandaron por fin el paquete?
- ○ Sí, *se lo* mandaron ayer.

- ¿*Le* diste a Linus la receta?
- ○ Sí, *se la* di por teléfono.

- ¿*Les* robaron las joyas a tus padres?
- ○ Sí, *se las* robaron todas.

- ¿Podrían cambiar las toallas?
- ○ Por supuesto, señores, ahora mismo *se las* subimos a la habitación.

- Señora, ¿*le* llevo el paquete al coche? ¿O *se lo* enviamos a su casa?

- ¿*Les* has comprado los bombones ya?
- ○ Todavía no.
- Ah, ¿no? Pues no *se los* compres, que son alérgicos al chocolate.

3 Ana and Andrés have had a baby girl, Lucía, who is doing well. However, Andrés can't stop worrying and asking Ana questions.

➲ Andrés: ¿Le has dado la manzanilla?

Ana: Sí, ..*se*.. ..*la*.. he dado hace un rato.

1. Andrés: ¿Le has puesto el chupete?

Ana: Sí, ... he puesto, pero no le gusta.

2. Andrés: ¿Le has cambiado el pañal?

Ana: No, Andrés, todavía no .... he cambiado.

3. Andrés: ¿Le has limpiado los oídos?

Ana: Sí, ... he limpiado.

4. Andrés: ¿Le han hecho los agujeros en las orejas?

Ana: No, no .... han hecho. ¿ .... vamos a hacer?

5. Andrés: ¿Le has dado el masaje?

Ana: Sí, ... he dado y le ha encantado.

4 Ana is a teacher in a nursery school. Complete as in the example.

➲ Lucía: Señorita Ana, ¿me puedes quitar el abrigo?

Ana: Sí, Lucía, ahora mismo ..*te lo quito*... .

1. Ana: Miguel, ¿le has devuelto las tijeras a Omar?

Miguel: Sí, seño, ... Creo que está cortando las cortinas de la ventana.

2. Ángela: Seño, ¿me puedes limpiar los mocos?

Ana: Sí, Ángela, ahora mismo ....

3. Sara y Sofía: Seño, ¿nos pones el vídeo de Cenicienta?

Ana: Dentro de un rato .... , ¿vale?

4. Ana: ¿Queréis leer un cuento?

Niños: No, seño. Tú .... Es que nosotros no sabemos leer todavía.

5. Ana: ¿Le has dado el rotulador verde a Adrián?

Leo: No, seño, no .... Es mío.

6. Lara: Seño, ¿me das una galleta?

Ana: Claro, Lara. .... ahora mismo.

7. Carmen y Andrés: Seño, ¿nos das la plastilina?

Ana: Sí, enseguida ....

8. Ana: ¿Os habéis lavado las manos?

Niños: No, seño, no ....

9. Ana: Omar, ¿les has echado la comida a los peces?

Omar: Sí, ... y .... han comido en un minuto.

10. Ana: Carmen, ¿tú le has dado un empujón a Sofía?

Carmen: No, yo no .... Ha sido Miguel.

D   With affirmative imperative, infinitive and gerund: *déjasela, dejársela, dejándosela...*

■ With the **affirmative imperative, infinitive** and **gerund** forms, object pronouns take the form of verb suffixes, coming after the verb and forming a single word with it:

AFFIRMATIVE IMPERATIVE + DO/IO	INFINITIVE + DO/IO	GERUND + DO/IO
Escríbela *Escríbele*	*Escribirla* *Escribirle*	*Escribiéndola* *Escribiéndole*

AFFIRMATIVE IMPERATIVE+IO+DO	INFINITIVE + IO + DO	GERUND + IO + DO
Escríbesela	*Escribírsela*	*Escribiéndosela*

• *Déjasela un momento a ella.*   • *Dejársela fue un error.*   • *Dejándosela no solucionas nada.*

👁 When we add the pronouns to the verb, the word stress does not change. For this reason, when the stressed syllable becomes the third or fourth in the word, we have to mark it with an accent (tilde).

Deja   *Dejar*   *Dejando*
Déjasela   *Dejársela*   *Dejándosela.*
   4   3   4

👁 With the pronoun *os* the final -*d* of the imperative form of **vosotros** is dropped: ➲ 34. Imperativo

• *Poneos los abrigos.* [*Ponedos los abrigos*]

➲ 20. Non-personal forms

5 *El baile del cachimbo* is the dance sensation of the summer.
The chorus repeats the actions using pronouns. Complete as in the example.

1ª estrofa	El coro dice:	El coro repite:
		¡ahora házselo a tu pareja!

Y uno, dos y tres. Levanta los brazos,   ➔ a. *Levantándolos*   ➔ b. *Levantándoselos*

mueve las manitas,   1 a. ....   1 b. ....

ahora dobla las rodillas   2 a. ....   2 b. ....

y un, dos, tres. Gira la cabecita.   3 a. ....   3 b. ....

Adelante y atrás, mueve las caderas,   4 a. ....   4 b. ....

sube la pierna derecha al compás,   5 a. ....   5 b. ....

y mueve el cuello sin parar.   6 a. ....   6 b. ....

¡Ay!, ¡qué gustito!, ¡ay!, ¡qué gustito!

6 The director of *La Bella Durmiente* (The Sleeping Beauty) and *La Cenicienta* (Cinderella)
is giving instructions to the actors. Put the correct pronouns in the gaps and don't forget the accents.

La Bella Durmiente

- Acércate despacio a la princesa. ➔ ..... Bésa.*la*.
  (1) ......coge...... la mano para ayudarla a levantarse.
  Estupendo, muy bien... Ahora (2) ....mira.......
  intensamente y (3) ....di....... que la quieres...
  ¡Genial, estupendo!
- A ver, ahora, todos vosotros (4) ....despertad.......;
  venga, (5) ...... levantad....... Si la Bella Durmiente
  está despierta, vosotros también.

La Cenicienta

- Bien, ahora tú, (6) ....prueba....... el zapato de
  cristal a Anastasia, la hermanastra. (7) ....coge.......
  el pie con mucha suavidad... Eso es, muy bien.
  Ahora (8) ....pon .... el zapato. Así, con delica-
  deza. Muy bien, estupendo...
- Ahora tú, Anastasia, muy enfadada, (9) ....tira.......
  el zapato a la cabeza. (10) ....di....... que es un
  inútil. ¡Espléndido! ¡Sublime!

E   **With periphrastic verbs:** *Tienes que comértelo / Te lo tienes que comer*

■ With **periphrastic verbs** (combinations of a conjugated and a non-conjugated
verb), the object pronouns can come either before the conjugated verb or after
the non-conjugated verb:

vas a comprar

+

te lo

Te lo <u>vas</u> a comprar.

Vas a <u>comprár</u>telo.

- *Te lo tengo que decir.*
- *Se lo voy a decir.*
- *Te lo estoy diciendo.*
- *Os la puedo enseñar.*

- *Tengo que decírtelo.*
- *Voy a decírselo.*
- *Estoy diciéndotelo.*
- *Puedo enseñárosla.*

👁 When the pronouns are put after the verb, they become suffixes and
form a single word (*Voy a regalárselo*); however, when the pronouns are
put before the verb they are written separately (*Se lo voy a regalar*).

➲ 33. Periphrastic verbs

7 Bea and Miguel are visiting a psychologist. Put the correct pronouns in the gaps and don't forget the accents.

➲ Bea: Miguel, ... lláma...*me*. alguna vez al trabajo.

1. Miguel: Bea, ... deja...... salir con mis amigos algún día. No pasa nada.

2. Bea: Tú siempre ...... estás regañando...... por hablar por teléfono con mis amigas.

3. Miguel: Y tú, ¿ ...... puedes dejar...... ver el fútbol en paz?

4. Bea: ....compra.... flores y .....di..... cosas bonitas.

5. Psicólogo: Tranquilos. No os enfadéis. ..... tenéis que decir..... siempre lo que pensáis el uno al otro.

6. Bea y Miguel: ¿ ..... tenemos que decir..... siempre, siempre lo que pensamos?, ¿en serio?

7. Psicólogo: Pues claro. Tenéis que recuperar el romanticismo. Tú, Bea, ... manda..... mensajes al móvil, ... diciendo..... que lo quieres. Y tú, Miguel, ... llama.... para ..... decir..... que estás deseando verla.

8 Lucía is a bit of a rebel. Put in the missing pronouns and don't forget the accents.

Mamá: Lucía, recoge tus juguetes. ➲ .....Recóge-.*los* , por favor, Lucía. (1) ¿ No ..... quieres recoger..... ? (2) Pues ..... vas a recoger..... , por las buenas o por las malas. (3) Venga, Lucía, ... tienes que recoger..... .

Lucía: (4) Ya ..... estoy recogiendo..... , mamá.

Mamá: Tómate la leche, Lucía.

Mamá: (5) Lucía, ¿ ..... vas a tomar..... la leche?

Lucía: (6) Ya ..... estoy tomando ..... , mamá.

Mamá: Lucía, apaga la televisión. (7) ..... Apaga..... , por favor. Lucía, (8) ..... tienes que apagar..... , ya es muy tarde. (9) ¿ ..... vas a apagar..... o no?

Lucía: (10) Ya ..... estoy apagando..... , mamá.

F In reflexive and opinion-expressing constructions: *Se las lava. Le gusta el chocolate.*

■ We can combine IO and DO pronouns in reflexive constructions. In these cases, **the reflexive pronoun goes before the non-reflexive pronoun:**

- *Se ha cortado las uñas pero no se las ha pintado.*

- *Ese vestido está muy bien. ¿Te lo pruebas?*

- *Me aprietan los zapatos.*
  ○ *Pues, quítatelos.*

- *Me lo puedo tocar pero no puedo vérmelo.*

■ In opinion-expressing constructions with verbs like *gustar*, *encantar*, *interesar*, *apetecer*, *preocupar*, *molestar*, *doler*, etc., we only use IO pronouns. They cannot be used with DO pronouns, as these constructions don't have a DO, only a subject and an IO:

➲ 18. Reflexive and opinion-expressing constructions

- *Me gustan mucho los garbanzos, pero es que ahora no me apetecen.*

- ¿*Te duele la garganta*?
  ○ *Me molesta un poco, sí.*

[Me ~~los~~ apetecen.]
[Me ~~la~~ molesta.]

Los garbanzos y la garganta son SUJETO y no CD.

9 This family has some rather strange habits. Complete with one or two pronouns.

➲ Mi madre se lava las manos continuamente. .*Se*... .*las*. lava unas veinte veces al día.

1. A mi padre .... duelen los huesos cuando va a llover. Le molestan especialmente las rodillas.

2. Yo me pongo normalmente dos pares de calcetines de lana. Siempre tengo los pies fríos. ¡ .... pongo incluso en verano!

3. A mis hermanos les gustan mucho los animales. .... interesan sobre todo los insectos. Son grandes coleccionistas.

4. A mi abuela le dan mucho miedo las tormentas. .... da pánico que le caiga un rayo en la cabeza.

5. Mis hermanas y yo nos pintamos las uñas de los pies de colores. .... pintamos así porque somos muy modernas.

6. En mi casa, nos acostamos todas las noches a las 10.30, y .... levantamos a las 6.30. En eso, mi padre es inflexible.

7. A mí me encanta mi familia. Y a vosotros, ¿qué .... parece?

83

17. Presence and redoubling of pronouns

A   Use of *lo, la, los, las / le, les*: *Lo ha comprado. Le ha dado un regalo a María.*

■ If we are referring to the **DO**, we use the **object pronouns** (*lo/la/los/las*) when talking about **things** or **people** we have already **identified**:

- ¿Dónde has puesto <u>la caja</u>?
- *La* he tirado. Estaba rota.

- ¿Y <u>mi equipaje</u>?
- Ya *lo* he guardado.

- <u>Las toallas</u> *las* he cambiado. Estaban mojadas.

- ¿Has encontrado <u>a tus amigos</u>?
- No, *los* estoy buscando.

👁 Unlike **IO** pronouns, we don't use **DO** pronouns if the **DO** has not been previously identified:

- He cogido las fotocopias.
- ¿Has llamado al camarero?
- Lleva a tus padres al cine.

[~~Las~~ he cogido las fotocopias.]
[~~¿Lo~~ has llamado al camarero?]
[Llévalo~~s~~ a tus padres al cine.]

■ If we are referring to the **IO**, we use the **object pronouns** (*le, les* or *se+lo/la/los/las*) both with an **IO** identified before and also **with an IO we identify after** the pronoun:

- *Quedé con <u>mis amigas</u> y les enseñé mi casa.*
- *Llama <u>a tu hermano</u> y dile que ya está la cena.*
- *Esto ya lo sabe <u>tu jefa</u>. Se lo he explicado yo.*
- *Ese libro es de <u>tu padre</u>. Se lo pedí prestado.*

- *¿Le dejarás el recado <u>a la secretaria</u>?*
- *Le he comprado este brillante <u>a Ana</u>.*
- *Llévales estos vasos <u>a tus padres</u>.*
- *Le he cambiado la rueda <u>al coche</u>.*
- *¿Y el niño?*
- *Se lo he llevado <u>a mis tías</u>.*
- *Esto tengo que decírselo <u>a mi marido</u>.*
- *¿Le has echado sal <u>a la comida</u>?*

OBJECT IDENTIFIED BEFORE THE NOUN

OBJECT IDENTIFIED AFTER THE NOUN

➡ 12. Personal pronouns
➡ 15. Object pronouns

---

1   Replace the underlined words with *lo/la/los/las* in some cases and with *le/les (se)* in others.

➡ Mamá: ¡Luis! ¿Has cogido tú <u>las tijeras</u>?
Luis: No, mamá, yo no ..*las*.. he cogido.

1. Mamá: ¡Luis! ¿Has escondido <u>el mando a distancia</u>?
Luis: No, mamá, no .... he escondido.

2. Mamá: ¡Luis! ¿Has encerrado <u>a tu hermana</u> en el armario de vuestro dormitorio?
Luis: Sí, mamá, ... he encerrado yo. Me estaba molestando todo el rato.

3. Mamá: ¡Carmen! ¿Has visto <u>las llaves del coche</u>?
Carmen: Creo que Luis .... ha tirado por la ventana hace un rato.

4. Mamá: ¡Luis! ¿Has visto <u>al gato</u>?
Luis: Creo que Carmen .... ha metido en la lavadora.

➡ Carmen: Hoy me he peleado con <u>Álvaro</u> en clase y ..*le*.. he dado una patada.

1. Luis: Pues yo me he caído de <u>la bici</u> y .... he roto el faro.

2. Luis: Y lo peor es que la bici no era mía, era de <u>José Enrique</u>. .... la había pedido prestada.

3. Carmen: ¿Por qué no llamamos <u>a los abuelos</u> y .... pedimos algo de dinero para chucherías?

4. Luis: No, mejor llamamos <u>a la tía Adoración</u> y .... decimos que nos lleve al cine.

5. Carmen: ¿Y las llaves del coche de <u>mamá</u>? ¿........ las has devuelto?

6. Luis: <u>Las llaves del coche</u> están llenas de barro. ¿........ lo quitas tú o .... lo quito yo?

2 **Cross out the unnecessary pronouns**.

➲ No sé dónde l̶a̶s̶ he puesto las gafas.

1. Ponle un poco más de sal al gazpacho.
2. Lo han descolgado el teléfono. No paraba de sonar.
3. Voy a comprarle un hueso de plástico nuevo al perro.
4. ¡Qué roscos más ricos! ¡Y qué buenos los hacía la abuela! ¿Te acuerdas?

5. A mi cuñada no la puedo soportar, es que es imbécil.
6. Les di mi más sincera enhorabuena a los novios.
7. La prepararé la ensaladilla y la meteré enseguida en el frigorífico.
8. Le hemos inflado las ruedas al coche y le hemos cambiado el aceite.
9. No las he metido las sábanas en la secadora. Las he tendido.

B   Redoubling: *Me ha mirado a mí*.

■ When we want to differentiate between the person identified as the DO or IO and other people, we use *a mí, a ti, a él, a ella, a usted, a nosotros/-as, a vosotros/-as, a ellos, a ellas, a ustedes*, in addition to the normal object pronouns:

[Not for them]

Me pinta un paisaje.   **Me** pinta un paisaje **a mí**.

[Not for him]

- *Me ha mirado **a mí** y no **a ti**.*
- *Les ha comprado el regalo **a ellos**, no **a ellas**.*
- *A nuestros vecinos no les gusta el nuevo ascensor, pero **a nosotros nos** encanta.*

- *Lo llamó **a él**, y no a su hermano. Estoy segura.*
- *Yo **os** mandé el fax **a vosotras**, pero lo recibió la secretaria.*
- *Les enseñaré el piso **a ustedes** a las dos, porque a las cuatro vienen otros señores a verlo.*

■ Redoubling is also used to clarify the meaning of the 3rd person object pronouns:

Buenas tardes, señora. Soy Carlos, compañero de trabajo de su hijo y amigo de su hija. Resulta que **la** llamé por teléfono **a ella** y **le** dejé un mensaje, pero no contestó. Ya **se lo** dije **a su hijo**, pero **la** llamo ahora **a usted** para que **se** lo recuerde **a ella**.

lo ⟶ *a él, a usted* (masc.)

la ⟶ *a ella, a usted* (fem.)

los ⟶ *a ellos, a ustedes* (masc.)

las ⟶ *a ellas, a ustedes* (fem.)

le ⟶ *a él, a ella, a usted*

se <

les ⟶ *a ellos, a ellas, a ustedes*

👁 Pronouns with prepositions can never be used by themselves to identify the DO or IO:

- *Me traerá un regalo **a mí**.*   [~~Traerá un regalo a mí.~~]
- *¿Nos ha llamado Pedro **a nosotros**?*   [~~¿Ha llamado Pedro a nosotros?~~]
- *Les pidieron un consejo **a ellos**.*   [~~Pidieron un consejo a ellos.~~]

3 Complete as in the model.

➲ I. ● Concha, ¿me quieres? a. te quiero

   ○ Claro que *te quiero* .... b. te quiero a ti

   II. ● Es verdad que en mi vida hay muchas mujeres, pero yo sólo *te quiero a ti* .

1. I. ● Fíjate qué mala suerte: de todo el bloque de vecinos sólo .... a. nos han robado

   II. ● ¿Qué os pasa? b. nos han robado a nosotros

   ○ Es que .... la cámara de vídeo.

2. I. ● ¡Camarero, la cuenta! Yo .... a. os invito

   II. ● Es que a mi fiesta .... , no a ellas. b. os invito a vosotras

3. I. ● A Rosa le preocupa mucho el dinero, pero .... a. a mí me da igual

   II. ● ¿Qué prefieres? ¿Pollo o ternera? b. me da igual

   ○ Pues, no sé, ...

4. I. ● Perdone, señor, ¿quiere ver la nueva enciclopedia que tenemos en oferta? a. no me interesa

   ○ No, gracias, ... b. a mí no me interesa

   II. ● A mi novio le encanta el fútbol, pero ....

5. I. ● A ti no, porque tú estás acostumbrado, pero .... a. le molesta mucho

   hablar en público. b. a ella le molesta mucho

   II. ● El humo .... Tiene un problema respiratorio.

4 The instructions for this game are a little complicated. Complete as in the model.

➲ Vamos a ver, Carmen, yo .*te*.. doy a ti la pelota y tú .*se*.. la das a Luis.

1. Y si no ...... encuentro a ti, ¿a quién se la doy?

2. No importa. Luis ...... la da a mí y yo ...... la doy a vosotras, ¿vale? Sara y Sofía, ¿lo habéis entendido?

3. No, no lo hemos entendido. ¿Tú ...... la das a nosotras? ¿Sí? Y nosotras, ¿a quién se la damos?

4. Vosotras ...... la dais a nosotros, a Luis y a mí.

5. Perdona, mamá, pero desde aquí no ...... veo a Luis y a ti.

5 Jerónimo and Alablanca are having problems in their relationship and with pronouns. Help them to use them correctly.

Alablanca: ➲ Jerónimo, ya no llevas a mí a las fiestas del poblado vecino.

Jerónimo: (1) Alablanca, ya no miras a mí como antes.

Alablanca: (2) Pasa algo a nosotros. (3) Antes besábamos a nosotros más.

Jerónimo: (4) Yo adoro a ti, mi bella luna llena.

Alablanca: (5) Y yo también quiero a ti mucho, más que al agua y al sol.

Jerónimo: (6) Pues si queremos tanto a nosotros, (7) ¿por qué no compramos a nosotros una pizza y vamos a ver el sol rojo detrás de las montañas?

➲ *No me llevas a las fiestas...* ....

1. ....

2. ....

3. ....

4. ....

5. ....

6. ....

7. ....

6 Indicate who the underlined pronoun in each sentence could refer to.

➲ Le di la enhorabuena... a. a Leticia ✓ b. a Felipe ✓ c. a ustedes d. a usted ✓ e. a los Reyes

1. Lo felicitó por su victoria... a. a él b. a ella c. a ustedes d. a usted e. a las animadoras

2. Les dieron el pésame... a. a su madre b. a sus hijos c. a ellas d. a usted e. a ustedes

3. La quise mucho... a. a mi novio b. a Corina c. a usted d. a mis gatas e. a mis canarios

4. Se la enseñó... a. a ella b. a su marido c. a ustedes d. a ellos e. a sus amigas

5. Los he suspendido... a. a ustedes b. a ella c. a ellos d. a usted e. a mi alumno

6. Las he aprobado... a. a él b. a ustedes c. a ellos d. a ellas e. a mi alumna

18. Reflexive and opinion-expressing constructions

A   Reflexive constructions: *Me baño. Me lavo los dientes*.

- In reflexive constructions, the **subject** and **object** (direct or indirect) are the same;
  in other words they refer to the same person or thing.
  When we conjugate a reflexive verb, **the effects of this verb are limited to the subject**:

Yo me afeito por las mañanas.

- *Poncio se lava las manos.*

- These are the **pronouns** used in the reflexive:

yo	**me** acuesto
tú	**te** acuestas
él/ella/usted	**se** acuesta
nosotros/-as	**nos** acostamos
vosotros/-as	**os** acostáis
ellos/ellas/ustedes	**se** acuestan

👁 The verb **ending** and the **pronoun** refer to the same person.

➡ 15. Object pronouns

---

1 Indicate which verbs are reflexive in the following sentences. Be careful with the pronoun-verb agreements.

➡ Mañana <u>me despierto</u> a las diez.

1. ¿Me dejas cincuenta euros?
2. Te acuestas siempre tempranísimo.
3. Te he visto esta tarde en el centro comercial.
4. ¿Se ha puesto ya Laura el abrigo?
5. Le he comprado un gorro a Encarna.

6. Nos vestimos y salimos, ¿vale?
7. La gente nos mira de una forma rara.
8. Si salimos, os llamo.
9. Si os ponéis delante, no veo nada.
10. A mis padres no les gusta esta música.
11. Mis padres se levantan a eso de las 7.

2 Link as in the example.

➡ a. Nos pintamos toda la cara de blanco.   a. Parecían fantasmas.
   b. Les pintamos toda la cara de blanco.   b. Parecíamos fantasmas.

1. a. Se ahogó en la piscina del hotel.   a. Fue un accidente. Él mismo se entregó a la policía.
   b. Lo ahogó en la piscina del hotel.   b. Fue un accidente. Tropezó y se dio un golpe en la cabeza.

2. a. Todas las noches se limpiaba los zapatos antes de acostarse.   a. Era un hombre muy metódico, obsesionado por su aseo personal.
   b. Todas las noches le limpiaba los zapatos antes de acostarse.   b. Estaba siempre pendiente de él.

3. a. Le tiró una copa encima y le manchó el pantalón.   a. Era muy torpe. Siempre llevaba la ropa sucia.
   b. Se tiró una copa encima y se manchó el pantalón.   b. Así fue como se conocieron.

4. a. Se quitaron la ropa.   a. Para meterse en la cama.
   b. Les quitaron la ropa.   b. Les robaron todo.

B Uses: *Te has mojado*. *Te has mojado el pelo*. *Te has mojado la blusa*.

■ In Spanish, the reflexive indicates that the subject is carrying out the action on themselves, on a part of their bodies or on something they are carrying or have:

	THE SUBJECT ON THEMSELVES	THE SUBJECT ON A PART OF THEIR BODIES	THE SUBJECT ON SOMETHING THEY ARE CARRYING OR HAVE
VERBS			
bañarse *ducharse* *vestirse* *etc.*	● *Yo me baño todos los días, nunca me ducho.* ● *Amalia se viste siempre de negro.*		
afeitarse *depilarse* *tatuarse* *etc.*	● *¿Todavía no te has afeitado?* ● *Estoy harto de depilarme.*	● *Pepe se está afeitando el bigote.* ● *Ana se depiló las piernas y las axilas.*	
cortarse *lavarse* *mancharse* *mojarse* *pintarse* *ponerse* *quitarse* *secarse* *etc.*	● *¿Me esperas un momento mientras me lavo?* ● *Vaya, ya te has manchado otra vez.* ● *¿Te pones al lado de Cati? Os voy a sacar una foto.* ● *¿Por qué nunca te secas al salir de la ducha?*	● *¿Os habéis lavado las manos?* ● *Nos vamos a manchar las manos.* ● *Se puso la dentadura.* ● *Pablo se seca el pelo con secador.*	● *Joan se lava la ropa a mano.* ● *¡Me he manchado el bolso con el café!* ● *¿Nos ponemos el pijama?* ● *¿Te has secado los zapatos antes de entrar?*

■ We can use the direct object pronouns *lo, la, los, las,* with this type of construction:

    ● *¿Pepe se ha afeitado <u>el bigote</u>?, ¿en serio?*   ● *¿Me pinto <u>las uñas</u> o me las corto?*
    ○ *Sí, se lo afeitó ayer.*

👁 In Spanish, this construction is used to refer to actions that in other languages (including English) are expressed with the possessive:

    ● *Me pongo la chaqueta.* ~~Pongo mi chaqueta.~~   ● *¿Te has cortado el pelo?* ~~¿Has cortado tu pelo.~~
    ● *Quitaos el abrigo.* ~~Quitad vuestros abrigos.~~   ● *Se rompió la nariz.* ~~Rompió su nariz.~~

    ➲ 7. Possessives   ➲ 16. Position and combination

❸ Complete the reflexive constructions for this children's song with the correct pronoun and/or verb ending.

Me acuesto y me levanto

Mamá ➲ *Se* lav*a*... los dientes.
Papá (1) se duch..... cantando.
Mis hermanitos (2) se acuest.....
y (3) ..... duerm..... en su cuarto.
Todos en casa bien pronto
(4) ..... metemos en la cama,

pues siempre (5) ..... levanta.....
a las seis de la mañana.
En cuanto el sol (6) ..... despierta,
yo (7) ..... levant..... y (8) ..... vist..... ,
papá (9) ..... afeit..... la barba,
mamá (10) ..... bañ..... y ..... pein..... .
Y tú, ¿cómo (11) ..... levant..... ?

4 Martita is finding being a teenager difficult. Look at the things she does and fill in the missing words.

➜ ..*Se*... come ..*las*.. uñas.

1. No .... quita nunca .... gafas de sol.

2. No .... lava .... manos antes de cenar.

3. No .... corta .... pelo nunca.

4. .... pone .... vaqueros más viejos que tiene.

5. .... pinta .... labios de color naranja.

6. .... ha tatuado .... brazos.

7. .... ha teñido .... pelo de lila.

5 Who will wake up whom tomorrow morning?

➜ (Yo solo)   a. Los despierto.

1. (Yo a ti)   b. Os despierta.

2. (Tú a mí)   c. La despiertas.

3. (Yo a mis amigos)   d. Me despierto.

4. (Tú a tu hermana)   e. Os despertáis.

5. (Nosotros a ti)   f. Te despierto.

6. (Ella a vosotros)   g. Me despiertas.

7. (Vosotros solos)   h. Te despertamos.

And who cuts whose hair at Pepe's hairdressing salon?

8. (Pepe a mí)   a. Le cortas el pelo.

9. (Pepe a sí mismo)   b. Te corta el pelo.

10. (Vosotros a vosotros mismos)   c. Me corta el pelo.

11. (Pepe a ti)   d. Se corta el pelo.

12. (Tú a Pepe)   e. Le corta el pelo.

13. (Laura y Pepe a sus hijos)   f. Les cortan el pelo.

14. (Laura a Pepe)   g. Les corta el pelo.

15. (Laura a unos clientes)   h. Os cortáis el pelo.

C   Reciprocity: *Nos conocemos. Nos queremos.*

■ By using the reflexive we can express that two or more subjects carry out an action reciprocally, or to each other:

- *Pepe y su primo se pegan por todo.*
  [Pepe hits his cousin + His cousin hits Pepe.]

- *Ana y tú os escribís, ¿no?*
  [Ana write letters to you + You write letters to Ana.]

- *Isabel y Fernando se quieren.*
  [Isabel loves Fernando + Fernando loves Isabel.]

---

6 Montse is telling Elvira things about her relationship with Ercan. Write in the correct pronoun.

Elvira: ¿Dónde ➜ ..*os*...... conocisteis Ercan y tú?

Montse: (1) .... vimos por primera vez en un viaje a Turquía. Él era el guía.

Elvira: ¿Y (2) .... enamorasteis enseguida?

Montse: ¡No, qué va! A principio sólo (3) .... caímos bien, pero un día me invitó a cenar, dimos un paseo y...

Elvira: Y (4) .... besasteis.

Montse: No, no: ¡me llevó a ver a su madre! Desde ese día su madre y yo no (5) .... entendemos.

Later on, Elvira gives Begoña a summary.

Montse y Ercan ➜ ...*se conocieron*.... en un viaje a Estambul, pero no (6) .... enseguida, al principio sólo (7) .... bien. El primer día que salieron juntos no (8) .... ; él es muy tradicional y la llevó a conocer a su madre. Y desde ese día la madre de Ercan y Montse no (9) ....

D   Opinion-expressing constructions: *Me gusta... Les da miedo... Nos parece bien...*

■ In this type of construction, there is an element (the **subject**) that produces an emotion, sensation, feeling or reaction... (expressed by the **verb**) in someone (the **indirect object**):

Me gusta mucho **el pan**.
IO   SUBJECT

SUBJECT

el fútbol
la comida japonesa
Nueva York
...

salir y cenar fuera
dormir la siesta
...

las gafas de sol
los días de lluvia
el café y el té
...

INDIRECT
OBJECT

Gustar

A mí	me		
A ti	te	*gusta*	
A él/ella/usted	le		
A nosotros/-as	nos		
A vosotros/-as	os	*gustan*	
A ellos/ellas/ustedes	les		

■ Apart from *gustar*, other verbs like **apetecer, doler, encantar, fastidiar, interesar, molestar, preocupar**, etc also work like this:

- *Pues hoy no **nos** apetece nada **salir**.*
- *A mi madre **le** duelen **los huesos** cuando cambia el tiempo.*
- *¿A usted **le** interesan **las películas de ciencia ficción**?*
- *¿No **te** preocupa nada **el futuro**?*

➡ 16. Position and combination

➡ 17. Presence and redoubling

👁 In these constructions, when the subject is a combination of various infinitives, or of infinitive plus noun, the verb goes in the singular. The verb only goes in the plural if there is a plural noun closer to the verb than the infinitive:

- *Me gusta **ir** al cine y **leer** en la cama.*
- *Me gusta **el cine** y **leer** en la cama.*
- *Me gusta **ir** al cine y **las novelas de misterio**.*
  PERO: *Me gusta**n** **las novelas de misterio** y leer en la cama.*

■ In some constructions of this type, the effect (emotion, reaction, sensation, etc) that the subject causes in someone is expressed with the verb plus an adjective, noun or adverb:

Dar + igual, miedo, pena, rabia, risa, vergüenza...
Resultar/Parecer + estupendo, increíble, raro...
Caer + bien, mal, regular...

- *Me dan asco **las ratas**.*
- *Les parece fatal **ir a la cena sin un regalo**.*
- *¿A ti te cae bien **mi padre**?*

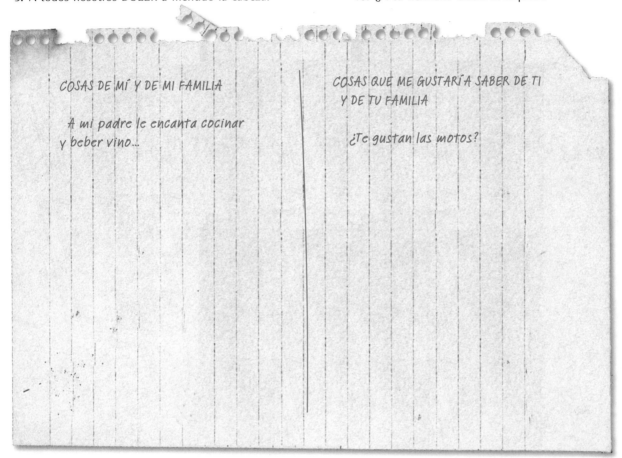

7 Sofía is preparing for a conversation exchange with Pierre, a French boy. Complete the list the things she plans to tell him about her family, and what she wants to ask him about his.

➲ A mi padre ENCANTAR cocinar y beber vino. ✓

1. A mi madre NO GUSTAR los chicos con el pelo largo.
2. A mis hermanas GUSTAR la ropa y salir por la noche.
3. A mí ENCANTAR sobre todo viajar y dormir.
4. A todos nosotros GUSTAR mucho el queso francés.
5. A todos nosotros DOLER a menudo la cabeza.

➲ ¿A ti GUSTAR las motos? ✓

6. ¿A tus padres MOLESTAR el tabaco?
7. ¿A tus hermanos INTERESAR la ecología?
8. ¿A vosotros GUSTAR la sangría y la paella?
9. ¿A vosotros MOLESTAR los gatos?
10. ¿A tu hermana GUSTAR esquiar?

COSAS DE MÍ Y DE MI FAMILIA

A mi padre le encanta cocinar
y beber vino...

COSAS QUE ME GUSTARÍA SABER DE TI
Y DE TU FAMILIA

¿Te gustan las motos?

8 Below you will find some extracts from a debate on sexist stereotypes. Complete with pronouns and the correct forms of the verbs, and then match them to their other halves.

Los hombres dicen:

➲ No es verdad. A nosotros sí (GUSTAR) ...*nos gusta*... la ropa.

1. ¡Qué tontería! A mí (ENCANTAR) .... ocuparme de las cosas de la casa. (GUSTAR) .... mucho ordenar los armarios.

2. ¿A vosotros (FASTIDIAR) .... hablar de vuestros sentimientos? ¿(DAR VERGÜENZA) .... compartir vuestros secretos?

3. No sé si a todos nosotros (MOLESTAR) .... cuidar a los niños.

4. ¿A ti no (GUSTAR) .... tomar algo con los amigos?

a. Yo creo que a nosotros no (MOLESTAR) .... contar nuestras cosas, pero somos más reservados.

b. A mí, por ejemplo, (ENCANTAR) ...*me encanta*........ ir de tiendas.

c. No obstante, reconozco que a muchos amigos míos (MOLESTAR) .... Sobre todo, planchar.

d. Pues a mí (ENCANTAR) .... ir al bar y charlar un poco después del trabajo. Es la mejor terapia.

e. A mí, la verdad, (FASTIDIAR) .... tener que ver la misma película de dibujos veinte veces.

Las mujeres dicen:

➜ A nosotras (ENCANTAR) *nos encanta* ir a la peluquería.

6. A mí personalmente (FASTIDIAR) .... ir de compras.

7. ¿Has dicho que a ti (MOLESTAR) .... el desorden?

8. A mí (ENCANTAR) .... meterme en la cocina y preparar la comida. (RELAJAR) .... ensayar nuevos platos.

9. ¿En serio piensas que a todas nosotras (GUSTAR) .... los bebés?

f. ¿A ti no (GUSTAR) *te gusta* cambiarte el color del pelo?

g. Porque a mí no (GUSTAR) .... mucho, la verdad; y eso que he tenido dos hijos.

h. A mí marido también, pero (MOLESTAR) .... mucho cómo deja el fregadero después.

i. A mí no (MOLESTAR) .... nada. Mi marido es igual. Nunca pongo nada en su sitio y a él no (IMPORTAR) ....

j. Pero a muchas amigas mías (ENCANTAR) .... comprar ropa.

9 Jerónimo and Alablanca are texting with smoke signals. Here are some of their messages. Help them to put their sentences into perfect Spanish.

➜ Encantar el pescado crudo y la danza del fuego. *Me encantan...*

1. Dar rabia ir de caza en invierno y coser zapatillas. ....

2. Alegrar la luna llena sobre las montañas y tu sonrisa. ....

3. Caer fatal la nieta del jefe Pluma Rojas. ....

4. Apasionar el olor a tierra mojada, pintarme la cara de colores y tu sonrisa. ....

5. Resultar espantoso lavar la ropa en el río y preparar tortas de maíz. ....

6. Dar alergia el humo de la pipa de la paz y los adornos de plumas. ....

Jerónimo then tells Crazy Horse what Alablanca is like.

Alablanca then tells Morning Dew what Jerónimo is like.

A Jerónimo le encantan el pescado crudo y la danza del fuego.

SECTION 4

Verbs

¿Tendrá mi edad?   Sí, la tendrá, pero todavía no.

19. Conjugation. The basic building blocks.

A Talking about a verb: the infinitive.

■ When we **talk about a verb**, we use the **infinitive**, which is the verb form that can be found in a dictionary. It is a non-personal verb form, meaning that it doesn't conjugate.

→ 20. Non-personal forms

■ In Spanish the infinitive has three endings, each with a different classifying vowel. All verbs are classified according to these endings:

ENDING IN -*ar*	ENDING IN -*er*	ENDING IN -*ir*
Estudiar	*Aprender*	*Decidir*
Hablar	*Comer*	*Decir*
Jugar	*Correr*	*Escribir*
Pasear	*Leer*	*Salir*
Trabajar	*Ver*	*Pedir*

pasear. (De *paso*.) intr. Ir andando por distracción o por ejercicio. **2.** Ir c

ver. (Del lat. *videre*.) tr. Percibir por los ojos los objetos mediante

decir. (Del lat. *dicere*.) tr. Manifestar con palabras el pensamiento. **2.** Asegurar

¿Tú querer casarte conmigo?

Sí, pero esperar nosotros un poco. Ser muy jóvenes.

¿Quieres casarte conmigo?
Sí, pero esperaremos un poco. Somos muy jóvenes.

👁 Verbs that have a reflexive form add the pronoun -*se* to the infinitive. For example: *ducharse, moverse, vestirse*.

→ 18. Reflexive and opinion-expressing constructions

1 Ms Morpheme is an instructor in the Grammex gym. Today she has prepared an exercise routine in order to perfect conjugation... Table 1: Here are a number of infinitives; put them into the appropriate group.

salir escuchar ✓ poner ser conducir oír entrar llamar tener poder decir aprender reproducir haber partir

-ar	escuchar	-er		-ir	

Put these other verbs into the same table. They are all verbs with a reflexive form.

levantarse irse ocuparse cortarse vestirse acostarse perderse ducharse ponerse

Look up some of these verbs in your dictionary. Notice the abbreviations that accompany them.

2 This quiz is the second exercise that Morpheme has prepared for today. You have three minutes to work out and write down the infinitives of the verbs in the box. Here's a clue: look at the vowel in the ending.

estudiamos ✓ salís cocina aprenden estás escribimos pedís vemos bebe
trabajan traen dormís comemos vivimos sentamos sentimos cantas lee

-ar ....estudiar...................

....

....

....

....

....

-er ....

....

....

....

....

....

-ir ....

....

....

....

....

....

B   Conjugar un verbo

■ In Spanish, the endings of the verb tenses are very important because they tell us about the tense and the person we are referring to. So conjugating a verb means using the correct form of the tense and the person that we are talking about.
To conjugate a **regular verb**, we change the ending of the infinitive for a tense and person ending. For example:

Estudiar	*Aprender*	*Escribir*
estudi + ENDING	*aprend* + ENDING	*escrib* + ENDING

estudio	[yo Presente]	*aprendo*	[yo Presente]	*escribo*	[yo Presente]
estudias	[tú Presente]	*aprendes*	[tú Presente]	*escribes*	[tú Presente]
estudié	[yo Indefinido]	*aprendí*	[yo Indefinido]	*escribí*	[yo Indefinido]
estudiaste	[tú Indefinido]	*aprendiste*	[tú Indefinido]	*escribiste*	[tú Indefinido]

■ To conjugate an **irregular verb**, apart from changing the endings, we have to know what sort of irregularity it has. This irregularity generally **affects the stem**, or first part of the verb. For example:

Jugar, in the *Presente*, in some persons changes the *-u-* for *-ue-*:
    jugar → [*jueg* + TENSE AND PERSON ENDING]

Querer, in the *Presente*, in some persons changes the *-e* for *-ie-*:
    querer → [*quie* + TENSE AND PERSON ENDING]

Pedir, in some tenses and in some persons changes the *-e-* for *-i-*:
    pedir → [*pid* + TENSE AND PERSON ENDING]

3 This is exercise 3. To be able to conjugate, it is very important to know how to separate or split verbs. In the list below, separate the stem from the ending.

cambiar	....cambi + ar....	poder	....	nacer	....
abrir	....	conducir	....	encantar	....
terminar	....	pedir	....	romper	....
escribir	....	recibir	....	prohibir	....
aprender	....	salir	....	soñar	....
comer	....	querer	....	dormir	....
desayunar	....	poner	....	pensar	....

C Concordar el verbo con el sujeto

■ In Spanish, the verb conjugation has **six different endings** for the six possible persons of the subject. The verb always agrees with the subject in whichever person it appears:

SINGULAR			
	1ª persona	*Yo*	*como*
	2ª persona	*Tú*	*comes*
	3ª persona	*Él, ella, usted*	*come*

PLURAL			
	1ª persona	*Nosotros/-as*	*comemos*
	2ª persona	*Vosotros/-as*	*coméis*
	3ª persona	*Ellos, ellas, ustedes*	*comen*

- *Tú sabes más de lo que dices.*
- *Lola y yo no sabemos nada de eso.*
- *¿Saben ellos ya lo que pasó?*

¡Creo que he descubierto algo importante! Pero no sé qué...

CANTA ABA-S

■ Some person endings are always the same and are repeated in all verb tenses. If you take a careful look at the endings below it will make conjugating easier:

PERSON		VERB ENDING
yo	→	*-vowel**
tú	→	*-s***
él, ella, usted	→	*- vowel**
nosotros/-as	→	*-mos*
vosotros/-as	→	*-is*
ellos, ellas, ustedes	→	*-n*

* There is no single vowel as this changes with the verb tense.

** Except in the *Pretérito indefinido* and the **Imperativo**.

4 And this is the last exercise in today's gym routine. Write each of these verb forms next to the corresponding person. There are forms from several different tenses, so pay special attention to the verb endings.

desayunas ✓	salimos	hacéis	tenemos	escribes	cantamos	envías	comunicáis	creo
llamarán	sabe	sabemos	fueron	decían	saldremos	tradujeron	sabes	estaban	venís

Yo ....

Tú *Desayunas* ....

Él, ella, usted ....

Nosotros/as ....

Vosotros/as ....

Ellos, ellas, ustedes ....

5 This evening, Mar has invited some friends for an evening meal. They have been talking about the occasion, and the fragments below are some of the things they have said. Complete the sentences with the verbs, paying special attention to the agreement with the subject.

➲ ¿Vosotros a qué hora _vais_............ a llegar?

1. Nosotros .... sobre las ocho.

2. ¿Tú .... llegar a esa hora?

   Como .... tan tarde del trabajo...

3. ¿Y Mar y su familia por qué .... tan pronto?

4. Bueno, ¿qué les ....?: ¿vino, postre, unas flores...?

5. Nada de chocolate, que los niños de Mar no .... comer.

6. Un buen vino siempre lo .... , ¿no?

7. ¿Vosotros .... en coche?

vais ✓	pueden	iréis	podrás	cenan
llegaremos	sales	llevamos	agradecerán	

20. Non-personal forms: *hablar, hablando, hablado.*

A   Meaning and form of the infinitive: *hablar, comer, vivir.*

■ The infinitive is a verbal noun. It is the **name** we give to an **activity**.

- *Pintar es hacer dibujos.*

■ The infinitive is the basic form of the verb, which is why it is the form you will find in a dictionary. In Spanish, the infinitive can have three endings.

1st CONJUGATION **-ar**	2nd CONJUGATION **-er**	3rd CONJUGATION **-ir**
Cantar	Comer	Salir
Saltar	Saber	Dormir
Volar	Tener	Venir
Soñar	Volver	Elegir
Comprar	Conocer	Abrir

➡ 19. Conjugation. The Basic...

➡ 37. Periphrastic verbs

1 Using your dictionary, find the infinitive that corresponds to the nouns below, as in the example.

la canción	➡ *cantar*	la entrada	5.	la ida	10. ....
el salto	1.	la venida	6.	el amor	11. ....
el cuento	2.	la venta	7.	la carrera	12. ....
la rueda	3.	el hecho	8.	la vuelta	13. ....
la salida	4.	el sentimiento	9.	el sudor	14. ....

B   The infinitive as a noun

■ As a noun, the infinitive is used in the same ways as a noun:

As SUBJECT	As DIRECT OBJECT	With PREPOSITIONS
• *La salida fue difícil.*	• *¿Quieres agua?*	• *No puedes salir sin paraguas.*
• *Salir fue difícil.*	• *¿Quieres beber?*	• *No puedes salir sin llevar paraguas.*
• *El descanso ayuda mucho.*	• *No sabe nada.*	• *¿Vas a Madrid?*
• *Descansar ayuda mucho.*	• *No sabe escribir.*	• *¿Vas a salir?*
• *Está prohibido el baño.*	• *Prefiero la soledad.*	• *Es la hora de la comida.*
• *Está prohibido bañarse.*	• *Prefiero estar solo.*	• *Es la hora de comer.*

■ With opinion-expressing constructions like *me gusta, me encanta, me pone nervioso, me da miedo,* etc., the thing that you like, love, makes you nervous or makes you frightened is the **subject**. This is why, in cases like these we use nouns or *infinitives*:

- *Me gusta mucho la natación.*
- *Me gusta mucho nadar.*

- *A mí no me da miedo la oscuridad.*
- *A mí no me da miedo salir de noche.*

- *Me tranquilizan tus palabras.*
- *Me tranquiliza saber que estás bien.*

Pues no sé... **salir** con los amigos, **hacer** deporte, **dormir** mucho, **ver** la tele... Lo normal.

¿Qué es lo que más te gusta **hacer** los fines de semana?

➡ 18. Reflexive and opinion-expressing ...

2 **Cross out the only option that is not a possible response to the questions.**

➲ ¿Qué quieres ahora?   ~~Comiendo un poco~~ / Comer un poco / Un poco de comida

1. ¿Qué te gusta más?   El coche rojo / Ver la tele / Conduciendo motos
2. ¿Qué es lo que te preocupa?   La carrera de mañana / Correr mañana / Corriendo mañana
3. ¿Qué haces?   Acabo de comer / Acabo de comiendo / Voy a comer
4. ¿Qué es lo que te da miedo?   Durmiendo sola / Estar contigo / Las moscas
5. ¿Qué es bueno para el resfriado?   Una infusión de menta / Durmiendo mucho / Llevar poca ropa

C   The infinitive as a verb

■ As a verb, the infinitive takes a **subject**. Normally the context is enough for us to tell what the subject is, so we only mention it explicitly to avoid possible confusion:

We don't mention the subject because the context makes it clear

- *Si quieres **comer**, tengo algo en el frigorífico.* [comer-tú]
- *No **le** gusta **esperar**.* [esperar-él/ella]
- *El sueño de Javi es **no trabajar**.* [no trabajar-Javi]
- *Los policías **nos** obligaron a **salir**.* [salir-nosotros]
- *¿Está prohibido **fumar**?* [fumar-en general]
- *Antes de **llegar**, la llamé.* [llegar-yo]

NO FUMAR

We mention the subject to avoid confusion

- *Antes de **llegar** <u>ellos</u>, la llamé.* [if I say only *llegar*, you might think I'm talking about 'llegar-yo']
- *Después de **llegar** <u>yo</u>, se fueron.* [if I say only *llegar*, you don't know if I'm talking about 'yo' or 'ellos']

■ The infinitive can take all the different types of object that any verb can:

DIRECT OBJECT (DO):   - ***Decir*** <u>eso</u> *me parece maleducado.*
INDIRECT OBJECT (IO):   - ***Decir**le eso <u>a tu madre</u> me parece maleducado.*
OBJECTS REPRESENTED BY A WHOLE PHRASE: - ***Decir**le eso a tu madre <u>a las cuatro de la madrugada y en su propia casa</u> me parece maleducado.*
SUBORDINATE OBJECTS: - ***Decir**le <u>que nunca vas a volver</u> a tu madre a las cuatro de la madrugada y en su propia casa me parece maleducado.*

3 **Write out the meanings of the following signs. The sentences provided in the box on the right may help you in choosing the verb.**

➲ *no girar a la izquierda*   1. ....   2. ....   3. ....

4. ....   5. ....   6. ....   7. ....

- No me **beses** aquí. No se puede.
- No pasa nada. Vamos un poco más lejos y **comemos** allí.
- No **gires** a la izquierda. Está prohibido. ✓
- ¿Te estás **haciendo pipí**? Pues espérate un poco a llegar a casa.
- Si te **duermes**, vamos a otro sitio.
- No es posible el **giro a la derecha**.
- ¿Por qué estás **tocando el claxon**?
- Si **adelantas**, nos multarán.

4 **What is the subject of the following infinitives?**

➜ **Trabajar** tanto no debe ser bueno. ..En general..........

➜ Siéntense. ¿Les apetece **tomar** algo? ...Ustedes.........

1. Me encanta **andar** por las montañas. ....

2. Yo dije que me iba antes de **salir** Cristina. ....

3. Yo dije que me iba antes de **salir**. ....

4. **Tener** hijos es una experiencia inolvidable. ....

5. Tus amigos saben **ser** muy amables con la gente. ....

6. ¿Os prohibió **pasar** la policía? ....

7. ¿Me permite **entrar**, Sra. López? ....

8. Mi profesor dice que es muy útil **hablar** varias lenguas. ....

9. No me obligues a **hacer** eso. ....

10. ¿No os ha invitado Pepe a **comer** en su casa, chicas? ....

11. ¡Antonio! ¡Luis! ¡Venid a **ayudar**me! ....

12. Ese trabajo es bueno. El problema es que te piden **tener** estudios superiores. ....

¡Me encanta andar por las montañas!

D **Meaning and form of the gerund: *hablando, comiendo, viviendo***

■ The gerund is a verbal adjective that talks about an activity being carried out:

■ Its regular form is made by changing the ending of the infinitive to the following endings:

• *Francisco se relaja **pintando** cuadros.*

-ar	-ando	Hablar → hablando

-er, -ir	-iendo	Comer → comiendo

Vivir → viviendo

👁 (vowel + *-iendo*) = *-yendo*   Caer → cayendo
Ir → yendo

■ Verbs ending in *-ir* with an *-e-* or a *-o-* in the last syllable of the stem (*e...ir, o...ir*) have an **irregular form**: these vowels are changed to *-i-* and *-u-* respectively:

-e- → -i-	-o- → -u-

Decir   diciendo [~~deciendo~~]   Morir   muriendo [~~moriendo~~]
Reír   riendo [~~reiendo~~]   Dormir   durmiendo [~~dormiendo~~]

👁 Examples of these verbs are: *pedir, repetir, seguir, sentir, mentir, competir, elegir, herir, medir, preferir, podrir,* or related compound forms: *contradecir, sonreír, impedir, perseguir, presentir,* etc.

---

5 **What can you see in these drawings? Choose from the verbs in the box.**

nadar
hacer
hablar ✓
poner
morder

➜ Veo a un chico   1. Veo a un niño   2. Veo a una niña   3. Veo a un policía   4. Veo un perro
..hablando.........   ....
con una chica.   en la piscina.   dibujitos.   una multa.   un hueso.

6 All these verbs end in *-ir*. Circle the irregular ones (*e...ir*, *o...ir*) and in each case write the appropriate gerund form.

➲ vivir ....*viviendo*.... 4. reír .... 8. ir .... 12. producir ....
1. (morir) ..*muriendo*...... 5. sufrir .... 9. salir .... 13. mentir ....
2. repetir .... 6. oír .... 10. competir .... 14. compartir ....
3. dormir .... 7. decidir .... 11. seguir .... 15. sentir ....

E Uses of the gerund: *Está subiendo. Subiendo a la derecha.*

■ *Estar* + GERUND enables us to talk about the development of an action **in any verb tense**:

[37. Periphrastic verbs]

¿Puedes venir un segundo?

Ahora no puedo. Me **estoy duchando**.

UNFINISHED ACTIONS	FINISHED ACTIONS
• *No hagas ruido. Los niños* ***están*** *durmiendo.* • ***Estábamos viendo*** *el partido tranquilamente y, de pronto, se fue.*	• *El pobre está muy cansado.* ***Ha estado trabajando*** *todo el día.* • ***Estuve hablando*** *dos horas con ella, pero no conseguí nada.*

---

7 Transform the verbs in bold, as in the example.

Acciones en sí mismas

• Mi primo ha **trabajado** tres años como camarero.
• Me encontré con Patricia cuando **entraba** al cine.
• Ilsa **estudia** español desde el mes pasado.
• Yo **salí** con una chica francesa dos años.
• Yo ya me **iba**, cuando de pronto ella me llamó.
• **Trabajé** en esa empresa hasta que me casé.

Acciones consideradas en su desarrollo

➲ ...*Ha estado trabajando*........... tres años...
1. ... cuando ....
2. Ilsa .... español...
3. Yo .... con una chica francesa...
4. Yo ya me .... cuando...
5. .... en esa empresa...

■ We also use the gerund to talk about the way to do something, or to get to a place:

¿**Cómo** se aprende mejor una lengua?

Estudiando y, sobre todo, **hablando** mucho.

Perdone, ¿dónde están los servicios?

Bajando las escaleras, a la izquierda.

---

8 Connect each question to the most logical answer.

➲ ¿Cómo has solucionado el problema?
1. ¿Cómo puedo mejorar, doctor?
2. Aparicio, ¿dónde está mi maleta?
3. Eso está muy lejos. ¿Cómo voy a ir?
4. ¿Dónde hay una farmacia, por favor?
5. ¿Cómo has conseguido adelgazar tanto?

a. Cuidando su alimentación y durmiendo 8 horas al día.
b. Pues fácil, yendo al gimnasio tres veces por semana.
c. Cogiendo un taxi. Sólo así llegarás a tiempo.
d. Pues siga recto y, subiendo aquella calle, a la derecha.
e. Mira, entrando al comedor, a la derecha de la puerta.
f. Simplemente hablando con ella.

➲ .*f.*.
1. .....
2. .....
3. .....
4. .....
5. .....

■ We do not use the gerund, we use the **infinitive**:

As SUBJECT:	● ___Pilotar___ *aviones* es emocionante.	[~~Pilotando~~ *aviones es emocionante.*]
As DO:	● *Ella odia* **llegar** *tarde*.	[*Ella odia* ~~llegando~~ *tarde.*]
With PREPOSITIONS:	● *Perdona* <u>por</u> no **llamarte**.	[*Perdona por no* ~~llamándote~~.]
	● *Lávate antes* <u>de</u> **comer**.	[*Lávate antes de* ~~comiendo~~.]

9 Margaret is studying Spanish and is still having difficulties with the gerund and infinitive. Correct her mistakes.

A mí me gusta mucho (➲) ~~haciendo~~ deporte, porque (➲) haciendo deporte estás mejor físicamente. Antes de (**1**) viniendo a España, yo jugaba en un equipo de baloncesto. (**2**) Jugando al baloncesto es muy divertido. Ahora estoy (**3**) buscando aquí gente para (**4**) hacer un equipo y poder jugar otra vez. Empecé a (**5**) buscando hace una semana, y ya somos seis. También me gusta (**6**) estudiar lenguas, claro, y (**7**) hablando con los españoles. Después de (**8**) estando en España dos meses, voy a ir a Argentina. (**9**) Viajar es muy interesante para mí.

➲ .... hacer ....
➲ ....✓..........................
1. ....
2. ....
3. ....
4. ....
5. ....
6. ....
7. ....
8. ....
9. ....

F   Meaning and form of the past participle: *hablado, comido, vivido.*

■ The past participle is a verbal adjective that expresses the **result of a process**:

● *Un cuadro* **pintado**.

[the result of the action of painting is a painted picture.]

■ Its regular form is made by changing the verb ending to the following endings:

-ar	**-ado**	*Hablar → hablado*
-er, -ir	**-ido**	*Comer → comido* *Vivir → vivido*

■ The most common **irregular past participles** are the following:

Hacer → **hecho**	*Romper →* **roto**	*Morir →* **muerto**
Satisfacer → **satisfecho**	*Volver →* **vuelto**	*Abrir →* **abierto**
Decir → **dicho**	*Poner →* **puesto**	*Cubrir →* **cubierto**
Ver → **visto**	*Escribir →* **escrito**	*Freír →* **frito** (*o freído*)
	Resolver → **resuelto**	*Imprimir →* **impreso** (*o imprimido*)

👁 All their compound forms have the same irregularity:

Deshacer → **deshecho**	*Contradecir →* **contradicho**	*Prever →* **previsto**
Devolver → **devuelto**	*Descubrir →* **descubierto**	*Reabrir →* **reabierto**

10 Carmencita is still very young, and thinks that all past participles are regular.
Help her by identifying and correcting the seven mistakes she has made.

➜ Esta mañana he ~~haeido~~ *hecho* un dibujo muy bonito, y la profesora

me ha **dicho** ....✓........ que dibujo muy bien.

1. Mi perrito Güili se ha **escapado** .... y no ha **volvido** ....

   Nadie lo ha **visto** .... A lo mejor se ha **morido** .... , el pobre.

2. Mi mamá me ha **ponido** .... hoy pollo **frito** ....

   para comer, pero no me gusta, y no he **comido** .... nada.

3. Yo estaba jugando y he **rompido** .... una lámpara del comedor,

   pero mis papás han **ido** .... a comprar y todavía no lo han

   descubrido ....

4. He **encontrado** .... una carta en un sobre. Entonces he **abrido**

   .... la carta, pero todavía no sé leer y no sé quién la

   ha **escribido** ....

G   Use as an adjective: *Una cosa terminada. Está terminada. La tengo terminada.*

■ When used as an adjective, the past participle **always agrees**
with the noun it refers to **in gender and number**:

Noun + PAST PARTICIPLE

- *Los <u>archivos</u> protegidos con contraseña no se pueden abrir fácilmente.*
- *En verano hay muchos <u>perros</u> abandonados en la carretera.*

Estar + PAST PARTICIPLE

- *No puedes abrir los <u>archivos</u> de mi ordenador. Están protegidos*
  con contraseña.
- *Mira esa pobre <u>perrita</u>. Está abandonada.*

Tener + PAST PARTICIPLE

- *No puedes abrir los <u>archivos</u> de mi ordenador. Los tengo protegidos*
  con contraseña.
- *Tienes abandonadas esas pobres <u>plantas</u>. Cuídalas un poco más,*
  hombre, que son muy bonitas.

Ya tengo los platos **fregados**.
¿Qué más hago ahora?

11 If somebody does a thing, that thing has been done. Complete the descriptions of the results
of the following actions with the correct form of the past participle.

- Alguien ha abierto una ventana.
- Has puesto la comida en la mesa.
- Ya has dicho todo lo que tenías que decir.
- Alguien ha roto tres platos en tu cocina.
- Borja ha hecho todas las tareas de casa esta mañana.
- Has sorprendido a tus amigos con una visita inesperada.
- Tu compañero te ha resuelto varias dudas sobre los pronombres.
- Ya has estudiado la mitad de los temas de Historia.

➜ Hay una ventana ...*abierta*... .

1. La comida está .... en la mesa.

2. Todo está ya ....

3. Hay tres platos .... en la cocina.

4. Ya las tiene ....

5. Están ....

6. Esas dudas ya están ....

7. Ya tienes .... la mitad de los temas.

H Use of the combined forms of the verb: *he salido, había salido, habré salido...*

■ With the auxiliary verb *haber* + PAST PARTICIPLE we can make the following compound verb forms:

Pretérito perfecto:	Presente of *haber* + PAST PARTICIPLE	*He comido, has comido, ha comido...*
Pretérito pluscuamp.:	Imperfecto of *haber* + PAST PARTICIPLE	*Había sido, habías sido, había sido...*
Futuro perfecto:	Futuro of *haber* + PAST PARTICIPLE	*Habré ido, habrás ido, habrá ido...*

■ In these forms, the past participle cannot be separated from the auxiliary *haber*:

- *Hemos hablado* mucho. [H̶e̶m̶o̶s̶ m̶u̶c̶h̶o̶ h̶a̶b̶l̶a̶d̶o̶.]
- *Han llegado* recientemente. [H̶a̶n̶ r̶e̶c̶i̶e̶n̶t̶e̶m̶e̶n̶t̶e̶ l̶l̶e̶g̶a̶d̶o̶.]

➲ 22. Pretérito perfecto

➲ 27. Pretérito pluscuamperfecto

➲ 29. Futuro perfecto

■ In addition, these forms do not change, meaning that they do not agree with any other element of the sentence:

- <u>Nosotras</u> hemos **salido** tarde. [Nosotras hemos s̶a̶l̶i̶d̶a̶s̶ tarde.]
- A <u>María</u> <u>la</u> he **llamado** ya. [A María la he l̶l̶a̶m̶a̶d̶a̶ ya.]

12 Order the words to make coherent sentences, putting the infinitive into the correct form of the past participle.

- Retrasar / Os / mucho / habéis.   ➲ *Os habéis retrasado mucho.*
- Resolver / han / bien / el / Los / problema / científicos   1. ....
- Convencer / Elena / me / había / explicación / no / con / su   2. ....
- Devolver / ¿no / Todavía / libros / has / los?   3. ....
- Asustar / habrá / la / Pedro / con / gritos / sus   4. ....
- Prever / Los / habían / economistas / crisis / una   5. ....

13 Complete with the correct past participle form of the verb indicated.

publicar
- ➲ La editorial Infusión ha *publicado*... muchos libros sobre comida dietética.
- ➲ Ése es un libro *publicado*... en Infusión.
- ➲ Ese libro que tú dices está *publicado*... en Infusión.
- ➲ Infusión tiene *publicadas*... muchas obras sobre comida dietética.

romper
1. ¿Qué le habrá pasado? ¿Tendrá las dos piernas .... ?
2. ¿La pierna derecha también está ....?
3. Con las dos piernas .... no se puede ni mover, el pobre.
4. Pobre Javi. Yo creo que se ha .... las dos piernas.

abrir
5. Si tienes niños, una ventana .... es un peligro.
6. ¿Por qué has .... la ventana?
7. ¿Por qué tienes todas las ventanas .... ?
8. ¿La ventana del dormitorio está .... ?

resolver
9. Si tú quieres, el problema está ....
10. Todavía no tengo los dos problemas más importantes ....
11. Se lo he dicho claramente y ya está. Problema ....
12. ¿Has .... tus problemas ya?

21. Presente de indicativo

A Regular verbs: *hablo*, *como*, *vivo*...

■ To form the *Presente de indicativo* we change the verb ending
to the following **endings**:

	-ar	-er	-ir	Hablar	Comer	Vivir
Yo	-o	-o	-o	*hablo*	*como*	*vivo*
Tú	-as	-es	-es	*hablas*	*comes*	*vives*
Él, ella, usted	-a	-e	-e	*habla*	*come*	*vive*
Nosotros/-as	-amos	-emos	-imos	*hablamos*	*comemos*	*vivimos*
Vosotros/-as	-áis	-éis	-ís	*habláis*	*coméis*	*vivís*
Ellos, ellas, ustedes	-an	-en	-en	*hablan*	*comen*	*viven*

■ The word stress always falls on the stem for *yo*, *tú*, *él* and *ellos*, and on the ending
for *nosotros* and *vosotros*, as shown by the underlining in the examples above.

1 Which person is the verb form talking about? Choose the possible subject or subjects from the options
in the box and circle the verb ending that tells you.

Tú	Lucía y Sole	Usted	Usted y su marido	Yo	El amigo de Hans	Elena y yo	Vosotros tres

➔ ¿Habl(a) español? (*Usted / El amigo de Hans*..........)

1. Como a las dos, más o menos, y **ceno** sobre las diez. (..)

2. No **puede** aprender español si no **estudia**, no **lee**, no **escribe**, no **practica**. (......................../........................)

3. Si **vives** en Móstoles, seguro que **comes** muchas empanadillas. (..)

4. Mira: **subes** hasta el segundo piso, **llamas** a la puerta C o **abres** con la llave, y **entras**. (................................)

5. ¿Qué **miráis**? (...)

6. Si **cantan** (............................/................................) , entonces **bailamos**. (................................)

7. ¿Dónde **vivís**? (...)

2 Complete with the right *Presente de indicativo* verb ending. You can work out the person
from the context.

➔ Mira, te present.*o*... a Sasha. Enseñ...*a*.. búlgaro en una escuela privada.

1. ● Perdona mis errores, es que todavía no toc...... la guitarra muy bien.

   ❍ Es verdad que no toc...... muy bien. ¿Por qué no dej...... la música
   para más tarde?

2. ● ¿Qué signific...... madrugar?

   ❍ Si un día tú te levant...... temprano, eso signific...... que madrug...... .

3. Por aquí pas...... un autobús cada cinco minutos.

4. ● Perdona, pero yo deb...... irme. Me esper...... mis padres arriba.

   ❍ Bueno, pero antes nos beb...... una cerveza más, ¿vale?

5. Alberto, ¿por qué no me escuch......? ¿Es que yo no signific......
   nada para ti?

6. ● Miroslaw y tú habl...... muy bien inglés.

   ❍ Bueno, ni él ni yo habl...... tan bien, pero es verdad que practic...... mucho.

7. Mafalda y tú hacéis muy buena pareja. ¿Cuánto tiempo llev...... de novios?
   ¿Viv...... juntos?

B Verbs with vowel changes: *quiero* / *puedo*, *juego*...

■ In many verbs, **the last vowel of the stem changes when the word stress falls on it**.
This means that it changes for all persons except *nosotros* and *vosotros*:

¡No cambian!

Entender

~~entiendo~~	→	en**tie**ndo
~~entiendes~~	→	en**tie**ndes
~~entiende~~	→	en**tie**nde
enten**de**mos		
enten**déis**		
~~entienden~~	→	en**tie**nden

■ With some verbs, this change means that the vowels *e*, *o* and *u* at the end
of the stem, lengthen into a diphthong *-ie-*, *-ue-* when they are stressed:

-e- → -ie-			-o- → -ue-			-u- → -ue-	
Querer	*Querer*		*Poder*	*Poder*		*Jugar*	*Jugar*
Sentar			Doler				
Cerrar	quiero		Morir	puedo			juego
Pensar	quieres		Dormir	puedes			juegas
Empezar	quiere		Volar	puede			juega
Comenzar	queremos		Recordar	podemos			jugamos
Perder	queréis		Encontrar	podéis			jugáis
Entender	quieren		Costar	pueden			juegan
Sentir			Volver...				
Preferir...							

3 Does the vowel change or not? Guess the verb, check the person markers and decide.

-e- → -ie-

➲ Qu.*ie*...ro comer temprano.

1. P........rden el tiempo.

2. ¿Emp........zo ya?

3. P........nsamos que no.

4. Pref......ren salir mañana.

5. Después c........rras la puerta.

6. No ent........ndéis nada.

7. Lo s........ntimos mucho.

-o-, -u- → -ue

8. Me d..........le la cabeza.

9. ¿Rec..........rdáis a Javi?

10. Sin agua, las plantas se m......ren.

11. ¿J........gamos al Trivial?

12. Me enc........ntro cansado.

13. D........rmes demasiado.

14. C......sta mucho dinero.

15. ¿Cuándo v........lves a Almería?

16. V........lamos a 700 km/h.

C Verbs with vowel changes: *pido, repito*...

■ With other verbs, the vowel *-e-* at the end of the stem changes to an *-i-*
when it is stressed:

-e- → -i-	(Only verbs with ...*e*...*ir*)		
Pedir	*Pedir*	*Repetir*	*Reír*
Impedir			
Seguir	pido	repito	río
Perseguir	pides	repites	ríes
Repetir	pide	repite	ríe
Competir	pedimos	repetimos	reímos
Reír	pedís	repetís	reís
Sonreír...	piden	repiten	ríen

👁 All verbs with ...*e...ir* and ...*o...ir*
change according to one of the
patterns explained in notes **B** and **C**.

4 Help us put Jerónimo and Alablanca's opinions into correct Spanish, with the correct form of the Presente de indicativo.

➲ *Rostro pálido serio y triste, no* **sonreír***.*
Nosotros alegres, sonreír a estrellas en cielo.

1. *Rostro pálido* **reír** *de nuestras costumbres.*
Nosotros no reír de costumbres de rostro pálido.

2. *Rostros pálidos* **pedir** *cosas imposibles a naturaleza.*
Nosotros sólo pedir alimento y vida.

3. *Rostro pálido* **perseguir** *animales para matar.*
Nosotros perseguir para comer.

4. *Rostros pálidos* **repetir** *errores mil veces.*
Nosotros no repetir cosas malas.

5. *Rostros pálidos* **competir** *entre ellos. Nosotros no competir, colaborar.*

6. *Rostro pálido* **medir** *la tierra. Nosotros no medir: tierra infinita.*

➲ El hombre blanco es serio y triste, no *sonríe* .
Nosotros somos alegres, *sonreímos* a las estrellas en el cielo.

1. El hombre blanco se .... de nuestras costumbres. Nosotros no nos .... de las suyas.

2. Los hombres blancos .... cosas imposibles a la naturaleza. Nosotros sólo le .... alimento y vida.

3. El hombre blanco .... animales para matarlos. Nosotros los .... para comer.

4. Los hombres blancos .... sus errores mil veces. Nosotros no .... las cosas malas.

5. Los hombres blancos .... entre ellos. Nosotros no .... , sino que colaboramos.

6. El hombre blanco .... la tierra. Nosotros no la .... : la tierra es infinita.

D First person irregular: *hago*, *pongo*, *salgo*...

■ There is a group of very common verbs that is **irregular only in the first person singular**:

Hacer	*hago, haces, hace...*	**Ver**	*veo, ves, ve...*		*-ecer, -ocer, -ucir*: *-zco*
Poner	*pongo, pones, pone...*	**Dar**	*doy, das, da...*	**Parecer**	*parezco, pareces...*
Salir	*salgo, sales, sale...*	**Saber**	*sé, sabes, sabe...*	**Agradecer**	*agradezco, agradeces...*
Valer	*valgo, vales, vale...*	**Caber**	*quepo, cabes, cabe...*	**Conocer**	*conozco, conoces...*
Traer	*traigo, traes, trae...*			**Conducir**	*conduzco, conduces...*
Caer	*caigo, caes, cae...*			**Introducir**	*introduzco, introduces...*
				Traducir	*traduzco, traduces...*
				Producir	*produzco, produces...*

■ When a verb has this irregularity, it will also be found in all its related **compound verbs**:

*Des**hacer** → des**hago**   Re**hacer** → re**hago***
*A**traer** → a**traigo**   Dis**traer** → dis**traigo***

*Su**poner** → su**pongo**   Com**poner** → com**pongo***
*A**parecer** → a**parezco**   Des**aparecer** → des**aparezco***

5 Joselito is learning to speak. Help him by identifying and correcting the mistakes he makes (there are five more of them).

➲ Ahora **pono** *pongo* el papel aquí.
y **escribo** ✓ , ¿ves?

1. Yo **hablo** .... mejor que Hanna, porque **sabo** .... más.

2. Hanna se **parece** .... a su papá, y yo me **parezo** .... a mi mamá.

3. Yo no **conozo** .... Alemania.

4. Yo no **salo** .... a la calle solo porque me **caio** ....

6 **Complete with the correct form of the verb.**

How different the two of us are! (¡Qué diferentes que somos tú y yo!)

➡ Tú siempre **haces** lo que quieres. Yo ...*hago*......... lo que es necesario hacer.

1. Tú **ves** problemas en todo. Yo .... problemas sólo donde realmente los hay.

2. Tú nunca **das** sin recibir algo a cambio. Cuando yo .... algo, no espero nada.

3. Tú **traes** a casa a todo el mundo. Yo sólo .... a mis mejores amigos.

4. Tú no **sabes** reconocer tus defectos. Yo .... perfectamente cuándo hago algo mal.

5. Tú **conduces** pensando que no hay nadie más en la carretera. Yo .... con cuidado.

6. Tú **desapareces** de pronto sin decirme nada. Yo nunca .... Siempre estoy cuando me llamas.

7. Tú siempre **supones** que todo está bien. Yo no .... nada.

8. Tú eres muy egoísta, pero no lo **reconoces**. Yo, por lo menos, ... que soy una pesada.

E **First person irregular and other changes**: *Tener, venir, decir, oír, estar*.

■ Some verbs have an irregular **first person singular** as well as some other **irregularity**. The syllable that carries the stress is underlined:

	1st pers. / *e* → *-ie-*		1st pers. / *e* → *-i-*	1st pers. / + *-y-*	1st pers. / *acento*
	Tener	*Venir*	*Decir*	*Oír*	*Estar*
Yo	<u>ten</u>go	<u>ven</u>go	<u>di</u>go	<u>oi</u>go	es<u>toy</u>
Tú	<u>tie</u>nes	<u>vie</u>nes	<u>di</u>ces	<u>o</u>yes	es<u>tás</u>
Él, ella, usted	<u>tie</u>ne	<u>vie</u>ne	<u>di</u>ce	<u>o</u>ye	es<u>tá</u>
Nosotros/-as	te<u>ne</u>mos	ve<u>ni</u>mos	de<u>ci</u>mos	o<u>í</u>mos	es<u>ta</u>mos
Vosotros/-as	te<u>néis</u>	ve<u>nís</u>	de<u>cís</u>	o<u>ís</u>	es<u>táis</u>
Ellos, ellas, ustedes	<u>tie</u>nen	<u>vie</u>nen	<u>di</u>cen	<u>o</u>yen	es<u>tán</u>
	Irregular 1st person singular and vowel changes			Irregular 1st person singular and a *-y-* is added.	Irregular 1st p. singular and accent/word stress change.

---

7 **1** **Complete the sentences with the most appropriate verb from the box in the *Presente de Indicativo*.**

decir	oír	venir	estar	tener

➡ Yo ...*vengo*........ aquí cada día sólo para verte. Tú ...*vienes*....... para verme también. Tú y yo ...*venimos*...... con la esperanza de vernos.

1. Cuando hablo de ti siempre .... cosas bonitas. Tú también .... cosas bonitas de mí. Tanto tú como yo .... cosas hermosas el uno del otro.

2. Yo .... bonitos recuerdos de ti, y tú .... bonitos recuerdos de mí. Es decir, que los dos .... bonitos recuerdos.

3. Yo me pongo nervioso cuando .... tu voz. Tú cierras los ojos cuando .... mi nombre. Nosotros dos sentimos algo cuando .... nuestras voces.

4. Creo que yo .... enamorado de ti y que tú también .... enamorada de mí. Está claro que tú y yo .... enamorados.

5. Si tú .... a mi casa, yo .... contento. Cuando yo te .... "te quiero", tú .... campanas en tu corazón. Cuando tú .... conmigo, yo no .... miedo.

¿Te quieres casar conmigo?

¡Vale!

107

F Very irregular verbs: *ir*, *ser*, *haber*.

	Ir	**Ser**	**Haber**
Yo	*voy*	*soy*	*he...*
Tú	*vas*	*eres*	*has...*
Él, ella, usted	*va*	*es*	*ha...* (hay)
Nosotros/-as	*vamos*	*somos*	*hemos...*
Vosotros/-as	*vais*	*sois*	*habéis...*
Ellos, ellas, ustedes	*van*	*son*	*han...*

Haber is an auxiliary verb. We use the *Presente* of *haber* to form the *Pretérito perfecto*: **he** comido, **has** ido, **ha** dicho...

Hay is an impersonal form:
- *Aquí hay mucha gente.*

Ser is not an auxiliary verb.

> 36. *Haber* and *estar*

> 35. *Ser* and *estar*

8 Complete with the correct verb, in the correct person.

> ir   ser   haber

➔ Hola, *soy* .... Ernesto. ¿Tú cómo te llamas?

1. ● ¿Por qué me dices eso ahora? ¡Todas las mujeres .... iguales!
   ○ Bueno, Antonio, tranquilo.

2. ● ¿Podéis hacerlo solas o .... yo a ayudaros?
   ○ No, gracias, ya .... terminado. Nos .... Adiós.

3. ● Perdone, ¿ .... un banco cerca de aquí?
   ○ Sí, ... dos al final de esta calle.

4. ● ¡Hola, guapa! ¿ .... venido para felicitarme por mi cumpleaños?
   ○ Pues no exactamente. Sólo .... venido a recoger mis cosas.

5. Carolina .... alemana, pero sus abuelos .... españoles.

6. Quiero comprarme una lámpara en Yanokea, pero no tengo coche. ¿Cuándo .... vosotros?

G Uses. Present affirmations: *Mi novio está en Madrid*.

■ We use the *Presente* to affirm things in present time, which we want to present as certain and completely under control. We are declaring **what we know about the present** or asking others what they know.

¿Qué gato **es** ése?

Es Julio César, el gatito de mi hermano.

> How things are in the **PRESENTE**:

THE QUALITIES OF THINGS
- *Es una casa antigua y **tiene** un patio interior precioso.*
- *Me gusta más el otro coche. **Corre** más y **gasta** menos gasolina.*

HABITUAL SITUATIONS
- *Yo **duermo** normalmente ocho o nueve horas al día.*
- *¿**Vives** todavía en aquella casa tan incómoda y fría?*

MOMENTARY SITUATIONS
- *Podemos vernos ahora. Mi novio **está** en Madrid.*
- *Manuela **tiene** fiebre y no **puede** ponerse al teléfono en este momento.*
- *¿**Está** todavía abierto el supermercado?*

■ If we want to present the information as not totally certain, we use the **Futuro**:

- *No sé. **Será** un gato jugando.*

> 28. Futuro

■ If we affirm situations that refer to things that have happened in the past, we use the **Pretérito imperfecto**:

- *Aquel gatito **era** Julio César.*

> 25. Pretérito imperfecto

9 **What can we know for sure now?**

➲ A Claudio le **encantaba** el Real Madrid.

1. Las llaves **están** en el bolso de Carmen.

2. Estuve en casa de Juan. **Tenía** un jardín precioso.

3. Rosa **es** una estupenda bailarina.

4. ¿Gerardo y Luisa? Hace mucho tiempo que se casaron. Ya **tendrán** hijos.

5. Ernestina **tiene** fiebre.

¿Es verdad ahora?	Es verdad	No lo sabemos
➲ Claudio **es** del Real Madrid.	....	....✓....
1. Carmen **tiene** las llaves.	....	....
2. Juan tiene un bonito jardín.	....	....
3. Rosa **baila** muy bien.	....	....
4. Gerardo y Luisa **son** padres.	....	....
5. Ernestina **está** enferma.	....	....

H Uses. Future affirmations: *Mi novio vuelve mañana*.

■ We also use the *Presente* to talk about future time (making it clear that we're talking about the future), when we want to present the information as certain and totally under control. We are talking about something we know and that will happen, regardless of what the weather is like. We are declaring **what we know about the future** or asking others what they know.

How things are in the **FUTURO**:

INFORMATION THAT IS CERTAIN
- *Mi novio **vuelve** <u>mañana</u>. Si quieres, nos vemos esta tarde.*
- *<u>El martes</u> no **hay** clase, pero <u>el jueves</u> **tenemos** dos exámenes.*
- *<u>El día 23</u> **es** el cumpleaños de Samuel. **Cumple** un año.*
- *Lola, ¿qué **haces** <u>mañana por la tarde</u>? ¿**Trabajas**?*

INSTRUCTIONS
- *Mira, **sales** por esa puerta, **giras** a la izquierda y **sigues** hasta el final...*
- *¿Primero **apago** la tele y luego le **doy** al botón o al contrario?*

¿Te vienes a estudiar mañana a mi casa?

Vale, a las cuatro en punto **estoy** allí.

■ If we want to present the information as a prediction, we use the **Futuro**:

- *A las cuatro **estaré** allí.*

➲ 28. Futuro

---

10 **Complete with the correct form of the *Presente*. Use the verbs in the box.**

● ¿Cuándo tienes un par de días para terminar nuestro trabajo?

○ Pues por ahora lo tengo difícil. A ver: el martes ..*ceno*... con Marta. El miércoles no .... nada, pero el jueves .... mis padres de Mallorca y tengo que ir a recogerlos al aeropuerto, y el viernes .... el cumpleaños de Mari. Luego, la semana siguiente, el lunes .... una reunión de trabajo muy importante. El día 11 .... el concierto de Rosa, y eso no me lo pierdo, y al día siguiente me .... a la playa al apartamento de Ramón, que está libre ese día. Pero el martes 9 y el miércoles 10 no .... ninguna obligación especial. ¿Trabajamos esos días?

cenar ✓
ir
tener
tener
tener
ser
ser
volver

1 Lunes		8 Lunes
___		_8:30 → Reunión de trabajo_
2 Martes		9 Martes
Cena con Marta a las nueve		___
3 Miércoles		10 Miércoles
___		___
4 Jueves		11 Jueves
Mis padres...		_Concierto de Rosa_
5 Viernes		12 Viernes
Cumpleaños de Mari		_PLAYA!!!!!!_
6 Sábado		13 Sábado
___		___
7 Domingo		14 Domingo
Septiembre Semana 35		Septiembre Semana 36

I   Uses. General affirmations: *Los hombres son así.*

■ We use the *Presente* to make or ask for statements about things in general that we present as certain and totally under control. We are saying **what we know about things in general**.

How things ALWAYS are:

KNOWN FACTS
- *Los niños **son** niños.*
- *Un león nunca **ataca** a un elefante.*
- *¿Cuánto **es** 9 x 8?*

11 Complete the text with the correct verb, and learn something about the Bengal cat. Use a dictionary if necessary.

> ser ✓ tener pesar poder poder ayudar medir

El Gato de Bengala ...*es*......... un felino salvaje, natural de Asia, pero también .... vivir como gato doméstico. Las madres .... de 2 a 4 cachorros después de una gestación de unos 65 días. A veces, el padre .... a criar a los cachorros. .... vivir de 12 a 15 años. .... normalmente 60 cm, aunque algunos autores indican hasta un metro, más la cola que alcanza los 45 cm. .... entre 3 y 8 kg.

> nadar mantener necesitar alimentar amar encantar

Se .... de mamíferos medianos y peque-ños, aves, reptiles y peces. Es de hábitos nocturnos, se .... activo desde el atardecer hasta el amanecer. A pesar de ser un animal de origen salvaje,

es de carácter noble, ... la vida familiar y .... cariño. Lo más curioso, quizá, es que le .... el agua y .... con gran agilidad.

12 Which concept are we talking about with these sentences in the *Presente*?

> Momento presente (P)   Momento futuro (F)   En general (G)

➡ Los triángulos **tienen** tres lados. (..*G*......)

1. Recuerda que **estamos** en una iglesia. (.........)
2. No te **preocupes**. **Estoy** en tu casa a las seis en punto. (.........)
3. Ya sé que la comida se está quemando. Ahora mismo **voy**. (.........)

4. Me **duele** la cabeza. ¿**Tienes** una aspirina? (.........)
5. Los elefantes no **vuelan**, hijo. (.........)
6. **Vas**, le **das** un beso y te **vienes** corriendo otra vez, ¿vale? (.........)
7. Oye, si **seguís** con ese tema, me **levanto** y me **voy**. (.........)
8. La paciencia **es** la madre de la ciencia. (.........)
9. ¿A qué hora **empieza** el partido? (.........)

13 Below you will find descriptions of different types of people. Complete them with the verbs in the box, and connect them to the person they describe.

➡ Una persona muy metódica... ➡ siempre ..*hace*..... las cosas de la misma manera.

1. Una persona egoísta...
2. Una persona sensible...
3. Una persona tacaña...
4. Una persona con sentido del humor...
5. Una persona pesimista...

a. .... las emociones con mucha intensidad.
b. .... de todo y también de sí misma.
c. .... mucho en sí misma y poco en los demás.
d. lo .... todo negro.
e. .... mucho y .... poco con los demás.

> hacer ✓
> gastar
> ver
> reírse
> pensar
> ahorrar
> sentir

22. Pretérito perfecto de indicativo

A — Meaning and forms: *he hablado*, *he comido*, *he vivido*...

■ The Pretérito perfecto is formed by:

The **Presente de indicativo** of the auxiliary verb **haber**.

he
has
ha
hemos
habéis
han

hablado
comido
vivido

The **past participle** corresponding to <u>finished</u> events.

→ 20. Non-personal forms

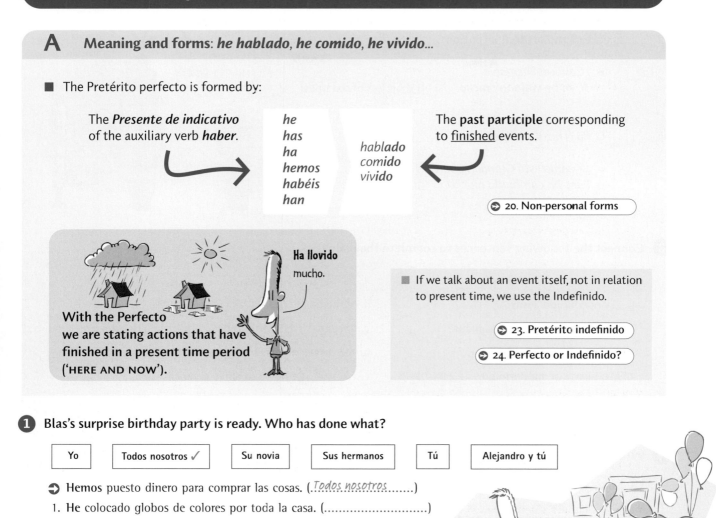

Ha llovido mucho.

With the Perfecto we are stating actions that have finished in a present time period ('HERE AND NOW').

■ If we talk about an event itself, not in relation to present time, we use the Indefinido.

→ 23. Pretérito indefinido

→ 24. Perfecto or Indefinido?

---

1 Blas's surprise birthday party is ready. Who has done what?

| Yo | Todos nosotros ✓ | Su novia | Sus hermanos | Tú | Alejandro y tú |

→ **Hemos** puesto dinero para comprar las cosas. (.*Todos nosotros*.......)

1. **He** colocado globos de colores por toda la casa. (...........................)

2. **Han** llamado por teléfono a todos los invitados. (...........................)

3. **Habéis** traído un montón de discos de flamenco. (.....................)

4. **Ha** hecho su comida preferida. (...........................)

5. No **has** hecho nada porque nunca tienes tiempo. (.........................)

---

2 Complete the sentences with the correct verb and person in the Perfecto and link each sentence to a picture.

| meter | salir | encender | tener | beber | llegar | hacer ✓ | ganar |

→ ¿ *Habéis hecho*.......... las tareas para casa? (..*C*..)

1. .... la estufa porque tengo frío. (.....)

2. Rebeca, ¿te .... en el agua tú sola? (.....)

3. ¡Qué suerte .... esta chica! (.....)

4. Eres un egoísta. Te lo .... todo (.....)

5. ¡ ....! ¡Somos los mejores! (.....)

6. ¡Qué bien! ¡......................... el sol! (.....)

7. Señoras y señores, ... al aeropuerto de Düsseldorf. (.....)

B   The recent past: *Ha llovido mucho. Este verano ha llovido mucho.*

■ We use the Perfecto when a completed event does not interest us in itself, but as **part of the present situation**:

Present situation:
Está muy grande.

Este árbol **ha crecido** mucho.

- ● *¿Conoces Tasmania?*
- ○ *Sí, yo **he viajado** mucho.*   [I know lots of countries]

- ● *¿Tienes las llaves?*
- ○ *Pues no, las **he perdido**.*   [I don't have the keys]

- ● *¿Y cómo está Granada ahora?*
- ○ *Pues **ha cambiado** mucho.*   [It is very different]

3 Connect the following sentences to complete the dialogues.

➲ Bueno, ya podemos irnos.

1. ¿Dónde **ha ido** Jesús?
2. ¿Por qué **has abierto** la ventana?
3. ¡Pepe, el niño se **ha caído**!
4. ¿Tu hija ya se **ha dormido**?
5. ¿**Has visto** mis gafas? No las encuentro.
6. ¿Ya estáis aquí?

a. Es que tengo mucho calor.
b. Sí, **hemos llegado** a las cuatro y cuarto, más o menos.
c. ¿Seguro? ¿**Has cerrado** bien la puerta? ¿**Has apagado** las luces?
d. Me parece que las **has puesto** al lado del teléfono.
e. No sé. Yo lo **he visto** antes en la cafetería.
f. Sí, se **ha levantado** muy temprano y estaba muy cansada.
g. Tranquila, no le **ha pasado** nada.

4 What has happened? Complete as in the example.

| Comer muchos dulces | Seguir un régimen ✓ | Ganar el gordo de la lotería |
| Bailar toda la noche | Ir a la playa | Salir en televisión muchas veces |

He pasado una noche estupenda...

➲ Está mucho más delgado que antes.   *Ha seguido un régimen.*

1. Están cansados.   ....
2. A los niños les duele el estómago.   ....
3. Lleva un coche carísimo.   ....
4. Están muy morenos.   ....
5. Ahora es muy famosa.   ....

¡Hmmm!

... pero no ha sido ésta.

■ We also use the Perfecto when we want to place completed events in **a present time period**:

PRESENT TIME PERIOD: **hoy** / today

Hoy **he plantado** un árbol.

Esta mañana **he plantado** un árbol.

MAÑANA
MORNING

TARDE
AFTRNOON

NOCHE
NIGHT

Hoy
Esta mañana
Esta tarde
Esta noche

PRESENT TIME PERIOD: **esta semana** / this week

Este martes **he plantado** un árbol.

Esta semana **he plantado** un árbol.

Este fin de semana
Esta semana
Esta Navidad
Este mes...

LUNES / MONDAY
MARTES / TUESDAY
MIÉRCOLES / WEDNESDAY
JUEVES / THURSDAY
VIERNES / FRIDAY

PRESENT TIME PERIOD: **este año** / this year

Esta primavera **he plantado** un árbol.

Este año **he plantado** un árbol.

Este verano
Este año
Este curso...

PRIMAVERA / SPRING
VERANO / SUMMER
OTOÑO / AUTUMN
INVIERNO / WINTER

PRESENT TIME PERIOD: **hasta ahora** / up to now

En mi vida **he plantado** árboles muchas veces.

He plantado árboles muchas veces.

Siempre, nunca,
toda la vida,
alguna vez,
muchas veces,
últimamente,
en los últimos
días/meses/años,
desde el martes,
hasta ahora...

5 Pedro is a lucky man. Angel has always had bad luck. Decide which things have happened to each of them?

➔ Pedro *ha tenido muchos amores* .... en su vida.
   Ángel *ha estado solo* .... toda su vida.

a. Estar solo.
b. Tener muchos amores.

1. Pedro siempre .... hasta ahora.
   Ángel .... muchas veces.

a. Conseguir buenos trabajos.
b. Tener trabajos difíciles.

2. Pedro .... en los últimos años.
   Ángel .... últimamente.

a. Perder mucho dinero.
b. Ganar mucho dinero.

3. Pedro .... este año.
   Ángel .... en los últimos meses.

a. Ponerse enfermo tres veces.
b. Tener muy buena salud.

4. Pedro .... esta semana.
   Ángel .... esta semana.

a. Conocer a una chica fantástica.
b. Separarse de su mujer.

5. Pedro .... esta mañana.
   Ángel .... esta mañana.

a. Encontrar una billetera.
b. Perder su billetera.

113

C The past in the future: *A las cinco he terminado*.

■ We also use the Pretérito perfecto to state with a degree of certainty, future events that are previous to another future moment. We do this when we explicitly adopt a specific point of reference in the future and want to declare things that will be finished at this point in time:

A las cinco ya **he llegado**.

- ● *¿Cómo va eso?*
- ○ *Casi terminado. <u>En dos horas</u> lo **hemos pintado** todo.*

- ● *Oye, dejadme algún dulce, ¿vale?*
- ○ *No te hagas ilusiones. Seguro que <u>cuando vuelvas</u>, la tarta **ha desaparecido**.*

- ● *¿Si salimos <u>mañana a las siete</u> está bien? ¿Estarás cansado para conducir?*
- ○ *No, con seis horas **he dormido** suficiente, no te preocupes.*

■ To do the same, but without the same degree of certainty, we use the Futuro perfecto:

- ● *A las cinco habré llegado.* ⮕ 29. Futuro perfecto

---

6 Are they talking about past or future time?

⮕ ¿Tú crees que para la cena **hemos llegado**? Es para avisar a mi madre...   (..*Future*..)

⮕ Si estás tan seguro de que **han llegado** ya, ¿por qué no te das más prisa?   (....*Past*...)

1. Yo **he hecho** todo lo que podía hacer. Ahora termina tú.   (.............)

2. Si veis un restaurante pintado de verde, eso significa que ya **habéis llegado** al pueblo.   (.............)

3. ¿**Has encendido** la calefacción? Aquí hace mucho frío...   (.............)

4. Pepe, que **han llamado** a la puerta. ¿Por qué no abres?   (.............)

5. Este tren es muy rápido. Antes de que nos demos cuenta, **hemos llegado** a Bilbao.   (.............)

6. ¡Vaya, hombre! ¡Ya **he olvidado** decirle a Rosa que los frenos del coche no funcionan!   (.............)

7. Venga, un poco de ánimo. Para las siete ya **hemos limpiado** toda la casa.   (.............)

8. ¿Qué **has dicho** de las siete? ¡Tenemos que irnos ya!   (.............)

---

7 Somebody made the predictions on the left, but the reality is what you can see on the right. Were the predictions correct or not?

⮕ No te preocupes: a las siete lo **he terminado**, seguro.   Terminó a las 6:30.   (..*Sí*......)

⮕ Ahora no puedo, pero a las siete lo **termino**, no te preocupes.   (..*No*....)

1. Te digo que para Navidad ya **ha nacido** Luisito, ya verás.   Nació en noviembre.   (.........)

2. Te digo que Luisito **nace** en Navidad, ya verás.   (.........)

3. Su avión **aterriza** a las 11:15 en el aeropuerto de Jizro.   Aterrizó a las 11:05   (.........)

4. A las 11:15, seguro que el avión ya **ha aterrizado**.   (.........)

5. ● Evaristo, ¿recuerdas que mi madre viene a comer el domingo   Lo arregló el jueves.   (.........)

   y que el horno no funciona?   (.........)

   ○ Que sí, mujer, que para el domingo ya **he arreglado** el horno...

6. El fin de semana, que tengo tiempo, **arreglo** el horno.

23. Pretérito indefinido

A Meaning and forms: *hablé*, *comí*, *viví*...

- The Pretérito indefinido is used to talk about a **finished** event, not connected to the present time period.

Llovió mucho aquel día.

> With the *Indefinido* we are narrating **finished** events that happened in a past time period ('THEN').

- The *Indefinido* of regular verbs is formed by changing the ending of the infinitive for the following **endings**:

	-ar	-er / -ir
Yo	-é	-í
Tú	-aste	-iste
Él, ella, usted	-ó	-ió
Nosotros/-as	-amos	-imos
Vosotros/-as	-asteis	-isteis
Ellos, ellas, ustedes	-aron	-ieron

When the stem ends in a vowel, the *-i-* becomes a *-y-* : caer, construir, creer, huir, influir, leer, oír, sustituir ...

-ió → -yó   Caer → cayó   ~~caió~~
            Oír → oyó   ~~oió~~

-ieron → -yeron Caer → cayeron ~~caieron~~
                Oír → oyeron   ~~oieron~~

> 👁 In the *Indefinido*, there is no final *-s* on the 2nd person singular (*tú*).

- In addition, with the Indefinido of regular verbs, the word stress is always on the final syllable, as shown by the underlining in the examples:

	Hablar	Comer	Vivir
Yo	Hablé	Comí	Viví
Tú	Hablaste	Comiste	Viviste
Él, ella, usted	Habló	Comió	Vivió
Nosotros/-as	Hablamos*	Comimos	Vivimos*
Vosotros/-as	Hablasteis	Comisteis	Vivisteis
Ellos, ellas, ustedes	Hablaron	Comieron	Vivieron

> 👁 The word stress is often the only way to tell the *Indefinido* apart from other verb forms:
>
> | [yo Presente] | [él Indefinido] |
> |---|---|
> | Hablo | → Habló |
> | Entro | → Entró |
> | Bailo | → Bailó |

* These forms are the same as those of the *Presente de Indicativo*.

---

1 Identify all the verbs that are in the *Indefinido* form, and then put all the others into this same form, as in the example.

compraron	➲ ...✓...	he decidido	9. *he decidido*	ha leído	19. *he leído*		*vir? ver?*
llamo	➲ *llamé*	pasó	10. *pasé*	vimos	20. *ve*		
abres	1. *abre*	invitabas	11. *invité*	encontrarás	21. *encontré*		
cerrábamos	2. *cerré*	ha salido	12. *he salido*	entraban	22. *entré*		
baila	3. *bailé*	comíamos	13. *comí*	estudió	23. *estudiar*		
canto	4. *canté*	dejaste	14. *dejaré*	han construido	24. *he construido*		
acabasteis	5. *acabé*	terminarán	15. *terminé*	saludé	25. *saludé*		
oías	6. *oír*	vivíamos	16. *vivé*	estudiabais	26. *estudié*		
hablo	7. *hablé*	cree	17. *creé*	escondes	27. *escondé*		
han huido	8. *he huido*	habéis bebido	18. *habé* *bebido*	decidiréis	28. *decidé*		

2 Is the verb in bold in the *Presente* or the *Indefinido*? Use the context to help you decide.

➡ Mi mujer y yo **dormimos** mucho. Si no dormimos, estamos siempre muy cansados. ➡ *...Presente............*

➡ Mi mujer y yo **dormimos** mucho. Ellos casi no dormían. Estaban haciendo turismo
a todas horas. ➡ *...Indefinido.........*

1. **Hablamos** de los problemas entre hombres y mujeres. ¿Te apetece participar? 1. ....
2. **Hablamos** de los problemas entre hombres y mujeres. Pero nadie dijo nada interesante. 2. ....
3. **Llegamos** a Madrid el martes y todavía no hemos visto el museo del Prado. 3. ....
4. **Llegamos** a Madrid el martes. ¿Nos vas a recoger en el aeropuerto? 4. ....
5. **Compramos** una botella de agua mineral y nos vamos, ¿vale? 5. ....
6. **Compramos** una botella de agua mineral que nos costó carísima. 6. ....
7. Le **escribimos** un e-mail y todavía no nos ha contestado. 7. ....
8. Le **escribimos** un e-mail y nos vamos, ¿de acuerdo? 8. ....

B Verbs with an irregular stem: *dijo*, *puso*, *estuvo*...

■ Most of the verbs that are irregular in the *Indefinido* have an **irregular stem**:

Verbs ending in
-ducir → -duj-

Saber → sup-	Tener → tuv-	Querer → quis-	Conducir → conduj-
Poder → pud-	Estar → estuv-	Venir → vin-	Producir → produj-
Poner → pus-	Andar → anduv-	Hacer → hic- e	Traducir → traduj-
Haber → hub-	Decir → dij-	hic- iste	Introducir → introduj-
Caber → cup-	Traer → traj-	hiz- o	Reducir → reduj-

👁 *Co*ntener, intervenir, deshacer, contradecir, reproducir, and their related compound verbs.

■ All the following verbs take a single, **special ending** in the *Indefinido*:

		Estar	Hacer	Decir
Yo	-e	es*tu*ve	*hi*ce	*di*je
Tú	-iste	estu*vis*te	hi*cis*te	di*jis*te
Él, ella, usted	-o	es*tu*vo	*hi*zo	*di*jo
Nosotros/-as	-imos	estu*vi*mos	hi*ci*mos	di*ji*mos
Vosotros/-as	-isteis	estu*vis*teis	hi*cis*teis	di*jis*teis
Ellos, ellas, ustedes	-ieron (-eron*)	estu*vie*ron	hi*cie*ron	di*je*ron

* If the stem ends in -*j*.

■ Unlike regularly conjugated verbs, the stress is on the stem in the 1st and 3rd persons singular
(*yo* y *él-ella-usted*), as indicated by the underlining in the examples above.

3 Lourdes is still very young and thinks that all verbs in the *Indefinido* are regular.
Help her by finding and correcting the six mistakes she's made (apart from the example).

➡ Ayer **estuvimos** ....✓.......... en casa
de Susi y sus papás nos ~~ponieron~~ ....
...*pusieron*... una película de dibujos animados muy bonita.

1. ¿Por qué no **veniste** ....*viniste*...... con
nosotras a la playa? **Hacimos** ...*hicimos*....
un castillo de arena y nos **bañamos** ....
....

2. Montse **condució** ...*condujo*... el cochecito
de Rosendo, y yo **quise** .... también
conducirlo, pero no **podí** ...*pude*.......
porque Rosendo me lo **quitó** ....

3. Papá me **dició** ...*dijo*......... que me ibas a
comprar un regalo. ¿Por qué no me lo **compraste** .... ? ¿Es que no **teniste**
...*tuviste*... tiempo?

4 Complete the following sentences with the correct verb from the box in the *Indefinido*.

➲ Cuando vi el fuego y el humo, me ..*puse*...... muy nervioso y no ..*supe*...... qué hacer.

1. El otro día me pasó una cosa muy rara en el ordenador del trabajo: cuando .... la contraseña, se .... un fallo general en el servidor de la oficina.

2. Yo te .... que tú sí podías venir conmigo. Si no .... , es porque no ....

3. Lo pasamos muy bien y, además, ... un viaje muy bueno, porque .... Miguel, y él conduce muy bien.

4. Me dieron un montón de folios para traducir, pero tenía demasiado trabajo en aquel momento. Sólo .... cuatro páginas. No .... hacer más.

5. Mira, es que se puso muy nerviosa. No .... manera de calmarla. Yo .... todo lo que pude.

> venir/decir/querer
> saber/poner ✓
> producir/introducir
> traducir/poder
> haber/hacer
> tener/conducir

C   Verbs with vowel changes: *pidió*, *durmió*...

■ **Verbs ending in -*ir* that have an -*e*- or an -*o*- in the last syllable of the stem** (*e...ir, o...ir*, that are also irregular in the *Presente*), change this vowel in the third persons singular and plural:

e → i *Pedir*		*o → u* *Dormir*
pedí		dormí
pediste		dormiste
pidió		durmió
pedimos		dormimos
pedisteis		dormisteis
pidieron		durmieron

¡Qué mal **dormí** ese día!

Ah, pues nosotros **dormimos** muy bien.

Pues el pobre Joaquín no **durmió** nada, ¿os acordáis?

👁 Verbs like *repetir, sentir, seguir, mentir, competir, elegir, herir, medir, reír, preferir, morir*, or related compound verbs: *sonreír, impedir, perseguir, presentir*, etc. The verb **oír** is regular (*oyó, oyeron*).

---

5 The following verbs are all from the 3ʳᵈ conjugation (ending in –*ir*), but five of them are regular and ten are irregular. Work out which is which, and write the third person singular and plural of all of them.

➲ morir *murió*
(irr.) *murieron*

➲ vivir *vivió*
(r.) *vivieron*

1. repetir *repitió*
repitieron

2. herir *hirió*
hirieron

3. discutir *discutió*
discutieron

4. oír *oyó*
oyeron

5. impedir *impidió*
impidieron

6. medir *midió*
midieron

7. salir *salió*
salieron

8. repartir *repartió*
repartieron

9. mentir *mintió*
mintieron

10. decidir *decidió*
decidieron

11. preferir *prefirió*
prefirieron

12. perseguir *persiguió*
persiguieron

13. reír ....
rieron

14. presentir *presintió*
presintieron

15. competir *compitió*
compitieron

D   *Dar, ir, ser*

Dar	*Ir / Ser*	
di	fui	*Ir* and *ser* have **the same form** in the *Indefinido*.
diste	fuiste	
dio	fue	
dimos	fuimos	
disteis	fuisteis	• *La manifestación **fue** un éxito: **fue** mucha gente.*
dieron	fueron	

6 Complete the sentences with one of the three verbs in the *Indefinido*.

ser	ir	dar

➲ Lo pasé muy bien, de verdad. ....*Fue*..... una fiesta de cumpleaños estupenda.

1. ● ¿Os ha dado Alberto algo para mí?

   ❍ Pues no. .... los dos con él al cine ayer, pero no nos .... nada.

2. ● ¿Qué tal ayer con Celia?

   ❍ Muy mal. Marta y yo .... a su casa para hablar tranquilamente. .... muy amables y muy educados, pero ella empezó a insultarnos y nos ....

3. Nosotros le .... una pastilla, pero ella empezó a temblar y se puso roja, roja... .... horrible.

E Uses: *El viernes pasado los vi. Cuando entraba, los vi.*

■ We use the *Indefinido* to place finished events "THEN", in the past where they happened. For this reason, the *Indefinido* contrasts with the *Perfecto*, which places events in the "HERE AND NOW", in a present time period:

- *Aquel día me **asusté** mucho. <u>He tenido</u> pesadillas desde entonces.*
- *El verano pasado **vi** dos o tres veces a Valeria, pero este verano no la <u>he visto</u>.*
- *Lo que te <u>ha dicho</u> hoy no me <u>ha sorprendido</u>. Lo que te **dijo** el otro día sí me **sorprendió**.*

➲ 22. Pretérito perfecto

➲ 24. Perfecto or Indefinido?

---

7 Change the present viewpoint on the left, for the past viewpoint on the right, using the same grammatical person.

('THEN')

Thinking of a present time period

➲ **Hemos comido** demasiado, ¿no crees?

1. Oye, **he oído** que te vas. ¿Es verdad?

2. Esta mañana no **he tomado** café. ¿Me invitas?

3. ¡Mirad, es Juan! ¡Por fin **ha llegado**!

4. ¿**Has llamado** al médico?

Thinking of a past time period

➲ Ayer ....*comí*........ demasiado.

1. El otro día .... que Lola se iba, ¿es verdad?

2. Aquella mañana no .... café. No tenía dinero.

3. Juan no aparecía, pero a las doce por fin ....

4. ¿............... al médico el lunes?

('HERE AND NOW')

■ We also use the *Indefinido* to **narrate finished events** in the past. It is always understood that the event started, unfolded and finished at the point in the narration where we find ourselves. This is why the *Indefinido* contrasts with the *Imperfecto*, which describes an event not yet finished at this point:

- *Cuando ya <u>estaba</u> llegando al trabajo, me **acordé** de Luis y **volví** a su casa a recogerlo.*
- *Antes me <u>llamaba</u> todos los fines de semana, pero el fin de semana pasado no me **llamó**.*
- *No <u>tenía</u> las llaves. Por eso **entré** por la ventana y **abrí** desde dentro.*

➲ 25. Pretérito imperfecto

➲ 26. Imperfecto, Indefinido or Pretérito perfecto?

---

8 Change the viewpoint from describing to that of narrating in the past, using the same grammatical personl.

Describing (unfinished processes)

➲ Mientras ella se **duchaba**, yo limpié el cuarto.

1. Antes **hablabas** francés peor que ahora.

2. En Galicia, todos los días **comíamos** marisco.

3. En aquel tiempo esas cosas **influían** mucho sobre mí.

4. Yo os estaba llamando, pero no me **oíais**.

5. Nosotros **bebíamos** y **bebíamos**, y ellas nos miraban.

Narrating (finished events)

➲ Cuando se ....*duchó*........ , nos fuimos.

1. ¿...*hablaste*.... francés en tu viaje a Marsella?

2. Ayer ...*comimos*... marisco en el restaurante de Luis.

3. Esas cosas ...*influyeron*...mucho en mi decisión.

4. ¿...*oísteis*.... las voces de Javi?

5. Al final, nos lo ...*bebimos*.... todo.

■ With the *Pretérito perfecto* and the *Indefinido* we are able to talk about the same reality (**finished** events in the past) from two different perspectives:

> When we use the *Indefinido* we are thinking about the event in itself and in the past time period in which this event happened (finished '**THEN**').

> When we use the *Perfecto* we are thinking about this event in relation to the present, and in a larger present time period that includes where we are now (finished '**HERE AND NOW**').

3 de enero...

('THEN')

...17 de enero

Me **compré** un vestido precioso.

Me **he comprado** un vestido precioso.

················> ('HERE AND NOW')

■ If we consider the event as not finished yet, we use the *Imperfecto*.

⬅ 25. Pretérito imperfecto

⬅ 22. Pretérito perfecto

⬅ 23. Pretérito indefinido

⬅ 26. Imperfecto, Indefinido or Pretérito perfecto?

A   Espacios actuales y no actuales: *Este año ha sido horrible / El año pasado fue horrible*

■ Some of the time adverbials that we use or are thinking of when talking about events in the past, can be easily identified with one or the other time periods ('**HERE AND NOW**'= the time period where we are and '**THEN**'= a past time period):

WHEN WE TALK ABOUT...	*Hoy, Esta tarde, Esta semana, Este mes, Este año, Este siglo, Esta Navidad, Este verano, Esta vez, Hasta ahora, Últimamente, Todavía no...*	■ WE USE THE **PERFECTO** BECAUSE WE ARE TALKING ABOUT '**HERE AND NOW**': The day, the week, the month, Christmas, the summer, the year, the century... **where we are in time.**
WHEN WE TALK ABOUT...	*Ayer, El jueves, La semana pasada, El mes pasado, En febrero, El 7 de abril, El otro día, Ese/Aquel día/mes/año..., En ese/aquel momento, Esa/aquella vez, La última vez, En 1987, Hace dos años, Cuando vivía en Madrid...*	■ WE USE THE **INDEFINIDO** BECAUSE WE ARE TALKING ABOUT '**THEN**': A day, a week, a month, a summer, a Christmas, a year... **in the past.**

Ha llovido mucho esta semana. ['HERE AND NOW']

Llovió mucho la semana pasada.   ['THEN']

Lunes   Martes...   ...Viernes   Sábado   Domingo

Lunes   Martes...   ...Viernes   Sábado   Domingo

1 **What are they talking about? Underline the most likely option.**

➲ ¿**Has visto** mis gafas de sol?

   a. La semana pasada.

   b. <u>Hoy.</u>

1. Alguien **ha matado** a Julio César.

   a. Julio César es el Emperador romano.

   b. Julio César es su gato.

2. Nadie **bailó**.

   a. En la fiesta del fin de semana pasado.

   b. En esta fiesta donde estamos.

3. He conocido a un chico maravilloso.

   a. El lunes pasado.

   b. Este verano.

4. Nos **compramos** un Mercedes.

   a. En 1999.

   b. Esta misma mañana.

5. **Fue** muy importante para la humanidad.

   a. El descubrimiento del fuego.

   b. La era de la informática.

6. No **ha dicho** ni una sola palabra.

   a. El día de su último cumpleaños.

   b. Desde esta mañana hasta ahora.

7. ¿**Comprasteis** toda la comida vosotros?

   a. Para la cena de hoy.

   b. Para la cena del otro día.

2 **Underline the most appropriate form for each context.**

➲ ● ¿Sabes si va a venir Julia al cine?

   ○ Esta tarde no la <u>he visto</u>/vi, pero ayer **he habla-do/<u>hablé</u>** con ella y me **ha dicho/<u>dijo</u>** que sí.

1. ● Estamos ya a viernes. ¿Todavía no **has arregla-do/arreglaste** el grifo?

   ○ Es que esta semana no **he tenido/tuve** tiempo.

2. ● Este fin de semana lo **hemos pasado/pasamos** muy bien con mis hermanas, ¿verdad?

   ○ Yo creo que el fin de semana pasado **ha sido/fue** mejor, sin tus hermanas.

3. ● Montserrat, ¿y tú? ¿No **has ido/fuiste** este año a ningún concierto?

   ○ Pues sí, en febrero **he ido/fui** a uno de Plácido Carreras, y este mes **he estado/estuve** en otro de José Domingo.

4. ● ¿Qué **has hecho/hiciste** hoy?

   ○ Nada interesante. Pero ayer **he salido/salí** con Rebeca a cenar, para celebrar nuestro aniversario. Nos **hemos casado/casamos** un 11 de julio, ¿no te acuerdas?

B **Unspecified time periods:** *Nunca ha pasado nada / Nunca pasó nada*

◼ With other markers that have a broader and less precise meaning, we can refer to either present or past periods, depending on the context. In these cases our use of the *Perfecto* or *Imperfecto* will indicate clearly which of the two time periods we are referring to ("here and now" = up to now / "then" = in a past time period):

WHEN WE TALK ABOUT...	*Siempre, Nunca, En la vida, Alguna vez, Varias veces, En los últimos días / meses / años, Al final...*	◼ WE USE THE **PERFECTO** IF WE ARE TALKING ABOUT 'HERE AND NOW'. Up to now.	◼ WE USE THE **INDEFINIDO** IF WE ARE TALKING ABOUT 'THEN'. In a past time period

¿**Has visto** a Cristina últimamente?

Sí, estas Navidades **he salido** muchas veces con ella. ['HERE AND NOW']

Navidades 2004

El año pasado **pasé** las Navidades en Madrid, y **salí** muchas veces con Cristina. ['THEN']

2005

3 Are we talking about 'HERE AND NOW' or 'THEN'?

➡ Dos veces la semana pasada... (...'THEN'...)

1. Dos veces este año... (..............)

2. Ahora mismo... (..............)

3. Un día, hace 5 años... (..............)

4. Nunca en mi vida... (..............)

5. Alguna vez hasta ahora... (..............)

6. Cuando terminé el curso, al final... (..............)

7. Cervantes, durante toda su vida... (..............)

8. Nunca en mi antigua relación con Susana... (..............)

9. Ese verano, ninguna vez... (..............)

10. De pequeño, yo nunca... (..............)

11. Con aquel amigo de la escuela primaria, siempre... (..............)

12. Esta semana, al final... (..............)

13. En aquellos tres últimos días... (..............)

14. El primer coche que tuve... (..............)

15. La política social del actual presidente... (..............)

4 Choose the most appropriate verb and complete with the correct form of the *Indefinido* or *Perfecto*.

| estar ir ir | | ➡ ● ¿Tú ...has ido... alguna vez a Disneylandia?
○ Yo sí, cuando era pequeño .fui......... tres veces.
● Pues yo no he estado.. nunca. |

| dar funcionar | 1. ● ¿Qué tal va tu ordenador nuevo?
○ Fatal, siempre está dando problemas.
● A mí el mío me .... muy bien hasta ahora.
○ Pues me alegro por ti. Yo echo de menos el que tenía antes. Aquel nunca me .... ningún problema. |

| decir decir decir | 2. ● Te .... mil veces que está muy feo meterse el dedo en la nariz.
○ Mil veces no. Hoy me lo .... una vez, y ayer me lo .... dos veces. Total, tres. ¡Prffrrrrffrrff! |

| pasar pasar casarse | 3. Mi bisabuelo, y también sus padres, ... la mayor parte de su vida en Argentina. Pero mi madre .... hace muchos años con un español. Por eso yo nací aquí en España y .... toda mi vida en Madrid. |

| estar decir tener | 4. ● ¿Cómo va la cosa con Julieta?
○ Mal. En este último mes .... muchos problemas. La última vez que nos vimos .... discutiendo todo el día, y el otro día, me .... que me dejaba. |

| cambiar enfadarse | 5. ● ¿Por qué .... la familia cuando murió?
○ Es que, antes de morir, Aureliano .... su testamento a favor de su amante. |

5 Write out the results of the competitions between the villages of Villatripa de Arriba and Villatripa de Abajo, using the verbs *ganar, perder* or *empatar* in the *Perfecto* or *Indefinido*.

	Cuándo	Qué
Competiciones ganadas	➡ Siempre.	El concurso anual de baile.
	1. En los años 90, siete veces.	El campeonato de fútbol.
	2. En los últimos diez años, dos veces.	El concurso de levantar piedras.
Competiciones perdidas	3. En las fiestas del verano pasado.	La carrera de sacos.
	4. Casi siempre en los últimos años.	El concurso de belleza masculina.
	5. Siempre hasta ahora.	El tiro al plato de espaldas.
Competiciones empatadas	6. En el año 2004.	En el concurso de paellas de marisco.
	7. Últimamente, muchas veces.	En el concurso de bandas de música.

➡ *Siempre hemos ganado el concurso anual de baile.*

1. ....

2. ....

3. ....

4. ....

5. ....

6. ....

7. ....

C   Recent time periods: *Ya he terminado / Ya terminé*

■ To talk about a very recent event, we can use the *Pretérito perfecto*, but we can also use the *Indefinido*. There is only a small difference in perspective between them.

With the *Perfecto* we present the event as *part of the present situation*:

- ¿Dónde está Pedro?
- No sé. Se **ha ido** <u>hace un par de minutos</u>.

With the *Indefinido* we present the event in itself, , taken in isolation and less connected to the present:

- ¿Dónde está Pedro?
- No sé. Se **fue** <u>hace un par de minutos</u>.

He **hablado** con Bea <u>hace un rato</u>, y me **ha dicho** que...

3:30   3:45

<u>Hace un rato</u> **hablé** con Bea, y me **dijo** que...

3:30   3:45

WHEN WE TALK ABOUT...	*Ya...* *A las diez y media* (de 'hoy')... *Hace un rato...* *Hace un momento...*	■ WE USE THE **Perfecto** or Indefinido

- ¡Vaya! ¡Se **ha ido** / **fue** la luz! ['ahora mismo']
- ¿**Has apagado** / **Apagaste** el horno? ['ya']
- ¡Por fin! ¡<u>Ya</u> **ha funcionado** / **funcionó**!

- Ya están aquí tus padres. **Han llegado** / **Llegaron** <u>a las diez</u>.
- ¿Luis? Pues, mira, <u>hace sólo un momento</u> que se **ha ido** / **fue**.

---

6 When they are talking about something that has just happened, Jerónimo always thinks of it at something connected to the present, whereas Alablanca sees it as an event in itself. They, however, can only think, because they don't know the *Perfecto* and the *Indefinido*, whereas you can also express it. Choose for them the correct form of the verbs in bold, as in the examples.

Jerónimo: ¡Dios mío, ya **empezar** (➜) (....*ha empezado*......) a llover!

Alablanca: Sí, ya **empezar** (➜) (....*empezó*......) a llover. ¿Y qué?

Jerónimo: Pues que nosotros no **traer** (1) (...*no*......) paraguas.

Alablanca: Pues en la casa yo **recordárte**lo (2) (...*te lo*......) .

Jerónimo: Sí, pero yo **olvidar**lo (3) (...*lo*......) .

Alablanca: Hace un momento yo **ver** (4) (......) una casa para refugiar de la lluvia.

Jerónimo: ¿Dónde, allí? **Ir** rápido. **Empezar** (5) (......) a llover más fuerte. ¡Menos mal! ¡**Entrar**! ¡Ya **estar** protegidos! ¿**Mojarte** (6) (...*¿Te*......) mucho?

Alablanca: No, **taparme** (7) (...*Me*......) la cabeza con el sombrero.

Jerónimo: ¿Tú **cerrar** (8) (......) la puerta?

Alablanca: Sí, **cerrar** (9) (......*cuando*......) cuando **entrar**.

Jerónimo: ¡Uf! ¡Nosotros **tener** (10) (......) suerte!

Alablanca: Nada de suerte. **Ser** yo la que **encontrar** (11) (......) refugio.

25. Pretérito imperfecto de indicativo

A   Meaning of the Imperfecto

The *Presente* expresses events that are **not yet finished in the present**:

- Sí, **hace** frío porque esta casa **es** un poco vieja y, además, por las noches no **funciona** la calefacción.

■ The *Imperfecto* changes this perspective to **a moment in the past**:

- Sí, en aquella casa **hacía** frío porque **era** un poco vieja y, además, por las noches no **funcionaba** la calefacción.

We use the Imperfecto to describe UNFINISHED EVENTS at a moment in the past.

¡Cuánto **llueve**!

Llovía mucho aquel día...

Mi novia **es** una chica muy inteligente.

Mi primera novia **era** muy inteligente.

Todas las noches **estudio** una hora.

Antes **estudiaba** una hora todas las noches. Ahora no.

Está un poco nervioso. **Es** la hora de su comida.

A las cinco ya **estaba** un poco nervioso. **Era** la hora de su comida.

---

1 José Luis got married and has changed a lot. Describe the changes, putting the following information in the correct column.

➲ Nunca leía novelas. ✓

a. No le gustaba ir a los restaurantes. ✓

b. Llevaba una ropa muy clásica. ✓

c. Nunca come en casa. ✓

d. Tiene tres perros.

e. Sale todas las noches con sus amigos.

f. No tenía amigos. ✓

g. Le encanta leer. ✓

h. Viste muy moderno. ✓

i. Quería tener muchos hijos.

José Luis **antes** de casarse:

➲ *Nunca leía novelas*

1. *no le gustaba...*
2. *llevaba una ropa*
3. *No tenía amigos*
4. *Quería tener muchos hijos*

José Luis **ahora**:

Le encanta leer

nunca come en casa
Viste muy moderno
Sale todas las noches
Tiene tres perros

B   Regular forms: *hablaba*, *comía*, *vivía*...

■ To form the *Imperfecto* of regular verbs we change the endings of the Infinitive for the following **endings**:

	-ar	*-er* / *-ir*	*Hablar*	*Comer*	*Vivir*
Yo	*-aba*	*-ía*	*ha**bla**ba*	*co**mía***	*vi**vía***
Tú	*-abas*	*-ías*	*ha**bla**bas*	*co**mías***	*vi**vías***
Él, ella, usted	*-aba*	*-ía*	*ha**bla**ba*	*co**mía***	*vi**vía***
Nosotros/-as	*-ábamos*	*-íamos*	*ha**blá**bamos*	*co**mía**mos*	*vi**vía**mos*
Vosotros/-as	*-abais*	*-íais*	*ha**bla**bais*	*co**mía**is*	*vi**vía**is*
Ellos, ellas, ustedes	*-aban*	*-ían*	*ha**bla**ban*	*co**mía**n*	*vi**vía**n*

The 1st and 3rd persons singular have the same form.

The word stress is always on the ending, as shown by the under-lining in the examples.

---

2 At Blas's party, everything changed in just two minutes when his parents rang the doorbell. Describe the first scene, by checking the information on the left.

Son las 5:45 pm

Blas y Silvia **están** bailando muy pegados. Casimiro, el novio de Silvia, no **para** de mirar a Blas. **Hay** varias botellas de cerveza en la mesa y el cenicero **está** lleno de colillas. La música **está** muy alta y todo el mundo se **ríe** sin parar. La hermana de Silvia y el hermano de Blas **duermen** en el sofá, cogidos de la mano. La foto de los padres de Blas **tiene** tres chicles pegados. En la cocina, cuatro chicos **están** tirándose aceitunas unos a otros.

Son las 5:47 pm
¿Qué estaba pasando a las 5:45?

Cuando los padres de Blas llamaron a la puerta, él y Silvia ...*estaban*.... bailando muy pegados. Casimiro, el novio de Silvia, no .... de mirar a Blas. .... varias botellas de cerveza en la mesa y el cenicero .... lleno de colillas. La música .... muy alta y todo el mundo se .... sin parar. La hermana de Silvia y el hermano de Blas .... en el sofá, cogidos de la mano. La foto de los padres de Blas .... tres chicles pegados. En la cocina, cuatro chicos .... tirándose aceitunas unos a otros.

---

3 Who are the verbs in bold talking about? Work it out from the context.

Yo	Usted	Ella	Él

➔ ¿No lo **sabía**, Sra. Elgorriaga? (..*usted*....)

1. ¿No **sabía** que teníamos una fiesta? Qué despistada es, ¿no crees? (............)

2. Buenas tardes. ¿Qué **quería**? (............)

3. ● ¿Qué **quería**? (............)
   ○ No sé. Se ha quedado callado y se ha ido.

4. La admiraban porque **jugaba** al tenis muy bien, ¿recuerdas? (............)

5. ● ¿Juegas al tenis los fines de semana?
   ○ **Jugaba**. Ya no. (............)

6. En realidad, no me **quería**. Sólo se quería a sí mismo. (............)

7. Nos separamos un año después de conocernos. No la **quería** de verdad. (............)

8. **Tenía** una perrita preciosa, pero se la regaló a su novio. (............)

9. **Tenía** un gato, pero donde vivo ahora no puedo tener animales. (............)

He venido porque tenía muchas ganas de verte.

¿Quién? ¿Tú o Toby?

C   Very irregular verbs: *ir*, *ser*, *ver*.

	Ir	Ser	Ver
Yo	iba	era	veía
Tú	ibas	eras	veías
Él, ella, usted	iba	era	veía
Nosotros/-as	íbamos	éramos	veíamos
Vosotros/-as	ibais	erais	veíais
Ellos, ellas, ustedes	iban	eran	veían

- *Juan **era** un poco raro: **iba** al cementerio los días de luna llena y sólo **veía** películas de zombis.*

Ir and *Ser* put the word stress on the stem.

---

4   Complete with the correct form of the *Imperfecto*.

➔ Ya no vemos mucho a nuestra hija. Antes sí la
...*veíamos*... .

1. Ya no voy a la playa en verano. Antes sí ...*iba*... .

2. Ya no soy tan optimista. Antes sí lo ...*era*... .

3. Sois muy antipáticos conmigo. Antes ...*erais*... más simpáticos.

4. No veo nada con esta luz. Con la que has puesto antes ...*veía*... mejor.

5. Mis padres ya no son tan estrictos conmigo. Antes ...*eran*... mucho más estrictos.

6. ¿Veis mucho a Roberta ahora? Antes la ...*veíais*... todos los días, ¿no?

7. Ya somos mayores. Cuando .... jóvenes, era diferente.

8. ¿Ya no vais a Madrid en Navidades? Antes .... siempre.

■ When we use the *Presente* we are in the present moment, describing what is happening at that moment. With the *Imperfecto*, our point of view moves to the past and we put ourselves **in a past moment** and **describe** what was happening **at that moment**. This is why the uses of the *Imperfecto* are the same as those of the *Presente*, but moved back to a moment in the past.

➔ 23. Presente de indicativo

D   Uses of the Imperfecto. Describing qualities: *Era una chica muy guapa*.

We use the *Presente* to describe how people or things are at the moment:

■ We use the *Imperfecto* to do this same thing, but remembering **people or things from the past**:

Es un ordenador muy bueno. **Tiene** un disco duro de 500 Mb y el procesador **va** a 348 MHz. **Puedes** hacer un montón de cosas con él.

<u>Mi primer ordenador</u> **era** muy malo. **Tenía** sólo 500 Mb de disco duro y el procesador **iba** lentísimo. No **podías** hacer casi nada con él.

5 Luisa is remembering the following people and things and is describing what they were like. Complete her description, using the verbs given.

1. La CASA donde vivía de pequeña.

ser	estar
haber	tener

..*Estaba*... en las afueras de la ciudad. .... unas vistas preciosas. .... un parque muy cerca. .... muy fresca en verano.

2. Un CHICO que conoció en una fiesta de disfraces.

parecerse	ir
llevar	ser

Manuel .... el hermano de mi mejor amiga, pero no .... en nada a ella. En aquella fiesta .... disfrazado de pollo y .... zapatos de tacón.

3. Su primer JEFE.

tener	gustar
saber	llamarse

.... Casimiro. .... una mirada un poco extraña. Le .... mucho mandar y .... que todos le teníamos mucho miedo.

4. El COCHE que tenía su jefe.

llegar	gastar
costar	ser

.... un deportivo rojo precioso. .... 25.000 euros, ... hasta 200 Km/h, y sólo .... 6,5 litros de gasolina cada 100 Km.

E   Uses of the Imperfecto. Describing habitual situations: *Antes dormía mucho*.

We use the *Presente* to describe habitual situations and events in the present:

■ We use the *Imperfecto* to do this same thing, but remembering events that we talk about as being habitual at a moment in the past:

Me **encanta** el agua. Mi madre me **lleva** todas las semanas a la piscina. Algunas veces **vamos** con mis amigos. Mi mamá **está** casi siempre conmigo, pero a veces me **baño** yo sola con mi flotador.

Cuando era pequeña me **encantaba** el agua. Mi madre me **llevaba** todas las semanas a la piscina. Algunas veces **íbamos** con mis amigos. Mi madre **estaba** casi siempre conmigo, pero muchas veces me **bañaba** yo sola con mi flotador.

---

6 Jerónimo and Alablanca have a new house and are very happy. Put their words into perfect Spanish.

➲ Antes **tener** que ir al río para buscar agua. Ahora **tener** agua dentro de casa.

1. Antes **cocinar** con fuego, y **ser** muy difícil. Ahora **tener** horno eléctrico y microondas.

2. Ahora **poder** ver el mundo entero en una televisión. Antes siempre **ver** el mismo paisaje.

3. Antes **buscar** comida en las montañas. Ahora **comprar** en tienda muy cerca.

4. Ahora **estar** calientes todo el invierno. Antes **pasar** frío si no **hacer** fuego todos los días.

➲ Antes ..*teníamos*.. que ir al río para buscar agua. Ahora ..*tenemos*.. agua dentro de casa.

1. Antes .... con fuego, y .... muy difícil. Ahora .... horno eléctrico y microondas.

2. Ahora .... ver el mundo entero en una televisión. Antes siempre .... el mismo paisaje.

3. Antes .... comida en las montañas. Ahora .... en una tienda que está muy cerca.

4. Ahora .... calientes todo el invierno. Antes .... frío si no .... fuego todos los días.

F   Uses of the Imperfecto. Describing temporary situations: *A las dos estaba durmiendo*.

We use the *Presente* to describe what is happening at a specific moment in the present:

Mira, creo que no **voy** a ir a la fiesta. **Estoy** cansada, **tengo** un montón de trabajo y, además, **hace** mucho frío y **está** lloviendo.

■ We use the *Imperfecto* to do this same thing, but remembering what was happening at **a specific moment in the past**:

Me llamó Guada a las cinco porque no **iba** a venir a mi fiesta. **Estaba** cansada, **tenía** un montón de trabajo y, además, **hacía** mucho frío y **estaba** lloviendo.

➲ 37. Periphrastic verbs

7 Yesterday, five crimes were commited in the city. Where were you at these times? Complete this brief report for the police.

8:40	11:05	14:20	16:00	21:45
En el Bar Ranco, desayunando con dos amigos.	En la oficina, hablando con el jefe.	En casa, comiendo solo.	En unos grandes almacenes, comprando ropa.	En el coche, besando a una chica.

¿Dónde estaba usted?
[What were you doing at the time?]

¿Qué hacía en ese momento?
[Where were you?]

➲ A las 8:40 ....*Estaba en el Bar Ranco.*..........   ......*Estaba desayunando con dos amigos.*.........

1. A las 11:05 ....

2. A las 14:20 ....

3. A las 16:00 ....

4. A las 21:45 ....

8 Lidia is remembering when she met the two great loves of her life.
Complete her memories by putting the verbs in the correct form of the *Imperfecto*.

Yo ➲ ..*estaba*.. sentada en un banco del parque. (1) .... las cinco de la tarde. (2) .... primavera. (3) .... un sol espléndido. En el parque (4) .... un olor maravilloso a hierba fresca y a flores. En los árboles, los pajaritos (5) .... La gente (6) ...., los niños (7) .... de un lado a otro, jugando. Ella (8) .... leyendo un libro en un banco enfrente de mí, y de vez en cuando me (9) .... Entonces llegó un hombre con un bebé y le dio un beso en la mejilla.

Ser	Estar
Ser	Mirar
Haber	Correr
Hacer	Cantar
Estar ✓	Pasear

Aquella noche yo estaba con unos amigos en una discoteca. Ella (10) .... amiga del amigo de una amiga, y yo no la (11) .... , pero me (12) .... una chica muy atractiva. Mientras yo (13) .... , ella me (14) .... , y yo no (15) .... dejar de mirarla a ella tampoco. (16) .... ya muy tarde, y yo (17) .... cansada y (18) .... irme a casa, pero me (19) .... aquel juego de miradas. De pronto, ella sacó unas gafas de miope de su bolso, se las puso y se fue corriendo.

Conocer	Poder
Bailar	Gustar
Parecer	Querer
Ser	Estar
Mirar	Ser

26. Imperfecto, Indefinido or Pretérito perfecto?

■ The **Imperfecto** is used to **describe** the past:

> With the **Imperfecto** we place ourselves 'INSIDE' a past event and describe an unfinished activity 'THEN'.

Llovía mucho aquel día.

Unfinished 'THEN'

■ The **Indefinido** is used to **narrate** the past:

> With the **Indefinido** we place ourselves 'AFTER' a past event and talk about an action or activity that finished 'THEN'.

Llovió mucho aquel día.

Finished 'THEN'

A Describing temporary situations or talking about completed events

■ With the **Imperfecto** we talk about an event as not yet finished at a <u>specific moment</u> in the past.
We describe a temporary situation:

- *Ayer, <u>a las cinco</u>, todavía estaba estudiando.*

- *Cuando bajaba las escaleras, [going down] me encontré una maleta.*

■ With the **Indefinido** we talk about that activity as having already finished <u>at that moment</u>.
We talk about a completed event:

- *Ayer estuve estudiando <u>hasta las siete</u>.*

> ⮕ 37. Periphrastic verbs

- *Cuando bajé las escaleras, [completely] me encontré una maleta.*

1 Decide which verb form goes with which explanation, as in the example.

Cuando **cruzaba** la calle, escuché una voz que me llamaba...

Cuando **crucé** la calle, escuché una voz que me llamaba.

➲ Ayer iba a la farmacia, y cuando **cruzaba/crucé** la calle, escuché una voz que me llamaba...

1. Cuando **volvíamos/volvimos** a casa nos encontramos un maletín lleno de joyas...

2. Cuando la **llevábamos/llevamos** al hospital, dijo que ya se sentía bien y volvimos a casa...

3. La pobre María estaba muy triste y yo muy nervioso. No **sabía/supe** qué decirle...

4. El otro día fui a ver "Continuator III". La película me **parecía/pareció** muy interesante...

5. Cuando los atracadores **escondían/escondieron** el dinero, apareció la policía...

Verb form:	Explanation:
a. (._crucé_......)	Ya estaba al otro lado de la calle.
b. (._cruzaba_....)	No había terminado de cruzar.
a. (................)	El maletín estaba en su casa.
b. (................)	El maletín estaba en la calle.
a. (................)	Llegaron al hospital.
b. (................)	No llegaron al hospital.
a. (................)	No le dijo nada.
b. (................)	No sabemos si le dijo algo o no.
a. (................)	Finalmente le gustó la película.
b. (................)	No sabemos si finalmente le gustó.
a. (................)	La policía vio dónde lo escondieron.
b. (................)	La policía no vio el dinero.

B Completed activities (Indefinido) and parts of an activity (Imperfecto)

■ We can talk about short activities (*comerse un bocadillo*) or longer ones (*estudiar Medicina durante cinco años*). The duration is not important.

SHORT ACTIVITIES	LONG ACTIVITIES

COMPLETED ACTIVITY: we place ourselves '**AFTER**' this activity and use the **Indefinido**.

*Me comí el bocadillo **en tres minutos**.*

*Juan José **estuvo** estudiando Medicina **cinco años**.*

····1:06····1:07····1:08···· ····1995····1996····1997····1998····1999····

PART OF AN ACTIVITY: we place ourselves '**INSIDE**' this activity and use the **Imperfecto**.

A la 1:07 estaba comiéndome un bocadillo.

En 1998 estaba estudiando Medicina.

👁 This is why, when we refer to the **total duration** of an activity (*en una hora, durante tres años, toda la tarde, dos días, hasta las 7, tres veces, mucho tiempo, etc.*), we use the **Indefinido**, and not the **Imperfecto**:

- *Ayer **trabajé** todo el día.*   [Ayer ~~trabajaba~~ todo el día.]
- *Anoche **estuvimos** jugando hasta muy tarde.*   [Anoche ~~estábamos~~ jugando hasta muy tarde.]
- ***Estuvo** en el hospital tres meses*   [~~Estaba~~ en el hospital tres meses.]

129

2 Are we talking about one part of an activity or about the complete activity?
Study the example and make sentences with the verb *estar* in the imperfecto or indefinido.

`18:06`   `18:15`   `18:38`   `18:40`

➲ **Cuando nos llamaste** al móvil, Daniela y yo
..*estábamos*.... esperando a Marta en la parada
del autobús. ..*Estuvimos*.... esperándola **más de
media hora**, hasta que, al final, nos cansamos y
nos fuimos.

1. Estoy cansado, sí. Es que ayer ....
trabajando **desde las 8 hasta** casi las 11. Vamos,
que **a las diez y media** de la noche todavía
.... revisando papeles allí solo, en la
oficina, como un idiota.

2. Mi jefe .... de viaje en Canadá **tres
meses** el año pasado. Cuando tuvimos el accidente
en la empresa nos llamó desde Toronto, porque **en
aquel momento** .... allí visitando a
una hermana suya.

3. ● **Cuando nació Carmen**, nosotros ....
viviendo en París.
   o Ah, ¿sí? ¿Y cuánto tiempo .... allí?
   ● Pues .... viviendo allí **hasta** que Carmen
cumplió dos años, y entonces volvimos a Almería.

4. ● Oye, te llamé el domingo **a las nueve** y no
.... en casa.
   o Sí, es que **a esa hora** .... durmiendo.
.... en la cama **toda la mañana**.

5. **El día de mi último cumpleaños** yo ....
haciendo un curso de español de dos semanas en
Granada. Pero sólo .... allí **diez días**.

6. Mira **esta foto**: aquí .... todos celebrando
la boda de Bea. .... bailando y contando
chistes **toda la noche**. Fue una noche magnífica.

C   Stative qualities (Imperfecto) or dynamic qualities (Indefinido)

■ When we are referring to the stative properties or characteristics of an object,
we remember an image from the past and describe the way the object **was**:

STATIVE QUALITIES: **Objects**

***Una chica* preciosa**

● *La chica que conocí ayer* ***era*** *preciosa.*

[*La chica que conocí ayer* f~~u~~~~e~~ *preciosa.*]

■ When we are referring to the dynamic properties or characteristics of an
activity, we remember a sequence of images from beginning to end and
we talk about how the activity was.

DYNAMIC QUALITIES: **Activities**

***Una fiesta* preciosa**

● *La fiesta del sábado* ***fue*** *preciosa.*

[*La fiesta del sábado* ~~era~~ *preciosa.*]

3 **How should you ask about the qualities of the following things? Chose between ¿Cómo era? or ¿Cómo fue?, as in the examples.**

⮕ La fiesta de cumpleaños   ● _¿Cómo fue la fiesta de cumpleaños?_   ○ Estupenda. Lo pasamos muy bien.

⮕ Tu profesora de español   ● _¿Cómo era tu profesora?_   ○ Un poco seria, pero muy buena profesional.

1. Tu primera casa   ● .... ○ Enorme. Teníamos cinco dormitorios.

2. El partido de fútbol   ● .... ○ Aburridísimo. No metieron ningún gol.

3. El perrito que tenías   ● .... ○ Pequeñito, con mucho pelo y un poco tonto.

4. La falda que llevaba Elena   ● .... ○ Roja, creo, y muy cortita.

5. Tu primer día de trabajo   ● .... ○ Un poco duro, porque no conocía a nadie.

6. Tu hermana de pequeña   ● .... ○ Muy alegre y muy cariñosa.

7. El ladrón   ● .... ○ Rubio, alto, con los ojos azules.

8. La conferencia   ● .... ○ Horrible. No había nadie, y ahora lo comprendo.

9. El hotel donde dormiste   ● .... ○ De tres estrellas, bastante nuevo.

10. El viaje   ● .... ○ Muy tranquilo. Un poco largo, pero tranquilo.

11. El curso de alemán   ● .... ○ Fue muy difícil, y el profesor era horrible.

12. El reloj que te regalaron   ● .... ○ Bonito, pero muy malo: sólo funcionó dos días.

👁 If we refer to the **total duration** of a quality (*una hora, durante dos semanas, todo el día, mucho tiempo...*), we are talking about a completed activity and **the Indefinido is the only option**:

● *Yo antes **tenía** el pelo largo.*
● ***Tuve** el pelo largo <u>dos o tres años</u>, pero luego me cansé.*
  [~~Tenía~~ el pelo largo dos o tres años.]

---

4 **Imperfecto or Indefinido? Complete with the verb on the left, as in the examples.**

llevar   ⮕ Recuerdo perfectamente que en aquella fiesta _llevabas_ puesto tu abrigo negro.

      ⮕ _Llevó_ puesto su abrigo negro toda la noche.

ser   1. Cuando yo la conocí, Elisa .... una buena estudiante. Luego cambió mucho.

     2. .... una buena estudiante durante un par de años. Luego cambió mucho.

estar   3. Gonzalo .... muy gordo una temporada, pero se puso a régimen y adelgazó.

     4. Gonzalo .... muy gordo, por eso se puso a régimen, para adelgazar.

ser   5. Cuando se construyó, el edificio del Ayuntamiento .... azul.

     6. El edificio del Ayuntamiento .... azul durante varios siglos, pero ahora es blanco.

llamarse   7. Este pueblo .... Guarromán mucho tiempo, pero le cambiaron el nombre por Limpiadillo.

     8. Antes, este pueblo .... Guarromán, pero ahora se llama Limpiadillo.

131

D Describing habitual situations (Imperfecto)

■ When we talk about events that we want to present as habits at a time in the past, we place ourselves 'INSIDE' that period and describe how the situation was 'THEN':

● *Yo, de pequeño, era muy buen estudiante. Escribía y leía todas las tardes...*

■ For this reason, **we use the Imperfecto** to indicate regularity (*antes, habitualmente, normalmente, frecuentemente, siempre, nunca, cada día, a veces, dos veces al día, una vez por semana...*):

● *En aquella empresa **trabajaba** normalmente todo el día.*

[*En aquella empresa ~~trabajé~~ normalmente todo el día.*]

● *Cuando éramos pequeños siempre **estábamos** jugando hasta muy tarde.*

[*Cuando éramos pequeños siempre ~~estuvimos~~ jugando hasta muy tarde.*]

● *Antes **íbamos** al cine todos los fines de semana.*

[*Antes ~~fuimos~~ al cine todos los fines de semana.*]

5 In each of the sentences below, decide what we are talking about and circle the correct form of the verb in each case

Imperfecto →	Habitual situation
Indefinido →	Completed event

➲ a. Antes **iba**/fui mucho al cine Ideal. (*situación regular*....)

➲ b. Ayer iba/**fui** al cine Ideal. (*hecho completo*.....)

1. a. Cuando era pequeño sólo **iba/fui** a un parque de atracciones una vez. (...........................)

   b. Cuando era pequeño, cada fin de semana **iba/fui** a los parques de atracciones. (...........................)

2. a. El verano pasado **estábamos/estuvimos** 15 días en la playa y 15 días en la sierra, pero este año no hemos salido de casa. (...........................)

   b. Cuando Carmen era pequeña, todos los veranos **estábamos/estuvimos** 15 días en la playa y 15 días en la sierra, pero ahora no quiere viajar con nosotros y nos quedamos en casa. (...........................)

3. a. Los padres no sabían qué nombre ponerle, pero al final la **llamaban/llamaron** Nicasia. (...........................)

   b. Se llamaba Nicasia, pero sus amigos la **llamaban/llamaron** normalmente "Casi". (...........................)

4. a. Estaba loco con su gato. Lo **llevaba/llevó** al veterinario dos veces al mes. (...........................)

   b. No cuidaba nada a su gato. Lo **llevaba/llevó** dos veces al veterinario en toda su vida. (...........................)

5. a. Aquel primer concierto de Broos Printing **era/fue** genial. (...........................)

   b. Cuando era más joven, sus conciertos **eran/fueron** geniales, pero ya no es lo mismo. (...........................)

E Narrating events

■ With the Imperfecto **we stop time** in a story to describe a momentary situation; with the Indefinido we indicate that something happened completely and **make time move forwards** towards a new situation:

EL OTRO DÍA **salíamos** del cine [en este punto de la historia, ellos están saliendo] cuando, de pronto, un señor con un aspecto muy raro **se acercó** a nosotros [en este punto de la historia, el señor está junto a ellos] y **empezó** a cantarnos una canción [en este punto de la historia, el señor ya está cantando] en una lengua muy extraña. Nosotros no **entendíamos** nada y no **sabíamos** qué hacer [en este punto de la historia, ellos están sorpendidos y desconcertados]. **Estuvo** cantando así dos o tres minutos [en este punto de la historia, el señor ya ha terminado de cantar], y cuando ya **se iba** [en este punto de la historia, el hombre ya se va] **llegó** una ambulancia [en este punto de la historia, la ambulancia ya está con ellos] y **se lo llevó** [en este punto de la historia, el señor ya está dentro de la ambulancia y la ambulancia se ha ido]...

6 Jerónimo is talking about an incredible thing that happened to him yesterday. Could you correct his little story? You'll have to choose either the Imperfecto or Indefinido form for each verb, whichever is appropriate.

Ayer, yo **caminar** tranquilamente por el bosque, porque **ir** a casa de Alablanca para llevarle pasteles y, de pronto, en el camino, un lobo muy malo **salir** de los árboles y **ponerse** enfrente de mí, con la boca abierta. Yo **estar** muerto de miedo, pero **salir** corriendo y, al final, **conseguir** escapar de él. **Poder** hacer dos cosas: o **volver** a mi casa o **intentar** llegar a casa de Alablanca, a pesar de todo. **Decidir** seguir andando para visitarla. Cuando **entrar** en la casa, ella **estar** acostada en la cama, pero **tener** una cara muy extraña con muchos pelos. Por eso yo, rápidamente, **dejar** la comida al lado de su cama y **volver** a mi casa corriendo. Yo **ser** Jerónimo, no ser Brus Güilis.

Ayer, yo caminaba tranquilamente por el bosque...
....
....
....
....
....
....

F Imperfecto or Pretérito perfecto? *Salía / Ha salido*

■ We decide between the Imperfecto and the Perfecto using exactly the same rules as we use to decide between the Imperfecto and the indefinido:

DESCRIBING **MOMENTARY SITUATIONS**	TALKING ABOUT **COMPLETED EVENTS**

• **Hoy**, *a las cinco*, todavía *estaba* estudiando.
• **Hoy** *he estado* estudiando *hasta las siete*.

7 Decide which verb form goes with which interpretation, as in the example.

➲ Pues iba yo a la farmacia, y cuando **cruzaba/he cruzado** la calle, he escuchado una voz que me llamaba...

a. (*cruzaba*....) Ha escuchado la voz cruzando la calle.
b. (*he cruzado*..) Ya estaba al otro lado de la calle cuando ha escuchado la voz.

1. Cuando la **llevábamos/hemos llevado** al hospital, ha dicho que ya se sentía bien y hemos vuelto...

a. (..................) No han llegado al hospital.
b. (..................) Sí han estado en el hospital.

2. La pobre María estaba muy triste, y yo muy nervioso. No **sabía/he sabido** qué decirle...

a. (..................) No sabemos si le ha dicho algo o no.
b. (..................) Sabemos que no le ha dicho nada.

3. La última novela de Agapito Tristán me **parecía/ha parecido** muy mala...

a. (..................) Ha leído la novela completa.
b. (..................) No sabemos si ha terminado de leerla.

8 Are we talking about part of an activity or the complete activity?
Look carefully at the example and make sentences with the verb *estar* in the Imperfecto or the Perfecto.

➲ Cuando nos has llamado al móvil, Daniela y yo
estábamos esperando a Marta en la plaza
Nueva. _Hemos estado_ esperándola **más de
media hora**, hasta que, al final, nos hemos cansado y nos hemos ido.

1. Mi jefe .... en Canadá **tres meses**
este año. Precisamente el día del accidente
.... en Toronto.

2. ● ¿Cuánto tiempo .... encerrados

Rosa y tú en la casa?
○ ¡Toda la tarde .... encerrados!
Cuando Jenaro ha llegado con la llave todos
.... ya desesperados.

3. ● Oye, te he llamado esta mañana **a las nueve** y
no .... en casa.
○ Sí, lo que pasa es que **a esa hora**
.... durmiendo. .... en la
cama hasta las diez y media, más o menos.

G Narratives happening now or not happening now

■ If the event is still unfinished at the point of the story where we find ourselves, we use the **Imperfecto**:

■ If the event has already finished and is complete at the point of the story where we find ourselves, we use the Indefinido or the Perfecto.

Perfecto to place the story in a present time period.

Indefinido to place the story in a past time period

The qualities of things Habitual events Momentary situations	Events completed 'HERE AND NOW' (Hoy, este mes, esta mañana, este año...)	Events completed 'THEN' (Ayer, aquel día, el lunes pasado, el mes pasado...)

TALKING ABOUT A PRESENT TIME PERIOD

Hoy...

Para:
CC:
Asunto:

Querido Evaristo:

No he podido ir con vosotros porque he estado toda la noche con Elena. Sí, aquella
profesora de español que era tan guapa y que me gustaba tanto. Ya sabes que desde que
la conocí hemos salido algunas veces a tomar café, que ella siempre me hablaba de sus
alumnos y que yo muchas veces intentaba sacar el tema de los novios sin
resultado. Pues esta tarde hemos ido al cine y la he invitado a cenar después en mi casa.
Lo tenía todo preparado: una comida perfecta, velas, música romántica... Pero Elena ha llegado a casa con un chico. Yo no sabía qué hacer ni qué decir, pero ella ha aclarado inmediatamente la situación: era su novio. Al final ha sido una cena un poco accidentada, como
ves.

TALKING ABOUT A PAST TIME PERIOD

Cuando estaba en Berlín...

Conocí a Elena en Berlín. Yo estaba en una oficina de la embajada y ella
trabajaba como profesora de español en una universidad. Elena tenía
entonces unos 25 años. Era un poco más joven que yo. Ella estaba muy
contenta con su trabajo allí, y muchas tardes salíamos a tomar un
café para hablar de sus alumnos. Me gustaba mucho aquella chica. Un
día salimos para ir al cine y la invité a cenar a mi casa. Lo tenía todo
preparado: una comida perfecta, velas, música romántica... Pero ella
llegó a casa con un chico. Yo no sabía qué hacer ni qué decir. Entonces
ella aclaró la situación: era su novio. Al final fue una cena estupenda.
La comida, quiero decir.

9 Imperfecto or Perfecto? In each case decide which.

Para:

CC:

Asunto:

Hola, Carolina. Te escribo este mail para contarte por qué no ➜ *he podido* ir a tu fiesta. Es que esta tarde
(1) .... al cine con Mario. Sí, ese chico que (2) .... tan feo, ¿recuerdas? Te lo presenté el otro
día en el café y, después, te (3) .... varias veces de él. Bueno, pues resulta que, después del cine, Mario me
(4) .... a cenar en su casa. Yo no (5) .... , pero, al final, (6) .... a cenar a su casa
con Hans. Mario no lo (7) .... , así que le (8) .... que Hans (9) .... mi novio, y el
pobre se lo (10) .... Al final, la cena (11) .... realmente horrible. El pollo (12) ....
quemado y la Coca-Cola (13) .... light sin cafeína y, además de todo, (14) .... que escuchar
durante toda la cena un disco de grandes éxitos de Julio Iglesias. Creo que (15) .... mi peor noche en
los últimos seis meses. Bueno, nos vemos mañana y te cuento más.

➜ poder ✓	1. ir	2. ser	3. hablar	4. invitar	5. querer	6. ir	7. conocer
8. decir	9. ser	10. creer	11. ser	12. estar	13. ser	14. tener	15. ser

10 Imperfecto or Indefinido? In each case decide which.

➜ .....*Conocí*..... a Mario en Berlín. Yo (1) .... como camarera en
una cervecería y él (2) .... empleado en una oficina de la embajada.
En aquel tiempo, yo (3) .... 32 años, y él 28. Un día me
(4) .... mi edad y le (5) .... Yo no (6) ....
contenta con mi trabajo, incluso me daba un poco de vergüenza decírselo, así
que le (7) .... que (8) .... profesora de español.
Él (9) .... muy enamorado de mí, pero yo no. (10) ....
demasiado feo para mi gusto, y no (11) .... una mente demasiado
brillante tampoco. Pero él siempre me (12) .... a tomar café,
y yo cada vez le (13) .... mentiras y más mentiras. Un día
(14) .... al cine y después él me (15) .... a su casa
para cenar. Yo no (16) .... qué hacer para no decirle directamente
que él no me (17) .... Así que (18) .... a un amigo
alemán y (19) .... los dos juntos a su casa. Le (20) ....
que (21) .... mi novio. El pobre Mario se (22) .... muy
triste. Al final, la cena (23) .... un desastre. Sobre todo la comida.

➜ conocer ✓	8. ser	16. saber
1. trabajar	9. estar	17. gustar
2. ser	10. ser	18. llamar
3. tener	11. tener	19. ir
4. preguntar	12. invitar	20. decir
5. mentir	13. contar	21. ser
6. estar	14. ir	22. poner
7. decir	15. invitar	23. ser

135

27. Pluscuamperfecto de indicativo

A Meaning and forms: *había hablado, había comido, había vivido...*

■ The *Pretérito pluscuamperfecto* is formed with:

➲ 20. Non-personal forms

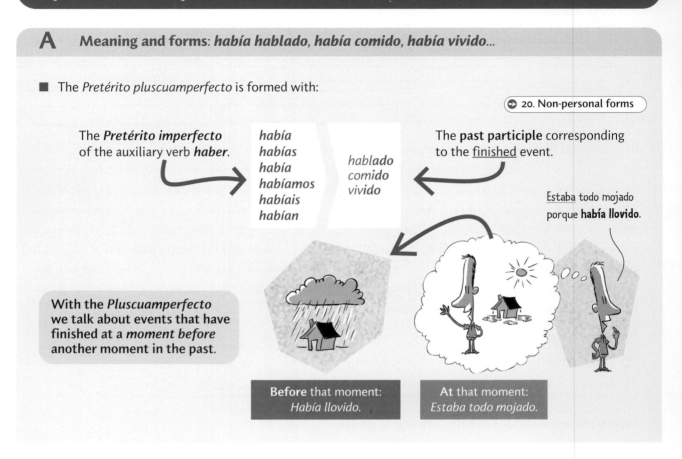

The *Pretérito imperfecto* of the auxiliary verb **haber**.

había
habías
había
habíamos
habíais
habían

hablado
comido
vivido

The **past participle** corresponding to the <u>finished</u> event.

<u>Estaba</u> todo mojado porque **había llovido**.

With the *Pluscuamperfecto* we talk about events that have finished at a *moment before* another moment in the past.

Before that moment:
Había llovido.

At that moment:
Estaba todo mojado.

1 Write each verb in the appropriate form of the *Pluscuamperfecto* and relate them to the corresponding drawing.

● ¿Sabes que Toby se escapó ayer por la tarde? No me lo explico.

○ Pues es fácil. Cuando se escapó, **tú** ➲ ..*habías salido (c)*.. con Antonio a dar una vuelta. Toby pudo salir perfectamente por la puerta principal, porque, cuando yo volví, me di cuenta de que **Antonio y tú** os (1) ....
......*dejado*..... la puerta abierta al salir. Yo, por mi parte, (2) ....*ido*........ a comprar al supermercado porque necesitábamos comida para la noche. También **las ventanas** se (3) ....*quedado*...... abiertas porque también las encontré abiertas al volver. Y **Marisa** se (4) ....*quedado*..... dormida después de la comida y ella, cuando duerme, duerme. Si, además de todo esto, recuerdas que **Toby** ya (5) ....*visto*.. por la ventana a Mopa, la nueva perrita de la vecina, está ya todo explicado, ¿o no?

B Use: the anterior past.

■ From the present, we can talk about finished events in the past with the *Perfecto* or the *Indefinido*. But, when we place ourselves at a specific point in the past, we use the **Pluscuamperfecto** to refer to events that had already finished **before this time in the past**:

No está. Se <u>ha ido</u> a trabajar esta mañana.

¿Y papá?

En aquel momento, mi padre no estaba en casa. Se **había ido** a trabajar.

Before that moment:
Se había ido a trabajar.

At that moment:
Mi papá no estaba.

¿Y papá?

No está. Se <u>fue</u> anoche a trabajar.

❷ **Move the sentences below, expressed in the Perfecto, into the past, and put the verbs into the correct tense and person.**

Antes de ahora

● "Oye, son las seis y todavía no **ha llegado** nadie".

● "¡Ya estoy aquí! ¡Qué bien, lo **habéis arreglado** ya todo!"

● "**He preparado** unas tapas. ¿Os apetecen?"

● "Sí, ella siempre **ha sido** muy buena conmigo."

● "Si tienes buenas notas es porque **has estudiado** mucho."

● "Nos **hemos dejado** las llaves dentro. ¿Cómo entramos ahora?"

● "Horror. Nuestro tren ya se **ha ido**. ¡Menudo lío! ¿Qué hacemos ahora?"

Antes de aquel momento

➲ A las seis todavía no *había llegado* nadie.

1. Cuando llegué, lo .... ya todo.

2. .... unas tapas, pero no comieron nada.

3. Le mentí diciéndole que .... muy buena conmigo.

4. Tenía muy buenas notas. Es lógico: .... mucho.

5. No pudimos entrar porque nos .... las llaves dentro.

6. Llegaron a la hora exacta a la estación, pero el tren se ....

3 **Move the sentences below, expressed in the *Indefinido*, into the past, changing the form of the verb.**

En un momento pasado

⮑ Lo siento. Patricia no está. **Salió** hace un rato.

1. Tenemos que ir a casa de Ángela. Se **compraron** un coche ayer y quieren enseñárnoslo.

2. Tranquila, se lo **conté** todo a Paco ayer.

3. ● ¿Entiendes lo que dice en este papel?
   ○ Más o menos. Yo **estudié** dos años ruso.

4. La semana pasada **hice** mi primera donación de sangre.

5. **Estuvimos** en la playa de Mónsul el año pasado y el anterior.

Antes de aquel momento

⮑ Corrí todo lo que pude, pero Patricia ya _había salido_ cuando llegué a su casa.

1. Fuimos a casa de Ángela. Se .... un coche nuevo y querían enseñárnoslo.

2. Me aseguró que ya se lo .... todo a Paco.

3. Casimiro pudo entender lo que decía aquel papel porque .... ruso dos años.

4. Estaba muy orgulloso porque la semana anterior .... su primera donación de sangre.

5. Ellos conocían muy bien el camino porque ya .... allí dos veces.

■ We can only use the *pluscuamperfecto* if we present an event as happening **before a very specific point** in the past:

Before I arrived ● *Cuando llegué, ya se habían comido toda la tarta.*

Before he told me ● *El otro día me encontré a Paco. Me dijo que había estado enfermo.*

Before he called her ● *A las seis la volví a llamar, pero se había ido.*

■ If this point of reference in the past is not clear, we use the *Indefinido* rather then the *pluscuamperfecto*:

● *Ayer fui al cine.*
○ *¡Ah! ¿Sí? ¿Y qué película fuiste a ver?*

Ayer había ido al cine.

¿Habías ido?

¿Antes de qué?

4 **Look at the following sentences and decide whether they are correct, or whether the *Indefinido* should be used.**

⮑ La sopa no estaba buena porque le **había echado** mucha sal. (.......✓............)

⮑ El sábado ~~habíamos ido~~ a un restaurante muy bueno, pero este restaurante es horrible. (..._fuimos_........)

1. Estábamos ya en la puerta, pero no pudimos entrar al concierto porque Jorge se **había dejado** las entradas en casa. (....................)

2. En marzo **había viajado** por primera vez a Madrid y, después, visité Valencia y Barcelona. (....................)

3. Le puso la dirección y el sello a la carta y la **había echado** en el buzón. (....................)

4. Héctor nació muy flaco, pero cuando lo vi por segunda vez, ya **había engordado** un montón. (....................)

5. Nosotros **habíamos comido** cuando llegamos. (....................)

6. El fin de semana pasado mi novio **había venido** a verme. (....................)

7. El programa no te funcionó porque no lo **habías instalado** correctamente. (....................)

28. Futuro

A Meaning

■ As with the *Presente*, the *Futuro* expresses a present or future reality.
It differs from the *Presente* in that with the *Futuro* we only **predict or suppose** what a reality that we have not yet experienced, might be.

Making affirmations about the present or the future:	Making a supposition about the present, or a prediction about the future:
● *Ahora* **tiene** *mucho trabajo.* 　A statement about something in the present.	● *Ahora* **tendrá** *mucho trabajo.* 　A supposition about something in the present.
● *Mañana* **acaba** *el trabajo.* 　A statement about something in the future..	● *Mañana* **acabará** *el trabajo.* 　A prediction about something in the future.

---

1 Which of the two moments are we talking about with these forms of the *Futuro*?

Future moment: (F)
Present moment: (P)

➜ Al mundo **vendrán** trece millones de naves. **Vendrá** una confederación intergaláctica de Ganímedes, de la constelación Orión, de Raticulín, de Alfa y de Beta. (..F..)

1. ● ¿El hijo pequeño de Alfredo es rubio?
   ○ Pues no sé, pero si todos sus hijos son rubios, éste también **será** rubio. (......)
2. Si tú se lo pides, no **dirá** nada. (......)
3. ● ¿Y tus amigos? No los veo.
   ○ **Estarán** en el banco. Tenían que sacar dinero. (......)
4. ● No nos queda dinero.
   ○ **Iré** al banco, no te preocupes. (......)
5. Mi hijo se **llamará** Nemesio. Me encanta ese nombre. (......)
6. ● ¿Cómo se llama el hijo de Inma?
   ○ Pues no sé, pero se **llamará** Nemesio. A ella le encanta ese nombre. (......)

B Regular forms: *hablaré, comeré, viviré...*

■ To form the *Futuro* of regular verbs we use the infinitive plus the endings of the *Presente* of *haber*:

	Presente of *haber*		-ar/-er/-ir	Hablar	Comer	Vivir
Yo	he		-é	hablar<u>é</u>	comer<u>é</u>	vivir<u>é</u>
Tú	has		-ás	hablar<u>ás</u>	comer<u>ás</u>	vivir<u>ás</u>
Él, ella, usted	ha	Hablar	-á	hablar<u>á</u>	comer<u>á</u>	vivir<u>á</u>
Nosotros/-as	hemos	Comer Vivir	-emos	hablar<u>emos</u>	comer<u>emos</u>	vivir<u>emos</u>
Vosotros/-as	habéis		-éis	hablar<u>éis</u>	comer<u>éis</u>	vivir<u>éis</u>
Ellos, ellas, ustedes	han		-án	hablar<u>án</u>	comer<u>án</u>	vivir<u>án</u>

■ **The word stress always falls on the ending**, as shown by the underlining in the examples above.

2 Transform the following statements into predictions or suppositions using the appropriate form of the verb.

Statements	Predictions or suppositions
⮕ Si no estudias, no **llegas** a ninguna parte.	⮕ Si no estudias, nunca ...*llegarás*..... a ninguna parte.
María Elena **vuelve** a las cinco.	1. María Elena .... a las cinco, más o menos.
Nunca **cambio** de opinión.	2. Nunca .... de opinión, nunca.
No hay problema. Si llueve, **comemos** dentro.	3. Mejor fuera, pero, si llueve, ... dentro.
No puede correr mucho. Le **duele** la rodilla.	4. Le .... la rodilla y, por eso, no corre mucho.
¿Me **invitas** a cenar esta noche?	5. ¿Me .... a cenar algún día?
Si no quieres hablar tú, **hablo** yo.	6. Si no quieres hablar tú, ... yo.
¿Puedo ir a veros mañana? ¿**Estáis** en casa?	7. ¿Puedo ir a veros mañana? ¿ .... en casa?
No se hablan. **Están** enfadados.	8. No sé. Si no se hablan, es que .... enfadados.

C Irregular verbs: *diré*, *querré*, *tendré*...

■ Irregularities in the *Futuro* always affect the stem, or first part of the verb. The most common verbs with irregular stems are listed below:

Decir	→	*dir-*	*Querer*	→	*querr-*	*Tener*	→ *tendr-*
Hacer	→	*har-*	*Haber*	→	*habr-*	*Poner*	→ *pondr-*
			Poder	→	*podr-*	*Venir*	→ *vendr-*
			Saber	→	*sabr-*	*Salir*	→ *saldr-*
			Caber	→	*cabr-*	*Valer*	→ *valdr-*

*Todavía eres muy pequeña, pero dentro de poco **sabrás** lo que quieres ser y **podrás** elegir. Y estoy segura de que **harás** cosas importantes. **Habrá** muchas cosas nuevas en tu vida. **Saldrás** de casa para vivir sola y **vendrás** a visitarme alguna vez, espero.*

■ The **ending** is always regular:

Decir	*Querer*	*Tener*
diré	*querré*	*tendré*
dirás	*querrás*	*tendrás*
dirá	*querrá*	*tendrá*
diremos	*querremos*	*tendremos*
diréis	*querréis*	*tendréis*
dirán	*querrán*	*tendrán*

👁 The corresponding compound verbs also have the same irregularity:

*Des**hacer*** → *desharé*   *Re**hacer*** → *reharé*
*Man**tener*** → *mantendré*   *Su**poner*** → *supondré*, etc.

*¿Cómo **seré** de mayor, mamá? ¿**Seré** guapa? ¿**Seré** rica?*

3 Little Samuel José thinks that all verbs are regular in the Futuro. Help him learn by finding and correcting his mistakes (there are eight more).

⮕ Yo **teneré** ..*tendré*.... una moto como mi papá, y **seré** ......✓........ muy fuerte, como mi papá.

1. Si me quitas mi libro de animales, se lo **deciré** .... a mi tito José, y **venirá** .... y te lo **quitará** .... y me **dará** .... muchos besos.

2. Mi mamá **volverá** .... pronto y me **ponerá** .... la tele para ver los dibujos animados.

3. Después de comer **saliré** .... a la calle y **jugaré** .... con mis amigos.

4. El año que viene **iré** .... a la escuela y así **saberé** .... leer cuentos y **poderé** .... escribir cartas a los Reyes Magos.

5. Los Reyes Magos me **traerán** .... juguetes, y los **poneré** .... en el suelo para jugar y luego los **recogeré** .... Y mi mamá me **quererá** .... mucho.

4 Complete with the correct form.

> ➔ Si tú no me **quieres**, alguien me ...querrá... .

1. Si el amor no **cabe** en tu corazón, en otro corazón ....
2. Si no **tienes** paciencia conmigo, otros la ....
3. Si tú no me **dices** cosas románticas, alguien me las ....
4. Si no **vienes** a buscarme cuando estoy triste, alguien ....
5. Si no **sales** al balcón para recibirme, otros ....
6. Si tú no **haces** lo que yo quiero, alguien lo ....
7. Si tú no **sabes** cómo tratarme, estoy segura de que alguien ....
8. Si tú no **vales** para ser un buen marido, alguien ....
9. Si contigo no **puedo** ser feliz, con otros .... serlo.
10. Si contigo no **hay** esperanza, con otros la ....

D Uses. Predicting the future: *Mi novio volverá mañana*.

■ When we use the *Futuro* to talk about future time, we are predicting the future. We do this to indicate that we are talking about events that can only be confirmed by the passage of time. We are predicting what the future will be, or asking others to make predictions:

| WHAT THE FUTURE MIGHT BE | ➤ Predictions | • *No debes preocuparte.* **Volverá** *mañana.*
• *El martes* **tendremos** *sol en la mitad sur y* **habrá** *nubes en el norte.*
• *Al final no se* **casará** *con ella, ya* **verás**.
• *A las cuatro y media* **estaré** *esperándote en el aeropuerto.*
• *¿Voy contigo o* **sabrás** *hacerlo tú solo?* |

¿Te vienes a estudiar mañana a mi casa?

Vale, a las cuatro en punto **estaré** allí.

PRESENT   FUTURE

■ If we want to present the information in a more objective way, we use the *Presente* or *Ir a* + INFINITIVO:

- *A las cuatro* **estoy** *allí.*
- *A las cuatro* **voy a estar** *allí.*

➤ 21. Presente de indicativo

➤ 37. Periphrastic verbs

---

5 Connect the sentences on the left with the ones on the right.

> ➔ Ven a tu concesionario Aupel y prueba nuestros coches. (..*g*...)   a. A tu novio le encantará.

1. Estás muy guapa con ese vestido. (.......)   b. Otro día me lo dirás.
2. Préstame el libro de cocina. (.......)   c. ¡No irás a ninguna parte con el dinero del banco!
3. ¿Tendrás tiempo mañana para ayudarme? (.......)   d. Ella me necesita.
4. Este niño será médico. (.......)   e. Te lo devolveré mañana.
5. Bueno, si no quieres hablar ahora, vale. (......)   f. Dentro de media hora te sentirás mejor.
6. Tómate estas pastillas. (.......)   g. Vivirás experiencias inolvidables. ✓
7. ¡Alto, Flanagan! ¡Deja el revólver! (.......)   h. Yo no puedo mover estos muebles solo.
8. Tarde o temprano, volverá. (.......)   i. Se pasa todo el día examinando a su prima.

6 Complete the fortune-teller's predictions by putting the verb into the correct form.

➡ Pronto te ...quedarás... calvo.

		Quedar ✓

1. Antes de un mes .... a una mujer guapísima
   y te .... muy enamorado de ella.

2. En ese momento tu vida .... completamente.

Quedar ✓
Sentir
Cambiar
Conocer

3. Tu mujer te ....
4. .... 100.000 euros en un concurso de televisión.
5. Tu mujer .... volver contigo.
6. .... siete hijos y cuatro perros.
7. Y si no me pagas, ... joven.

Morir
Tener
Querer
Ganar
Abandonar

7 The Rocamora-Holehole marriage is not going well. On the left you can see the things that are happening, but how will they end? Chose the appropriate consequences in each case.

➡ Casi no se hablan.   Se romperá la comunicación...

1. Él sale mucho y conoce a mucha gente nueva.   ....
2. Ella esquía y navega con nuevos amigos.   ....
3. Los dos gastan demasiado.   ....
4. Nunca están juntos en las fiestas importantes.   ....
5. Cada vez tienen menos cosas en común.   ....

Romperse la comunicación ✓
La próxima Navidad no estar juntos
Arruinarse
Salir con otra
Separarse
Conocer a otra persona más interesante que él

E   Uses. Making suppositions about the present: *Mi novio estará en Madrid ahora*.

■ We use the *Futuro* to talk about present time, when we are talking about something we are not in complete control of, and that we do not consider certain. We are just supposing what the present may be, or asking others to make suppositions:

Estará en Madrid ahora.	=	*Supongo que está en Madrid ahora.*

WHAT THE PRESENT MIGHT BE	**Suppositions**	• *No debes preocuparte por el niño.* **Estará** *con su hermano mayor.* • **Será** *una casa antigua, porque le ha costado muy poco dinero.* • *Este coche no está mal, pero ¿no crees que el Peyó* **correrá** *más?* • *Yo duermo ocho horas diarias, pero Rosa* **dormirá** *más.* • *¿* **Vivirá** *Claudio todavía en aquella casa tan incómoda y fría?* • *Manuela se encuentra mal.* **Tendrá** *fiebre.* • *¿* **Estará** *todavía abierto el supermercado? ¿Tú qué crees?*

¿Qué **será** eso que se mueve?

No sé, **será** un gato buscando comida.

REALITY NOT FULLY KNOWN

■ If we are talking about present activities in an objective and certain way, we use the *Presente*:

• *Es un gato buscando comida.*

➲ 21. Presente de indicativo

8 Be economical. Change the part of the sentence in bold for the corresponding future.

➲ Me da la impresión de que no le gusta estar con nosotros.

1. Me imagino que **tiene** cosas más interesantes que hacer.
2. Yo pienso que no **sabe** dónde estamos.
3. Posiblemente **tiene** demasiado trabajo.
4. Supongo que no le **gustan** las fiestas.
5. Seguro que **viene** más tarde.
6. Quizá **está** enfermo, ¿no?
7. A mí me parece que no **quiere** encontrarse con Rosa.
8. Probablemente no **sabe** nada sobre la fiesta.
9. A lo mejor **tiene** que cuidar a su hermanito.

➲ No le ....*gustará*..... estar con nosotros.

1. .... cosas más interesantes que hacer.
2. No .... dónde estamos.
3. .... demasiado trabajo.
4. No le .... las fiestas.
5. .... más tarde.
6. .... enfermo.
7. No .... encontrarse con Rosa.
8. No .... nada sobre la fiesta.
9. .... que cuidar a su hermanito.

9 Connect the things that Pepe says (on the left) with the most probable explanation in each case (on the right).

➲ Es mejor no molestar a Luis ahora.
Estará cenando. ——————————

a. Pepe sabe qué está haciendo Luis ahora.
b. Pepe imagina qué puede estar haciendo Luis.

1. ● ¿Quién llama a la puerta?
   ○ **Será** el cartero.

a. Pepe está mirando por la ventana.
b. Pepe está duchándose.

2. ● ¿De quién es este bolígrafo?
   ○ **Será** mío. Déjalo ahí.

a. Pepe reconoce perfectamente su bolígrafo.
b. Pepe no recuerda exactamente si ese boli es suyo.

3. ● Pepe, ¿quién sabe que somos novios?
   ○ Tranquilo, sólo lo **sabe** Emilio.

a. Sin duda, Emilio conoce su relación.
b. Posiblemente, Emilio conoce su relación.

4. ● Barti no ha comido nada.
   ○ No le **gustará** el pescado.

a. Barti es el gato de Pepe.
b. Barti es el gato del amigo de Pepe.

5. Oye, Claudia, ¿cuántos años **tendrá** Alonso?

a. Alonso es el hijo de Claudia.
b. Alonso es el vecino del cuarto piso.

6. ● ¿Tiene sal la carne, Pepe?
   ○ **Tendrá** un poco.

a. Pepe ha probado ya la carne.
b. Pepe no ha probado todavía la carne, pero conoce los gustos del cocinero.

7. ● A Rosita le duele mucho la cabeza.
   ○ Es que **está** con gripe. **Tendrá** fiebre.

a. Pepe conoce la enfermedad de Rosita, pero no tiene termómetro.
b. Pepe no sabe qué le pasa a Rosita, pero ha comprobado su temperatura con un termómetro.

10 You are at a party with a friend and see someone you quite fancy, but neither of you know her. You can talk to her directly or talk to your friend about her. Put the verbs into the correct form.

Si hablas con ella:

➲ ¿Cómo te ..*llamas*...?
1. ¿Cuántos años ....?
2. ¿De dónde ....?
3. ¿A quién .... en esta fiesta?
4. ¿Te .... bailar?
5. ¿Qué perfume ....?
6. ¿............ con alguien?
7. ¿............ salir a tomar algo fuera de aquí?
8. ¿Me .... tu número de móvil?
9. ¿Te .... que te llame?

Si hablas con tu amigo:

➲ ¿Cómo se ..*llamará*...?
1. ¿Cuántos años ....?
2. ¿De dónde ....?
3. ¿A quién .... en esta fiesta?
4. ¿Le .... bailar?
5. ¿Qué perfume ....?
6. ¿................ con alguien?
7. ¿ .... salir a tomar algo fuera de aquí?
8. ¿Me .... su número de móvil?
9. ¿Le .... que la llame?

| querer |
| salir |
| ser |
| tener |
| importar |
| conocer |
| gustar |
| dar |
| llamar ✓ |
| usar |

143

29. Futuro perfecto

A · Meaning and forms: *habré hablado, habré comido, habré vivido...*

■ The *Futuro perfecto* is formed with:

➲ 20. Non-personal forms

The **Future** of the auxiliary verb **haber.**

habré
habrás
habrá
habremos
habréis
habrán

hablado
comido
vivido

The **past participle** corresponding to the <u>finished</u> event.

¿Porqué está todo tan mojado?

No sé. **Habrá llovido.**

We use the Futuro perfecto to **predict** or **suppose** events that are FINISHED already or before a given moment in the future.

1 Transform the following statements into suppositions by using the appropriate *Futuro perfecto* form of the verb.

If we are making a statement...

➲ Esto no funciona. **Hemos hecho** algo mal.

1. **Has trabajado** mucho, pero no veo el resultado.
2. La perra está ladrando. ¿La **habéis asustado**?
3. Creo que **hemos tomado** la carretera equivocada.
4. Ya no me llama. Me **ha olvidado**.
5. Tus amigos no van a llegar. Se **han perdido**.
6. María **ha salido** un momento a comprar pan.

If we are only supposing...

➲ Esto no funciona. ....*Habremos hecho*.... algo mal.

1. .... mucho, pero no veo el resultado.
2. La perra está ladrando. ¿No la ....?
3. .... la carretera equivocada, no sé.
4. Ya no me llama. Me ....
5. Si no llegan, es que se ....
6. ¿María? No sé. .... un momento.

B · Uses. Imagining the recent past: *Habrá dormido poco, supongo.*

■ We use the *Futuro Perfecto* in **the same cases we use the *Pretérito Perfecto*,** but with one **difference**:

➲ 22. Pretérito perfecto

Pretérito Perfecto: We are talking about a past reality that we control: We state this as fact.

Futuro Perfecto: We are talking about a past reality that we are not fully in control of: We only **suppose** this reality.

| Habrá salido | = | Supongo que *ha salido* |

Affirming the event:
We control the information.

- *¿Por qué estás tan cansado?*
- *Es que esta noche <u>he dormido</u> poco.*

- *¿Dónde están las llaves?*
- *Las <u>he puesto</u> encima del televisor.*

- *Ayer no vinieron para arreglar el grifo.*
- *No, pero <u>han venido</u> esta mañana.*

Supposing the event:
We **are not totally in control of** the information.

- *¿Por qué está Luisa tan cansada?*
- *Habrá dormido poco.*

- *¿Dónde están las llaves?*
- *Las **habré puesto** encima del televisor.*

- *Ayer no vinieron para arreglar el grifo.*
- *No, pero **habrán venido** esta mañana.*

2 Read carefully what Ana says about her boyfriend: What does Ana know, and what is she only supposing?

Para:

CC:

Asunto:

Hola, Andrea.
Te escribo porque estoy desesperada. Esteban está
últimamente muy raro conmigo. No ha salido con sus
amigos en las últimas semanas y, sin embargo, siempre
está fuera y dice que no tiene tiempo de nada. Se
habrá creído que soy tonta y que no me doy cuenta de
nada. Tampoco me ha regalado nada para mi cumpleaños.
Dice que es culpa de su mala memoria. Seguramente se
le habrá olvidado, pero es que son tantas cosas…
Habrá conocido a alguna chica y se habrá enamorado,
seguro. Esta semana ha estado todas las tardes con una
compañera de trabajo que no me gusta nada. Ella le ha
ayudado mucho siempre, pero ya es demasiado tiempo
juntos, ¿no crees? Dime qué piensas.
Besos, Ana.

➲ Su novio no sale últimamente con sus amigos. (_Lo sabe_........)

➲ Su novio cree que es tonta. (_Lo imagina_...)

1. Su novio no le ha hecho ningún regalo de cumpleaños. (................)

2. Su novio ha olvidado hacerle el regalo. (................)

3. Su novio ha conocido a otra chica. (................)

4. Su novio se ha enamorado de otra persona. (................)

5. Su novio ha estado esta semana muchas veces con una compañera de trabajo. (................)

6. La compañera de su novio le ha ayudado muchas veces. (................)

C   Uses. Predicting the past in the future: *Mañana habré terminado*.

■ We use the *Futuro Perfecto* to make statements about **future events that will happen before a given point in the future.** We do this when we specifically place ourselves at **a precise point of reference** in the future and predict what will be done by this time:

- ● ¿*Cómo va eso?*
- ○ *Ya queda poco.* <u>En dos horas</u> *lo **habremos pintado** todo.*

- ● *Oye, dejadme algo de tarta, ¿vale?*
- ○ *No sé. Me temo que* <u>cuando vuelvas</u> *la tarta **habrá desaparecido**.*

- ● ¿*Si salimos* <u>mañana a las siete</u> *está bien? ¿Estarás cansado para conducir?*
- ○ *No, con seis horas **habré dormido** suficiente.*

■ To do the same thing with a greater degree of certainty, we use the *Pretérito Perfecto*:

- ● *A las cinco he llegado.* (➲ **22. Pretérito perfecto**)

*A las cinco ya **habré llegado**.*

---

3 Somebody made the predictions on the left. On the right you have what really happened. Did they predict correctly, or not?

➲ A las siete **habré terminado**.   Terminó a las 6:30. (._Sí_....)

➲ Terminaré a las 7.   (._No_....)

1. En marzo ya **habrá nacido** Luisito.   Nació en febrero.   (.........)

2. En marzo **nacerá** Luisito.   (.........)

3. Cuando venga tu madre el domingo **arreglaré** el horno.   Lo arregló el jueves. (.........)

4. Cuando venga tu madre el domingo, ya **habré arreglado** el horno.   (.........)

5. El avión **aterrizará** a las 11:15 en el aeropuerto de Jizro.   Aterrizó a las 11:05 (.........)

6. A las 11:15, el avión ya **habrá aterrizado** en Jizro.   (.........)

30. Condicional

A   Regular and irregular forms: *hablaría*, *comería*, *viviría*, *querría*...

■ To form the *Condicional simple* of regular verbs, we use the **infinitive** plus the **endings** of the *Imperfecto* of *haber*:

	Imperfecto of *haber*		-ar/-er/-ir	Hablar	Comer	Vivir
Yo	había		-ía	hablaría	comería	viviría
Tú	habías		-ías	hablarías	comerías	vivirías
Él, ella, usted	había	Hablar	-ía	hablaría	comería	viviría
Nosotros/-as	habíamos	Comer	-íamos	hablaríamos	comeríamos	viviríamos
Vosotros/-as	habíais	Vivir	-íais	hablaríais	comeríais	viviríais
Ellos, ellas, ustedes	habían		-ían	hablarían	comerían	vivirían

■ **The word stress is always on the ending,** as shown by the underlining in the previous examples.

- *Después de vuestra experiencia allí, ¿volveríais a vivir en un pueblecito?*
- *Pues dependería de las circunstancias.*

● 28. Futuro

■ The verbs that are irregular in the *Condicional simple* are exactly the same as those that are irregular in the *Futuro*:

Decir → diría   Querer → querría   Tener → tendría
Hacer → haría   Haber → habría   Poner → pondría

- *¿Tú qué harías? ¿Saldrías con ella y le dirías algo?*
- *Yo tampoco sabría qué hacer, la verdad.*

- *¿Dónde pondrías el sofá? ¿Al lado de la ventana o en esa pared?*

1 Little Pablito thinks that all verbs in the *Condicional* are regular.
Help him to learn by finding and correcting his mistakes, as in the example
(you have to find nine more).

➔ Si yo fuera grande, ~~tenería~~ ....*tendría*.... muchos libros muy gordos, y **leería** ......✓......... mucho todos los días.

1. Y así **sabería** .... mucho de gramática y **podría** .... hablar perfectamente.

2. Y también **salería** .... yo solo a la calle, porque ahora no me dejan mis papás, y **pasearía** .... por toda la ciudad, y **hacería** .... todo lo que me gusta, y tú **venirías** .... conmigo.

3. Si yo fuera ya mayor, **sería** .... un profesor muy inteligente y **daría** .... conferencias y **deciría** .... cosas muy interesantes.

4. Yo **querería** .... escribir una gramática, pero no sé escribir todavía.
En esa gramática **ponería** .... cosas muy interesantes, y no **habería** .... ninguna gramática mejor que ésa, y me **haría** .... rico.

5. Yo, en tu lugar, no me **reiría** .... tanto de mí y de mi hermano. **Poderías** .... tener problemas si se lo decimos a nuestra mamá.

B   Making suppositions about the past: *Serían las cinco, más o menos*.

With the *Futuro* we make or ask for suppositions about things in the present that we are not certain about:

■ With the *Condicional* simple we make suppositions about a past reality or ask for suppositions about this past time:

¿Qué **será** eso que se mueve ahí? — No sé. **Será** un gato jugando.

No sé. **Sería** un gato jugando. — ¿Qué **sería** aquello que se movía allí?

| Saldría | = | Supongo que salía/salió |

Affirming the past:

- <u>Eran</u> las cinco, más o menos.

- Estaba muy caliente. ¿<u>Tenía</u> fiebre?
- Llegamos tarde porque <u>perdimos</u> el autobús.

Making suppositions about the past:

- En aquel momento **serían** las cinco, más o menos.
- Estaba muy caliente. ¿**Tendría** fiebre?
- **Perderían** el autobús y, por eso, llegaron tarde.

---

2 Change the form of the verb to show that they are making suppositions about something in the past.

The party on Sunday

¿Por qué no ha venido Jorge a la fiesta?

➲ Pues no sé, **estará** enfermo...

   o no **sabrá** la dirección...

   o **estará** enfadado con nosotros...

   o **tendrá** cosas más interesantes que hacer...

   o no le **apetecerá**... ¿Quién sabe...?

A day later

¿Por qué no vendría Jorge a la fiesta de ayer?

➲ Pues no sé, _estaría_ enfermo...

1. o no .... la dirección...

2. o .... enfadado con nosotros...

3. o .... cosas más interesantes que hacer...

4. o no le .... ¿Quién sabe...?

3 People are saying that yesterday in the village square Jorge was seen kissing someone very passionately. How does the form of the verb change if the people speaking know what happened or are merely supposing?

If they know, they say...

No ➲ ...era....... Jorge. ➲ ..Era........ otro chico.

(1) .... su novia y (2) .... despidiéndose.

Es que no la **veía** desde hacía mucho tiempo.

(4) .... un poco bebidos.

No (5) .... besando a una chica.

(6) .... a un chico.

Querían escandalizar a la gente.

If they are only supposing, they say...

No ➲ ..sería..... Jorge. ➲ ...sería.... otro chico.

Sería su novia, y **estarían** despidiéndose.

No la (3) .... desde hacía mucho tiempo.

Estarían un poco bebidos.

No **estaría** besando a una chica.

Sería a un chico.

(7) .... escandalizar a la gente.

C **Making hypothetical statements about the present and the future:** *Yo no diría nada...*

■ When we use the *Condicional simple* to refer to something in the present or the future, we are talking or asking about a **hypothetical reality**:

We state (or ask) hypothetically:

- Yo, _en tu lugar_, **iría** al médico. [But I am not you and cannot go for you.]
- Te **ayudaría** con mucho gusto, pero es que _tengo que irme_. [I cannot help you.]
- Eres muy alta. **Serías** muy buena _como jugadora de baloncesto_. [But you are not a basketball player.]
- _Si tuvieras tiempo_, ¿**harías** más deporte? [Because you do not take much exercise.]

■ Because of this hypothetical sense, we can also use the *Condicional simple* to make a request or a suggestion **more indirect or polite**:

- ¿_Puedes_ ayudarme a cambiar este mueble?
- ¿_Tienes_ un boli rojo, por casualidad?
- ¿Le _importa_ si abro un poco la ventana?
- Yo creo que lo mejor _es_ no decir nada.

Expressed more politely:

- ¿**Podrías** ayudarme a cambiar este mueble?
- ¿**Tendrías** un boli rojo, por casualidad?
- ¿Le **importaría** si abro un poco la ventana?
- Yo creo que lo mejor **sería** no decir nada.

---

4 Decide whether the two options are possible or not, and cross out any that are not.

➲ ¿Tienes/Tendrías unas monedas para prestarme?

➲ ¿Tienes/Tendrías muchos hijos si fueras rico?

1. Me **gusta**/Me **gustaría** mucho tu camisa. ¿Dónde la has comprado?

2. Si fueras un animal, ¿qué animal **serás**/**serías**?

3. ¿Qué tres cosas os **llevaréis**/**llevaríais** a una isla desierta?

4. Mi mujer ideal es la actriz Charo Nestón. Me **casaré**/**casaría** ahora mismo con ella.

5. Si yo pudiera, no lo **contrataré**/**contrataría**.

6. ¿Cómo **será**/**sería** tu mundo ideal?

7. Me **gusta**/**gustaría** ser muy guapa y atractiva, y quedarme embarazada, pero soy un hombre.

8. ¿Os **importa**/**importaría** hablar más alto?

9. ¿**Puedes**/**Podrías** venir conmigo mañana al banco?

10. Ha sido muy amable con nosotros. Yo creo que **debemos**/**deberíamos** regalarle algo.

11. Me **encantaría**/Me **encanta** ser rubia y alta. Pero soy japonesa.

12. Han estado muy antipáticos durante todo el día. **Podríamos**/**Podemos** hablar con ellos para aclarar las cosas.

31. Condicional compuesto

A Forms: *habría hablado, habría comido, habría vivido*...

■ The *Condicional Compuesto* is formed with:

| The **Condicional** of the auxiliary verb **haber**. | habría
habrías
habría
habríamos
habríais
habrían | hablado
comido
vivido | The **past participle** corresponding to the <u>finished</u> event. |

➔ 20. Non-personal forms

---

1 Complete the form of the Condicional Compuesto in the correct person.

● ¿Recuerdas cuando el león se enfadó y casi se sale de la jaula? ¡Qué miedo!, ¿no?
¿Te imaginas que se hubiera escapado? ¿Qué habría pasado?

○ Bueno, todos los que estábamos allí ➔ *habríamos.* salido corriendo, supongo. En concreto, yo me (1) .... metido inmediatamente en el coche, y creo que Rosa también. Y tú también te (2) .... asustado. No digas que no.

Rosa y tú os (3) .... asustado tanto como yo.

● Es posible. Pero estoy seguro de que Lou no (4) .... tenido tanto miedo.

○ No, ella no se asusta fácilmente, es verdad. ¿Y Alex y Jenaro?

● Pues seguro que le (5) .... explicado al león que no está bien comer personas. Ellos son así...

B Making suppositions about the anterior past: *Habría salido, porque no abría*.

With the *Futuro perfecto* we make or ask for suppositions about the recent past:

■ With the *Condicional compuesto* we speculate about a past before a moment in the past or ask for speculation about this time:

Making statements about the anterior past:

● *Ya lo sabía, porque se lo <u>había dicho</u> Rosario.*
● *Ayer tenías mala cara. ¿Es que <u>habías dormido</u> mal?*
● *No pudo llamar: le <u>habías dado</u> el número equivocado.*

Speculating about the anterior past:

● *¿Ya lo sabía? Se lo **había dicho** Rosario, seguro.*
● *Tenía mala cara, el pobre. ¿**Habría dormido** mal?*
● *Le **habrías dado** el número equivocado y no pudo llamar.*

2 Change the form of the verb to show that they are making suppositions about a situation before a moment in the past.

The party on Sunday

- ¿Por qué no ha venido Jorge a la fiesta?
- ○ Pues no sé, **habrá tenido** algún problema...

 o no le **habrán avisado** a tiempo...

 o se **habrá puesto** enfermo...

 o **habrá tenido** que ir a otro sitio...

 o **habrá olvidado** que era hoy... ¿Quién sabe...?

A day later

- ¿Por qué no vendría Jorge a la fiesta del domingo?
- ○ Pues no sé, *habría tenido* algún problema...

 1. o no le .... a tiempo...

 2. o se .... enfermo...

 3. o .... que ir a otro sitio...

 4. o .... que era ayer... Quién sabe...

C **Making hypothetical statements about the recent past:** *Yo no habría dicho nada...*

■ When we use a *Condicional compuesto* to refer to the recent past, we are making statements or asking about a hypothetical reality that cannot be true, as we know that the truth is different:

➲ 42. Joining sentences

We state (or ask) hypothetically:

- Yo, <u>en tu lugar</u>, **habría ido** al médico hace ya meses.
- Te **habría ayudado** con mucho gusto, pero es que <u>tenía mucha prisa</u>.
- Eres muy alta. **Habrías sido** muy buena <u>como jugadora de baloncesto</u>.
- <u>Si hubieras tenido tiempo</u>, ¿**habrías hecho** más deporte?

[But I am not you and didn't go.]

[I could not help you.]

[But you were not a basketball player.]

[Because you have never taken much exercise.]

---

3 Jerónimo and Alablanca have a platonic love. Last night they spent three hours together, just gazing into each other's eyes. What would Alablanca have done if Jerónimo had behaved differently? Complete what would have happened, putting their thoughts in the boxes into perfect Spanish.

➲ Si Jerónimo le hubiera propuesto casarse, *no habría aceptado, porque es joven todavía.*

1. Si le hubiera recitado un poema, ...

2. Si se hubiera enfadado con ella, ...

3. Si le hubiera dicho que amaba a otra, ...

4. Si le hubiera dado un beso, ...

5. Si hubiera llorado, ...

6. Si le hubiera confesado que es gay, ...

7. Si le hubiera hecho proposiciones deshonestas, ...

8. Si le hubiera prometido amor eterno, ...

| Yo darle otro a él |
| Yo consolarlo a él |
| Yo también enfadarme con él |

| Yo escuchar con mucho gusto | Yo sentirme ofendida y rechazarlas | Yo no aceptar, porque ser joven todavía ✓ |

| Yo sorprenderme mucho, pero comprender | Yo jurar también quererlo siempre | Yo preguntarle a quién |

32. Forms of the subjuntivo: *hable, haya hablado...*

A Regular forms of the Presente de subjuntivo: *hable, coma, viva...*

■ We form the *Presente de subjuntivo* by changing the classifying vowels of the *Presente de indicativo* in the following way:

Presente de indicativo	-ar	-er	Hablar	Comer	Vivir
Yo	-o	-o	hablo	como	vivo
Tú	-as	-es	hablas	comes	vives
Él, ella, usted	-a	-e	habla	come	vive
Nosotros/-as	-amos	-emos	hablamos	comemos	vivimos
Vosotros/-as	-áis	-éis	habláis	coméis	vivís
Ellos, ellas, ustedes	-an	-en	hablan	comen	viven

Presente de subjuntivo	-ar	-er/-ir	-ar → e		-er/-ir → a
Yo	-e	-a	hable	coma	viva
Tú	-es	-as	hables	comas	vivas
Él, ella, usted	-e	-a	hable	coma	viva
Nosotros/-as	-emos	-amos	hablemos	comamos	vivamos
Vosotros/-as	-éis	-áis	habléis	comáis	viváis
Ellos, ellas, ustedes	-en	-an	hablen	coman	vivan

■ The **word stress** remains in the same place as in the Presente de indicativo: on the stem in the *yo, tú, él* and *ellos,* persons, and on the ending in the *nosotros* and *vosotros,* persons, as shown by the underlining in the examples above.

■ If we need to use the subjunctive, we use the *Presente* to express both the **present** and the **future**, in the following way:

If in the **indicative** we say...	In the subjunctive we say...
Está en Berlín. / **Estará** en Berlín. ⟶	No creo que **esté** allí.

⊙ 33. Indicativo or subjuntivo?

1 *Presente de indicativo* or *Presente de subjuntivo*? Identify the verb form in each case and write the other form in the same person in the appropriate column.

	Indicativo	Subjuntivo		Indicativo	Subjuntivo
cantan	➲ ....✓....	....*canten*....	camines	10.	....
hablemos	➲ ..*hablamos*..	......✓......	corras	11.	....
bebes	1.	....	rompáis	12.	....
camina	2.	....	limpiamos	13.	....
perdona	3.	....	mires	14.	....
rompo	4.	....	perdone	15.	....
vivís	5.	....	partimos	16.	....
miráis	6.	....	beban	17.	....
limpies	7.	....	corro	18.	....
cocina	8.	....	mejoran	19.	....
cuide	9.	....	saludemos	20.	....

B   Verbs with vowel changes: *pedir, sentir, dormir...*

Verbs with vowel changes in the *Presente de indicativo*, also have them in the *Presente de subjuntivo*. Almost all the changes are the same, but there are some verbs that have additional changes.

➔ 21. Presente de indicativo

■ If, in the *Presente de indicativo* the vowel -*e*- at the end of the stem changes to an -*i*- in the *yo, tú, él* and *ellos*, persons, in the *Presente de subjuntivo* this change affects all persons:

Pedir *Impedir* *Seguir* *Perseguir* *Repetir* *Competir* *Reír* *Sonreír* *Medir...*			*Pedir*		¡También cambian!
		Presente de indicativo	**Presente de subjuntivo**		
	Yo	pi*d*o	pi*d*a		
	Tú	pi*d*es	pi*d*as		
	Él, ella, usted	pi*d*e	pi*d*a		
	Nosotros/-as	pe*d*imos	pi*d*amos		
	Vosotros/-as	pe*d*ís	pi*d*áis		
	Ellos, ellas, ustedes	pi*d*en	pi*d*an		

■ Other verbs with *...e...ir* and *...o...ir*, that do not change this vowel in the *nosotros* and *vosotros* persons, do introduce this change in the *Presente de subjuntivo*:

	e → i			*o → u*	
	Mentir	*Sentir*	*Preferir*	*Dormir*	*Morir*
Nosotros/-as	*mintamos*	*sintamos*	*prefiramos*	*durmamos*	*muramos*
Vosotros/-as	*mintáis*	*sintáis*	*prefiráis*	*durmáis*	*muráis*

2   **Jerónimo and Alablanca are having an argument with their neighbours Jed and Amy. Complete the missing verbs in the correct person.**

Vosotros reír de nosotros.

Es verdad que nos **reímos** mucho pero no es verdad que nos **riamos** de vosotros.

➔ ● Vosotros **mentir** siempre.
1. ● Nosotros **sonreír** por cualquier cosa.
2. ● Nosotros **amar** naturaleza y **sentir** gran respeto por animales.
3. ● Nosotros ser solidarios y vosotros **competir** continuamente entre vosotros.
4. ● Nosotros ser ecológicos: **preferir** flor a televisor y montaña a carretera.
5. ● Nosotros **dormir** sólo con estrellas en cielo, y todos vosotros dormir con pastillas químicas.

Presente de indicativo	Presente de subjuntivo
➔ ○ Bueno, a veces sí *mentimos* ,	pero no es verdad que siempre ...*mintamos*... .
1. ○ Sí, muchas veces .... ,	pero es mentira que .... por cualquier cosa.
2. ○ Sí, es verdad que vosotros .... la naturaleza,	pero es falso que .... tanto respeto por los animales: ayer os comisteis dos pollos...
3. ○ Vale, nosotros .... muchas veces,	pero no creemos que .... continuamente.
4. ○ Sí, es evidente que vosotros .... las flores,	pero no vemos que .... la montaña a la carretera. ¿Por qué tenéis un coche deportivo?
5. ○ Es cierto que nosotros, a veces, ... con pastillas,	pero no es cierto que todos nosotros .... con pastillas.

C Verbs with irregular roots: *salga, diga, ponga...*

■ When a verb has an irregular stem in the first person singular in the *Presente de indicativo*,
we use this irregular stem to form **the whole of the *Presente de subjuntivo***:

➲ 21. Presente de indicativo

Hacer	Presente de indicativo	Presente de subjuntivo
Yo	**hag**o →	**hag**a
Tú	hac*es*	**hag**as
Él, ella, usted	hac*e*	**hag**a
Nosotros/-as	hac*emos*	**hag**amos
Vosotros/-as	hac*éis*	**hag**áis
Ellos, ellas, ustedes	hac*en*	**hag**an

■ This affects verbs such as:

Decir	→	**dig-**	*Venir*	→	**veng-**
Traer	→	**traig-**	*Caer*	→	**caig-**
Poner	→	**pong-**	*Tener*	→	**teng-**
Salir	→	**salg-**	*Oír*	→	**oig-**

Conocer	→	**conozc-**
Parecer	→	**parezc-**
Agradecer	→	**agradezc-**
Conducir	→	**conduzc-**

And their compound forms:

*Contra**decir***	→	*contra***dig-**
*Su**poner***	→	*su***pong-**
*Desa**parecer***	→	*desa***parezc-**
...		

3 Little Lucía and Ángela sometimes make mistakes with some of the irregular subjunctives.
Find and correct their five mistakes, not counting the example.

➲ ● Mira a papá, Ángela. ¿No ves cómo te pareces a él?

➲ ○ Es extraño que **digas** ......✓........ eso. Yo no veo que me ~~pareza~~ ..*parezca*.. a papá en nada.

1. ● ¿Quieres que **ponamos** .... el vídeo de dibujos animados?
   ○ Sí, está en el cajón. Espera que lo t**raiga** .... y lo ponemos.

2. ● ¿Quieres que **salamos** .... a jugar al parque con papá?
   ○ Vale, pero no creo que papá **tena** .... tiempo. Está siempre jugando con el ordenador.
   ● Voy a decirle que **vena** .... con nosotras, a ver qué dice...

3. ● Papá conduce mucho mejor que mamá.
   ○ Yo no creo que **conduza** .... mejor. Si no sabe ni aparcar...
   ● ¡Calla! Es mejor que no te **oiga** .... decir eso...

D Very irregular verbs: *ser, estar, ver, ir, haber, saber*.

	Ser	*Estar*	*Ver*	*Ir*	*Haber*	*Saber*
Yo	*sea*	*esté*	*vea*	*vaya*	*haya...*	*sepa*
Tú	*seas*	*estés*	*veas*	*vayas*	*hayas...*	*sepas*
Él, ella, usted	*sea*	*esté*	*vea*	*vaya*	*haya...*	*sepa*
Nosotros/-as	*seamos*	*estemos*	*veamos*	*vayamos*	*hayamos...*	*sepamos*
Vosotros/-as	*seáis*	*estéis*	*veáis*	*vayáis*	*hayáis...*	*sepáis*
Ellos, ellas, ustedes	*sean*	*estén*	*vean*	*vayan*	*hayan...*	*sepan*

The verb *estar* is only irregular in its word stress, which always falls on the ending.

Haber is an auxiliary verb. The *Pretérito perfecto de subjuntivo* is formed with the *Presente de subjuntivo* of *haber*: **haya** comido, **hayas** ido...

Haya corresponds both to the personal form (*ha*) and the impersonal form (*hay*) of the *Presente de indicativo*.

4 María has received a strange love letter. Complete her indignant reply with the *Presente de subjuntivo* in the correct person.

Quiero **saber** si me amas,
quiero **verte** cada día.
Quiero **estar** en tu pijama,
quiero **ir** contigo, María.
Quiero **ser** el que te llama,
pues sin ti no **hay** luz del día.

Corazón de Melón

Querido Corazón de Melón:
Comprendo tus deseos, y haré lo posible para no satisfacerlos.
Te diré que me pareces ridículo y quiero que ➜ ...*sepas*...
que no te amo. Me iré a otra ciudad para que no me
(1) .... cada día. Quemaré toda mi ropa, si es
necesario, para que no (2) .... nunca en mi pijama.
Llamaré a la policía para que no (3) .... conmigo
a ninguna parte. Te taparé la boca para que no (4) ....
el que me llama. Y te regalaré una buena lámpara para que
por fin (5) .... luz suficiente en tu vida y no vuelvas
a escribirme nunca más.

María

E Forms of the Pretérito imperfecto de subjuntivo: *hablara(-se), comiera(-se), viviera(-se)...*

■ There is a simple and completely regular rule that makes it easy to form the *Pretérito imperfecto de subjuntivo*: Take the **third person plural** (*ellos*) of the regular or irregular **Indefinido** of the verb you want to conjugate, and change the final –*ron* for the following endings:

Hablar *habla~~ron~~*	Imperfecto de subjuntivo	*Ser* *fue~~ron~~*	Imperfecto de subjuntivo	*Salir* *salie~~ron~~*	Imperfecto de subjuntivo
	hablara		*fuera*		*saliera*
	hablaras		*fueras*		*salieras*
	hablara		*fuera*		*saliera*
	habláramos		*fuéramos*		*saliéramos*
	hablarais		*fuerais*		*salierais*
	hablaran		*fueran*		*salieran*

■ The **word stress** in the *Imperfecto de subjuntivo* always falls in the same place as the *Indefinido*, as shown by the underlining in the examples above.

■ If we need to use the subjunctive, we use the *Imperfecto* to talk about both the **past** and the **hypothetical present or future**, in the following way:

If in the **indicative** we say...		In the **subjunctive** we say...
Estuvo/Estaba en Berlín.	*Estaría en Berlín ayer.* [I suppose.] *Estaría en Berlín ahora.* [But he missed the plane.] *Estaría en Berlín mañana.* [If he catches the plane.]	*Es posible que estuviera allí.*

➜ 33. Indicativo or subjuntivo?

5 Write the verbs in bold on the left in the third person plural of the *Indefinido*. Then, based on the forms you have just written, complete the answers on the right in the *Imperfecto de subjuntivo*.

	Indefinido (ellos)	Imperfecto de subjuntivo
➲ • ¿Pudiste ver si **estaban** ya preparados?	_estuvie-ron_	➲ ○ No, no parecía que _estuvieran_ todavía preparados.
1. • Mi perro **vivió** 20 años.	....	1. ○ No es posible que .... tanto...
2. • ¿De verdad **probasteis** los gusanos fritos?	....	2. ○ Sí, pero sólo dos o tres. Ellos querían que .... la comida típica de allí.
3. • Yo, en tu lugar, le **mentiría**.	....	3. ○ No. Sería muy injusto que le ....
4. • Antes **veníamos** mucho aquí.	....	4. ○ Sí, y a tu madre no le gustaba que nosotros ....
5. • ¿**Elegisteis** vosotros el color para pintar la casa?	....	5. ○ ¡Qué va! No nos dejaron que lo ....
6. • Y cuando se lo dije, se **rió** de mí.	....	6. ○ ¡No puedo creer que se .... de ti!
7. • ¿Tú crees que yo **podría** conseguir ese trabajo si hablara búlgaro?	....	7. ○ No, la verdad es que no creo que .... conseguirlo.
8. • ¿Recuerdas el viaje a Lisboa? ¡Qué mal **conducía** Ana!	....	8. ○ Sí, fue horrible. Nadie quería que .... ella, pero condujo...
9. • Me propuso ir a su casa, pero yo no **quería**.	....	9. ○ Pues me parece muy raro que tú no .... , la verdad.
10. • No sé qué pasó con Toby. Supongo que se **escaparía**.	....	10. ○ Sí, es muy posible que se .... No le dabas casi nada de comer...

■ Apart from the *-ra,* form of the *Imperfecto de subjuntivo*, there is an alternative *-se* form that means exactly the same. We make this form by changing the *-ron* ending of the *ellos* person of the *Indefinido* for the following endings:

Hablar *habla~~ron~~*	Imperfecto de subjuntivo	*Ser* *fue~~ron~~*	Imperfecto de subjuntivo	*Salir* *salie~~ron~~*	Imperfecto de subjuntivo
	hablase		*fuese*		*saliese*
	hablases		*fueses*		*salieses*
	hablase		*fuese*		*saliese*
	hablásemos		*fuésemos*		*saliésemos*
	hablaseis		*fueseis*		*salieseis*
	hablasen		*fuesen*		*saliesen*

6 Which is the odd one out?

➲	aceptara	estuviese	tenga	(salimos)	_Es la única forma que no es subjuntivo_
1.	hubiera	dijéramos	supiesen	tuvisteis	....
2.	vieron	fuese	oyéramos	agradecieseis	....
3.	trajeras	trajeses	conduzca	viniéramos	....
4.	cayese	caería	caíamos	caigo	....
5.	oyes	oís	oiremos	oyera	....

¡Ojalá lloviera!

¡Sí, ojalá lloviese!

F — Forms of the Pretérito perfecto de subjuntivo: *haya hablado/comido/vivido...*

■ The *Pretérito perfecto de subjuntivo* is formed with:

The *Presente de subjuntivo* of the auxiliary verb **haber**.

haya
hayas
haya
hayamos
hayáis
hayan

hablado
comido
vivido

The **past participle** corresponding to the <u>finished</u> event.

➲ 20. Non-personal forms

■ If we need to use the subjunctive, we use the Perfecto to talk about both the **recent past** and the **past in the future**, in the following way:

➲ 33. Indicativo or subjuntivo?

If in the **indicative** we say...	In the **subjunctive** we say...
Ha estado en Berlín. / *Habrá estado* en Berlín.	*No creo que* **haya estado** *allí.*

7 Change the verbs in bold in the following dialogues into the corresponding forms of the subjunctive.

➲ ● Dicen que **han estado** un año viviendo en Oslo.
   ○ No creo que <u>hayan estado</u> tanto tiempo allí.

1. ● ¡Ya **hemos encontrado** la película de Jarri Sonfor!
   ○ ¡Es imposible que la .... tan pronto!

2. ● ¿**Ha llegado** ya el paquete de la tía Remedios?
   ○ No recuerdo que .... ningún paquete...

3. ● No te preocupes: a las dos lo **he terminado** todo.
   ○ Dudo mucho que para esa hora lo ....

4. ● No sé dónde están las llaves. Las **habrás perdido**.
   ○ Es imposible que yo las ....

5. ● **Habéis acertado** totalmente con el regalo. Gracias.
   ○ ¡Pues qué bien que .... !

G — Forms of the Pluscuamperfecto de subjuntivo: *hubiera(-se) hablado/comido/vivido...*

■ The *Pretérito pluscuamperfecto de subjuntivo* is formed with:

The *Imperfecto de subjuntivo* of the auxiliary verb **haber**.

hubiera (-*se*)
hubieras (-*ses*)
hubiera (-*se*)
hubiéramos (-*semos*)
hubierais (-*seis*)
hubieran (-*sen*)

hablado
comido
vivido

The **past participle** corresponding to the <u>finished</u> event.

➲ 20. Non-personal forms

■ If we need to use the subjunctive, we use the *Pluscuamperfecto* to talk about the **anterior past**, in the following way:

➲ 33. Indicativo or subjuntivo?

If in the **indicative** we say...	In the **subjunctive** we say...
Había estado en Berlín. / *Habría estado* en Berlín.	*No creo que* **hubiera estado** *allí.*

8 José Rodríguez was supposed to get lunch ready, but he didn't, and his wife has no time for any of his excuses. Complete her replies with the corresponding form of the subjunctive

¿Por qué no hiciste la comida?

➲ Es que las sartenes se **habían perdido**...

1. Es que me **había cortado** un dedo con el cuchillo...

2. Es que la luz se **había ido**...

3. Es que pensé que quizá **habrías cambiado** de opinión...

4. Es que **habíamos decidido** comer fuera...

➲ No es verdad que las sartenes se <u>hubieran perdido</u> ...

1. No es verdad que te ....
   un dedo con el cuchillo...

2. No es verdad que la luz se ....

3. No es verdad que yo ....
   de opinión...

4. No es verdad que .... eso.

33. Indicativo or subjuntivo?

A Making statements (indicativo) or non-statements (subjuntivo)

■ We use a verb in the **indicative** when **we want to state** the meaning of the verb in question: we want to express what someone knows (a statement) or thinks (a supposition) about a particular reality.
We can state information directly (in a simple sentence) or after an OPINION MARKER that introduces a statement (in a subordinate clause).

	SIMPLE SENTENCE	OPINION	SUBORDINATE CLAUSE
	WE STATE (INDICATIVE)	**MARKER**	**WE STATE (INDICATIVE)**

We state
We suppose   Susana **tiene / tendrá** novio.

Está claro
Yo creo
Él piensa
Supongo

que   Susana **tiene / tendrá** novio.

¿Qué gato **es** ése?

Es Julio César.

¿Qué será eso que se mueve ahí?

Me imagino que **será** Julio César.

■ We use a verb in the **subjunctive** (or the infinitive) when **we do not want to state** the meaning of the verb in question, because we do not want to make either a statement or a supposition: we only want to express a **desired reality**. A verb in the subjunctive is always dependent on a OPINION MARKER that we use to express wishes, denial, possibility or value judgments:

OPINION MARKER	SUBORDINATE CLAUSE
	WE DO NOT STATE (SUBJUNCTIVE)

👁 **We never use the subjunctive** to express a direct opinion (in a simple sentence):

Queremos
No creo
Es posible
Es mentira

que   Susana *tenga* novio.

Susana ~~tenga~~ novio.

Es posible que sea Julio César.

Yo no creo que sea Julio César.
A él no le gusta jugar con la basura.

157

1 The famous inspector, Cherlog Jol, is questioning one of the people suspected of committing a theft. Are the notes the secretary took during his statement absolutely correct?

Lo que ha dicho el detenido:	Lo que ha escrito el secretario:	Sí/No
➲ Me **llamo** Mario Roldán..	➲ Ha declarado que se **llama** Mario Roldán	*Sí*
1. **Tenga** paciencia conmigo, inspector.	1. Ha declarado que el inspector **tiene** paciencia con él.	....
2. <u>Sé que</u> Pablo Margi **tiene** una parte del dinero.	2. Ha declarado que Pablo **tiene** una parte del dinero.	....
3. <u>Creo que</u> Alejandro Cascas se **llevó** las joyas.	3. Ha declarado que, en su opinón, Alejandro se **llevó** las joyas.	....
4. <u>Supongo que</u> Jenaro Orol **estará** ya en otro país.	4. Ha declarado que, en su opinión, Jenaro **está** ya en otro país.	....
5. <u>Es posible que</u> Lourdes Milo **esté** todavía en España.	5. Ha declarado que Lourdes todavía **está** en España.	....
6. La verdad es que <u>yo necesitaba</u> **conseguir** dinero.	6. Ha declarado que **consiguió** dinero.	....
7. <u>Me alegro de que</u> me **haga** esa pregunta.	7. Ha declarado que el inspector le **hace** esa pregunta.	....
8. <u>No creo que</u> Rosa Alora **esté** implicada en el robo.	8. Ha declarado que Rosa **está** implicada en el robo.	....
9. <u>Quiero que</u> **venga** mi abogado inmediatamente.	9. Ha declarado que su abogado **viene** inmediatamente.	....
10. <u>Es muy triste</u> **ir** a la cárcel.	10. Ha declarado que **va** a la cárcel.	....

B Expressing wishes and desired outcomes: *Quiero que venga.*

■ When we talk about wanting something, the thing that we want **never takes the form of a statement**. It is only a **desired reality** concerning something that may or may not happen, and that we propose as an objective:

- ● ***Quiero*** <u>*que me ayudes*</u>.
  [I cannot state "me ayudas", as it is only a wish.]

(Desired outcome)

[It is **not** a statement, only a desired outcome.]

Quiero...
Deseo...
Necesito...

que te ~~casas~~ *cases conmigo / casarme contigo.*

- This is why we always use the subjunctive (or the infinitive) with verbs that are subordinate to OPINION MARKERS and that express wishes or desired outcomes:

(No) Quiero...
(No) Desea...
(No) Esperan...
Él (no) prefiere...
(No) Me apetece...
(No) Tiene ganas de...
...

[What I am going to say **is not a statement**: it is only **something that is wished for or not wished for.**]

que te cases conmigo.

(No) Te pido...
(No) Te ha prohibido...
(No) Permite...
(No) Te aconsejo...
(No) Es importante...
(No) Es necesario...
...para...
...

[What I am going to say **is not a statement**: it is **something that should or should not happen.**]

2 Put the opinion markers in the correct place in the table, according to their meaning.

No le exijo que... ✓   Está claro que... ✓   Ellos creen que... ✓   ¿Le han propuesto que...? ✓

¿Me permite que...?   ¿Me recomiendas que...?   Estamos seguros de que...   Sé que...

Es fundamental que...   Me parece que...   No me puedes pedir que...   Me han contado que...

¿No preferís que...?   ¿Necesitas que...?   Todos imaginan que...   Pensamos que...

Introducing a statement or supposition

Está claro que...
Ellos creen que...

....
....
....
....
....
....

...**habla** con ella.

(INDICATIVO)

Introducing a wish or desired reality

No le exijo que...
¿Le han propuesto que...?

....
....
....
....
....
....

...**hable** con ella.

(SUBJUNTIVO)

- When we express wishes or desired outcomes, we can put the subordinate verb into a personal form of the **subjunctive** (introduced by *que*), or use a simple **infinitive**:

	We use the **infinitive**	We use the **subjunctive**
With OPINION MARKERS such as...	If the subject of the main and subordinate verbs is the same:	If the subject of the main and subordinate verbs are different:
Querer..., Desear..., Necesitar, Pedir..., Preferir..., Tener ganas de..., Intentar..., Conseguir..., Tratar de...,	*Quiero salir.* (yo) = (yo)	*Quiero que salgas / salgan...* (yo) ⟷ (tú) ¡ellos)
With OPINION MARKERS such as...	To generalise:	To emphasise the person of the verb:
Es importante/necesario/mejor... Hay que intentar/conseguir...	*¿Es necesario pasar por ahí?* (en general) = (tú, yo, nosotros...)	*¿Es necesario que pasemos por ahí?* (en general) ⟷ (nosotros, en concreto)

3 Identify the subject of the verbs in bold.

➲ ¡No te vayas, Mariana, que Elena quiere que le **cortes** el pelo!   ➲ ...*Mariana*...

➲ Vamos a esperar. Es mejor **tomarse** las cosas con calma.   ➲ ...*En general*...

1. Se ha puesto muy nerviosa. Vamos a intentar **tranquilizarla**.   1. ....

2. Trata de **tranquilizarte**, Pitita. Tu marido vendrá pronto...   2. ....

3. Para aprender español es necesario **estudiar** con una buena gramática.   3. ....

4. Creo que ella debe saberlo. Es mejor que se lo **digas** ya.   4. ....

5. Si conseguimos **aprobar** el examen, vamos a hacer una fiesta.   5. ....

6. Tengo unas ganas locas de que **vengáis** a visitarme.   6. ....

7. ¿Te apetece **descansar** un poco antes de seguir?   7. ....

8. No te rindas, mujer. ¿Por qué no intentas **hablar** con ella otra vez?   8. ....

9. No me gusta nada la idea de comer en Mcdonuts. Prefiero que **comamos** aquí.   9. ....

4 Aladetrés, Alablanca's best friend, wants to send her a letter, but she's a bit confused about how to form the verbs in bold. Can she use the simple infinitive or should she use *que* + subjunctive? Help her.

➲ <u>Necesito</u> yo **escribir** mi tristeza.   ➲ Necesito *escribir mi tristeza.*

➲ <u>Deseo</u> tú **saber** mis sentimientos.   ➲ Deseo *que sepas mis sentimientos.*

1. Estoy enamorada de Toro Cansado, y yo <u>tengo ganas de</u> yo **ver** a Toro Cansado.   1. Tengo ganas de .... a Toro Cansado.

2. Pero él no me <u>permite</u> yo **hablar** por teléfono con él.   2. Pero él no me permite .... por teléfono con él.

3. Mi hermana tampoco <u>quiere</u> yo **hablar** por teléfono con él.   3. No quiere .... por teléfono con él.

4. Ella <u>prefiere</u> yo **no pensar** más en él.   4. Prefiere .... más en él.

5. Me <u>prohíbe</u> yo **llamar** a su casa.   5. Me prohíbe .... a su casa.

6. Pero yo <u>espero</u> él **llamar** a mi casa.   6. Espero .... a mi casa.

7. Tenemos que <u>intentar</u> él **pensar** en mí.   7. Tenemos que intentar .... en mí.

8. Tienes que ayudarme <u>para</u> él y yo **poder** ser novios.   8. Tienes que ayudarme para .... ser novios.

9. ¿Me <u>recomiendas</u> yo **confesar** mi amor?   9. ¿Me recomiendas .... mi amor?

10. ¿Crees que <u>es mejor</u> yo **esperar** un poco?   10. ¿O crees que es mejor .... un poco?

11. <u>Es</u> muy importante yo **saber** tu opinión.   11. Es muy importante .... tu opinión.

5 Alablanca has received Aladetrés's letter, and has written a reply. She also needs your help to decide between the infinitive, indicative or subjunctive for all the verbs in bold.

Querida Aladetrés:

En mi opinión, está claro Toro Cansado **no estar** enamorado de ti. Pero tenemos que hacer algo, porque yo quiero tú **ser** feliz. Creo que lo mejor será **actuar** con tranquilidad. En primer lugar, si él no quiere él **hablar** por teléfono contigo, te recomiendo tú **no insistir** en llamarlo y tú **buscar** otra forma de comunicar con él. En segundo lugar, tienes que intentar tu hermana **cambiar** de actitud y ella **no estar** siempre diciéndote qué tienes que hacer. Finalmente, no te aconsejo tú **confesar** tu amor todavía. Es mejor tú **esperar** unos meses, porque yo creo él **no estar** preparado todavía para comprender este amor. Pero puedes estar tranquila: tú sabes yo siempre intento tú **estar** bien y yo **ayudar** a ti en lo posible. Tu amiga,

Alablanca

Querida Aladetrés:

En mi opinión, está claro que Toro Cansado ...*no está*... enamorado de ti. Pero tenemos que hacer algo, porque yo quiero que ...*seas*... feliz. Creo que lo mejor es ...*actuar*... con tranquilidad. En primer lugar, si él no quiere .... (1) por teléfono contigo, te recomiendo que .... (2) en llamarlo y que .... (3) otra forma de comunicar con él. En segundo lugar, tienes que intentar que tu hermana .... (4) de actitud y que .... (5) siempre diciéndote qué tienes que hacer. Finalmente, no te aconsejo que .... (6) tu amor todavía. Es mejor que .... (7) unos meses, porque creo que él .... (8) preparado todavía para comprender este amor. Pero puedes estar tranquila: tú sabes que yo siempre intento que .... (9) bien y .... (10) en lo posible.

Tu amiga,

Alablanca.

■ With the *Que* + **Presente de subjuntivo** formula, we can express conventional good wishes or warnings in standard situations where we normally use fixed expressions:

Good wishes

- ¡*Que aproveche*!
  ['I hope you enjoy your meal': when someone is about to start eating.]
- ¡*Que te lo pases bien*!
  ['Have a good time', 'have fun': when someone is going to a party, for example.]

Warnings

- ¡*Que tengas cuidado*!
  ['Be careful': when someone is going to do something dangerous.]
- ¡*Que no corráis*!
  ['Don't speed': when someone is setting off on a car journey.]

---

6 Aladetrés always knows what her brother, Jerónimo, is doing and is quick to offer him her best wishes. But her expressions into good Spanish and link them to the circumstances in which they are said, from the box below.

➲ ¡Tú **mejorarte**!   ¡Que te ...*mejores*...!   *e*

1. ¡Tú **cumplir** muchos más!   ¡Que .... muchos más! ....
2. ¡Tú **tener** suerte!   ¡Que .... suerte! ....
3. ¡Tú **divertirte**!   ¡Que te ....! ....
4. ¡Tú **descansar**!   ¡Que ....! ....
5. ¡Tú **tener** buen viaje!   ¡Que ....buen viaje! ....
6. ¡Vosotros **ser** felices!   ¡Que ....felices! ....

a) Jerónimo se va a una fiesta.	e) Está enfermo y Aladetrés se despide de él. ✓
b) Va a hacer un examen.	f) Aladetrés despide a Jerónimo en el aeropuerto.
c) Ha dicho "buenas noches": se va a la cama.	
d) Jerónimo se ha casado con Alablanca.	g) Es el día del cumpleaños de Jerónimo.

---

7 Little Camilita is going on a school trip with her friends and her mother gives her five pieces of advice about how she should behave. Chose which they are, and write them out with *Que* + Presente de subjuntivo, as in the example.

- Tienes que comer muchos caramelos.
- Tienes que ser buena. ✓
- No debes pelearte con nadie.
- Debes comerte tu bocadillo entero.
- Tienes que decir muchas palabras feas.
- Tienes que ir siempre cerca de la maestra.
- No debes obedecer a tu maestra.
- No quiero que te ensucies la ropa.

➲ *Que seas buena...* ....
1. ....
2. ....
3. ....
4. ....

C Stating or querying information: *Creo que viene / No creo que venga*

■ We use a subordinate verb in the **indicative** when **we want to state** as factual the information that this verb expresses:

	subordinate verb
Todos saben *Está claro* *Yo creo* *Es verdad* ...	*que **tienes** novio.* [This is a **statement**. It is the opinion of the subject.]

■ We use a subordinate verb in the **subjunctive** when **we do not want to state** as factual the information that this verb expresses:

	subordinate verb
Puede ser *Dudo* *No creo* *Es mentira* ...	*que tengas novio.* ~~TIENES~~

[This is a not a **statement**. It is not the opinion of the subject, but only an idea.]

■ This is why we use the indicative after OPINION MARKERS that introduce opinions (more or less firmly held), but use the subjunctive after OPINION MARKERS that express the subject's questioning or doubt about the subordinate information:

OPINION MARKERS THAT INTRODUCE INFORMATION

Está claro que **es** la Tierra.

(Stating)

| *Yo sé que...*
Me han contado que...
Está claro que...
¿Es verdad que...?
No hay duda de que... | *es la Tierra.* |

[**We state** that the information presented is the opinion of the subject.]

(Supposing)

| *Ellos creen que...*
¿Piensas que...?
Nos parece que...
Supongo que...
Me imagino que... | *es/**será** la Tierra.* |

Me parece que **es** la Tierra.

INDICATIVE

OPINION MARKERS THAT QUESTION INFORMATION

Es posible que **sea** la Tierra.

(Only considering the **possibility**)

Es posible que...
¿Es probable que...?
Puede ser que...
Dudo que...

~~sea~~ la Tierra.

[**We are not stating.** The information presented is not the **opinion** of the subject.]

No está claro que **sea** la Tierra.

(**Rejecting**)

Es mentira que...
No es verdad que...
No creemos que...
No está segura de que...
No está claro que...
No me imagino que...

~~sea~~ la Tierra.

SUBJUNCTIVE

---

8 **Complete the table by ordering the opinion markers by category.**

Es indudable que... ✓   No es verdad que... ✓   ¿Puede ser que...? ✓   Pensamos que... ✓

Suponen que...   A ellas les parece que...   Es falso que...   Es posible que...

No es cierto que...   Me parece probable que...   Te aseguro que...

Es evidente que...   Sospecho que...   Es bastante posible que...

Introducing a statement
Es indudable que...
....
....

Introducing a supposition
Pensamos que...
....
....
....

...es la Tierra.

(INDICATIVE)

Rejecting an idea
No es verdad que...
....
....

Considering a possibility
¿Puede ser que...?
....
....
....

...sea la Tierra.

(SUBJUNCTIVE)

163

9 Following Doctor Ginés Labella's conference on sexual equality, six of the participants comment on her most controversial statements. Complete what they say with the correct form (Presente de indicativo / Presente de subjuntivo) of the three verbs in bold below.

... y, como iba diciendo, hay que reconocer que las mujeres son claramente superiores a los hombres, al menos en tres aspectos: en primer lugar, **aprenden** lenguas con mucha más facilidad; en segundo lugar, **son** más hábiles para resolver problemas de lógica; y, por último, está demostrado que **tienen** más sentido estético...

1. Para mí, **está claro que** las mujeres ..*aprenden*.. lenguas más fácilmente. También **es verdad que** .... más hábiles en la lógica, y **no hay duda de que** .... más sentido estético.

3. **Yo también creo que** las mujeres .... una lengua más rápido, y **me parece que** sí, que también .... más hábiles con la lógica. Del sentido estético no sé qué pensar, pero sí, **supongo que** .... más que los hombres.

5. ¡Mentira, mentira y mentira! **No es verdad que** .... lenguas mejor, **no es cierto que** .... mejores con la lógica, y también **es falso que** .... más sentido estético.

2. Pues yo **dudo mucho que** *aprendan* lenguas más fácilmente. Además, **no está demostrado que** .... más hábiles en la lógica, y **tampoco creo que** .... más sentido estético.

4. Hombre, sí, **puede ser que** .... las lenguas más fácilmente, y también admito **la posibilidad de que** .... más hábiles en la lógica. Pero **no me parece nada probable que** .... un sentido estético especial, la verdad...

6. Bueno, vamos a ver: **es indudable que** .... mucho mejor las lenguas, y **es perfectamente posible que** .... más hábiles con la lógica, pero **no es en absoluto verdad que** .... más sentido estético: los grandes artistas siempre han sido hombres...

10 Doctor Ginés Labella's husband takes advantage of the conference break to give a little talk on his pet subject: snails. However, not everything he says is true. Identify and write out below the three truths and the three errors in what he says.

Pues yo creo que los caracoles <u>son unos mamíferos apasionantes.</u> <u>Llevan su casa en la espalda,</u> <u>tienen dos antenas</u> preciosas que sacan y esconden a voluntad, y <u>pueden ver la comida a varios kilómetros de distancia.</u> Parecen tontos, pero, en realidad, <u>tienen una inteligencia muy parecida a la humana.</u> Por ejemplo, aunque <u>son muy lentos,</u> a veces se <u>suben encima de la cabeza de las palomas</u> para viajar más rápido. Y, además, estos animalitos <u>son muy pacíficos.</u> Y, bueno, les dejo ya de nuevo con la conferencia de mi esposa. Yo tengo que terminar de cocinar unos caracoles para la cena. Muchas gracias por su atención.

➜ Es verdad que .*los caracoles tienen dos antenas.*...

1. Todo el mundo sabe que ....

2. Está claro que ....

3. A mí también me parece que ....

➜ No es verdad que .*sean mamíferos*.................

4. Es mentira que ....

5. No creo que ....

6. Yo no pienso que ....

D Making statements or requests: *Dice que viene* / *Dice que venga*

■ We can use many verbs like *decir,* to introduce statements or requests. When *decir* means '**to state**', we use the indicative: when it means '**to request**', we use the subjunctive:

	The subordinate information is a **statement**	The subordinate information is a **request**.
Decir	*Me han dicho que **vienes** a la fiesta, ¿es verdad?*	*Me han dicho que vengas a la fiesta. ¿Te apetece?*
Repetir	*Te repito que no **tengo** ganas de salir.*	*Te repito que te vayas tú solo.*
Insistir en	*Insisto en que este puente **es** muy peligroso.*	*Insisto en que crucemos el río por allí.*

11 What are the people below saying? You'll have to think hard to decide whether it's information (indicative) or if they're asking for something to be done (subjunctive).

➲ "Las llaves **están** en el dormitorio."

Dice que las llaves ....*están*........ en el dormitorio.

➲ "**Compra** papel higiénico, por favor."

Dice que ...*compre*.. papel higiénico.

1. "**Baila** conmigo. **Bailo** muy bien."

Dice que .... con él, que .... muy bien.

2. "Yo **no quiero** ir contigo."

Dice que .... ir conmigo.

3. "¡Que **no quiero** ir contigo!"
Me ha repetido que .... ir conmigo.

4. "**Ten** más cuidado con ese jarrón."

Dice que .... más cuidado con el jarrón.

5. "**No digas** más tonterías."

Dice que .... más tonterías.

6. "**Deja** de decir tonterías."

Insiste en que .... de decir tonterías.

7. "**Pareces** una persona inteligente."

Dice que .... una persona inteligente.

8. "**Eres** muy egoísta, ¿no crees?"

Dice que .... muy egoísta.

9. "**Sé** un poco menos egoísta, ¿quieres?"

Dice que .... un poco menos egoísta.

10. "**Puedo** ayudarte si quieres"

Dice que .... ayudarme si quiero.

11. "**Vas** muy rápido. **Ve** más despacio."

Dice que .... muy rápido, que .... más despacio.

12. "**Come** un poco más. **Comes** muy poco."

Dice que .... un poco más, que .... muy poco.

E Expressing an opinion about information: *Es estupendo que venga*.

■ Remember: when we want **to state** the information that a subordinate verb expresses, we use the indicative. When we want **to query** it, we use the subjunctive:

We state the subordinate information	*Yo sé que Leo **habla** inglés.* *Supongo que **hablará** inglés.*	[We want **to state** that Leo **speaks** English.]
We query the subordinate information	*Es posible que hable inglés.* *No creo que hable inglés.*	[We do not want **to state** that Leo **speaks** English.]

■ However, when the information **is generally accepted** as true or possible, and we only want to **make a comment or give a personal opinion on it**, we always use the **subjunctive** (or infinitive):

We only give our opinion on the subordinate information

A mí no me gusta
Me parece bien
Es lógico
No es normal
Me da igual

que hable inglés.

[We do not want to state that he "speaks English": we only want to say what we know or think about the possible or real fact that he "speaks English".]

¡Tan joven, qué pena...!

No es nada interesante...

¿No os parece un poco extraño...?

Hija, tienes que saber que papá y mamá han encargado un hermanito a la cigüeña, y que ya está de viaje por el cielo.

Me alegra mucho...

...que esté embarazada...

¡Dios mío, qué miedo...!

¡Qué bien que mamá **esté** embarazada!

No es una casualidad...

Es una sorpresa...

Bueno, yo creo que es normal...

Stating → • *¿Sabes qué? Me han dicho que Paula **está** embarazada, y que **es** una niña.*

Questioning → • *¿En serio? No puedo creer que esté embarazada.*

Stating → • *Que sí, mujer, que sí. **Ha ido** al médico, y le ha confirmado que **está** embarazada.*

Only commenting
- *Pues me parece muy extraño...*
- *¿Qué te parece extraño: que esté embarazada o que sea una niña?*
- *No, lo que me parece extraño es que haya ido al médico. Ella odia ir al médico...*

12 Put the opinion markers in the correct place in the table below, depending on their meaning.

Es evidente que... ✓	¿Te parece mal que...? ✓	Sospechamos que... ✓	Me parece lógico que... ✓
Me imagino que...	Es verdaderamente extraño que...	He oído que...	Odio que...
No me importa que...	Su marido piensa que...	Es difícil que...	Yo he visto que...
Es estupendo que...	¿Crees que es importante que...?	¿Ana te ha contado que...?	Me parece que...

Introducing an affirmation or supposition

Es evidente que...

Sospechamos que...

....

....

....

....

....

...**está** embarazada.

(INDICATIVE)

Giving a personal opinion about an idea

Me parece lógico que...

¿Te parece mal que...?

....

....

....

....

....

...**esté** embarazada.

(SUBJUNCTIVE)

13 **2. What do you think? Use the opinion markers in the box (or any others that express your opinion) to say what you think about some of the news items below, as in the example. Use the correct person and tense of the subjunctive in each case.**

➲ Una anciana de 80 años **sobrevive** después de caer desde un sexto piso. ✓

1. Groenlandia **suspende** su festival de nieve por una ola de calor.

2. Dos ex ladrones **presentan** un programa de televisión sobre robos.

3. Más de la mitad de los ministros del gobierno español **son** mujeres.

4. Los japoneses ya **pueden** pagar en los supermercados con la huella dactilar.

5. Una conocida marca de helados **investiga** en la fabricación de un helado para perros.

6. Un juez **manda** a prisión a un hombre por hacer chistes sexistas.

7. Un perro **espera** diez días en la puerta de la comisaría hasta que liberan a su amo.

8. El gobierno **paga** 500 euros mensuales por cada hijo menor de tres años.

Es increíble que una anciana sobreviva después de caer de un sexto piso (➲)

....

....

....

....

....

....

....

....

Me alegra mucho...

Me parece muy triste...

Es increíble...

Es normal...

Me parece muy cómico...

Es curioso...

Me parece muy justo...

Es una tontería...

Está muy bien...

Me parece muy mal...

Me parece ridículo...

Me parece exagerado...

A mí me da igual...

Yo pienso que es lógico...

Me parece preocupante...

...

■ When we express value judgements about information, we can put the subordinate verb
into a personal form of the **subjunctive** (introduced by *que*) or use the simple **infinitive**:

	We use the **infinitive**	We use the **subjunctive**
With OPINION MARKERS like these...	If the subject of the subordinate verb is the same as that of the OPINION MARKERS:	If the subject of the subordinate verb is different to that of the OPINION MARKERS:
Me gusta..., Nos encanta..., Me da igual..., Les alegra..., (No) me importa...	*Le encanta jugar al fútbol.* (a él) = (**él**)	*Le encanta que juguemos al fútbol.* (a él) ⟷ (**nosotros**)
With OPINION MARKERS like these...	To generalise:	To make the person clear:
Es estupendo / extraño / bueno... Está bien / mal... No me parece bien / mal / lógico...	*Es maravilloso estar enamorado.* (in general) = (**tú, yo, nosotros...**)	*Es maravilloso que estés enamorada.* (in general) ⟷ (**specifically you**)

⑭ Identify the subjects of the verbs in bold.

¡Está muy feo **meter**se el dedo en la nariz, Jaimito!

➲ A Lucas no le gusta nada **conducir** de noche.   _Lucas_

➲ Tienes razón, Florentino: es un privilegio **tener** amigos como vosotros.   _En general_

1. Te agradezco mucho que me **digas** eso.
2. Les ha parecido muy emocionante **asistir** a la boda.
3. Perdone, señora. ¿Le importa que me **siente** a su lado?
4. Perdone, señora. ¿Le molestaría **sentar**se en otra parte? La mesa está reservada.
5. Pasen ustedes primero. A mí no me importa **esperar**.
6. Me alegro de que por fin se **acuesten**. ¡Qué pesados estaban hoy los niños!
7. Ya he hecho yo la compra. ¿No te alegras de no **tener** que ir a comprar?
8. Es de muy mal gusto **hacer** esperar a la gente. A ver si otro día llegas antes.
9. No es lógico **pasar** toda la vida esperando un sueño que nunca va a llegar.

F   Identifying or not identifying people, things or places

■ We can give information about the characteristics of people, things or places with an **adjective**, but we can also use a **phrase**:

➲ 42. Joining sentences

	With an adjective:	With a phrase:
A PERSON:	● <u>una chica</u> **mala**...	...es <u>una chica</u> **que hace cosas malas**.
A THING:	● <u>una película</u> muy **divertida**...	...es <u>una película</u> **que da mucha risa**.
A PLACE:	● <u>un sitio</u> **tranquilo**...	...es <u>un sitio</u> **donde te puedes relajar**.

■ When we use a phrase of this type, we express it in the indicative to show that the entity we are talking about (a person, thing or place) **has been identified**, and we use the subjunctive to show that it **has not been identified yet**:

- *He conocido a <u>una chica</u> que **vive** en Móstoles.*   [A specific girl: Lorena.]
- *¿Conoces a <u>alguna chica</u> que **viva** en Móstoles?*   [The specific girl is not important.]

- *Hoy vamos a hacer <u>la comida</u> que más te **gusta**.*   [A specific food: fish.]
- *Hoy vamos a hacer la <u>comida</u> que más te **guste**.*   [Whatever food you choose.]

- *Hemos estado en <u>una playa</u> donde todo el mundo **iba** desnudo.*   [A specific beach: Cantarriján.]
- *¿Tú has visto <u>una playa</u> donde **podamos** ir desnudos?*   [The specific beach is not important.]

¡¡¡Guillaume, c'est moi. Grrrr!!!

Yo tengo un loro que **se llama** Guillermo y que **habla** francés.

¡¡¡Bonjour. Ça va? Grrrr !!!

¡Qué chulo! ¡Yo también quiero tener <u>un loro</u> que **hable** francés!

INDICATIVO	SUBJUNTIVO
Entities already identified	Entities not identified yet
• We are talking about a specific person thing or place with this characteristic.	• We are talking about any person, thing or place with this characteristic.

15 Connect each of the things Jenny says with the most likely explanation.

➔ Hola. Estoy buscando una gramática que **tiene** dibujos en color. ..*b*....

    ~~a. Jenny busca cualquier gramática con dibujos en color.~~

    b. A Jenny le han hablado antes de esa gramática.

1. Bueno, una lengua que **sea** fácil de aprender, por supuesto. ....

    a. Jenny habla del español.

    b. Jenny quiere aprender otra lengua y todavía no ha decidido cuál.

2. ¿Nos llevamos el microondas que **tiene** más potencia o el que **sea** más barato? ....

    a. Han visto varios microondas, pero no saben cuál será más barato.

    b. Están buscando el microondas más potente.

3. Pon esta bandeja en la cocina, donde **estén** los platos. ....

    a. Jenny ha llevado los platos a la cocina antes.

    b. Otra persona ha llevado los platos a la cocina antes.

4. La opinión que Ana **tenga** sí me importa, pero lo que **dice** Jorge me da igual. ....

    a. Jenny ha hablado con Jorge, pero no con Ana.

    b. Jenny ha hablado con Ana, pero no con Jorge.

5. ¿Por qué no comemos en el sitio donde **comimos** la otra vez, en una mesa que **esté** un poco apartada? ....

    a. Jenny se refiere a la segunda mesa a la izquierda.

    b. Jenny se refiere al restaurante "Bona Petí".

16 Decide which of the possible sentence continuations is <u>not</u> possible.

➔ ¿Tienes un cuchillo que... (.*a*.....)
- a. ...corta bien? Éste es malísimo. ~~...corta bien? Éste es malísimo.~~
- b. ...corte bien? Éste es malísimo.
- c. ...corta bien? ¿Y por qué no me lo has dicho antes?

1. Yo voy a casarme con un hombre que... (.......)
- a. ...sabe cómo tratar a una mujer como yo. Si no lo encuentro, no me caso.
- b. ...sabe cómo tratar a una mujer como yo. Tengo suerte, ¿no?
- c. ...sepa cómo tratar a una mujer como yo. Eso lo tengo claro.

2. Yo quiero comprar un apartamento que... (.......)
- a. ...tiene unas vistas al mar preciosas. Lo vimos el otro día en Motril, pero es muy caro.
- b. ...tenga vistas al mar, pero no encuentro ninguno.
- c. ...tiene vistas al mar. ¿Sabes tú de alguno no muy caro?

3. Mira, voy a poner la lámpara donde... (.......)
- a. ...tú has dicho. Me parece lo mejor.
- b. ...tú digas. Así que, por favor, decídete.
- c. ...tú dices. ¿Dónde la pongo?

4. ¿Preparados? El estudiante que... (.......)
- a. ...me diga antes la respuesta gana un chupa-chups.
- b. ...me dice antes la respuesta es siempre Adam. ¿No hay otro que quiera un chupa-chups?
- c. ...me dice antes la respuesta ganará un chupa chups.

■ We can also refer to the characteristics of other entities, like the way of doing something, with an adjective or a phrase:

➔ **42. Joining sentences**

	With an adjective:	With <u>a phrase:</u>
A WAY OF DOING SOMETHING:	● Hazlo de <u>la manera</u> **correcta**.	● Hazlo (de <u>la manera</u> en que) *como* **tú sabes hacerlo**.

■ When we use a phrase of this type with the verb in the indicative, we are referring to a **known** way of doing something. However, if we use the subjunctive, we are talking about a way of doing something that **we cannot** or **do not want to identify**:

- ● Vale, haré la sopa *como* tú **dices**.   [The specific way you say: with meat and vegetables.]
- ● Vale, haré la sopa *como* tú **digas**.   [In whatever way you may say, it doesn't matter how.]

17 Decide which of the two options is best, as in the example.

➔ ● ¿Cómo quieres que haga el arroz? ¿Con pollo o con pescado?
  ○ Como tú ~~quieres~~ / quieras. A mí me da exactamente igual.

1. Perdona, pero así, de la manera en que lo **estás** / estés haciendo, no va a funcionar.

2. Como **dice** / diga un amigo mío, un problema deja de ser un problema si no tiene solución.

3. Lo mejor es hacerlo como **dice** / diga Elena. Pregúntale y lo terminamos ahora.

4. Yo no tengo la culpa de que el ordenador no funcione. Yo lo monté como **dice** / diga el libro de instrucciones. Si el libro está equivocado, no es problema mío.

5. ● ¿Adónde vamos a ir de vacaciones este año, cariño?
  ○ Adonde tú **quieres** / quieras, amor mío. ¿Adónde te gustaría más ir?

6. ● ¡Lo siento! ¡No puedo controlar el avión!
  ○ ¡Aterrice como **puede** / pueda, comandante, pero aterrice ya!

7. No, hijo, no. Tienes que coger la cuchara así, como te **dice** / diga mamá.

8. Agustina es una chica simpatiquísima. Habla con ella. Es la que **lleva** / lleve la minifalda roja.

9. Este verano quiero trabajar en un bar para ganar todo el dinero que **puedo** / pueda y poder viajar un poco.

G   Relating two things in time

■ To relate two events in time, we use expressions like *cuando...*, *hasta que...*, *en cuanto...*, *mientras...* or *siempre que...*

● 42. Unir frases

■ We use the **indicative** in the phrase that introduces these expressions when referring to the **past** or the **habitual present**. We use the **subjunctive** when referring to a moment in the **future**:

Past: *Cuando **salí** del trabajo, me fui a casa.*
Habitual: *Cuando **salgo** del trabajo, voy directo a casa.*
Future: *Cuando salga del trabajo, me iré a casa.*

> 👁 We do not use the subjunctive in questions about the future introduced by the question word *cuándo*:
>
> *¿Cuándo **vuelve** Ricardo?*   *¿Cuándo vuelva Ricardo?*
> *¿Sabes cuándo **terminaremos**?*   *¿Sabes cuándo terminemos?*

18 All the people below are responding to a question asked in a survey. Decide whether they are talking about the past (P), about something habitual (H) or about the future (F)?

¿Y usted?
¿Hace usted deporte?

➲ Yo, siempre que tengo tiempo.   ...H...

➲ Bueno, cuando estaba en la escuela, sí.   ...P....

➲ En cuanto me compre la bici, seguro.   ...F...

1. No, sólo hasta que me casé.   ....

2. Sí, cuando me siento muy estresado.   ....

3. Un poco, hasta que me canso.   ....

4. Sí, mientras espero el autobús hago flexiones.   ....

5. Mientras pueda, sí.   ....

6. Claro que sí: en cuanto salgo del trabajo.   ....

7. Cuando sea un poco mayor, quizá.   ....

19 First, decide whether the sentences are about the past (P), habits (H), or the future (F), then write in the correct forms of the verbs.

➲ .F..   Te llamaré cuando ....*pueda*........ , mañana antes de las 10 si es posible.

1. .....   Cuando .... cocino yo, pero normalmente no tengo tiempo.

2. .....   Antes iba a la playa siempre que .... , pero ahora ya no voy nunca.

3. .....   Cuando .... una cerveza, tengo que ir al baño inmediatamente.

4. .....   Vi a Marta mientras .... unas cervezas con Lourdes y Javier.

5. .....   Voy a ir a verles en cuanto .... una decisión definitiva, no te preocupes.

6. .....   Clara y yo nos conocimos cuando .... la carrera: estudiamos juntos.

7. .....   Lo siento, pero tendrás que esperar hasta que .... ese examen.

8. .....   Me duele muchísimo la cabeza cuando .... aerobic.

Poder

Tomar

Hacer

H   Corresponding time references between the indicativo and the subjuntivo.

■ The forms of the subjunctive that we use to refer to different tenses,
correspond to the forms of the indicative in the following way:

If in the **indicative** we say...	In the **subjunctive** we say...
Está / Estará en Berlín.	*Es posible que esté allí.*
Ha estado / Habrá estado en Berlín.	*Es posible que haya estado allí.*
Estaba / Estuvo / Estaría en Berlín.	*Es posible que estuviera allí.*
Había estado / Habría estado en Berlín.	*Es posible que hubiera estado allí.*

20 Complete the responses by putting the verbs in bold into the appropriate form of the subjunctive.

If we state:

- La niña **lloraba** cuando veía a Emilio.
- Yo, en tu lugar, creo que me **callaría**.
- Alguien nos **encontrará**. No te preocupes.
- Aquí hay dos personas que **tienen** más de 30 años.
- Laila me **visitó** el verano pasado.
- Sólo tomamos un café. Ya **habíamos comido**.
- No ha dicho nada porque no **ha querido** molestar.
- Me imagino que **habrán previsto** esa posibilidad.
- Ya sabes que me **voy** mañana.
- No te contestó porque se **habría quedado** dormido.
- Yo antes **pensaba** que el subjuntivo significaba duda.

If we do not state:

→ ○ A mí no me extraña que la niña ...*llorara*... .
1. ○ Pues si yo fuera tú, no creo que me ....
2. ○ No, no creo que nadie nos .... Preocúpate.
3. ○ ¿Hay alguien aquí que .... más de 30 años?
4. ○ Yo le pedí que me ....
5. ○ Sí, y les sorprendió mucho que ya ....
6. ○ Es lógico que no .... molestar.
7. ○ Sí, puede ser que .... esa posibilidad.
8. ○ ¡Pero yo no quiero que te .... !
9. ○ Sí, es probable que se .... dormido.
10. ○ ¿En serio? ¡No me puedo creer que .... eso!

21 Nemesio Contreras is still questioning everything that Dr Ginés Labella says.
Complete the notes that he took during the conference with the form of the
subjunctive that corresponds to the verbs in bold.

→ "La mujer **ha sido** siempre poco valorada."
1. "La mujer **es**, en realidad, la base de la historia del hombre."
2. "La historia **ha ocultado** grandes verdades sobre la mujer."
3. "Algunos documentos históricos aseguran que Cristóbal Colón **era** una mujer."
4. "Diversas fuentes sugieren que la rueda la **inventó** una mujer."
5. "Nunca un hombre **podrá** quedarse embarazado."
6. "Mi marido siempre **ha estado** de acuerdo con mis ideas."
7. "Y esto es todo, lo siento. No sé quién me ha robado la última página
   de la conferencia. **Habrá sido** mi marido."

→ No es del todo cierto que la mujer ...*haya sido*... siempre poco valorada.
1. Yo no pienso que la mujer .... la base de la historia.
2. No es cierto que la historia .... nada sobre la mujer.
3. ¡Es mentira que Colón .... una mujer!
4. La verdad, no puedo imaginarme que una mujer .... la rueda.
5. Dudo mucho que un hombre no .... quedarse embarazado.
6. Francamente, no me creo que su marido siempre .... de acuerdo con ella.
7. No es verdad que .... su marido, porque he sido yo.

34. Imperativo

A   Uses

■ We use the imperative to **make a direct request** for someone else to do something. A direct request can take many different forms:

Give instructions	● **Seguid** todo recto unos 100 metros y, luego, **girad** a la derecha.
Polite request	● **Ayúdame**, por favor, **dime** qué te ha dicho.
Order	● ¡**Sal** de ahí ahora mismo!
Advise	● Tienes mala cara. **Descansa** un poco y luego seguimos.
Invite	● **Venid** a mi casa mañana. Hago una fiesta.
Give permission	● ¿Puedo pasar?
	○ **Pasa, pasa.**

1 In all the following sentences, someone is asking another person to do something. Identify the type of request being made. Use a dictionary if necessary.

➲ ¡Dejad de molestar a Samuel, que es muy pequeño! ..*order*............

1. Hazlo tú, por favor. Yo no puedo. ....

2. ¡Bajad de ese árbol ahora mismo! ....

3. Ve a la ventana de "Herramientas", **pulsa** "Opciones" y ahí está. ....

4. ● ¿Puedo probar tu postre?

   ○ Claro, **pruébalo**, está buenísimo. ....

5. **Entrad** y **poneos** cómodos. Estáis en vuestra casa. ....

6. ● ¿Y qué puedo hacer yo, si no estoy enamorada de él?

   ○ **Dile** que eres todavía muy joven para casarte. A lo mejor así te deja tranquila. ....

> Request
> Order ✓
> Invitation
> Permission
> Order
> Instruction
> Advice

B   Imperativo with *tú*: *come*...

■ The **regular form** of the imperative for the *tú* person is the same as the third person singular of the *Presente de indicativo*, in all conjugations:

Yo	*como*	
Tú	*comes*	
Él, ella, usted	**come**	¡*Come*!
Nosotros/-as	*comemos*	
Vosotros/-as	*coméis*	
Ellos, ellas, ustedes	*comen*	

● Maribel no <u>habla</u>. **Habla** tú, por favor.
● Si él no <u>come</u> nada, **come** tú algo al menos.
● Todo el mundo <u>vive</u> su vida. **Vive** tú la tuya.

■ There are only eight **irregular** forms:

Ir	→	*Ve*	Poner	→	*Pon*
Salir	→	*Sal*	Decir	→	*Di*
Venir	→	*Ven*	Tener	→	*Ten*
Hacer	→	*Haz*	Ser	→	*Sé*

👁 The corresponding compound verbs have the same irregularity:

Pro**poner**	→	*propón*	Man**tener**	→	*mantén*
Sos**tener**	→	*sostén*	Entre**tener**	→	*entretén*
Su**poner**	→	*supón*	Des**hacer**	→	*deshaz* etc.

Toma. Esto es tuyo.

2 The robot AC-69 can do 69 different things. Ask him for a demonstration

➦ AC-69 **habla** en ruso:

¡ ..*Habla*.......... en ruso, 69!

1. AC-69 **enciende** las luces de la casa a distancia:

¡ .... la luz ahora!

2. AC-69 **llora** como un niño:

¡ .... un poco, 69!

3. AC-69 **sube** y **baja** escaleras:

¡ .... y .... esas escaleras!

4. AC-69 **bebe** whisky con Coca-cola:

¡ .... un poco de whisky!

5. AC-69 **baila** sevillanas:

¡ .... unas sevillanas!

6. AC-69 es educado con la gente cuando quiere:

¡ .... **educado** conmigo, 69!

7. AC-69 **viene** volando hasta donde estás tú:

¡ .... aquí volando, robotito!

8. AC-69 **va** volando a todas partes:

¡ .... a la cocina volando, 69!

9. AC-69 **pone** los pies en la cabeza:

¡ .... el pie izquierdo en la cabeza!

10. AC-69 **dice** "chiripitifláutico" muy rápido:

¡ .... "chiripitifláutico" rápido!

11. AC-69 **sale** de cualquier sitio en 1,5 segundos:

¡ .... de la habitación!

12. AC-69 **hace** paella de marisco:

¡ .... una paella para mí!

13. AC-69 **propone** planes:

¡ .... algo para el fin de semana!

C Imperativo with *vosotros*: *comed*...

■ The vosotros form of the imperative is formed by changing the **-r** of the infinitive to a **-d**. There are no irregularities. In informal language, you can also use the infinitive:

INFINITIVE

Comer → ¡*Comed*! / ¡*Comer*!

Tomad. Esto es vuestro.

- *Si queréis **hacer** algo, **haced**/hacer la ensalada.*
- *Yo no voy a **ir** a la fiesta. **Id**/Ir vosotros.*
- *¡Hay que **salir** rápido! ¡**Salid**/Salir ya!*

■ In spoken language, these **-d** or **-r** endings are often not pronounced clearly. For this reason, it is very important to identify the stressed syllable, to differentiate between the *tú* and *vosotros* in many regular forms:

We request something from one person (*tú*)	We request something from several people (*vosotros*)
¡B**a**ila! ¡C**o**me! ¡L**e**e!	¡Bail**a**d! ¡Com**e**d! ¡Le**e**d! ¡Bail**a**r! ¡Com**e**r! ¡Le**e**r!

3 What changes if *mamá* has two children?

➦ **Escucha** lo que voy a decirte.

..*Escuchad*..... lo que voy a deciros.

1. **Ve** a casa de la abuela.

.... a casa de la abuela.

2. **Toma** el camino del río.

.... el camino del río.

3. **Sigue** ese camino sin entrar en el bosque.

.... ese camino sin entrar en el bosque.

4. **Ten** cuidado de no ensuciarte la ropa.

.... cuidado de no ensuciaros la ropa.

5. **Habla** con ella un poco. A ella le gusta oírte.

.... con ella un poco. A ella le gusta oíros.

6. **Haz** tus deberes con ella. Necesita compañía.

.... vuestros deberes con ella. Necesita compañía.

7. **Sé** bueno con ella. Es muy viejecita.

.... buenos con ella. Es muy viejecita.

8. Y **ven** pronto: antes del anochecer.

Y .... pronto: antes del anochecer.

9. **Vuelve** antes de las siete.

.... antes de las siete.

D Imperativo with *usted* and *ustedes*: *coma, coman...*

■ To make a direct request in formal situations, we use **the third person singular or plural of the *Presente de subjuntivo***:

USTED	USTEDES
Tome, señora. Esto es suyo.	**Tomen**, señoras. Esto es suyo.

- *Bueno, vamos a ver.* **Dígame** *dónde le duele.*
- *Pasajeros del vuelo HL-323,* **diríjan**se *a la puerta B-5.*
- **Oiga**, *¿puede decirme la hora?*
- **Perdone**, *¿para ir a la calle Pallá?*
- **Miren** *a su derecha y verán el palacio del sultán.*

➲ 32. Forms of the subjuntivo

4 How does the form of these requests change if you are talking in a formal situation?

➲ Ve al médico. No tienes buena cara.

....*Vaya*........ al médico. No tiene buena cara.

1. ¡Ahora, rápido, **sal**!

   ¡Ahora, rápido, ... !

2. ¿Puedes hacerme un favor? **Traduce** esto.

   Martínez, ... esto, por favor.

3. ¿Qué os ha pasado? **Hablad** sin miedo.

   ¿Qué les ha pasado? .... sin miedo.

4. **Perdona**. No sabía que estabas aquí.

   .... No sabía que estaba usted aquí.

5. **Ten**. Este dinero es tuyo.

   .... Este dinero es suyo. Gracias.

6. **Oye**, Julio, ¿me puedo ir ya o me necesitas?

   ...., señor Carreras, ¿me puedo ir un poco antes?

7. **Haced** el favor de callaros un poco, ¿vale?

   .... el favor de callarse. Estamos en un hospital.

8. **Pon** aquí tu nombre y dirección, y te lo mando.

   .... aquí su nombre y dirección, y se lo mando.

9. **Venid** mañana, que hoy estoy muy ocupado.

   La doctora ha tenido que salir. .... mañana.

E Imperativo negativo: *no comas, no comáis, no coma, no coman...*

■ To make negative requests, we **always** use the *Presente de subjuntivo*, in all persons:

➲ 32. Forms of the subjuntivo

	POSITIVE IMPERATIVE	NEGATIVE IMPERATIVE
Tú	*Come*	*No **comas***
Vosotros/-as	*Comed*	*No **comáis***
Usted	**Coma**	*No **coma***
Ustedes	**Coman**	*No **coman***

👁 We can make negative requests with *no* or with any other expression with a negative meaning:

- *No beba, **ni** fume. **Tampoco** coma grasas.*
- ***Jamás** me mientas.*

- ***Nunca** vuelvas a hacer eso.*

5 Esteban has a lot of problems. Give him some advice, as in the example.

➲ • Como demasiado.

   ○ Pues no ....*comas*........... tanto, hombre.

1. • Fumo demasiado.

   ○ Pues no .... tanto.

2. • **Salgo** todas las noches hasta muy tarde.

   ○ Pues no ....

3. • **Bebo** mucho, y despúes conduzco.

   ○ Hombre, si conduces, no ....

4. • **Conduzco** muy rápido.

   ○ Pues ten cuidado y no .... tan rápido.

5. • Siempre **pienso** negativamente.

   ○ Pues de ahora en adelante no .... así.

6. • **Tengo** miedo de hablar con la gente.

   ○ Pues no .... miedo. Nadie te va hacer nada.

7. • **Creo** que nadie me quiere.

   ○ No .... eso. Mucha gente te quiere.

6 **What changes if the problems are now for both Esteban and his brother Sebastian?**

➔ ● Comemos demasiado.

   ○ Pues no ...*comáis*...... tanto.

1. ● Fumamos demasiado.

   ○ Pues no .... tanto.

2. ● Salimos todas las noches hasta muy tarde.

   ○ Pues no ....

3. ● Bebemos mucho y después conducimos.

   ○ Hombre, si conducís, no ....

4. ● Conducimos muy rápido.

   ○ Pues tened cuidado y no .... tan rápido.

5. ● Siempre **pensamos** negativamente.

   ○ Pues de ahora en adelante no .... así.

6. ● **Tenemos** miedo de hablar con la gente.

   ○ Pues no .... miedo. Nadie os va a hacer nada.

7. ● **Creemos** que nadie nos quiere.

   ○ No .... eso. Mucha gente os quiere.

F   **Imperativo with pronouns:** *Dímelo / No me lo digas*

■ With the positive imperative, the pronouns come after the verb, and form a single word. With the negative imperative the pronouns come in their normal order, in front of the verb and separate.

➔ 16. Position and combination

➔ 44. Accentuation

Normal order	POSITIVE IMPERATIVE	NEGATIVE IMPERATIVE
● Ella **me lo** <u>cuenta</u> todo.	● <u>Cuéntamelo</u> todo.	● No **me lo** <u>cuentes</u> todo.
● Pepa **nos** <u>ayuda</u> mucho.	● <u>Ayúdanos</u>, ¿quieres?	● No **nos** <u>ayudes</u>. No es necesario.
● Su tía **le** <u>regala</u> siempre juguetes.	● <u>Regaladle</u> ese juguete.	● No **le** <u>regaléis</u> ese juguete.
● **Se los** <u>regala</u> porque lo quiere.	● <u>Regáleselos</u> usted.	● No **se los** <u>regale</u>.

---

7 **Give José some advice.**

➔ Alejandro habla con cariño a Claudia. ....*Háblale*.... tú también así.

1. Alejandro le escribe poesías y se las lee. .... tú poesías y ....

2. Alejandro la llama por teléfono cada día. .... tú también.

3. Alejandro la quiere y se lo dice a todas horas. .... tú también.

4. Alejandro la acompaña cuando va de compras porque no le gusta ir sola. .... tú también.

5. A Alejandro no le molestan sus caprichos y se los perdona. .... tú también.

6. A ella no le gusta hacer la comida y Alejandro se la hace muchas veces. .... tú también.

7. Alejandro se ducha todos los días y se pone guapo cuando va a verla. .... y .... guapo tú también, hombre.

¿Por qué Claudia está enamorada de Alejandro y no de mí?

8 **Complete the table with the missing verb forms, as in the example. Be careful with the position of the pronouns!**

Tú	Dímelo.	Dáselas.	....	....	Tráenoslo.
	No me lo digas.	No se las des.	No	No	No ....
Vosotros	Decídmelo.	*Dádselas*	Pensadlo.	....	....
	No me lo digáis.	No	No	No os sentéis.	No ....
Usted	Dígamelo.	Déselas.	....	....	....
	No me lo diga.	No	No lo piense.	No	No ....
Ustedes	Díganmelo.	Dénselas.	....	Siéntense.	....
	No me lo digan.	No	No lo piensen.	No	No ....

35. *Ser* and *estar*

A *Ser*: *Julio César es un gato.*

■ We use the verb *ser* to:

Define words or concepts

- *Un planeta **es** un astro sin luz que puede tener satélites.*
- *Un gato **es** un felino doméstico.*

Express the particular characteristics of an object

- *La Tierra **es** redonda.*
- *Julio César **es** blanco y marrón.*

Define or classify an object

- *La Tierra **es** un planeta.*
- *Julio César **es** un gato.*

Identify the object we are referring to

- *La Tierra **es** el tercer planeta del sistema solar.*
- *Julio César **es** el gato de Ainhoa.*

➲ 4. Adjective

Thus, we can use the verb *ser* to talk about:

Identity:
- *Ésa **es** <u>María</u>.*

Character:
- *Manuel **es** <u>muy tímido</u>.*

Characteristics:
- *¡Oh! **Es** <u>muy bonito</u>. Gracias.*
- *El examen **ha sido** <u>fácil</u>.*

Classification:
- *Esto **es** <u>un abanico</u>.*
- *Los perros **son** <u>mamíferos</u>.*

Origin:
- *Rodolfo **es** <u>cubano</u>.*

Material:
- *¿Este anillo **será** <u>de oro</u>?*

Profession:
- ***Era** <u>médico</u>. Bueno, **era** <u>radiólogo</u>.*

Shape:
- *Mi dormitorio **es** <u>rectangular</u>.*

Make:
- *Mi móvil **es** <u>Mokia</u>.*

Colour:
- *No, mi coche **era** <u>verde</u>.*

Family relationships:
- ***Es** <u>mi sobrino</u>.*
- *Antonio **fue** <u>mi novio</u>.*

Date and time:
- *El lunes **es** <u>Navidad</u>.*
- *¿Ya **son** <u>las cinco</u>?*

👁 In Spanish we do not use the verb *ser* to talk about age. We use the verb *tener*:
- ***Tengo** veinte años.* [~~Soy veinte años.~~]

**1 1 At the Lost Property Office, Señora Olvido Pertinaz is describing all the things she has lost.
Link up the words in the different columns.**

Mi bolso — negro. — de piel. — bastante grande.

Mis guantes — **es** — de lana. — **Es** — Ricsson. — **Es** — pequeñísimos.

Mis gafas — **son** — de sol. — **Son** — rojos. — **Son** — cuadradas.

Mi móvil — rojo. — muy oscuras. — un poco antiguo.

B   *Estar*: Julio César está dormido.

■ We use the verb *estar* to talk about the **situation** of an object.
"Situation" can be **location** in space (**where** the object is) or **state**
(**how** the object is):

⊙ 4. Adjective

Locate objects in space

State in which an object is

Está debajo   Está en   Está   Está
de la mesa.   el árbol.   lejos.   cerca.

Está   Está   Está   Está
tumbado.   sentado.   asustado.   dormido.

- ● ¿*Dónde* **está** el banco?
- ○ **Está** <u>muy cerca de aquí</u>.
- ▲ **Está** <u>a unos cien metros</u>.

- ● Madrid **está** <u>en el centro de España</u>.

- ● ¿Dónde dejaste las llaves?
- ○ **Estaban** <u>en la mesa del recibidor</u>.

- ● ¿Y Martín?
- ○ **Está** <u>en la ducha</u>.

- ● ¿Qué tal Paloma?
- ○ Bueno, **está** <u>bien</u>. La verdad es que **está**
  <u>más animada</u>, pero aún **está** <u>un poco
  triste</u> a veces.

- ● Oye, la puerta **está** <u>abierta</u>.
- ○ Sí, es que **está** <u>rota</u>.

Estar bien/mal...	*Estar de buen humor/*
Estar solo/acompañado...	*de mal humor...*
Estar roto/arreglado...	*Estar harto/aburrido...*
Estar vacío/lleno...	*Estar vivo/muerto...*
Estar abierto/cerrado...	*Estar enfermo/sano/*
Estar de pie/sentado/	*loco...*
tumbado...	*Estar cansado/agotado...*
Estar alegre/triste/	*Estar dormido/*
contento/animado...	*despierto...*

⊙ 36. *Haber* and *estar*

---

2 Ernestina is very absent-minded and can never find anything. Her partner has left her a message
written in a series of notes, telling her where the things she has lost are. Complete it.

Nena:

   ¿Dónde tienes
   la cabeza?

El anillo ➡ ..está..
encima de la mesilla
de noche.

Las llaves (1) ....
dentro del cajón de
la mesa del estudio.

Los regalos para tus
sobrinos (2) ....
dentro del armario
de tu habitación.

Tu bolso (3) ....
en la percha de la
entrada.

Y yo, yo (4) ....
en Las Bahamas.
(5) .... cansado
de buscar todas tus
cosas.

Volveré.
Sólo necesito
un DESCANSO.

Ah, los billetes de
tren para ir a casa
de tu madre no
(6) .... en casa,

(7) .... en la
agencia de viajes.

¿Te acuerdas de en
qué calle (8) ....
la agencia?

Eso espero. Un beso,

   TONY

3 Compete the correct answer with *ser* or *estar* and cross out the incorrect one.

➲ Dos más dos...
a. ..*son*.. cuatro.
b. ..~~...~~.. seis.

3. La capital de Perú...
a. .... Montevideo.
b. .... Lima.

6. Sevilla...
a. .... en Galicia.
b. .... en Andalucía.

9. El Atlántico...
a. .... un océano.
b. .... un mar.

1. El Sol...
a. .... a 180.000 km. de la Tierra.
b. .... a un año luz de la Tierra.

4. Los Pirineos...
a. .... unas montañas que separan España de Francia.
b. .... unas islas.

7. Las islas Baleares...
a. .... en el mar Cantábrico.
b. .... en el mar Mediterráneo.

10. La Tierra...
a. .... más lejos del Sol que Marte.
b. .... más cerca del Sol que Marte.

2. La Luna...
a. .... un satélite.
b. .... un planeta.

5. La bandera española...
a. .... roja.
b. .... roja y amarilla.

8. Una persona agotada es una persona que...
a. .... cansada.
b. .... dormida.

11. El régimen político español...
a. .... una monarquía.
b. .... una república.

4 Write short descriptions, like those in the example, of Pedro and Juan. Use the words in the box and either *ser* or *estar*.

> Contento
> Un chico
> Joven
> Rubio
> Sentado
> Deportista
> Moreno
> Un hombre ✓
> Mayor
> Triste
> Bajo
> Tumbado ✓
> Alto
> Oficinista

Juan es un hombre.
....
....
....
....
....
....

Pedro está tumbado.
....
....
....
....
....
....
....

5 Pedro is showing his friend Rocío a photo. Circle the correct verbs.

Mira, ésta ➲ (es)/ está mi familia. (1) Éramos / Estábamos en un restaurante. Ese día (2) estaba / era el cumpleaños de mi madre. (3) Éste soy / estoy yo. (4) Tenía / Era 10 años. (5) Ese día era / estaba muy enfadado porque no me gustaban los zapatos que llevaba. El del bigote (6) es / está mi padre, y el chico que (7) es / está a su lado (8) es / está mi hermano mayor, Andrés. Ésas que (9) están / son sentadas (10) están / son mis primas. (11) Son / Están gemelas. Ése del fondo (12) es / está mi tío Raúl. (13) Estaba / Era jugador de fútbol pero ahora (14) está / es retirado. La que (15) es / está detrás (16) es / está mi madre. El bebé que tiene en brazos (17) es / está Clara, mi hermana pequeña. (18) Estaba / Era dormida. ¿La ves?

36. *Haber* and *estar*

A   Forms of *haber*: *hay*, *había*, *habrá*...

■ The verb *haber* has two forms, the personal and the impersonal.

The **personal form** is used to make compound tenses. For example:

PRETÉRITO PERFECTO	PRET. PLUSCUAMPERFECTO	FUTURO PERFECTO
Presente of *haber*	Imperfecto of *haber*	Futuro of *haber*

he has ha hemos habéis han PAST PARTICIPLE	había habías había habíamos habíais habían PAST PARTICIPLE	habré habrás habrá habremos habréis habrán PAST PARTICIPLE

- Eugenia no **ha** <u>venido</u> a trabajar, ¿sabes?
- ¿**Has** <u>ido</u> al concierto de los Repanocha?

- En esa época yo ya **había** <u>terminado</u> la universidad.
- Cuando llegó la policía, los ladrones **habían** <u>huido</u>.

- Tómese estas pastillas. Dentro de una hora el dolor **habrá** <u>desaparecido</u>.
- Las lentejas ya se **habrán** <u>enfriado</u> un poco. Ya te las puedes comer.

- 22. Pretérito perfecto
- 23. Pret. pluscuamperfecto
- 29. Futuro perfecto

The **impersonal form** is made with the **third person singular** of the verb *haber* in the tense in question, with the exception of the *Presente de indicativo*, which has a special form. For example:

PRESENTE	PRET. PERFECTO	INDEFINIDO	IMPERFECTO	FUTURO	F. PERFECTO
hay	*ha habido*	*hubo*	*había*	*habrá*	*habrá habido*

- En España **hay** más de cuarenta millones de habitantes.
- Esta mañana **ha habido** un problema y no hemos podido llegar a tiempo.
- Al final **hubo** un problema y no pudimos llegar a tiempo.
- **Habrá habido** algún problema, porque no han llegado a tiempo.
- Dentro de unos años ya no **habrá** ordenadores grandes. Sólo **habrá** de bolsillo.
- Hace unos años en este pueblecito no **había** coches. **Había** gallinas, cabras, vacas... pero no **había** coches.

👁   The impersonal forms never change:

[En mi escuela ~~habían~~ muchos estudiantes extranjeros.]
    había

[Este verano ~~han habido~~ bastantes tormentas.]
    ha habido

1 Choose the appropriate form of the present of the verb *haber* and link the two halves of the dialogues.

➥ ● Perdone, ¿sabe si ...*hay*. un banco por aquí cerca? —————— a. ○ Sí, aquí en la esquina hay uno. El Mangal.

1. ● Lo siento, pero no .... gazpacho. Se .... terminado.   b. ○ Sí, y todos son muy agradables con los turistas.

2. ● Pepón no .... aprobado casi nada. Tiene que repetir curso.   c. ○ No, todavía no. Llamarán más tarde, imagino.

3. ● ¿En el Cabo de Gata .... playas tranquilas?   d. ○ Es que ha estudiado poquísimo.

4. ● ¿........ llamado los Hernández?   e. ○ Buenas, pero cortas. Muy cortas.

5. ● ¿Y vosotros? ¿........ tenido unas buenas vacaciones?   f. ○ ¿Ya está mejor?

6. ● En este pueblo .... gente muy amable. Ya verás.   g. ○ Sí, y muy bonitas, además.

7. ● Chicos, no .... berberechos. ¿Queréis patatas fritas?   h. ○ No, que engordan muchísimo.

8. ● Esta mañana mi padre y yo .... ido a ver a la abuela al hospital.   i. ○ ¿Y tienen alguna otra sopa fría?

2 Guiri Forastérez does not know much Spanish. Correct the following notes about the city of Granalona, taken from his exercise book, where he makes several mistakes with the verb *haber.*

➥ El verano pasado en esta ciudad habían muchos turistas. ...*había*...........

➥ Antes había muchos niños por las calles y plazas. Ahora casi no hay niños. .....✓.............

1. Hace años no habían coches ni motos, pero hubieron muchos cambios
   y ahora hay muchos coches. ....

2. Antes había mucho silencio. No habían ruidos. ....

3. Pero antes no había ordenadores ni cibercafés. ....

4. Este año han habido unas fiestas maravillosas. ....

5. En las fiestas del año próximo habrán más petardos que este año. ....

6. Ha habido más gente en el mes de agosto que en todo el año. ....

B   Uses of *haber* in the impersonal form: *¿Hay un hospital por aquí cerca?*

■ We use the impersonal forms of the verb *haber* to express **the fact that something exists.** We do this when we think or know that our interlocutor does not have this information:

He alquilado un piso amueblado con un salón precioso.

Ah, ¿y cómo es el salón?

Pues, mira, a la izquierda **hay** un sofá azul. Enfrente del sofá **hay** una mesa alta y junto a la mesa **hay** una ventana grande con unas cortinas verdes.

Ummm, parece bonito...

● *Perdone, ¿**hay** una farmacia por aquí?*
○ *Sí, **hay** una a unos cien metros.*

[The person speaking does not know if there is a Chemist's.]
[The person speaking tells their listener that there is a Chemist's, and knows that they do not have this information.]

● *En mi barrio **hay** varias galerías de arte contemporáneo.*

[The person speaking assumes that their listener does not know that these galleries exist in their neighbourhood.]

● *¿Ves ese edificio? Pues antes ahí **había** unos árboles centenarios preciosos.*

[The person speaking assumes that their listener does not know that there used to be trees in that area.]

3 With the help of the Ojubber telescope, Casimiro has found two new planets: Vepiturno and Marsatón. He now has to write a report on everything there is on the two planets, and has to cover the points listed below. Help him to write it.

➲ Animales (vacas, caballos): ......*En Vepiturno hay vacas. En Marsatón no hay vacas, pero hay caballos.*......

....

1. Vegetación (plantas, árboles): ....

....

2. Geografía (ríos, montañas, mares): ....

....

3. Vivienda (casas, rascacielos): ....

....

4. Habitantes (muchos, pocos, niños, personas mayores): ....

....

....

C   *Haber/Estar: Hay varios hospitales, pero el Hospital General está en la esquina.*

■ The verb **haber** can be combined with elements that enable us to talk about objects that cannot be identified by the listener:

- ● ¿En tu país **hay** <u>olivos</u>?
- ○ Sí, **hay** <u>muchísimos</u>. Producimos mucho aceite.

- ● ¿**Hay** <u>un</u> mercado por aquí?
- ○ Sí, **hay** <u>dos</u>. El Central y el de Santa María.

- ● En esta zona **habrá** <u>diez o doce monumentos famosos</u>.

- ● Creo que en esa avenida **había** <u>algunas tiendas</u> bastante baratas.

- ● Uf, vamos a otro restaurante. Aquí no **hay** <u>nadie</u>. Seguro que no es bueno.

- ● ¿**Hay** <u>algo</u> que tengas que decirme?
- ○ No, nada.

■ The verb *estar* can be used to locate elements that can be identified by the listener:

¿Y el cuadro que te regalé?

Está encima del sofá.

> 35. *Ser* and *estar*

- *Perdone, ¿**hay** <u>una farmacia</u> por aquí?*
- *Sí, **hay** una a unos cien metros.*
- *¿Y dónde **está**?*

[In this exchange, the two people are talking about whether there is a *farmacia*: one is asking and the other answering]
[Now that the *farmacia* has been identified and they know it exists, it is a question of locating the *farmacia* that has been identified.]

- *Oiga, ¿sabe dónde **está** <u>El Corting Less</u>?*

[The person speaking assumes that the other knows of the existence of El Corting Less.]

- *¿<u>Madrid</u> **está** cerca de Salamanca o no?*

[The person is talking about the city of Madrid, something they assume is perfectly well identified.]

- *¡Socorro!, ¿dónde **están** <u>mi cartera y mis llaves</u>?*

[The person is talking about something that is perfectly identified.]

👁 When we use **haber** in the impersonal form (hay, había...), the nouns can be used without a determiner or accompanied by indefinite determiners, cardinal numbers or quantifiers. When we use **estar**, the nouns can be accompanied by definite articles, demonstratives and possessives

- *¿<u>Hay</u> **algún** médico en la sala?*
- *¿<u>Está</u> **el** médico de guardia en la sala?* [¿Hay el médico de guardia en la sala?]

- *<u>Hay</u> **tres** informes que no encuentro por ninguna parte.*
- *Aquí <u>están</u> **aquellos** informes que buscabas.* [Aquí hay aquellos informes que buscabas.]

4 Casimiro is telling his friend Ada Mir what he has seen on Vepiturno. Complete the dialogue with the verb *estar* or with *hay*.

Casi: ➜ ...*Hay*.... bastantes vacas, pero las vacas tienen más de cuatro patas.

Ada: ¿En serio (1) .... vacas? ¿Y dónde (2) ....?

Casi: En el polo norte, al lado de unos árboles.

Ada: ¡Ah!, pero ¿ (3) .... árboles?

Casi: Sí, (4) .... todos en el Norte. En el Sur sólo (5) .... nieve, mucha nieve.

Ada: ¿Y no (6) .... gente?

Casi: Bueno, (7) .... uno o dos pueblos. Parecen pueblos porque (8) .... unas casitas que (9) .... todas juntas...

Ada: ¿Y (10) .... coches?

Casi: No, no (11) .... ninguno. Pero (12) .... algo que parece un pájaro verde muy grande. ¿Puede ser un avión?

Ada: ¿Dónde (13) .... ? ¿En el campo?

Casi: No, no, (14) .... cerca del pueblo. Sí, seguramente es un avión o una nave espacial... ¿Sabes qué (15) .... al lado del poblado?

Ada: No, ¿qué?

Casi: Es terrible, Ada. (16) .... un anuncio de Cocacuela y un edificio de Yanoquea. Estamos perdidos.

5 Anita is very worried because she doesn't know whether the Three Wise Men will be able to find her new home, to deliver her toys on the night of 5th January, so she writes them a letter. Help her choose the right verbs.

Queridos Reyes Magos:

Este año hemos cambiado de casa y quiero explicaros dónde hay/está la nueva. En Barcelona hay/está una calle que se llama Vía Layetana. En esta calle no hay/está mi casa. Es una calle muy larga que va al mar. En esta calle hay/están muchos edificios bastante altos. A mitad de la calle, hay/está un trozo de las murallas romanas. Enfrente de las murallas romanas hay/está una callecita muy estrecha y en la esquina hay/está "La Colmena", que es una pastelería muy buena. Bueno, pues al lado de esa pastelería hay/está un portal muy grande, de madera. Ésa es la puerta de mi casa. Cuando entras, hay/está una puerta de hierro muy grande. Es la puerta del ascensor. Tenéis que subir al quinto piso. Al salir hay/están dos puertas, una, a la derecha, y otra, a la izquierda. La de la derecha es la de mi casa. En mi casa hay/están cuatro dormitorios. Mucho cuidado, mi dormitorio hay/está al final del pasillo. En la puerta hay/está un cartel que pone "Anita". Yo soy Anita. Traedme muchos regalos, que he sido muy buena este año.

Un beso para los tres,

Anita

Dibujos de Ángela Castañeda González

37. Periphrastic verbs: *Va a salir. Está saliendo...*

A *Ir a* + INFINITIVE: *voy a comer, iba a comer...*

■ With the **Presente of *Ir a*** + INFINITIVE we can talk about a future event as a logical result of things that we know in the present. This multi-word or periphrastic verb is used to predict or ask about a future that we consider to be **obvious**:

- *El tren tiene un problema mecánico.* **Va a salir** *con retraso.* [It is obvious.]
- *No comas tanto.* **Vas a ponerte** *enfermo.* [It is logical.]

voy
vas
va   **a**   INFINITIVE
vamos
vais
van

Esta tarde **va a llover**.

¿Cuándo **va a nacer** mi hermanito, mamá?

---

❶ What is going to happen? It is fairly clear, isn't it? Use the following verbs.

| saltar |
| suspender |
| caerse ✓ |

Una niña pequeña está jugando encima de una mesa.

➥ .....*Se va a caer*.............

Juanito no ha estudiado nada para este examen.

| entrar |
| explotar |
| nevar |

1. ....

Unos señores se dirigen a un restaurante.

2. ....

Hace mucho frío y el cielo está gris.

3. ....

Una bomba está activada.

4. ....

Un deportista corre hacia una valla.

5. ....

■ We can also use this periphrastic verb to talk about decisions or plans, or to ask about the intentions, decisions or plans of others:

- *Livio* **va a ir** *a la fiesta de Bea. Me lo ha dicho hoy.* [It is his intention or plan.]
- *El año que viene* **voy a estudiar** *más.* [It is his/her decision or plan.]
- *¿Qué* **vas a hacer** *este fin de semana?* [We are asking about his/her plans.]
- *Bueno, ¿* **vas a ayudarme** *o no?* [We are waiting for a decision.]

➲ 16. Position and combination

---

❷ All your friends have plans. Ask them what they are with *Ir a* + INFINITIVE.

➥ Rosa quiere **hacer** muchas cosas el próximo verano.

  1. Pedro y Ángel quieren **estudiar** algún idioma.

  2. Alberto quiere **comer** y está preparando algo en la cocina.

  3. Xavi está en Francia y piensa **volver** pronto a España.

  4. Patricio tiene la intención de **comprar**se un coche nuevo.

  5. Jaume y Carme piensan **ir** a algún país de América.

➥ ¿Qué ....*vas a hacer*..... el verano que viene?

  1. ¿Qué idioma .... ?

  2. ¿Qué .... ?

  3. ¿Cuándo .... ?

  4. ¿Qué coche te .... ?

  5. ¿A qué país .... ?

■ With the **Pretérito imperfecto** of *Ir a* + INFINITIVE we can convey the same information, but referring to a situation in the past:

- El tren tenía un problema mecánico. **Iba a salir** con retraso, pero lo repararon muy rápido y, al final, salió a la hora prevista.

- Era evidente que, si comía tanto, **iba a ponerse** enfermo. No me hizo caso y, claro, se puso enfermo.

iba		
iba		
ibas		
iba	**a**	INFINITIVE
íbamos		
ibais		
iban		

Estaba claro que **iba a llover**. Por eso, decidimos no salir...

Esta tarde **va a llover**.

Yo siempre le preguntaba a mamá cuándo **ibas a nacer**...

¿Cuándo **va a nacer** mi hermanito, mamá?

3 Remember the situations from exercise 1, and complete the sentences to say how they worked out, as in the example.

➡ Parecía que se ...*se iba a caer*..........., pero su madre la salvó.

2. Cuando ya .... en el restaurante, vimos que estaba cerrado, y volvimos a casa.

4. Pues sí, yo salí corriendo porque estaba claro que la bomba ....

1. No había estudiado nada, y todo el mundo me decía que .... Y tenían razón: al final suspendí.

3. La mañana era muy fría y el cielo estaba muy gris. Todos pensábamos que ...., pero luego salió el sol.

5. Yo iba el primero, pero, cuando .... la última valla, tropecé.

B Tener que / Haber que + INFINITIVE: Tienes que comer / Hay que comer

■ We use **tener que / haber que** + INFINITIVE to express necessity or obligation in two different ways:

Indicating who has the necessity or obligation	**Without indicating** who has the necessity or obligation

tengo
tienes
tiene   **que** INFINITIVE
tenemos
tenéis
tienen

hay **que** INFINITIVE

● **Tienes que comer** *más frutas y verduras. Te lo ha dicho el médico.* [You need to.]

● **Hay que comer** *muchas frutas y verduras para tener buena salud.* [It is necessary in general.]

■ We can use this periphrastic verb in any tense:

➔ **16. Position and combination**

● *Yo* **tenía que hacer** *la comida, pero al final la hizo Francisca, por suerte.* [I was supposed to.]

● *Había que hacer la comida y Francisca se ofreció inmediatamente para hacerla.* [Somebody had to.]

● *¿***Habéis** *solucionado el problema con el ordenador o* **habéis tenido que llevarlo** *a arreglar?* [Did you (plural) have to?]

● *¿***Ha habido que llevar** *el ordenador a arreglar o está ya todo solucionado?* [Did somebody have to?]

Hoy **tienes que** fregar tú. Yo me voy corriendo.

Pues yo tampoco tengo tiempo.

Bueno, pues ahora **hay que** fregar todo esto.

Ya lo hago yo. Tú descansa.

4 Are both options possible? If one of them is wrong, cross it out.

➔ ~~Tienes que~~ / Hay que ✓ ir a comprar azúcar. ¿Vas tú o voy yo?

➔ Estuvo toda la tarde sintiéndose muy mal. Al final, **tuvimos que** ✓/ **hubo que** ✓ llevarla al médico.

1. Por favor, **tienes que / hay que** decirme qué te ha dicho. Me muero de curiosidad.

2. ● Había mucha nieve en la carretera. Casi tuve un accidente con el coche...

   ○ Claro, es que en invierno **tienes que / hay que** tener mucho cuidado.

3. ● ¿Cómo hago el gazpacho?

   ○ Para hacer bien el gazpacho, **tienes que / hay que** pelar los tomates.

4. El otro día vi a Rosa con un hombre que no era su marido y llamé a Jesús: **tenía que / había que** saberlo.

5. Mi vecino del segundo se ha encontrado la casa llena de agua y **ha tenido que / ha habido que** llamar al fontanero. Le ha costado carísimo.

6. Verónica vendrá conmigo, así que tú **no tienes que / no hay que** acompañarme.

7. Cuando estabais en la calle, ha empezado a salir humo de vuestra casa. **Habéis tenido que / Ha habido que** llamar a los bomberos. Habíais olvidado apagar el tostador.

187

C Estar + GERUND: *Está durmiendo / Duerme*

■ With the verbs by themselves, we can talk about **states** (a situation that stays the same for a time) or **actions** (events that produce a change of state):

States	Actions

States

- *Está de pie.*
- *Está cansado.*
- *Está solo.*
- *Sabe mucho.*
- *Es listo.*
- *Tiene sueño.*

Actions

- *Lleva los regalos del cumpleaños al coche.*
  [The presents have changed place.]

■ With the periphrastic verb **Estar** + GERUND we can talk about the intermediate state of an action. We can observe an action as it develops; after it has started and before it has finished, as a situation that can stay the same for a time:

- *Está llevando los regalos del cumpleaños al coche.*

5 What are these people doing? Complete the sentences with the verbs in the box using *Estar* + GERUNDIO. Link each sentence to its corresponding illustration.

comprar ✓	aparcar	dormir
	sonreir	planchar

➔ ● ¿Y Javier?

　○ *Está comprando* .... en el súper. Pronto volverá.

1. Llegamos en cinco minutos. ....

2. Dicen que Loreto es muy seria, pero en esta foto ....

3. No hagas ruido. El niño ....

4. ● ¿Y mi camiseta?

　○ La ....

■ Whenever we are referring to a very specific moment in the development of an action, we prefer to use *Estar* + GERUND rather than a non-periphrastic verb:

In general	Momentary situations	
• *Los gatos no **beben** cerveza.*	• *¡Corre, Jenaro, mira! ¡Tu gata se **está bebiendo** mi cerveza!*	Right now
• *Antes siempre me **escribías** poesías, y ahora, nada. ¿Qué ha pasado con tu amor?*	• *No te contesté al teléfono porque **estaba escribiendo** una poesía para Dionisia y no quería desconcentrarme.*	In that moment in the past

6 Link the two parts of the sentence with the appropriate periphrastic or non-periphrastic verb.

➡ Estaba solo en casa cuando me llamaron de la tele.

1. Los planetas no **dan / están dando** luz propia.

2. El agua **hierve / está hirviendo** a 100 grados centígrados.

3. El agua **está hirviendo / hierve.**

4. **Estamos dando / Damos** vueltas al mismo sitio todo el rato.

5. No me puedo subir en los columpios que **dan / están dando** vueltas.

6. Cuando llamó la policía, me puse nerviosísimo.

7. Antes no **íbamos / estábamos yendo** a los bancos.

a. Ya puedes poner el té.

b. Marisa **trabajaba** / **estaba trabajando** en ese momento.

c. **Estaba guardando / Guardaba** el dinero del robo.

d. **La reciben / están recibiendo** de las estrellas.

e. ¿Por qué no paras y preguntas?

f. A esa temperatura se convierte en vapor.

g. Me **mareo / estoy mareando** con mucha facilidad.

h. **Guardábamos / Estábamos guardando** el dinero en casa.

■ We use *Estar* + GERUND to talk about **momentary situations** with action or activity verbs, but not with stative or qualitative verbs:

MOMENTARY SITUATIONS

	Estar + GERUND (With action verbs)	NON-PERIPHRASTIC VERB (With stative verbs)
Talking about the present	• El bebé **está llorando**. • **Están estudiando**. • Tu hermana **está leyendo**.	*Tiene* hambre y *parece* cansado. No **pueden** venir. Está **sentada** en la terraza. [Está sentando en la terraza.]
Talking about the past	• El bebé **estaba llorando**. • **Estaban estudiando**. • Tu hermana **estaba leyendo**.	*Tenía* hambre y *parecía* cansado. No **podían** venir. **Estaba** sentada en la terraza.

👁 Some verbs mean "action in progress" when they are used with *Estar* + GERUND and mean "state" when used non-periphrastically. In English we might even use a different verb:

• *Estoy viendo* la tele. [My activity is watching the TV.]

• *Desde aquí no veo* la tele. [I can't see it.]
 [Desde aquí no estoy viéndola.]

• *Está llevando* los sombreros al almacén.

• *Lleva* un sombrero muy bonito.
 [Está llevando un sombrero.]

---

7 Complete with *Estar* + GERUND for the action or activity verbs and with the non-periphrastic verb for the stative verbs.

Talking about the present

entrar ✓   parecer

1. Mira, mi novio es ése que ...está entrando... ahora. ¿Te .... guapo?

hacer (vosotros)   tener (él)

2. .... mucho ruido. El niño .... sueño y así no se va a dormir.

ver (nosotros)   ser

3. Espera un poco Es que .... el final de una película. .... muy interesante.

Talking about the past

4. ● ¿Y ...veías..... algo?

○ Casi nada, ese día .... todo muy oscuro.

ver (tú) ✓   estar

5. ● Mira esta foto. ¡Qué gracia! Aquí Pedro .... la tarta. .... muy guapo vestido de novio.

○ Pero .... el pelo muy largo, ¿no?

cortar   estar   llevar

6. ● ¿Llamaste tú? ¿Qué ....?

○ Nada, una tontería. Es que .... un crucigrama y no .... una palabra.

querer (tú)   hacer (yo)   saber (yo)

189

D Estar + GERUND with completed events: *Estuvo comiendo / Comió…*

■ When we use tenses that express finished events (Indefinido, Pretérito perfecto, Pluscuamperfecto, etc), with a non-periphrastic verb, we are talking about actions that are completely finished:

● **Ha llevado** *los paquetes. Ya no tiene que hacer nada más.*	Recent past
● **Llevó** *los paquetes. Ya no tenía que hacer nada más.*	Past
● **Había llevado** *los paquetes. Ya no tenía que hacer nada más.*	Anterior past

➔ 23. Indefinido

➔ 22. Pretérito perfecto   ➔ 27. Pluscuamperfecto

■ With the periphrastic verb *Estar* + GERUND we are talking about the development of an action over a period of finished time (*durante dos días, toda la mañana, hasta las 7, mucho tiempo, dos horas…*):

● **Ha estado llevando** *paquetes dos horas.*	Recent past
● **Estuvo llevando** *paquetes dos horas.*	Past
● **Había estado llevando** *paquetes dos horas.*	Anterior past

■ With *Estar* + GERUND we are not interested in whether the action has finished completely or not. We can use it to talk about actions that have finished completely that we see over the whole of their development:

● *Estuvimos comiendo en ese bar tan famoso.*   ● *Esta tarde **he estado comprando** la tele.*

Or we can talk about actions carried out over a certain period of time, but not finished completely:

● **He estado fregando** *el suelo de la casa toda la mañana, pero no he podido fregar el salón.*
● **Estuvo escribiendo** *una novela durante tres años y, al final, la dejó sin terminar.*

But:

● **He fregado** *el suelo de la casa. Tú puedes fregar los platos y poner la lavadora.*
● **Escribió** *una novela en tres años. Es mucho tiempo, pero ahora se ha hecho rico con las ventas.*

8 If somebody says this:

➔ Aquella tarde estuve visitando a mis padres.
1. Ha estado corrigiendo los exámenes.
2. Habíamos estado planchando la ropa.
3. Habían estado dándole la noticia a Isabel.
4. Estuvo leyendo el libro.

Can we draw these conclusions?

➔ Visitó a sus padres. (...*sí*...)
   Ha corregido todos los exámenes. (..........)
   No quedaba ropa sin planchar. (..........)
   Cuando llegué, Isabel ya lo sabía. (..........)
   Acabó el libro. (..........)

9 Are we talking about the process of doing an activity or of the activity being completely finished? Circle the most appropriate option.

➔ (He estado pintando) / He pintado el cuadro esta mañana, pero no he podido terminarlo.
1. **Hicieron / Estuvieron haciendo** el camino de Santiago en cuatro días. Un tiempo récord.
2. Mi madre **estuvo naciendo / nació** antes que mi padre. Es mayor que él.
3. **He estado leyendo / He leído** el informe toda la tarde, pero no he podido acabarlo.
4. Estaba muy triste: ese día **había estado perdiendo / había perdido** un juicio muy importante.
5. **Estuve escribiendo / Escribí** la carta más de una hora. Pero no sabía cómo despedirme.

SECTION 5

Prepositions

¿Qué hay entre Roberto y tú?

Una y.

Prepositions are used to identify the location of some things in relation to other things: in space, time or in the abstract space of ideas and concepts.

A   *De, a*

■ *De* indicates a starting point or origin:

- *Ese chico es **de** Segovia.*

- *¿**De** dónde venís?*
- ***De** Rabat.*

■ The preposition *de* introduces information that characterises, recognises, specifies or identifies another thing. With *de* we indicate:

Material, substance or contents of something

*Traje **de** algodón, novela **de** amor, estatua **de** mármol, bocadillo **de** jamón, camión **de** fruta, gota **de** aceite, hoja **de** papel, metro **de** tela, hablar **de** alguien o **de** algo, etc.*

Family relationship, possession

*El padre **de** Amina, el trabajo **de** Laura, la escuela **de** Ana, la libreta **de** Juan, etc.*

Type of object

*Casa **de** campo, cuchara **de** postre, billete **de** ida y vuelta, cuarto **de** baño, ropa **de** abrigo, libro **de** bolsillo, etc.*

Point of reference to locate another thing

- *El cementerio está enfrente **de** la Catedral.*
- *Esa chica trabaja cerca **de** mi oficina.*
- *A la derecha **de** la gasolinera está mi casa.*
- *Te dejo las llaves encima **de** la mesa, ¿vale?*
- *Llegamos a las diez **de** la mañana.*
- *Seguro que cuestan más **de** veinte euros.*

👁 *De* and *a* are the only two prepositions that always form a single word with the article *el*:

de + el = **del**   a + el = **al**
*Vengo **del** trabajo.   Voy **al** trabajo.*   → 5. Articles

👁 We say: *Vive **en** Palo Alto.* [~~Vive a Palo Alto.~~]

■ *A* indicates a point of arrival or destination:

- *¿Hoy no vas **a** la escuela?*

- *¿**A**dónde te han enviado?*
- ***A** la base de la Antártida.*

■ The preposition *a* indicates a point of reference towards which one is going, is positioned or is associated with. With *a* we indicate:

Positioning towards a part or a side of something

*A la derecha, **a** la izquierda, **a** la entrada, **al** frente, **al** principio, **al** final, **al** fondo, **a** las diez de la mañana, **a** la una en punto, **al** norte, **al** sol, **al** viento, **a** la espalda, etc.*

👁 - *Francia está **al** norte de España.*
     [Nearer to the North Pole than Spain.]
   - *Zaragoza está **al** norte de España.*
     [We will find Zaragoza in Spain, positioning ourselves in the northern part.]
   - *Zaragoza está **en** el Norte de España.*
     [Within the northern part of Spain.]

Point of reference

*Junto **a** la escuela, frente **a** la playa, etc.*

Direct object of a person and an indirect object

- *¿Has llamado **al** médico?*
- *Dale eso **a** mi madre.*
- *A mí no me gusta.*   → 12. Pronouns

The manner in which some things are done or made to work

*A gritos, **a** pie, **a** caballo, **a** mano, **a** máquina, **a** la fuerza, etc.*

1 Jabúlez is a company that specialises in the import and export of Serrano ham. To find out how it works, complete the text with *a*, *de* or *en*. (Be careful: *a + el = al*; *de + el = del*).

Jabúlez es una empresa familiar dedicada a la elaboración ...*de*... jamones. Su sede central es un edificio (1) .... tres plantas situado (2) .... el sur de España, (3) .... un pueblecito (4) .... Extremadura. Los jamones se secan (5) .... el viento dentro (6) .... grandes locales cuidadosamente ventilados. Mientras se secan, los jamones son observados, día a día, durante más de dos años y, al final, se empaquetan (7) .... mano. Más (8) .... cien camiones salen cada día (9) .... la empresa para ir (10) .... todas las ciudades (11) .... España

y, desde hace algún tiempo, también (12) .... varios países europeos.

Un hombre entre jamones

Jacinto Jabúlez es el hijo (13) .... el fundador y lleva más (14) .... doce años (15) .... el frente (16) .... la empresa familiar. Su trabajo es el (17) .... supervisar toda la actividad (18) .... la empresa y, además, invitar (19) .... diferentes firmas extranjeras (20) .... visitar sus instalaciones. (21) .... Jacinto le apasiona su trabajo. Vive (22) .... un magnífico chalé, (23) .... una urbanización que está muy cerca (24) .... su empresa. Todos los días llega (25) .... la empresa (26)................. pie (27) .... las seis en punto (28) .... la mañana.
Sus jamones son tan famosos que la prensa internacional ha hablado muchas veces (29) .... él e, incluso, en Estados Unidos y Japón se ha publicado su famoso libro (30) .... cocina: *No hay vida sin jamón.*

2 Count Lorénsez has been found dead in Arabia. The police have questioned eight people, but the main suspects are the four who don't speak good Spanish. Identify them, write the numbers and correct the mistakes.

1. Esta pistola es de un amigo mío que es policía. (.........)
2. Tengo un billete a avión con ida y vuelta. (.........)
3. Vivo en una zona muy apartada de aquí, en Dunas Bajas. (.........)
4. Yo ya he llamado a un amigo mío que es abogado. (.........)
5. ¿Por qué estamos aquí? Me han traído de la fuerza. (.........)
6. ¿Han venido en Arábiga sólo a interrogarnos? (.........)
7. Exijo una hoja de papel para poder escribir una declaración. (.........)
8. Perdone, inspector, ¿hay un teléfono cerca a aquí? Tengo que hablar con mi mujer. (.........)

B   Desde, hasta

■ **Desde** indicates the starting point of a journey or the **initial limit** of a spatial or temporal space within which something is located or happens:

DESDE

- *La Gran Via va **desde** la Plaza de Colón...*
- *Corrió descalzo **desde** la salida...*
- *No he tomado nada **desde** anoche...*
- *Ha curado **desde** elefantes...*
- ***Desde** estos asientos se ve mucho mejor.*
- ***Desde** ese punto de vista, sí lo entiendo.*

■ **Hasta** indicates the end of a journey, or the final limit of a spatial or temporal space within which something is located or happens:

HASTA

- *...**hasta** la Plaza Mayor.*
- *...**hasta** la meta.*
- *...y no puedo tomar nada **hasta** esta tarde.*
- *...**hasta** personas.*
- ***Hasta** mañana.* [We won't see each other until tomorrow.]
- ***Hasta** ahí estamos de acuerdo.*

👁 **Hasta** can also be used with the meaning *even*:
- *Lo ha felicitado **hasta** [even] el Rey.*

■ We can indicate the start and end of a journey, a space or a period of time
  with *de... a* or *desde... hasta*:

  ● *Fueron **de**/**desde** Madrid **a**/**hasta** Bombay en avión.*
  ● *Hay 60 kilómetros **de**/**desde** una ciudad **a**/**hasta** la otra.*
  ● *Tenemos vacaciones **de**/**desde** julio **a**/**hasta** septiembre.*

👁 To mark the spatial or temporal limit of something, ***desde*** and ***hasta***
  can be used by themselves, whereas ***de*** and ***a*** cannot:

  ● *Tuvimos un viaje muy malo, estuvo lloviendo **desde** Madrid.* [To an unspecified destination.]
    [*Estuvo lloviendo ✗ Madrid.*]
  ● *Tenemos vacaciones **hasta** el tres de septiembre.* [From an unspecified date.]
    [*Tenemos vacaciones ✗ tres de septiembre.*]

3 **Link the sentences on the left to the most appropriate explanation**.

➲ a. Un viaje **desde** Sevilla.   a. Dirección: Sevilla.
   b. Un viaje **a** Sevilla.   b. Dirección: otra ciudad.

1. a. Un taxi ocupado **del** aeropuerto.   a. El cliente ha llegado en avión.
   b. Un taxi ocupado **al** aeropuerto.   b. El cliente va a coger un avión.

2. a. Subir **a** la planta segunda.   a. El objetivo es llegar a esa planta.
   b. Subir **de** la planta segunda.   b. El objetivo es llegar a otra planta.

3. a. **Hasta** su abuelo cantó.   a. En homenaje a su abuelo.
   b. Cantó **a** su abuelo.   b. Incluso su abuelo.

4. a. Un novio **desde** los 30 años.   a. Cuando tenía 30 años.
   b. Un novio **a** los 30 años.   b. De los 30 años en adelante.

5. a. Un piso **desde** 350.000 euros.   a. Que vale esa cantidad o más.
   b. Un piso **de** 350.000 euros.   b. Que vale esa cantidad.

6. a. Espérame **hasta** las seis.   a. Las seis es la hora de la cita.
   b. Espérame **a** las seis.   b. Las seis es el límite de la espera.

7. a. Una carta **de** Granada.   a. Quiere enviar una carta.
   b. Una carta **a** Granada.   b. Ha recibido una carta.

8. a. Un tren **hasta** Santiago de Compostela.   a. Su destino final es Santiago de Compostela.
   b. Un tren **de** Santiago de Compostela.   b. Su origen es Santiago de Compostela.

4 **Find the most appropriate ending for these sentences**.

➲ El pobrecito Pepe ha estado estudiando...   a. de agosto.
         b. desde agosto.

1. Al final, a su mujer la ha aceptado...   a. desde la suegra.
         b. hasta la suegra.

2. Mi abuela murió...   a. hasta los noventa y tres años.
         b. a los noventa y tres años.

3. Mi abuelo vivió...   a. a los noventa y tres años.
         b. hasta los noventa y tres años.

4. El hijo de Carmina es un pesado. Estuvo llorando...   a. desde Cádiz.
         b. de Cádiz.

5. Para reservar el hotel tienen tiempo...   a. hasta la segunda quincena de mayo.
         b. a la segunda quincena de mayo.

6. El crucero va de Barcelona...   a. en Egipto.
         b. a Egipto.

C *En, entre*

■ The preposition *en* indicates that something is inside a space defined or limited by another thing (a place, an object, a surface, a unit, a period of time, a process, an idea, etc.):

Irene está en el trabajo, en su mesa, pero ¿qué hay en su mente?

EN

Las flores están en el florero.
El florero, en la mesa.
La mesa, en el centro de la habitación.
El sillón, en el rincón.
El cuadro, en la pared.
La lámpara, en el techo.
Los muebles, en la habitación.
La habitación, en la mente de Irene.

Thus we can use the preposition *en* to situate something in either a physical or an abstract space:

En casa, en Málaga, en coche, en el cajón, en el pasillo, en la cola, en vacaciones, en el trabajo, en la conversación, en ese sentido, etc.

■ With the preposition *en* we can indicate:

The means of transport	The way in which we do certain things	Being within a period of time
En autobús, en coche, en metro, en tren, en barco, en avión, en taxi, en burro, en camello, etc.	*En general, en particular, en serio, en broma, en público, en privado, en resumen, en secreto, en conjunto, etc.*	*En septiembre, en 2009, en Navidad, en verano, en ese momento, etc.*

👁 But: *a caballo, a pie...*
 [~~en caballo, en pie~~]

👁 We do not use *en* when talking about a physical destination. We use *a*:
 • *En Italia he ido a muchos sitios.* [I have been to many places in Italy.] [~~He ido muchas veces en Italia~~ / a]

The time it takes us to finish doing something

En tres horas, en cinco minutos:
• *Escribió el informe en tres horas.*
 [It took him/her three hours.]
• *Llegaremos en cinco minutos.*
 [In five minutes time no later.]

■ *Entre* indicates the limits of the space within which something is located or happens:

• *Málaga está entre Granada y Cádiz.*
• *Entre abril y mayo aquí llueve mucho.*
• *La B está entre la A y la C.*

■ *Entre* can indicate either two or more limits:

ENTRE

• *Hay una heladería entre el quiosco y el bar.*
• *Esto tiene que terminarlo entre hoy y mañana.*

• *Tengo que decidirme entre dos o tres ofertas.*
• *Las llaves están entre esos papeles.*

■ We can also use *entre* to express the fact that various subjects are working together to do something:

• *Lo hacemos entre Iñaqui, tú y yo, ¿no?*

• *Entre todos podéis arreglar ese problema.*

5 Nacho and Carolina are very active and keep themselves busy. Complete the text with the prepositions *en* or *a*.

1. Carolina nunca va ..*en*.. autobús ni .... metro.
   Siempre va .... pie a todas partes.
2. Sin embargo, Nacho va mucho .... moto, pero los fines
   de semana, por las mañanas, monta .... caballo.
3. Pero Carolina prefiere pasar todo el fin de semana
   paseando .... bicicleta.
4. .... verano van .... barco y nadan muchísimo.
5. .... invierno esquían. Van .... los Pirineos .... coche.
6. Y .... Semana Santa hacen senderismo. Recorren unos
   150 kilómetros .... pie.
7. Sólo se están quietos .... Navidad para estar con toda
   su familia.

Va a Barcelona
con avión.

Va a Barcelona
en avión.

6 Everyone in the Ortiz family is very untidy. Complete with the prepositions *en* or *entre* and link.

➲ Mis botas estaban ..*en*.. el armario de la entrada
y ya no están. ¿Alguien sabe dónde están?

1. ¿Y mi vestido de fiesta de Capriche? Ya no está
   .... mi armario.
2. ¿Alguien ha visto unos guantes negros que me compré
   el otro día y que dejé .... mi mesilla de noche?
3. Dios mío, ¿y mi blusa nueva? No está .... ningún
   cajón de esta casa.
4. ¿Qué es esto que está aquí, ... mis dos bolsos
   Blandik?
5. No encuentro mi crema superhidratante. Ayer la
   dejé .... el estante del armario del baño.
6. ¿Y mi anillo de prometida? No lo veo .... el joyero.

➲ Sí, las cogió Cuca ayer por la noche y las puso
..*en*.. la terraza porque estaban mojadas.

a. Yo los vi ayer .... la entrada.
b. Está .... la lavadora. Estaba muy sucia
   y decidí lavarla.
c. Sí que está allí. Búscalo bien. Está .... el de
   Cuchi y el de Ermani.
d. Seguro que está .... tu mesa del estudio,
   .... todos tus papeles. Y como es pequeño...
e. La tiene mamá. Ayer se puso un poco
   y la dejó .... la nevera.
f. A ver... Ah, es un peluche de Pitita.
   Déjalo .... su dormitorio.

7 Identify the three correct sentences and find out where the police discovered
the body of Lorénsez.

1. A un bosque que está bastante cerca de
   su residencia en Arábiga.
2. Entre seis palmeras del oasis más cercano
   a su residencia.
3. Al interior de una de las tiendas.
4. Al centro de unas dunas.
5. Entre una palmera muy alta y frondosa.
6. En un agujero junto a una charca de agua.
7. Envuelto a una alfombra.
8. Enterrado en la arena del desierto.

D *Para, por*

■ *Para* indicates the end objective that something is being directed towards:

■ *Por* indicates the space that is travelled through to get from one place to another:

*Vamos **para** Alicante **por** la carretera de la costa.*

PARA

POR

■ With *para* we can indicate:

■ With *por* we can indicate:

Purpose or reason

- *Vamos a Madrid **para** ver a Les Luthiers.*
- *Las toallas sirven **para** secarse.*

Recipient or destined audience

- *No es una película **para** niños.*
- *¿**Para** quién es este pastel?*

Towards a destination

- *Vamos **para** casa.*

Time period

- *La publicación es **para** otoño.*

- 👁 You do not need to use prepositions to express how long a situation lasts for. You can use the time expression by itself:
  - *Estuve **dos meses** en Alemania.*
  - *Voy a estar en Praga **dos semanas**.*

Imprecise location

In space
- *Me he dado una vuelta **por** el Retiro.*
  [Exploring el Retiro or the area near el Retiro.]
- *La panadería está **por** aquí.*
  [Somewhere in or near this place.]

In time
*Por la mañana/tarde/noche, **por** mayo, **por** vacaciones, **por** Semana Santa, etc.*
- *Vendremos por Navidad.* [The days of Christmas itself or around that time.]

Cause

- *Nos fuimos de la playa **por** el viento.*
- *¿Y **por** qué has invitado a Lidia?*
- *Muchas gracias **por** el regalo.*

Distribution

- *He repartido dos globos **por** niño.*

Means

- *Hemos hablado **por** teléfono.*
- *Le ha enviado las fotos **por** e-mail.*
- *Me he enterado **por** mi hermano.*

Exchange

- *Te cambio a tu novio **por** el mío.*
- *Lo compramos sólo **por** 20 euros.*

❽ Complete with *por* or *para*.

➲ Voy a Matalascañas ..*para*.. ver a mi novia.

1. Nos perdimos .... un bosque y tardamos cuatro horas en encontrar el camino.

2. Bueno, aquí están las galletas. Nos tocan cuatro .... persona.

3. Encontrar este piso fue una suerte. Lo compramos .... la mitad de lo que vale ahora.

4. Rafael dice que ha dejado la carrera .... su novia, pero yo creo que lo ha hecho .... él, sólo .... él.

5. ¿ .... quién son estos regalos?

6. Queremos hablar con la directora .... ver qué nos dice.

7. Oye, no iremos a la playa .... aquella carretera que tiene tantas curvas, ¿verdad?

8. Vale, perfecto, ¿por qué no me lo envías .... fax?

9. ¿Puedes firmar tú .... mí? Es que me duele muchísimo la mano y no puedo escribir.

10. El libro va a tardar un poquito, pero llegará a tiempo .... ese día.

11. ¿Quedamos mañana .... la mañana?

12. Señoras, señores: les estoy muy agradecida .... este homenaje. Gracias, de verdad.

9 **Connect the fragment on the left with the most likely interpretation on the right.**

➲ a. Vamos en taxi **para** el aeropuerto de Barajas...   a. Dando vueltas en Barajas.

 b. Vamos en taxi **por** el aeropuerto de Barajas...   b. Con dirección al aeropuerto.

1. a. Hemos visto unas flores **por** la ventana...   a. Han visto las flores al otro lado de la ventana.

 b. Hemos visto unas flores **para** la ventana...   b. Han visto las flores en la tienda.

2. a. Buscamos un documento **para** Internet...   a. Lo vamos a poner en Internet.

 b. Buscamos un documento **por** Internet...   b. Lo buscamos en Internet.

3. a. Han sacado una alfombra **para** la puerta...   a. La alfombra decorará la entrada.

 b. Han sacado una alfombra **por** la puerta...   b. La alfombra ha pasado a través de la puerta.

4. a. Compuso una canción **para** Elisa...   a. Elisa ha sido la causa de esta canción.

 b. Compuso una canción **por** Elisa...   b. Dedicada a Elisa. Elisa recibirá este regalo.

10 **The police have arrested the four suspects in the murder of Count Lorénsez, but two of them are innocent. The murderer and his accomplice don't know how to use *por* and *para*. Find and correct the mistakes to find out who they are.**

1. Mire, inspector, yo vine a Arábiga para ➲ ..✓.. trabajar en una empresa. Vine para (1)...... pasar tres meses pero, por (2)...... problemas de papeles, tuve que quedarme un mes más. Vivo en un hotelito que está por (3)...... la salida del oasis de Chilab. Ayer tenía que volver a mi país pero, por (4)...... culpa de este asesinato, me he tenido que quedar aquí. Espero estar libre para (5)...... poder volver cuanto antes.

3. No sé por (15)...... qué estoy aquí. Yo no he hecho nada, absolutamente nada. Estaba paseando tranquilamente por (16)...... el palmeral y, de repente, me entero por (17)...... unos amigos de que el conde Lorénsez ha muerto. Asesinado, el pobre. Voy para (18)...... casa y allí me encuentro a la policía y me traen aquí para (19)...... interrogarme. ¿Pero por (20)...... qué a mí? Yo creo que la policía no sabe nada... Y si la policía detiene a inocentes, ¿para (21)...... qué sirve? Y ahora, por (22)...... este horrible asunto, voy a tener que dormir en la cárcel.

2. Yo me vine aquí por (6)...... mi hermano, que ya trabajaba aquí. Cuando llegué, me propuso cambiar su negocio para (7)...... el mío. Me quedé a vivir en su casa. Se la compré para (8)...... 400.000 euros. Estoy muy a gusto. Mi trabajo es como un juego por (9)...... mí. Es muy fácil. Por (10)...... la mañana, envío paquetes para (11)...... correo y para (12)...... la tarde los recojo. Me enteré de la muerte del conde Lorénsez para (13)......mi hermano, que me llamó por (14)...... el móvil. Yo no conocía de nada al conde. Sólo le había entregado un paquete.

4. Ayer por (23)...... la tarde yo estaba por (24)...... el bazar, comprando una alfombra por (25)...... mi mujer. Una alfombra muy bonita, realmente, que, al final, compré para (26)...... 280 dólares. Cuando salía de la tienda para (27)...... llevar la alfombra al coche, la policía me detuvo como sospechoso de un crimen. ¿Pero cuándo fue ese crimen? Hasta ayer para (28)...... la mañana yo estuve en la habitación de mi hotel para (29)...... la gripe. Salí para (30) ...... comprar la alfombra y dicen que yo soy el culpable. Esto es una locura. Es una broma, ¿no?

11 Thanks to your help with the prepositions exercises, the police know who the culprit was.
Cross out the incorrect options.

➲ La policía ya sabe quién es el asesino **por/para** tu ayuda.

1. Todo lo ha descubierto **por/para** los problemas con
   las preposiciones.

2. Los inocentes ya pueden volver **por/para** sus casas.

3. Pero los culpables tienen que ir a la cárcel **por/para**
   ser juzgados.

4. El juicio está previsto **por/para** dentro de
   un mes.

5. La policía está muy agradecida **por/para** tu
   trabajo y te van a nombrar policía de honor
   del reino de Chilab.

E *Con, sin*

■ *Con* indicates association. We use it to say that
one thing goes with another, or is a component
or instrument of another. It can also indicate the
way we do something:

- *Está **con** el novio.*

■ *Sin* is the negation of *con*:

- *Está **sin** el novio.*

CON

SIN

A los dos les gusta:

- *El gazpacho **con** ajo...*
- *Dormir **con** pijama...*
- *Comer **con** palillos...*
- *Viajar **con** amigos...*
- *Las ciudades **con** mar...*

*...y el café **sin** azúcar.*
*...y **sin** calcetines.*
*...y cenar **sin** mantel.*
*...y pasear **sin** prisa.*
*...pero las playas **sin** gente.*
*No pueden vivir el uno **sin** el otro.*

👁 We can also use the gerund (*cantando, comiendo, viviendo,* etc.)
to talk about the way of doing something. In this case, the negation
is formed by ***sin* + INFINITIVE**:

- *Sí, vale, ha corrido diez kilómetros pero **descansando** y **bebiendo** agua.*
- *¡Ha corrido diez kilómetros **sin** descansar y **sin** beber nada!*

[~~bebiendo~~, ~~descansando~~]

➲ 20. Non-personal forms

12 We all have very strong ideas about certain things. Complete with *con* or *sin* and underline your preferences.

➔ El café, ¿.*con*... azúcar o *sin*..... azúcar?

1. La cerveza, ¿ .... espuma o .... espuma?

2. Las mujeres, ¿......... falda o .... pantalones?

3. Los hombres, ¿......... corbata o .... corbata?
¿......... bigote, ... bigote o .... barba?

4. Los paseos por la ciudad, ¿comprando o .... comprar?

5. Un piso para vivir, ¿......... mucha luz o .... mucha luz?

6. Los macarrones, ¿......... o .... pan?

7. La ensalada, ¿......... vinagre o .... vinagre?

8. Las películas, ¿......... subtítulos o traducidas?

9. El café, ¿......... cafeína o normal?

10. Conducir tu propio coche, ¿en silencio o .... música?

11. La pasta italiana, ¿......... queso o .... tomate?

12. Las fotos, ¿sonriendo o .... sonreír?

13. Ir al cine, ¿......... amigos o solo?

F   *Contra, hacia*

■ *Contra* is used to indicate that one element is opposed to another, that it offers a certain amount of resistance:

CONTRA

- *Chocamos **contra** el escaparate.*
- *Votarán **contra** nuestra propuesta.*
- *¿**Contra** quién juega su equipo?*
- *Corre **contra** el viento.*

■ *Hacia* indicates the spatial or temporal point towards which something is orientated:

HACIA

- *El meteorito se dirige **hacia** aquí.*
- *¿**Hacia** dónde apunta una brújula?*
- *Han ido **hacia** allí pero no han llegado.*
- *Mira **hacia** la derecha y dime qué ves.*
- *Empezamos a comer **hacia** las tres.*
  [At about three o'clock.]

13 Joseba is an ecologist and is writing a protest song. Insert *contra* or *hacia* according to the meaning.

➔ .*Contra*.. el consumo,
.*hacia*.... la libertad,
juntos iremos
con este cantar.

1. Juntos iremos
con este cantar,
.... los colorantes,
.... lo natural.

2. .... la contaminación,
.... la purificación,
todos lograremos
mejor vegetación.

3. ¿............ dónde vamos?,
te preguntarás.
.... el arco iris,
.... la verdad.

4. .... un verde futuro,
.... una mejor vida,
.... un aire puro,
.... una utopía.

5. .... las marcas,
.... lo auténtico,
todos viviremos
un mejor momento.

A *Encima (de)*, *debajo (de)*, *delante (de)*, *detrás (de)*...

■ To indicate the position of one object in relation to another we use the following prepositional phrases: *encima (de)*, *debajo (de)*, *detrás (de)*, *delante (de)*, *enfrente (de)*, *al lado (de)*, *cerca (de)*, *lejos (de)*, *a la derecha (de)*, *a la izquierda (de)*, *alrededor (de)*:

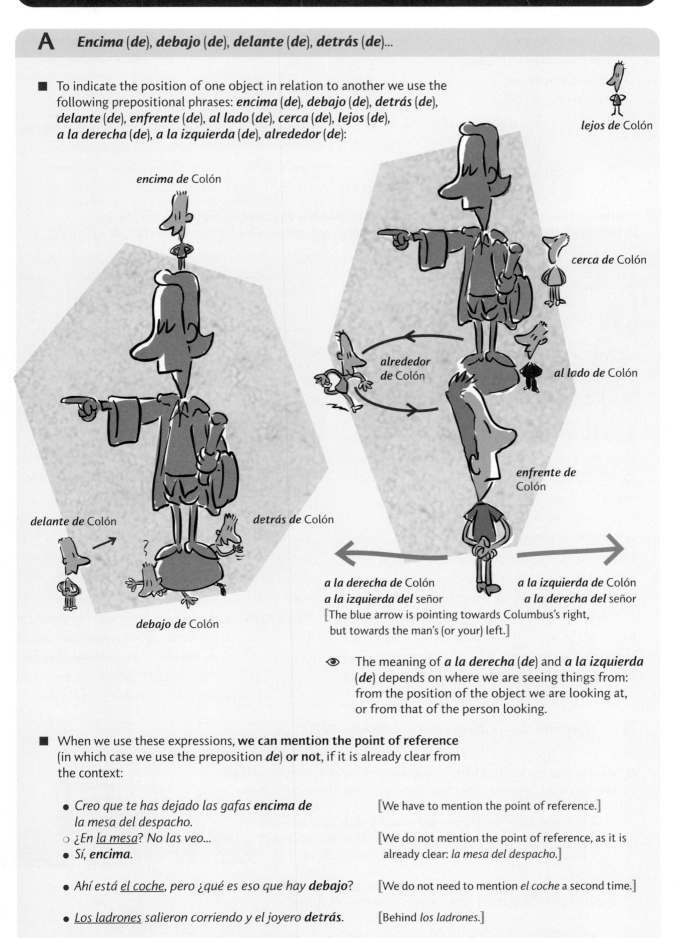

lejos de Colón

encima de Colón

cerca de Colón

alrededor de Colón

al lado de Colón

enfrente de Colón

delante de Colón

detrás de Colón

debajo de Colón

a la derecha de Colón
a la izquierda del señor

a la izquierda de Colón
a la derecha del señor

[The blue arrow is pointing towards Columbus's right, but towards the man's (or your) left.]

👁 The meaning of *a la derecha (de)* and *a la izquierda (de)* depends on where we are seeing things from: from the position of the object we are looking at, or from that of the person looking.

■ When we use these expressions, **we can mention the point of reference** (in which case we use the preposition *de*) **or not**, if it is already clear from the context:

- *Creo que te has dejado las gafas **encima de** la mesa del despacho.* [We have to mention the point of reference.]
- ○ *¿En <u>la mesa</u>? No las veo...* [We do not mention the point of reference, as it is
- *Sí, **encima**.* already clear: *la mesa del despacho*.]

- *Ahí está <u>el coche</u>, pero ¿qué es eso que hay **debajo**?* [We do not need to mention *el coche* a second time.]

- *<u>Los ladrones</u> salieron corriendo y el joyero **detrás**.* [Behind *los ladrones*.]

1 Ambrosio and Luisa have been married for thirty years and never agree with each other. They will always say the opposite of what the other has said.

➲ A.: Cariño, siéntate ahí a la izquierda.
L.: No, mejor me voy a sentar *a la derecha* .

1. A.: Aparca el coche **detrás del** autobús.
L.: Ahí no cabe, mejor aparco ....

2. L.: ¿Ponemos el retrato de mi madre **delante de** los libros?
A.: Yo prefiero ....

3. L.: Pon las toallas **encima de** las sábanas, haz el favor.
A.: Mejor voy a ponerlas ....

4. A.: La tele está demasiado **cerca de** la mesa.
L.: Pues yo creo que está demasiado ....

5. A.: Coloca las latas **debajo de** los cartones de leche.
L.: No, las voy a poner ....

2 Rigoberto Severo is a very tidy man, but an earthquake has displaced all his things. Fill the gaps by looking at the pictures (sometimes there is more than one possibility; remember that: *de + el= del*).

Aquella noche, como todas las noches, Rigoberto comprobó que todo estaba en su sitio. La cama estaba justo
➲ *enfrente del / delante del* el espejo, por supuesto, y la silla (1) .... Los zapatos estaban (2) .... la cama; el despertador estaba preparado: (3) .... la mesita de noche y a las seis en punto, como siempre. La ropa para el día siguiente estaba en orden: la camisa planchada y los calcetines limpios estaban (4) .... la silla, con los pantalones, bien estirados. Había puesto su reloj de pulsera (5) .... el despertador y ya le había dado un beso a la foto de su mujer. Comprobó que la linterna que había (6) .... la estantería tenía pilas. Por último, miró por la ventana. "Es probable que mañana llueva", pensó. Y se acostó.

De pronto, sintió un fuerte temblor y unos ruidos extraños. Le parecía que la habitación daba vueltas (7) .... su cabeza. Cuando se levantó, vio que los zapatos ya no estaban (8) .... la cama sino (9) .... la mesita de noche. (10) .... la cama había libros y, milagrosamente intacta, la foto de su mujer. No había nada (11) .... la mesita de noche. La camisa estaba tirada en el suelo; los dos relojes estaban ahora (12) .... la camisa. Además había un calcetín (13) .... la lámpara y los pantalones estaban (14) .... la puerta. Rigoberto se puso (15) .... el espejo para comprobar si seguia vivo.

B ¿Delante (*de*) or detrás (*de*) or enfrente (*de*)?

■ We use *delante* (*de*) to situate something in the area in front of an object. We use *detrás* (*de*) to locate something in the area behind an object:

● *El coche azul está **delante del** amarillo. El de color amarillo está **detrás del** azul y **delante del** verde. El verde está **detrás de** todos. El coche azul está **delante** y el verde **detrás**.*

■ We also use *delante* (*de*) or *detrás* (*de*) to locate objects situated before (*delante de*) or after (*detrás de*) other objects in our line of vision:

● *Los coches están **delante del** autobús. El autobús está **detrás de** los coches.*

■ We use *enfrente (de)* when the objects we are situating are "face to face":

    ● *El coche rojo está **enfrente del** camión azul, el coche naranja está **enfrente del** coche de color lila y el camión está **enfrente del** coche rojo.*

    👁 We use the preposition *de* only when we have to mention the point of reference:

       ● *El coche lila no está **al lado de**l <u>naranja</u>, está **enfrente**.*

3 Write in the missing words in this exercise in logical thinking. Be careful with *al* and *del*.

➲ Si Iván está enfrente de María, María
   .<u>está enfrente de Iván</u>....... .

1. Pero si Iván está delante de María, María está
   ....

2. Si el Banco Capital está enfrente del Banco Fortis,
el Banco Fortis está ....

3. Si la vecina rubia vive enfrente de mi casa, yo vivo
   ....

4. Si tenéis un coche rojo delante del vuestro,
vosotros estáis ....

5. Si una moto está a la derecha de un árbol,
el árbol está ....

6. Si en el cine estás sentado detrás de una persona muy alta, tienes una persona muy alta
   .... ti.

7. Si miras la cara de la estatua de Colón, estás
   ....

8. No puedo ver bien la tele porque Marisa se ha puesto .... mí.

9. Si en el teatro María está a mi derecha y Felipe detrás de mí, yo estoy ....
de María y .... Felipe.

10. Si las gafas están encima de los libros, los libros están .... las gafas.

C   *Al principio (de), al final (de), dentro (de), después (de)...*

■ Other prepositional phrases used for positioning are ***al principio** (de)*, ***al final** (de)*, ***en el centro** (de)*, ***en medio** (de)*, ***al otro lado** (de)*, ***al fondo** (de)*, ***dentro** (de)*, ***fuera** (de)*, ***antes** (de)*, ***después** (de)*:

*Un hotel **al final** de la calle.*

*Una estatua **en el centro** de/**en medio** de la plaza.*

*Un museo **antes de** la plaza.*
[If we are going towards the square, we will see the museum first and then the square.]

*Una escuela **después del** paso de peatones.*
[If we are going towards the square, we will reach the zebra crossing first and then the school.]

*Unos árboles **al fondo del** parque.*

*Un parque **al otro lado** de la plaza.*

*Un pato **dentro del** estanque y otro **fuera**.*

*Un paso de peatones **al principio de** la calle.*

■ We only use the preposition *de* with these prepositional phrases when
we mention the point of reference:
- *Hay una zapatería **dentro de** ese centro comercial.*
  [The shopping centre is the point of reference
  and has to be mentioned.]
- *Siga recto. Allí verá una plaza. Pues justo **antes**, está Correos.*
  [Before the square. We do not need to mention it again.]
- *¿Ve esa calle? Pues el Banco Estragox está **al final**.*
  [At the end of the street.]

4 The renowned archaeologists Jones and Indiana know that there is treasure hidden in the centre
of a well-known Spanish city. To find it they have to follow the instructions below, but the instructions
are not clear. Look at the map and complete them with the expressions from the box. (Be careful with
de + el = del).

al final (de)
al final (de)
al fondo (de)
al otro lado (de)
al principio (de) ✓
antes (de)
dentro (de)
dentro (de)
dentro (de)
dentro (de)
después (de)
después (de)
en el centro (de)
en medio (de)
fuera (de)

A ver... Tenéis que ir ➔ *al principio* de la Gran Vía,
al número 1. Seguid por esa calle hasta la tercera a la
derecha. Coged esa calle y allí, (1) .... , hay
una plaza. Entrad en ella y, (2) .... , en
una esquina, veréis una estatua. Cruzad la plaza hacia
la estatua, pero (3) .... llegar a la estatua,
tomad la calle que hay a la derecha y enseguida veréis
una plaza pequeña con una fuente (4) ....
Inmediatamente (5) .... la fuente, a la izquierda, hay una calle. Coged esa calle y, (6) .... ,
hay un parque. Entrad. (7) .... encontraréis

árboles y bancos para sentarse. (8) .... hay
un lago y un pequeño templo. Pues bien, el tesoro está
(9) .... el templo. Llegaréis a él (10)
.... atravesar un largo pasillo. Pero eso no es
todo: el tesoro está (11) .... un cofre. Para abrir
el cofre, necesitáis una llave que está escondida (12)
.... el templo. Salid de allí cuanto antes y
entrad en el laberinto. (13) .... el laberinto hay una estatua. La llave está (14) ....
el ojo izquierdo de la estatua. Ah, y una cosa fundamental: quiero la mitad del valor del tesoro...

Sentences

Te quiero más que a mis ojos,

Te quiero más que a mi vida,

más que al aire que respiro

y más que a la madre mía...

Cariño, ¿por qué no subes ya? ¿No ves que se van a despertar los niños?

40. Questions and exclamations

A   Yes/no questions: *¿Vienes con nosotros?*

■ In Spanish, questions that can be answered by yes/no do not have a special
structure. They can be distinguished from affirmations by the rising intonation at the end:

> 👁 When writing questions we put a question mark at both
> the beginning and the end (*¿...?*).

■ We can ask questions to confirm one possibility out of various:

- *¿Vienes o te quedas?*
- *La verdad es que no sé qué hacer.*

- *¿Seguimos andando o descansamos un poco?*
- *Yo prefiero descansar. Estoy agotado.*

■ With questions with the question tag *¿no?* and *¿verdad?* at the end,
we are asking for confirmation of something that we said before:

- *Tienes amigos en Alemania, ¿no?*
- *Sí, en Baden Baden, porque voy mucho en verano.*

- *Cervantes nació en Alcalá de Henares, ¿verdad?*
- *Creo que sí.*

Tú no eres de aquí, ¿verdad?

---

① Put the question marks into the following transcription of a man being questioned by the police.

P: Policía; J: Javier Rosales

P: Usted se llama Javier Rosales, ¿verdad?

J: Sí, efectivamente.

P: Trabaja en la universidad de verano de Laponia, no.

J: Sí, así es.

P: Es evidente que usted conocía a la difunta Mercedes Clarín. Eran amigos o algo más.

J: Éramos simplemente amigos.

P: Sabía que Mercedes Clarín salía con otro hombre.

J: No tenía ni idea. Tampoco me importa.

P: Estuvo en casa de Mercedes el viernes 28 de enero alrededor de las 22.30.

J: Tengo que contestar a eso. Es mi vida privada.

P: Es mejor colaborar. Créame.

J: De acuerdo, estaba en el bingo. Canté línea. Aquí tiene el cartón. Puedo irme ya, verdad.

B Place, time and manner: *¿Dónde...? ¿Cuándo...? ¿Cómo...?*

■ We use *dónde*, *cuándo* and *cómo* to ask about PLACE, TIME and MANNER:

The PLACE →	*dónde*
The TIME →	*cuándo*
The MANNER →	*cómo*

- *¿Dónde vive Julián ahora?*
- *¿Cuándo nos presentará Rita a su novio?*
- *¿Cómo vamos a Madrid? ¿En tren o en coche?*

¿Cómo te llamas?
¿Dónde vives?
¿Cuándo quedamos?

👁 These question words come at the start of the question.
The other elements of the sentence come after the verb,
except the object pronouns.

■ We can use *qué tal*, instead of *cómo*, when we are asking for a general
opinion about something or someone:

- *¿Qué tal se vive en Barcelona?* [What is life like in Barcelona?]
- *Muy bien, aunque es una ciudad un poco cara.*

- *¿Qué tal está tu madre?* [How is your mother?]
- *Bien, está muy bien ahora.*

■ Question words can be used by themselves, if it is clear what we are talking about:

- *Hemos hablado con Rafael.*
- *¿Cuándo?* [When did you speak?]

- *Ya he arreglado el grifo.*
- *¿Cómo?* [How did you fix it?]
- *He llamado al fontanero.*

- *¿Nos vemos el sábado por la tarde?*
- *Vale. ¿Dónde?*
  [Where shall we meet on Friday afternoon?]

- *Hola, ¿qué tal?* [How are you?]
- *Muy bien, ¿y tú?*

👁 *Qué tal* can be used without a verb when it is clear what we are talking about:

- *¿Qué tal la película?*
  [What was the film like?]
  ¿Cómo la película?

- *¿Qué tal anoche?*
  [What was last night like?]
  ¿Cómo anoche?

---

2 Complete the following questions from a test about Spain with *dónde, cuándo, cómo*
and then connect the questions with the answers.

➲ ¿...*Cómo*... se llama el río que pasa por Valladolid? — a. En Málaga.

1. ¿................ fue la Guerra Civil española? b. La jota.

2. ¿................ está El Teide? c. Pisuerga.

3. ¿................ se llama el baile típico de Aragón? d. Entre 1936 y 1939.

4. ¿................ es el día de la Constitución? e. En Tenerife. En las Canarias.

5. ¿................ nació Picasso? f. El 6 de diciembre.

3 Complete with *qué tal* or *cómo*. Sometimes both forms are possible.

➲ ¿...*Cómo*............ te has hecho esa herida? ¡Qué barbaridad!

1. ¿........................... te encuentras? ¿Mejor?

2. ¿........................... funciona el microondas? No sé a qué botón hay que darle para abrir la puerta.

3. ¿........................... tus padres? Hace mucho que no los veo.

4. ¿........................... han podido entrar? Yo creía que no tenían llave.

5. ¿........................... te ha salido el examen? ¿Era difícil?

6. ¿........................... el viaje? ¿Habéis esperado mucho rato en el aeropuerto?

7. ¿........................... la clase de aerobic? ¿Se suda mucho?

C   Quantity: ¿*Cuánto*...?

■ To ask about **quantity** we use:

> **Cuánto** (invariable) + VERB

- • ¿**Cuánto** <u>cuestan</u> estos abrigos?
- • ¿**Cuánto** <u>dura</u> el viaje en coche hasta Cuenca?

> **Cuánto/-a** (singular) + UNCOUNTABLE NOUN

- • ¿**Cuánto** <u>dinero</u> sacamos del banco?
- • ¿**Cuánt**a <u>gasolina</u> le ha echado Pablo al coche?

> **Cuántos/-as** (plural) + COUNTABLE NOUN

- • ¿**Cuánt**os <u>años</u> tienes?
- • ¿**Cuánt**as <u>entradas</u> te ha regalado Andrés?

👁 **Cuánto/-a/-os/-as** and the word that they refer to (verb or noun) come at the start of the sentence. The other elements of the sentence come after the verb, except for object pronouns.

■ **Cuánto/-a** and **cuántos/-as** can be used without an object when it is clear what we are talking about:

- • Hay que ir al banco: no tenemos <u>dinero</u> en casa.
  - ○ Vale, ¿y **cuánto** sacamos?

- • He comprado <u>pasteles</u> esta tarde y ya no quedan.
  - ○ ¡Ah! ¿Sí? ¿**Cuántos** nos hemos comido?

---

4 Complete these further questions from the test about Spain with *cuánto/-a/-os/-as* and link them to the answers.

➜ ¿..*Cuántos*... habitantes tiene Madrid?

1. ¿................. dura el viaje en avión de Madrid a Barcelona?
2. ¿................. lenguas se hablan en España?
3. ¿................. gente habla español en el mundo?
4. ¿................. tiempo duró la dictadura de Franco?
5. ¿................. mide El Teide, la montaña más alta de España?
6. ¿................. gente vive en Barcelona?
7. ¿................. personas hablan catalán?

a. 36 años.
b. Cuatro.
c. Más de un millón y medio.
d. 3. 718 m.
e. Unos cuatro millones.
f. 50 minutos.
g. Seis millones, aproximadamente.
h. Unos quinientos millones.

---

5 Complete the following questions with *cuánto/-a/-os/-as.*

➜ • ¿...*Cuántos*.... pisos tiene tu casa?
  ○ Tres: el sótano, la planta principal y un ático.

1. • ¿................. se tarda hasta Zaragoza?
   ○ No sé... Unas dos o tres horas en coche.

2. • ¿................. sal le pongo a la ensalada?
   ○ Poca, poca, que Ramón casi no toma sal.

3. • ¿Tiene plátanos?
   ○ Sí, ¿................. le pongo?

4. • ¿................. abono le echo a las plantas?
   ○ Bastante, que están muy tristes.

5. • ¿............ horas necesitas para acabar el trabajo?
   ○ En tres horas he terminado.

6. • ¿............ te falta para terminar eso?
   ○ Media hora o así.

7. • ¿Tenéis folios?
   ○ Sí, ¿............ necesitas?

D   Reason: ¿*Por qué*...?

■ To ask about the cause of something, we use *por qué*:

> ● ¿**Por qué** no ha venido Alberto?
> ○ No lo sé, pero creo que ha tenido un problema con el coche.

Papá, ¿**por qué** la luna es blanca?
¿Y **por qué** las estrellas no se caen?
¿Y **por qué** no tengo un hermanito?

👁 Whereas the 'because' word, which explains the cause, is written as a single word with no accent (*porque*), the 'why' word, which asks the question about the cause, is written as two words, and with an accent (*por qué*):

> ● ¿**Por qué** hay tantos coches parados?
> ○ **Porque** ha habido un accidente.

➲ 42. Joining sentences

👁 Asking why an activity is not being done (¿***Por qué no***...?) can also serve as a proposal to someone that this activity be done:

> ● ¿**Por qué** no vamos a cenar esta noche a una pizzería?
> ○ ¿Y **por qué** no cenamos en casa y salimos después?

6 Complete with *por qué*, *porque* or *por qué no*.

➲ ● ¿..*Por qué*.... has cerrado la ventana? Hace mucho calor.
  ○ ..*Porque*..... hay muchísimo ruido y así no se puede trabajar.

1. ● ¿................ me ayudas y hacemos la cama?
  ○ ¿Y .... la dejamos sin hacer y nos echamos una siesta?

2. ● ¿................ te comes el yogur?
  ○ .... soy alérgica a los lácteos. Si me lo como, me tienes que llevar al hospital.

3. ● ¿................ me miras así? ¿Tengo algo en la cara?
  ○ No, mujer. Te miro .... me gusta mirarte.

4. ● ¿................ te has peleado otra vez con tu hermana? ¿Me lo puedes explicar?
  ○ Pues .... ella siempre me quita las cosas y no me deja jugar.

5. ● ¿................ habrá venido a la cena? ¿Estará mala?
  ○ Seguro, ... ella no se pierde nunca una cena con nosotros.

6. ● Estoy completamente agotada. No puedo más.
  ○ ¿................ descansas un rato? Túmbate en el sofá.

7 Complete with *¿dónde?*, *¿cómo?*, *¿cuánto?*, *¿cuándo?*, *¿por qué?* or *¿por qué no?* Sometimes two solutions are possible.

➲ ● No va a venir la tía Lola a cenar.
  ○ ..¿*Por qué?*...........
● No sé, creo que está muy cansada.

1. ● El concierto de esta noche es a las ocho.
  ○ ....
● En el Teatro Calderón, como siempre.

2. ● Nos vamos a Madrid esta noche.
  ○ Ah, ¿sí? ....
● En autobús, en tren era imposible.

3. ● ¿Sabes que María y Luis se casan?
  ○ ....
● Este domingo.

4. ● ¿......................... vas a tardar?
  ○ En diez o quince minutos estoy ahí.

5. ● ¿Me puedes dejar algo de dinero?
  ○ Sí, claro, ...
● 20 euros es suficiente.

6. ● ¿Sabes? Este año no voy de vacaciones.
  ○ ....
● Tengo que terminar un trabajo la primera semana de septiembre.

7. ● Yo, a la fiesta de Toni, no pienso ir.
  ○ ¿ ....? ¿Ya no sois amigos?
● Estamos pasando una mala época.

8. ● ¿Sabes que Carlos se ha roto un brazo y una pierna?
  ○ ¿De verdad? ¿ ....?
● Pues escalando el Monte Perdido.

E   Things: *¿Qué compramos? ¿Qué disco compramos? ¿Cuál compramos?*

■ We use *qué* when we ask for things:

¿**Qué** le compramos a Adela?

Creo que quiere una cámara de fotos.

■ We use *qué* + NOUN when we want to mention **the type of thing** we are asking about:

¿**Qué** <u>cámara</u> le compramos?

Una digital. Es un poco más cara, pero es mejor.

■ We use *cuál/-es* when we are asking for one (or various) things from a **group** that has already been identified, either because it has been mentioned before or because the context makes it clear:

Vale, le compramos una <u>cámara digital</u>. ¿**Cuál** es la mejor?

La Kinon. Es estupenda.

👁   We can use *qué* with a noun (*¿Qué vestido...?, ¿Qué película...?*), but we cannot do this with *cuál*:

~~¿Cuál vestido...?~~   ~~¿Cuál película...?~~

👁   *Cuál* is the singular and *cuáles*, the plural:

- *Te regalo <u>uno de estos cuadros</u>. ¿**Cuál** te gust**a**?*
- *Te regalo <u>dos de estos cuadros</u>. ¿**Cuáles** te gust**an**?*

8 **Complete with *qué*, *cuál* o *cuáles*.**

1. ● ¿.*Qué*..... te apetece cenar?

   ○ No sé. ¿................. hay en la nevera?

   ● Nada.

   ○ Vale. ¿A .... restaurante vamos?

   ● A uno cerca, estoy muy cansada.

   ○ Ya, pero ¿a ....?

2. ● ¿Me prestas unos pantalones?

   ○ Depende, ¿................. quieres?

   ● Los vaqueros.

3. ● ¿Me dejas un momento ese disco?

   ○ ¿................. disco?

   ● El que está ahí encima.

   ○ Hay tres. ¿................. quieres?

4. ● ¿Sabes que he aprobado el examen?

   ○ ¿................. examen?

   ● El de conducir.

5. ● Ese radiador no funciona.

   ○ ¿................. radiador? ¿El de debajo de la ventana?

6. ● Y a tu padre, ¿................. le compramos?

   ○ Un vino de reserva está bien.

   ● Sí, vale, pero ¿.................? Hay muchísimos.

   ○ ¿................. te gusta más a ti?

7. ● Pásame los libros.

   ○ ¿.................? ¿Éstos?

   ● Sí, sí, ésos.

F **People: *¿Quién? ¿Qué niño? ¿Cuál?***

■ We use *quién/quiénes* when we ask after people:

¿**Quién** me ha llamado?

Tu tía Encarna y una chica.

■ We use *qué* + NOUN when we want to mention **the type of person** we are asking about:

¿**Qué** chica?

No sé. Ha dicho que era amiga tuya.

■ We use *quién/-es* or *cuál/-es* when we are asking for one (or various) people from **a group that has already been identified**, either because it has been mentioned before or because the context makes it clear:

¿Una amiga mía? ¿**Quién**?

No recuerdo su nombre. Me parece que era una compañera de clase.

Vale, alguna compañera de clase. Pero ¿**cuál**?

👁 We can use *qué* with a noun (¿*Qué médico*...?, ¿*Qué chica*...?) but we cannot do this with *cuál*:

¿C̶u̶á̶l̶ ̶m̶é̶d̶i̶c̶o̶...,? ¿C̶u̶á̶l̶ ̶c̶h̶i̶c̶a̶...?

👁 *Quién* and *cuál* are singular; *quiénes* and *cuáles*, are plural:

● ¿**Quién** tien<u>e</u> la llave?

● ¿**Quiénes** tien<u>en</u> la llave?

● Necesito <u>un masajista</u>. ¿**Cuál** <u>es el mejor</u>?

● Necesito <u>dos masajistas</u>. ¿**Cuáles** <u>son los mejores</u>?

211

9 Complete with *quién, quiénes, qué, cuál* or *cuáles*. Sometimes there are two possibilities.

➜ ● Ha venido Ana.
  ○ ¿Ana? ¿..*Qué*.... Ana?
  ● ¡Ah! No sé, tú sabrás.

1. ● ¿............. ciclista español ganó ocho veces el Tour?
  ○ Ninguno.

2. ● De tus tres hijos, ¿............. es el más estudioso?
  ○ El pequeño. Es el que más se parece a mí.

3. ● ¿Qué? ¡Pero, Juan, por Dios, eso era un secreto...! ¿A .... se lo has dicho?

4. ● Espejito, espejito: ¿............. es la más bella del reino?
  ○ Blancanieves, mi señora.

5. ● ¿............. son Melchor, Gaspar y Baltasar?
  ○ Los Reyes Magos.

6. ● A ver, niños. ¿............. ha escrito eso en la pizarra?
  ○ Ha sido Álvaro, señorita. Yo lo he visto.

7. ● De todos tus amigos, ¿............. viven más o menos cerca?
  ○ ¿Por qué?
  ● Para ponernos de acuerdo para ir al trabajo.

8. ● Oiga, por favor, ¿............. atiende en esta ventanilla?
  ○ El señor de las gafas, pero ahora está ocupado. Espere en la cola.
  ● Perdone, pero hay dos señores con gafas. ¿A .... se refiere?

9. ● ¿............. es el hombre más rico del mundo?
  ○ Vil Gueits, creo.

10 Complete the sentences with words from the box and match them to their continuation.

| qué ✓ |
| quién |
| qué |
| quiénes |
| qué |
| cuál |
| cuáles |
| qué |

➜ ¿..*Qué*........ es eso?

1. ¿................ os vais de viaje?

2. ¿................ comes?

3. ¿................ es?

4. ¿................ música pongo?

5. No acabo de decidirme. ¿................ de los dos me recomienda usted?

6. Al final, de las diez películas, ¿................ van al festival de Venecia?

7. ¿................ equipo ha ganado la Liga?

a. Todos: Edu, Ana, Lucía y Merche.
b. Soy yo, Nuria. Abre la puerta.
c. Ensalada de apio. ¿Quieres?
d. No sé. Parece un regalo para alguien.
e. El Betis.
f. Bluf, Anaconda II y Noches ardientes.
g. El rape está más fresco que el atún.
h. Algo tranquilo, si no te importa.

11 Write the questions that a journalist asks Francisco Zapatero, following his extraordinary discovery.

➜ ● ¿..*Cuándo*.... la encontró usted?
  ○ Ayer por la noche, después de cenar.

1. ● ¿Y .... la encontró?
  ○ Pues en un armario. Yo me acabo de mudar a esta casa y nunca había entrado en esa habitación.

2. ● Bueno, ¿y .... es exactamente?
  ○ Una momia, una momia en perfecto estado.

3. ● Increíble. ¿................ es? ¿Lo sabe usted?
  ○ Sí, sí, por supuesto. Es la tatarabuela de mi prima Casilda.

4. ● Ajá. ¿Y .... años calcula que tiene?
  ○ Tendrá unos doscientos años, más o menos.

5. ● ¿................ estaba vestida? ¿Llevaba alguna ropa?
  ○ No, no. Estaba envuelta en vendas: igual que las egipcias, igual.

6. ● ¿................ piensa usted que la guardaron en el armario?
  ○ No tengo ni idea. Quizá porque fue una mujer muy querida por la familia. Era muy buena.

7. ● ¿Y usted .... se encuentra?
  ○ Un poco sorprendido, la verdad.

8. ● ¿Y .... va a hacer con la momia?
  ○ Pues creo que voy a llevarla al Museo Arqueológico de la ciudad. Es una joya.

G ¿Cuál es la capital de Perú? / ¿Qué es Tegucigalpa?

■ To ask for something or someone to be identified, we can use
¿Cuál/-es + *ser* + CONCRETE NOUN?:

👁 If we are referring
to people, we can also
use *¿Quién/-es...?*

¿**Cuál es** la capital
de Perú?

Things	People
• *¿Cuáles son <u>sus peores defectos</u>?* [Among your defects, identify the worst.]	• *¿Cuál es <u>el profesor</u>?* [Among this group, identify the teacher.]
• *¿Cuál es <u>el horóscopo de Maite</u>?* [Among the signs of the zodiac, identify Maite's.]	• *¿Quién es <u>tu hermana</u>?* [Among these people, identify your sister.]
• *¿Cuál es <u>la oferta más barata</u>?* [Among today's special offers, identify the cheapest.]	• *¿Quiénes eran <u>tus cantantes preferidos</u>?* [Among all singers, identify your favourites.]

■ To ask for a definition or classification of something or someone, we use
¿Qué + *ser* + NOUN?:

• *¿Qué es Lima?*
○ *Una ciudad. La capital de Perú.*

• *¿Qué es un neurólogo?*
○ *Un médico especialista en el sistema nervioso.*

---

12 If you complete this test, you will find out several things about the universe; some are true and others are not.

➲ (I) ¿Qué es una galaxia?   a. Un inmenso conjunto de estrellas, gas y polvo.
(II) ¿Cuál es la galaxia más cercana   b. Andrómeda.
    a la Vía Láctea?

1. (I) ¿Quién es Marte?   c. Uno de los planetas del sistema solar.
  (II) ¿Qué es Marte?   d. El dios de la guerra.

2. (I) ¿Quién fue Laika?   e. El primer animal que se lanzó al espacio en
  (II) ¿Qué era Laika?   1957 en un satélite artificial ruso.
        f. Una perrita.

3. (I) ¿Qué son los satélites?   g. Ío, Europa y Calisto.
  (II) ¿Cuáles son los satélites más grandes   h. Astros sin luz propia que giran alrededor
    de Júpiter?   de un planeta.

4. (I) ¿Qué es un robot?   i. C-3PO y R2-D2.
  (II) ¿Quiénes son los robots que acompañan   j. Una máquina que hace cosas
    a Luke Skywalker en sus aventuras?   automáticamente.

5. (I) ¿Quiénes fueron Amstrong, Aldrin y Collins?   k. Astronautas.
  (II) ¿Qué eran Amstrong, Aldrin y Collins?   l. Los primeros seres humanos que viajaron a la luna.

6. (I) ¿Cuál es el planeta más grande del   m. Júpiter.
, sistema solar?   n. El rey del Universo, el soberano
  (II) ¿Quién es Júpiter?   de todos los dioses.

7. (I) ¿Qué era Darth Vader?   o. El padre de Luke Skywalker.
  (II) ¿Quién era Darth Vader?   p. Un caballero Jedi convertido al lado oscuro de la Fuerza.

13 Would you get on well with this person? Complete the questionnaire and then answer it.

➔ ¿..*Cuál*... es tu comida preferida? El pescado crudo.

1. ¿............. prefieres? ¿El frío o el calor? El frío.

2. ¿............. es tu pintor preferido? Miquel Barceló.

3. ¿............ te gusta más? ¿El día o la noche? El día.

4. ¿............. es tu color preferido? El negro.

5. ¿En .... ciudad te gustaría vivir? En Londres.

6. ¿.......... prefieres? ¿Dormir desnudo o en pijama? Desnudo.

7. ¿......... son tus manías? El orden y la puntualidad.

8. ¿......... tipo de música prefieres? El jazz.

H   ¿De dónde...? ¿Hasta cuándo...? ¿Por cuánto...? ¿Para qué ...?

■ *Cuándo, dónde, cuánto/-a/-os/-as, qué, quién, cuál* are used following a preposition if the element we are asking for is introduced by a preposition:

- *Trabajo en Desfalcosa <u>desde XCVZ</u>.*
  ○ *¿Desde cuándo?*

- *¿De dónde es tu mujer?*
  ○ <u>De Ávila</u>, pero sus padres son de Burgos.

- *¿A cuántos kilómetros está Málaga de aquí?*
  ○ <u>A doscientos cincuenta</u>, más o menos.

- *¿Con quién has quedado esta tarde?*
  ○ *No puedo decírtelo. Es un secreto.*

- *Creo que los ladrones se fueron <u>por KHJHKK</u>.*
  ○ *¿Por dónde?*

- *¿Con cuántos chicos has salido?*
  ○ *Uf, <u>con muchos</u>, pero en serio sólo con dos.*

- *¿Para qué has sacado la caja de herramientas?*
  ○ <u>Para arreglar</u> la puerta.

- *Estamos <u>en un hotel</u>.*
  ○ *¿En cuál?*

👁 To ask *¿A qué lugar?* we can use the form *adónde* (preposition *a + dónde*) or just *dónde*:

- *¿Adónde vais?* ¿Dónde vais?
  ○ *Al cine. La película empieza dentro de cinco minutos.*

---

14 Natalia has just had four teeth taken out and is not able to speak properly. Complete the questions on the right to ask about the bits that cannot be understood.

➔ He visto a KKKK en la sauna. — ¿..*A quién*... has visto?

1. Me acuerdo mucho de mis WWW. Viven tan lejos... — ¿.............. te acuerdas?

2. El coche ha chocado contra un KKJKJH y está destrozado. — ¿.............. ha chocado?

3. Después de ver muchos pisos, al final me he decidido por el ÑLÑL. — ¿.............. te has decidido?

4. Las películas de dibujos animados son de mis HTYFRJJJ. — ¿.............. son las películas de dibujos?

5. Abrieron la puerta con una KJHKYYG. — ¿.............. la abrieron?

6. Pienso en KKJJH y en su forma de hablar constantemente. — ¿.............. piensas?

7. Al final se casó con IIKKKJHHJ. — ¿.............. se casó?

---

15 There is some information missing from the following breaking news items. Write the questions you need to ask to obtain it

EFE. A las 19:30 de hoy, un avión de la compañía Zigzagair que se dirigía hacia

(➔) ***** con (1) ***** pasajeros a bordo, ha desaparecido en pleno vuelo.

REUTERS. El tenor español Agapito Vozarrón permanecerá en nuestra ciudad hasta

(2) *****. Ese mismo día se trasladará a (3) *****, donde tiene programado un recital.

AGENCIAS. El Banco de Argentina ha comprado la empresa InterGas por (4) ***** millones de dólares. InterGas pertenece al empresario Carlos Etéreo desde (5) *****.

➜ ¿Hacia dónde se dirigía el avión? .... 3. ....

1. .... 4. ....

2. .... 5. ....

I Indirect questions: *No sé si te conozco. No sé cómo te llamas*.

■ Sentences with *qué, quién/-es, cuál/-es, dónde, cuándo, cuánto/-a/-os/-as, cómo, por qué*, can be used **within other sentences** when we are referring indirectly to a question or its contents:

¿Quién ha ganado el premio?

- • *Iñaqui no sabe **quién** ha ganado el premio.*
- • *Los niños preguntan **dónde** estás.*
- • *No he oído **cuándo** les va a enviar Alberto el paquete.*
- • *¿Tú has comprendido **cómo** funciona la lavadora?*
- • *Los padres quieren averiguar **cuánto** tiempo estarán los niños en la escuela.*

👁 The question words come at the start of the indirect question, and the other parts of the sentence, except object pronouns, come after the verb.

■ To form indirect questions without using an interrogative, we can use *si*:

¿La lavadora funciona bien?

- • *Cristina quiere saber **si la lavadora funciona bien**.*
- • *No sé **si Alberto va a enviar los paquetes**.*
- • *Los padres no han averiguado **si los niños tendrán clase mañana**.*
- • *Mari Paz ha preguntado **si tus amigos van a ir a la fiesta**.*

👁 With indirect questions introduced by *si* the word order does not change.

---

16 Julie and Enrique have a blind date. Complete their thoughts, as in the example.

No sé...

➜ *cómo* .... tiene las manos.

1. en .... trabaja.

2. .... dinero gana.

3. .... vive.

4. .... tiene hermanos.

5. .... será su familia.

6. .... es su actriz favorita.

7. .... películas le gustan.

8. .... es su comida preferida.

9. .... lleva camiseta interior o no.

10. .... vive con sus padres.

No sé...

11. .... años tiene.

12. .... tiene los ojos.

13. .... besa.

14. .... tiene coche.

15. .... perfume usa.

16. .... es su deporte preferido.

17. .... vive en mi barrio.

18. .... le ha dado mi teléfono.

19. .... son sus medidas.

20. .... ha tenido muchos novios.

cómo ✓	cómo	si	si	cuál	si
cuánto	dónde	cuál	qué	qué	

si	cómo	si	cuáles	cuántos
si	qué	cómo	cuál	quién

215

J Exclamations: *¡Ha nevado esta noche!* *¡Qué raro!*

■ Any sentence can be an exclamation. A distinguishing feature is that the intonation rises sharply at the beginning and falls sharply at the end:

- *¡Ha llegado Carlos!*
- *¡No vengas!*
- *¡Luis tiene novia!*

Ha llegado Carlos.   *No vengas.*

¡Ha llegado Carlos!   *¡No vengas!*

- *¡Está lloviendo!*
- *¡Sal de aquí!*
- *¡No!*

👁 In writing, Spanish puts exclamation marks both at the beginning and at the end (¡....!).

■ For exclamations concerning intensity, quantity or manner, we use *qué*, *cuánto*, and *cómo*:

la INTENSITY	→	*Qué*
la QUANTITY	→	*Cuánto/-a, -os, -as*
el MANNER	→	*Cómo*

- *¡Qué feo!*
- *¡Cuánta agua lleva el río!*
- *¡Cómo canta Carla!*

¡Cómo baila Rodolfo!

¡Qué delgada está Catalina!

■ *Qué* can refer to an **adjective**, **adverb** or **noun**:

- *¡Qué <u>simpática</u> es la novia de Carlos!*   She is great fun.
- *¡Qué <u>rápido</u> pasa el tiempo!*   It passes very quickly.
- *¡Qué <u>ojos</u> tiene Ana!*   Her eyes are very beautiful.

■ In this type of construction, the exclamation word (*qué*, *cuánto*, *cómo*) goes **at the beginning**:

- *¡Qué inteligente es tu hija!*
- *¡Cómo grita el entrenador!*

And the **subject** of the sentence, when it needs to be mentioned, **at the end**.

■ When we know what we are talking about, the subject does not need to be mentioned:
- *¡Qué bonito!* your jersey is
- *¡Cómo duerme!* the baby
- *¡Cuánto sabe!* the person giving the conference / the person speaking

17 Link the exclamation with the topic to find out what Claudia is talking about.

¡Qué rico !

↪ ¡Qué vieja!	a. Una casa
1. ¡Qué bonitos!	b. Un bocadillo de calamares
2. ¡Cómo cocina!	c. El chef de un restaurante
3. ¡Qué rico!	d. Unos zapatos nuevos
4. ¡Cuántos libros!	e. Su novio
5. ¡Cuánta gente!	f. Un concierto de rock
6. ¡Cuánto lo quiero!	g. El perro del vecino
7. ¡Cómo ladra!	h. La biblioteca de un amigo
8. ¡Qué rápido!	i. La casa de la vecina
9. ¡Qué vestido!	j. Una modelo
10. ¡Qué saladas!	k. Un coche de carreras
11. ¡Qué jardín!	l. Las patatas fritas

■ We use *cuánto* to remark on the **quantity** of a given **verb**:

- ¡*Cuánto* <u>fuma</u> Luisa!   [Luisa smokes a lot.]
- ¡*Cuánto* <u>come</u> tu hijo!   [Your son eats a lot.]

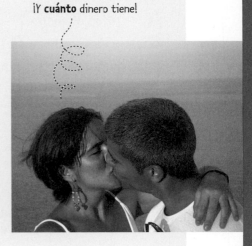

¡Cómo besa! ¡Y qué guapo es!...
¡Y **cuánto** dinero tiene!

■ We use *cuánto/ -a* (with uncountable nouns) and *cuántos/-as* (with countable nouns) to remark on the **quantity** of a given **noun**:

- ¡*Cuánta* <u>gente</u> hay en la cola!   [There are a lot of people in the queue.]
- ¡*Cuántos* <u>libros</u> tienes en casa!   [You have lots of books at home.]
- ¡*Cuántas* <u>novias</u> ha tenido Plácido!   [Plácido has had lots of girlfriends.]

👁 The noun agrees with *cuánto/-a/-os/-as* in gender and number.

■ To express the opposite idea, we use *qué poco* (with verbs), *qué poco/-a* (with uncountable nouns) and *qué pocos/-as* (with countable nouns):

- ¡*Qué poco* <u>fuma</u> Luisa!
- ¡*Qué poca* <u>agua</u> lleva el río!
- ¡*Qué pocos* <u>libros</u> tienes en casa!

18 Read the text below about Romualdo Vargas, and then write his neighbours' exclamations using *cuánto/-a/-os/-as* or *qué poco/-a/-os/-as*. Note the words in bold.

Romualdo (➔) **se ha casado siete veces** y tiene (1) **14 hijos**. (2) Antes **pesaba 132 Kg.** y **fumaba** muchísimo: más de dos paquetes al día, pero ahora está a régimen y **come muy poco** (sólo ensaladas y zumos) y (3) **fuma** también muy poco: un cigarrillo por semana. A Romualdo (4) **le gusta** mucho la música y también el cine: tiene una discoteca enorme con más de mil (5) **discos**, y lo (6) **sabe** todo sobre actores, directores y películas. Pero ahora casi nunca (7) **va al cine**: sólo una vez al mes.

➔ ¡Cuántas veces se ha casado!
1. ....
2. ....
3. ....

4. ....
5. ....
6. ....
7. ....

■ We use *cómo* to focus on the way in which an action has been carried out:

- ¡*Cómo* <u>come</u> tu hijo!   [I am surprised at how your son eats: very well or very badly.]
- ¡*Cómo* <u>vive</u> mi tío Alberto!   [I am surprised at how my uncle Alberto lives: very well, very badly or in an unusual way.]

19 Doña Angustias, Romualdo's mother, is going to stay with her son for a few days, and is surprised by the changes since her previous visit. Write sentences with *cómo*.

➔ Romualdo ha adelgazado de forma sorprendente. ¡Cómo ha adelgazado Romualdo!

1. Clara, su hija, ha crecido mucho. ....
2. Rufo, el perro, ladra sin parar. ....
3. La cocina está muy desordenada y sucia. ....
4. El jardín también está sucio y sin cuidar. ....
5. Los precios en el supermercado han subido mucho. Todo cuesta el doble. ....

41. Comparisons

A ¿Más or menos?

■ To compare two things that are different in some respect, we use:

| VERB | **más**
menos | que |

| **más**
menos | ADJECTIVE
ADVERB
NOUN | que |

- *En la ciudad la gente se <u>estresa</u>* **más que** *en el campo.*

- *En la ciudad los niños <u>juegan</u>* **menos que** *en el campo.*

- *La ciudad es* **más** <u>ruidosa</u> **que** *el campo.*
- *En el campo la gente se acuesta* **más** <u>temprano</u> **que** *en la ciudad.*
- *En el campo hay* **menos** <u>contaminación</u> **que** *en la ciudad.*

■ To be more precise with the comparison, we use quantifiers such as **un poco, bastante** or **mucho/muchísimo** before **más/menos**:

- *Sevilla es* **bastante** <u>más</u> *grande que Granada.*
- *Jaime ha comido* **un poco** <u>menos</u> *que Ángel.*
- *Ir en avión es* **mucho** <u>más</u> *rápido que en barco.*

➲ **11. Quantifiers**

■ When it is clear what we are talking about, we do not state the second element in the comparison:

- *Tu jefe gana* **más que** *tú.*
- *Sí, aunque yo trabajo* **más**. [que él]

- *El radiador nuevo es* **más** *grande pero calienta* **menos**. [que el viejo]

■ When the second element in the comparison is a pronoun without a preposition, we always use subject form:

- *Tu hermano habla más que* **tú**. [Tu hermano habla más que ~~ti~~]
- *Tu hermano habla más de mí que <u>de</u>* **ti**.

➲ **13. Subject pronouns**

➲ **14. Pronouns with prepositions**

---

1 Here are some basic facts about the inhabitants of two planets in the Pelambres galaxy. Compare them, as in the example.

	Rizus	Lisus	Más / menos
Nº de antenas	6	1	➲ Los Rizus tienen *más antenas que los Lisus.*
Nº de ojos	2	6	1. Los Rizus tienen ....
Altura media	220 cm	150 cm	2. Los Rizus son .... altos ....
Coeficiente intelectual	170	60	3. Los Lisus son .... inteligentes ....
Hora de levantarse	Entre 10 y 11 a.m.	Entre 6 y 7 a.m.	4. Los Lisus se levantan .... temprano ....
Hora de acostarse	00:00	22:00	5. Los Rizus se acuestan .... tarde ....
Litros de alcohol por habitante y año	420 litros	1 litro	6. Los Rizus beben ....
Expectativas de vida	123 años	67 años	7. Los Lisus viven ....

2 Write what you think the old lady and the young woman might be saying.

En mis tiempos la gente *se lavaba menos* que ahora.

Ahora hay *más libertad que* antes.

1. La vida ser tranquila

....

2. Los trenes ir despacio

....

3. La gente casarse joven

....

4. La fruta tener sabor

....

5. Haber igualdad entre hombres y mujeres

....

6. La gente divorciarse

....

7. La gente vivir años

....

8. La gente viajar

....

B Igual, tan / tanto, el mismo...

■ To say that two things are the same in Spanish, we use:

With ADJECTIVES and ADVERBS

| igual de | ADJECTIVE ADVERB | que |
| tan | | como |

- *Paco es **igual de** <u>atractivo</u> **que** José.*
- *Paco no baila **igual de** <u>bien</u> **que** José.*

- *Paco es **tan** <u>atractivo</u> **como** José.*
- *Paco no baila **tan** <u>bien</u> **como** José.*

And also:
- *Paco y José son **igual de** <u>atractivos</u>.*
- *Paco y José no bailan **igual de** <u>bien</u>.*

With VERBS

| ... | igual que | ... |
| | tanto como | |

Igual que
(IN THE SAME WAY OR AMOUNT)

- *Mi hija <u>duerme</u> **igual que** mi marido.*
  In exactly the same way (face upwards)
  or the same number of hours.
- *Mi hija no <u>ronca</u> **igual que** mi marido.*

And also: • *Mi hija y mi marido <u>duermen</u> **igual**.*

Tanto como
(SAME AMOUNT)

- *Mi hija <u>duerme</u> **tanto como** mi marido.*
  The same number of hours.
- *Mi hija no <u>ronca</u> **tanto como** mi marido.*

👁 When we refer to the object of a verb, we also use **lo mismo** (**que**) to indicate "the same amount" or "the same thing/s":

- *Mis dos hijos estudian* **lo mismo**: *arquitectura y piano.*
- *He dormido* **lo mismo** *que tú, doce horas.*
- *Pidieron* **lo mismo** *que vosotros: una subida de sueldo.*

■ When it is clear what we are talking about, we don't state the second half of the comparison:

- *El hotel Plasta es* **igual de** *caro* **que** *el Jilton e* **igual de** *cómodo.* [as the Jilton.]

👁 But with **tanto** we **only** eliminate the second part **when the sentence is in the negative**:

- *Paco bebe* **tanto como** *José pero no fuma* **tanto**. [as José.]
  [*Paco bebe tanto como José y fuma tanto.*] ⌐como él.

③ Lola Menta and Carmen Druga are two famous actresses who are very alike. Using the adjectives and adverbs in the box to make sentences with *igual de...* and *tan... como* to describe the ways in which they are similar and the ways in which they are not.

alta	delgada	joven ✓	rica	rápido	tarde	cerca

	Lola	Carmen
Edad	35	45
Altura	173 cm	173 cm
Peso	60 Kg	55 Kg
Hora de desayunar	12:00	12:00
Velocidad conduciendo	170 Km/h	170 Km/h
Distancia de casa al trabajo	5 Km	30 Km
Dinero	2 millones de euros/año	10 millones de euros/año

➔ *Carmen no es tan joven como Lola. / Carmen no es igual de joven que Lola.*

1. ....
2. ....
3. ....
4. ....
5. ....
6. ....

④ Compare what Lola Menta and Carmen Druga do, *igual que*, *tanto como* and *lo mismo* (*que*). Note that you can only use *tanto como* when comparing quantities.

➔ Lola se ha operado la nariz, los labios y las orejas. Carmen sólo se ha operado la nariz.

➔ *Carmen no se ha operado lo mismo que Lola.*
Carmen no se ha operado tanto como Lola.

1. Lola fuma tres paquetes de Güiston al día. Carmen también.

1. ....
....

2. Lola habla con falso acento argentino. Carmen también.

2. ....
....

3. Lola se bebe una botella de ron Palique al día. Carmen también.

3. ....
....

4. Lola se pinta los ojos, los labios, las uñas de las manos y de los pies.

   Carmen también.

   4. ....
   ....
   ....

5. Lola duerme con antifaz y en colchón de agua.

   Carmen también.

   5. ....
   ....

6. Lola desayuna dos docenas de ostras, salchichas y huevos.

   Carmen desayuna café solo.

   6. ....
   ....
   ....

With **NOUNS**:

IDENTITY AND AMOUNT	*el mismo* *la misma* *los mismos* *las mismas*	*que*
	NOUN	
ONLY AMOUNT	*tanto* *tanta* *tantos* *tantas*	*como*

IDENTICAL / SAME AMOUNT
COUNTABLE AND UNCOUNTABLE

- *Pedro lleva **el mismo** <u>móvil</u> **que** Juan.*
- *Pedro usa **la misma** <u>talla</u> **que** Juan.*
- *Pedro tiene **los mismos** <u>gustos</u> **que** Juan.*
- *Pedro tiene **las mismas** <u>amigas</u> **que** Juan.*
  [The same friends or the same number of friends.]
- *Pedro bebe **el mismo** <u>vino</u> **que** Juan.*
  [The same make of wine or the same quantity.]
- *Pedro no lleva **el mismo** <u>jersey</u> **que** Juan.*

And also:

- *Pedro y Juan tienen **el mismo** <u>móvil</u>.*
- *Pedro y Juan tienen **la misma** <u>talla</u>.*
- *Pedro y Juan tienen **los mismos** <u>gustos</u>.*
- *Pedro y Juan tienen **las mismas** <u>amigas</u>.*

SAME AMOUNT
UNCOUNTABLE (In singular)

- *Tomo **tanto** café **como** mi marido.*
- *Esa casa tiene **tanta** luz **como** la vuestra.*
- *Ya no tengo **tanto** pelo **como** antes.*

COUNTABLE (In plural)

- *Tengo **tantos** problemas **como** tú.*
- *Este hotel tiene **tantas** habitaciones **como** el de la playa.*
- *Tú no tienes **tantos** problemas **como** yo, ¿no?*

■ When it is clear what we are talking about, we don't state the second half of the comparison. But with **tanto/-a/-os/-as** we **only** eliminate the second part **when the sentence is in the negative:**

- *Mi ordenador tiene **tanta** memoria **como** el tuyo pero <u>no</u> lleva **tantos** programas.* [como el tuyo.]
  [*Mi ordenador tiene tanta memoria como el tuyo y lleva tantos programas.*]
  └ *como el tuyo.*

Yo voy a coger el 7, ¿y tú?

Ejem...yo, yo... el mismo.

N-14

BUS

5 Here is some further information about Lola Menta and Carmen Druga.
Complete the sentences as in the example.

	Lola	Carmen
Maridos	4	4
Pastillas para dormir	3 (Morfidal)	6 (Morfidal)
Agua mineral	Vichí	Vichí
Yates	3	3
Peluquera personal	Paquí Tijeras	Rocío Mechas
Entrenador personal	Jesús Cachas	Jesús Cachas
Amigas íntimas	Cari, Bea y Ana	Luci, Rosa y Pepi
Tazas de café al día	5 tazas (Colombiano)	5 tazas (Brasileño)

➲ Lola ha tenido ..*tantos*........ maridos como Carmen.

1. Carmen bebe .... agua que Lola.

2. Carmen tiene .... entrenador personal que Lola.

3. Carmen toma .... café .... Lola, pero no toma ....

4. Lola toma las mismas .... que Carmen pero no toma ....

5. Lola y Carmen tienen .... yates.

6. Lola tiene tantas .... como Carmen pero no ....

7. Carmen no tiene .... peluquera .... Lola.

6 Pablo and Paula have only just met, but have already found out that they are made for each other.

➲ Van a los ..*mismos*........ restaurantes: vegetarianos.

1. Se duchan .... : con agua fría.

2. Los dos son .... tímidos: no hablan con nadie.

3. Los dos tienen .... trabajo: son fontaneros.

4. Los dos cocinan .... bien: hacen maravillas.

5. Oyen .... tipo de música: jazz y zarzuela.

6. Les gustan .... películas: japonesas y turcas.

7. Los dos son .... altos: miden 1,72.

8. Tienen .... terapeuta, pero lo van a dejar.

9. Les gusta .... vino: Sotontano.

10. Los dos se acuestan .... tarde: a las 2 de la mañana.

11. Los dos tienen .... manía: morderse las uñas.

C   Relative superlative: *El hombre más rápido del mundo*.

■ When we want to highlight one thing or person above all the others in the group, we use:

el/la/los/las	(NOUN)	más/menos	ADJECTIVE	de + WHOLE UNIT
				que + SENTENCE

- *El edificio azul es **el** rascacielos **más** alto **de** la ciudad.*
- *Es **el** (rascacielos) **más** alto **que** he visto en mi vida.*

■ When it is clear from the context, it is not necessary to mention the unit being referred to:

- *Me has dicho quién es la más simpática de tus amigas, pero no quién es **la más rica**.*
  [The wealthiest of your friends.]

7 Connect the elements in the three columns to form sentences.

➲ Mi novio es	a. la menor	a. de la clase.
1. El Quijote es	b. el tren más rápido	b. que conozco.
2. Antoñito es	c. el libro más emocionante	c. de toda nuestra vida.
3. El AVE es	d. el hombre más guapo	d. de las cinco hermanas.
4. Los tres primeros años son	e. el niño más torpe	e. que he leído.
5. Sofía es	f. los más importantes	f. de España.
6. Los Polos son	g. el cuadro más famoso	g. de los últimos cinco años.
7. Este verano ha sido	h. la habitación más tranquila	h. del planeta.
8. Su dormitorio es	i. el peor día	i. de la semana.
9. El Guernica es	j. el más seco	j. de la casa.
10. El lunes es	k. las zonas más frías	k. de Picasso.

D Absolute superlative: *Una mujer cariñosísima*.

■ To express that something demonstrates a very high degree in some respect, but without relating it to other objects of the same type, we use:

| ADJECTIVE ADVERB | → | -*ísimo*/-*a*/-*os*/-*as* |

- *Este rascacielos es altísimo.*
- *El sitio está bien pero la cafetería es carísima.*
- *Lola siempre llega tardísimo.*

■ When -*ísimo* is added to an adjective, it agrees in gender and number with the noun to which it refers:

- *Tus hijos están altísimos.*
- *¡Qué barbaridad! Es una tienda carísima.*

👁 With adjectives that already express a considerable degree of intensity (such as *precioso, horrible, magnífico, estupendo, espantoso,* or *maravilloso*) you do not need to use -*ísimo*.

■ The -*ísimo* ending is added to the singular form of adjectives and some adverbs:

If the adjective or adverb ends in a vowel, you change the vowel to -*ísimo*:

> *alto/-a* → *altísimo/-a* *interesante* → *interesantísimo/-a*
> *temprano* → *tempranísimo* *tarde* → *tardísimo*

If the adjective or adverb ends in a consonant, you add -*ísimo*:

> *útil* → *utilísimo/-a* *fácil* → *facilísimo/-a* *difícil* → *dificilísimo/-a*

If the adjective ends in -*ble*:

> *amable* → *amabilísimo/-a* *sensible* → *sensibilísimo/-a*

With **adverbs** that end in -*mente* (formed from **the feminine singular of the adjective**) you add -*ísima*- to the adjective form:

> *lentamente* → *lentísimamente* *rápidamente* → *rapidísimamente*

👁 ADJECTIVES *joven* → *jovencísimo* *fuerte* → *fortísimo/fuertísimo*
  nuevo → *novísimo/nuevísimo* *antiguo* → *antiquísimo*
  poco → *poquísimo* *fresco* → *fresquísimo*
ADVERBS *cerca* → *cerquísima* *lejos* → *lejísimos*

➲ 44. Accentuation

223

8 Add the ending *-ísimo /-a /-os /-as* to these adjective, making sure you respect the agreements.

pocas	*poquísimas*	feliz	....	salado	....
simpáticos	....	joven	....	interesantes	....
antipático	....	amables	....	fácil	....
secas	....	agradable	....	divertido	....

9 Write the adjectives that correspond to these forms.

fortísimos	*fuertes*	fragilísimo	....	tontísimos	....
jovencísimas	....	grandísima	....	felicísimas	....
amabilísimo	....	blanquísimo	....	agradabilísimo	....

10 Add the ending *-ísimo* to these adverbs.

cerca	*cerquísima*	mucho	....	recientemente	....
lejos	....	poco	....	claramente	....
tarde	....	lentamente	....	fácilmente	....
pronto	....	tranquilamente	....	temprano	....

11 Ana and Puri are talking about their friend Felix's birthday party and love to exaggerate. Put the words in brackets into the *-ísimo/-a/-os/-as* form, though you will have to be careful, as some of the words do not work in this way. Also, watch out for the agreements.

Ana: Tú estabas (mona), ➔ *monísima* y el vestido que llevabas era precioso. Pero Mimín, la novia de Félix, estaba fatal, con ese pelo (1. **corto**) .... y (2. **rubio**) .... Y ese vestido (3. **largo**) .... y esos tacones (4. **altos**) .... Nada, fatal, (5. **horrible**) .... Y el bolso, ¿viste el bolso? Era (6. **feo**) .... , (7. **espantoso**) ....
Puri: El que está (8. **feo**) .... es Félix... Con esa barba (9. **largo**) .... , y (10. **despeinado**) .... Llevaba unos vaqueros (11. **gastado**)

.... y una camisa (12. **normal**) .... Seguro que la camisa era (13. **barato**) ....
Ana: Sí, es verdad. Pero el que está (14. **magnífico**) .... es Alejandro. (15. **Guapo**) .... y (16. **elegante**) .... Llevaba un traje (17. **precioso**) .... Y es (18. **educado**) .... Y, además, es (19. **simpático**) ....
Puri: Yo no lo vi en toda la noche. Estaba (20. **lejos**) .... ¡Qué suerte, hija! Tú estabas (21. **cerca**) .... de él...

Contesta a estas preguntas: ¿Quiénes iban mal vestidos? ....
¿Quiénes iban bien vestidos? ....

12 Complete as in the example. In two cases you cannot form the superlative, but will have to repeat the adjective.

➔ ● El profesor es muy agradable, ¿verdad?
   ○ Sí, es *agradabilísimo* .

1. ● No, prefiero no comprar este vino... Es muy caro.
   ○ Sí, es ....

2. ● Basta, no quiero ver más a José. Es muy creído.
   ○ Sí, es .... Me cae fatal.

3. ● ¿Qué pensáis? A mí me parece muy feo.
   ○ Es .... , la verdad.

4. ● Es un cuadro precioso. ¿Te gusta?
   ○ Sí, es ....

5. ● Es una situación horrible.
   ○ Sí, es .... ¿Nos vamos?

E   Mejor, peor, mayor, menor.

■ The adjectives **bueno, malo, grande, pequeño** and the adverbs **bien, mal**
have special forms to express a greater degree:

Mejor = (más + bueno) / (más + bien)	**Peor** = (más + malo) / (más + mal)

- El aceite de oliva es **mejor** que la mantequilla.
- Mi madre cocina **mejor** que tú.
- Es el **mejor** libro que he leído.

- La película es **peor** que el libro.
- Mi marido conduce **peor** que tú.
- ¿Quién es el **peor** de la clase?

Mayor = más grande (de más edad)	**Menor** = más pequeño (de menos edad)

- Mi hermana es un poco **mayor que** yo.
- Es el **mayor** pero no es el más listo.

- Tu novio es bastante **menor** que tú, ¿no?
- Sólo conozco al **menor** de los hermanos.

👁 When **mejor, peor, mayor** and **menor** are adjectives, they only agree in number:

- Las **bromas** de José son **mejores** que las de Alex.

13 Complete with *mejor, peor, mayor* and *menor*. Be careful with the agreements.

➡ ¡Veinte años más! Tu marido es bastante
...*mayor*..... que tú.

1. No me ha gustado nada la película. El libro es
mucho ....

2. El hotel era muchísimo .... que el del año
pasado. Había cucarachas y ratones. Lo hemos
pasado fatal.

3. Doctor, me siento mucho .... Estas
pastillas son fabulosas.

4. ¡Claro que Jesús es .... que yo!
Él tiene 28 y yo 37.

5. En mi país los autobuses son .... :
son más puntuales y más cómodos.

6. Aquellos cursos fueron bastante ....
que los de otros años. No aprendimos nada.
Un desastre.

7. Está claro que estas gambas son ....
Aunque son más baratas, están bastante más frescas.

14 Fernando spends all his time comparing himself with Jorge, his best friend at school. Read this page
from his diary and cross out the second half of the comparison whenever possible.

Querido diario:

Hoy voy a hablar de mi amigo Jorge. ➡ Su padre no le puede pegar al mío
porque mi padre es más fuerte (que el suyo) (1) A mí me hacen más regalos
en Navidad que a él porque mi padre gana mucho más dinero que el suyo.
(2) Cuando hacemos carreras yo corro tanto como él, pero cuando jugamos
al fútbol yo no meto tantos goles como él. (3) Yo me tengo que ir a la
cama a las nueve y no entiendo por qué Jorge se acuesta más tarde que yo.
No es justo. (4) Como vamos a la misma clase, nos mandan los mismos
deberes, pero yo no tardo tanto como él en hacerlos. Yo soy mucho más rápido
que él. (5) Él vive tan cerca del colegio como yo, pero siempre va en coche.
Yo voy andando o en autobús. (6) A Jorge y a mí nos gusta la misma niña,
Susana, pero ella me mira a mí más que a él. (7) Yo soy mejor que él con
los videojuegos, pero él es mejor que yo con las canicas. (8) Los dos hemos
pasado la gripe a la vez. Un día me llamó y me dijo que tenía tanta fiebre
como yo y que le dolía la garganta tanto como a mí, pero que él no lloraba
tanto como yo, que era más valiente que yo. (9) Jorge es mi mejor amigo y
yo soy su mejor amigo. La verdad es que no sé si a Susana la quiero más que
a él, pero cuando estamos de vacaciones me acuerdo más de Jorge que de ella.

42. Joining sentences: *y, o, pero, sino, porque, cuando, si...*

A   *Y, o, ni*

■ With *y* we join one element to another:

- *Han venido Luis y María a vernos.*
- *Vamos a cenar y a ver una película.*
- *Fuimos a la fiesta y lo pasamos muy bien.*

■ When there are more than two elements, the *y* only needs to be put before the last one:

- *Tenemos que comprar patatas, tomates, lechuga y ajos.*
- *Me levanto, me ducho, desayuno y voy a trabajar.*

But you can also say:

- *Hay que comprar patatas y tomates y ajos.*

👁 We use *e* (instead of *y*), especially when writing, if the next word starts with *i-* or *hi-*:

- *En el barrio viven paquistaníes e indios.*   • *Tienen que ir a la reunión padres e hijos.*

■ With *o* we indicate and **choice** between one or more elements:

- *¿Sacas tú la basura o la saco yo?*
- *De regalo, quiere unos guantes o un collar.*

- *Podemos ir al cine esta noche. ¿O vamos al teatro?*
- *O a la discoteca. Tengo ganas de bailar.*

O can be put before all the elements referred to, except in questions:

- *Iré el jueves o el viernes, aún no lo sé .*

And also:
- *Iré o el jueves o el viernes, aún no lo sé .*   But: *¿Oyte apetece un té o prefieres un café?*

👁 We use *u* (instead of *o*), especially when writing, if the next word starts with *o-* or *ho-*:

- *Los López tienen siete u ocho hijos.*   • *¿Vertical u horizontal?*

---

1 **Match up the two halves of the sentences.**

➲ Están aquí Clara y	a. después al cine.	6. ¿Quieres un café o	g. a la playa?
1. Vamos a ir a cenar y	b. sus amigas del colegio.	7. El viaje dura dos o	h. Holanda. No me acuerdo.
2. Tenemos clase esta tarde y	c. inglés. Es traductor.	8. ¿Vamos al campo o	i. Alemania, me parece.
3. Vino tu madre e	d. mañana por la tarde.	9. Lola quiere visitar Bélgica u	j. ocho horas en el avión.
4. Julián habla muy bien francés e	e. me encuentro con Ana.	10. Y Paco quiere visitar Italia o	k. prefieres una cerveza?
5. Esta mañana salgo de casa y	f. hizo la cena para todos.	11. Vamos a estar siete u	l. tres horas en barco.
		12. Setenta u	m. ochenta personas son demasiadas.

■ With *ni* we add one negative element to another:

- ○ <u>No</u> ha venido Juan.
- ○ **Ni** María. ¡Qué raro!

- ○ <u>No</u> quiero té **ni** café.
- ○ Luis <u>no</u> sabe inglés **ni** quiere aprender.

We can put *ni* before all the elements referred to.
Thus we can indicate from the very beginning that
all these elements will be negative:

- ○ **Ni** ha venido **ni** ha llamado.
- ○ **Ni** tengo novio **ni** estoy casada **ni** quiero casarme.

2 Carmen and her mother are buying presents for the family. How many things will they buy for each person?

➔ Para Ana, un perfume, o un bolso y una camiseta. ....1 ó 2.............

1. Para Mercedes, ni juguetes ni dulces: un cuento. ....

2. Para Antonio, un libro, un póster o un disco. ....

3. Para Julia, un marco de fotos o un cuadro. ....

4. Para Elisa, ni un piano, ni una guitarra ni nada. ....

5. Para Carla, una camisa y un chaleco o unos pantalones y un cinturón. ....

6. Para Juan, una toalla y un jabón. ....

7. Para Jordi, una planta y un disco, o unos zapatos. ....

8. Para Menchu, ni libros ni discos. Un collar o una pulsera. ....

3 Some friends are suggesting ideas for the weekend. Complete with *y*, *ni*, or *o*.

Carla: El sábado ➔ ....o.... el domingo por la mañana podemos ir al zoo (1) .... después a pasear por el campo.

Goyo: No hay tiempo para las dos cosas: (2) .... vamos al zoo (3) .... vamos al campo.

Merche: A mí no me apetece (4) .... una cosa (5) .... la otra. ¿Por qué no vamos a pasar el día a casa de Tomás?

Carla: ¿A casa de Tomás (6) .... a casa de Luis? La casa de Luis es más grande y tiene jardín.

Goyo: Pero (7) .... Luis (8) .... Tomás saben nada de nuestros planes. En vez de eso, podemos ir todo el fin de semana a la playa a tomar el sol (9) .... a descansar.

Merche: Sí, mejor. A la playa por la mañana (10) .... a bailar por la noche, ¿de acuerdo?

4 Look at the picture and complete the descriptions with *y* or *ni*. Which of the two is Cristina's husband?

El tipo de hombre ideal de Cristina...

➔ No lleva ..ni.. barba ni.... bigote.

1. Tiene el pelo corto ...... liso.

2. Lleva chaqueta ...... corbata.

3. No es ...... muy alto ...... muy delgado.

4. No tiene los ojos azules ...... el pelo rubio.

El marido de Cristina...

5. Lleva barba ...... bigote.

6. No tiene el pelo ...... corto ...... liso.

7. No lleva ...... chaqueta ...... corbata.

8. No es ...... muy bajo ...... muy gordo.

9. Tiene los ojos azules ...... el pelo rubio.

B   *Pero, sino*

■ *Pero* introduces an idea which **contrasts with** or **limits** a previous idea:

- Tengo una piscina en casa, ***pero*** *no sé nadar.*
- Quiero mucho a Lorenzo, ***pero*** *no me voy a casar con él.*

- Tu hermano no ha llegado, ***pero*** *sí tu cuñada.*
- La casa de Luisa es fantástica ***pero*** *un poco cara.*

---

5 Put *y*, *o*, or *pero* into the sentences below, as most appropriate.

⟳ Julián quiere ganar mucho dinero

....Y.... ha hecho entrevistas con tres empresas.

....O.... casarse con una chica millonaria.

.pero. no quiere trabajar.

1. Los López tienen una casa en la playa

.... siempre van a la montaña.

.... en la montaña. No me acuerdo.

.... otra en la montaña.

2. Rogelio está enamorado de Marta

.... de Alicia. No estoy seguro.

.... de Clara al mismo tiempo.

.... no quiere irse a vivir con ella.

3. El nuevo empleado trabaja muy bien

.... trabaja muy mal, depende del día.

.... mucho. Es el mejor de todos.

.... poco: sale siempre el primero.

4. Mañana vamos al cine

.... no antes de las 7 porque tengo que trabajar.

.... , mejor, a dar una vuelta si no llueve.

.... a cenar después.

5. Rosa todos los días va al gimnasio

.... hace ejercicio en casa, una de dos.

.... todavía no está tan fuerte como Alex.

.... , además, come sólo frutas y verduras.

■ We can use *pero* to **add an idea** that **contrasts** with another, previous negative idea:

Jane no habla español, ***pero*** *lo comprende.*

- Tú no has pedido jamón, ¿verdad?
- No, no he pedido jamón, ***pero*** *me lo han traído.*

- No tengo azúcar, ***pero*** *tengo miel.*
- No has hecho bien el examen, ***pero*** *has aprobado.*

■ We use *sino* to correct. **We negate** an element of an idea and **substitute** it for another:

Jane no habla español ***sino*** *inglés.*

- Usted ha pedido jamón, ¿verdad?
- No, yo no he pedido jamón ***sino*** *salmón.*

- Esas galletas no llevan azúcar ***sino*** *miel.*
- En el examen no has sacado un 6, como yo creía, ***sino*** *un 8.*

👁 [Mopa no pasea con su dueño
~~pero~~ con su dueña.]
sino

👁 When *sino* introduces a conjugated verb,
it becomes *sino que*:

- El ladrón no huyó por la ventana, **sino que** <u>estuvo</u> escondido en la casa
  hasta que llegó la policía.
- Y esta tarde no vas al parque, **sino que** <u>te vas a quedar</u> en casa
  y sin televisión.

6 The actress Guadalupe Chamorro is losing her memory. Help her sons correct
the information she's giving to a journalist using *sino* or *sino que*.

⤷ Nací en Reus en 1933.

(Nació en Barcelona en 1933.)

No nació en Reus sino en Barcelona.

1. En 1950 me casé. Mi marido se llamaba Paco
Frutales. (Su marido se llamaba Antonio Frutales.)

....

2. En 1985 mi marido me abandonó por otra.
(En 1985 su marido murió de un infarto.)

....

3. Mi primera película fue un gran éxito.
(En realidad fue un fracaso.)

....

4. En el 52 fui la protagonista de "Historia de G".
(Tuvo un papel secundario en la película.)

....

5. Tengo siete hijos.
(Tiene sólo tres hijos.)

....

6. Mi hijo mayor, Julián, es director de cine.
(Julián trabaja en el circo.)

....

7. Gané un Óscar por la película "José y yo".
(Ganó el premio "Ciudad de Teruel".)

....

7 Guadalupe Chamorro is also rather pessimistic and forgets to tell the journalist the positive
things about her life. Help her sons once more as they complete the information she gives.

⤷ No tengo ninguna hija.

(Tiene cinco nietas preciosas.)

No tiene ninguna hija, pero tiene cinco

nietas preciosas.

1. Ya no tengo casa en Hollywood.
(Tiene casas en París y en Roma.)

....

....

2. Gregory Peck nunca me quiso.
(Tuvo romances con varios actores de Hollywood.)

....

....

3. Nunca he tenido una buena crítica.
(Ha ganado mucho dinero en el cine.)

....

....

8 The journalist who has interviewed Guadalupe is foreign and doesn't know how to use *sino*.
Correct the five mistakes he has made.

⤷ No tiene siete hijos ~~pero~~ (.*sino*.) tres.

No es joven, pero (...✓....) todavía es atractiva.

1. No se casó en 1940 pero (........) en 1950.

2. No tiene avión privado pero (........) la productora
le regaló un barco de recreo.

3. Su primera película no fue "Historia de G" pero
(........) "Las aventuras del conde Drágila".

4. No es una buena actriz, pero (........) ha ganado
mucho dinero.

5. Su hijo no trabaja en el cine pero (........) en el circo.

6. No le gustan los periodistas, pero (........) a veces
habla con ellos.

7. Ahora no vive en Barcelona pero (........) en Reus.

8. No vive sola pero (........) con su hermana pequeña.

229

C Porque, como, es que

■ With **porque** we explain the cause for something:

Tengo que irme a casa **porque** mi hija está enferma.

Ah, ¿qué le pasa?

[Jaime explains why he has to go home: his daughter is ill.]

The cause introduced by **porque** will normally come last.

● No puedo ir a la fiesta de Jimena **porque** me voy a Madrid.

👁 Unlike the 'why' word, which asks the question about the cause, and is written as two words, with an accent (**por qué**), the 'because' word, which explains the cause, is written as a single word with no accent (**porque**):

● ¿**Por qué** no vas a trabajar?
○ **Porque** tengo 39 de fiebre.

➲ 40. Questions and exclamations

■ With **como** we introduce a fact that must be taken into account in order to understand another fact that follows:

Como está lloviendo, mejor nos quedamos en casa, ¿no?

Sí, mejor nos quedamos.

[If the boy takes the rain into account, he will understand the girl's suggestion.]

The cause introduced by **como** will normally be put first.

● **Como** trabaja tanto, Raquel no tiene tiempo para su familia.

¿Por qué llegas tan tarde?

Es que no ha sonado el despertador.

■ **Es que** is used to introduce a cause as the justification for something:

● No he hecho los deberes. **Es que** no he tenido tiempo en toda la semana. [The person justifies him or herself.]
● Me gustaría ir al cine contigo esta noche, pero no puedo. **Es que** mañana tengo que madrugar. [The person apologises.]

9 Complete these sentences with the most appropriate explanation. Be careful with the order of the elements.

como no hay nada interesante en el cine ✓
porque me he quedado sin batería en el móvil
como ya teníamos las entradas para el concierto
porque se han ido al parque con su madre

como Catalina sabe latín
porque ésta se nos ha quedado pequeña ✓
como el banco estaba cerrado
porque necesitábamos ocho

➲ *Como no hay nada interesante en el cine,* mejor alquilamos una película. ....

➲ ...., Dentro de un mes nos mudamos de casa *porque ésta se nos ha quedado pequeña.*

1. .... le he pedido que me ayude con la traducción ....

2. .... los niños no están en casa ....

3. .... he tenido que pedirle dinero a mi hermano ....

4. .... no te he llamado por teléfono ....

5. .... no tuvimos que hacer cola ....

6. .... hemos puesto un ejemplo más ....

10 Complete the dialogues with the most appropriate response.

> Pues porque María no me invitó. ✓   Sí, porque, si no, se va a enfriar el pescado.   Es que mi madre es de Milán.
> No, porque no hay mucho que hacer en la oficina.   Es que no tenemos a nadie con quien dejar al niño.
> Es que no tengo cepillo.   Porque ya estamos en junio y los días son más largos.   Es que no había huevos.

➲ • ¿Por qué no viniste a la fiesta anoche?
   ○ *Pues porque María no me invitó.*

1. • ¿No has preparado la tortilla?
   ○ ....

2. • ¿Podemos empezar a comer ya nosotros?
   ○ ....

3. • ¿Vas a trabajar este fin de semana?
   ○ ....

4. • ¿Por qué no te has lavado los dientes?
   ○ ....

5. • ¿Vais a venir esta noche a casa?
   ○ ....

6. • Oye, ¡qué bien hablas italiano!
   ○ ....

7. • ¿Por qué amanece tan pronto?
   ○ ....

D   *Que, donde, como, cuando*

■ We can use phrases to **give information** about objects, people or places that we name with **nouns**. We use the relative *que* (for objects and people) or *donde* (for places) to join the phrases to the nouns:

• Ese <u>perro</u> se llama Bruch.

• Ese <u>perro</u> **que** tiene Ana en brazos se llama Bruch.

[The dog is called Bruch. Ana is holding the dog in her arms.]

• La <u>novela</u> es fantástica.

• La <u>novela</u> **que** me regalaste es fantástica.

[The novel is fantastic. You gave me the novel.]

• El <u>hotel</u> está en la playa.

> ➲ 33. Indicativo or subjuntivo?

• El <u>hotel</u> **donde** trabaja Carlos está en la playa.

[The hotel is by the beach. Carlos works in the hotel.]

231

11 Some words have got rubbed out in the letter that Ángela wrote to the Three Wise Men. Help them reconstruct the sentences, using the expressions from the box.

Queridos Reyes Magos:

Este año quiero el libro de los animales ...que tiene mi amiga..... Sandra; la muñeca de Juguetosa (1) .... sola y (2) .... muchas canciones de Los Changuitos; la película de dibujos animados (3) .... con mis padres (es de una princesa india (4) .... con un marinero (5) .... muy lejano); el disco del cantante (6) .... de Neurovisión este año; y un traje de enfermera. Para mi hermana Lucía, (7) .... , os pido la bicicleta (8) .... para ir al colegio.

que tiene mi amiga ✓
que vive en un país
que puede andar
que tiene nueve años
que se enamora y se casa
que ha ganado el festival
que vi ayer en el cine
que quiere comprarse
que canta

12 Gianni is learning Spanish and is writing some curious facts about his family, but is having problems forming sentences with *que*. Can you help him?

➲ Mi tío Humberto tiene una casa preciosa. La casa de mi tío está en la costa.
 Mi tío Humberto tiene una casa preciosa que está en la costa.

1. Un primo mío está casado con una japonesa. La japonesa se llama Machiko.
 ....
 ....

2. Mi madre es traductora en una empresa. La empresa está a 10 Km. de nuestra casa.
 ....
 ....

3. Paola, mi hermana, escribe novelas. Las novelas de mi hermana tienen mucho éxito.
 ....
 ....

4. Ferdinando, mi hermano, tiene una cámara y se dedica a la fotografía. La cámara era de mi abuelo.
 ....
 ....

5. Y yo tengo un trabajo pero también tengo tiempo para estudiar español. Mi trabajo no me gusta nada.
 ....
 ....

13 When Gianni writes about his friends, he has problems forming sentences with *donde*.

➲ Gian Carlo trabaja en un casino. En ese casino yo tengo prohibida la entrada.
 Gian Carlo trabaja en un casino donde yo tengo prohibida la entrada.

1. Bianca es azafata en una compañía aérea y también es bailarina. En la compañía aérea gana mucho dinero.
 ....
 ....

2. Silvia trabajaba antes en una editorial, pero ahora se dedica a escribir guías de viaje. Yo trabajé también en esa editorial.
 ....
 ....

3. Lucca vive todo el año en un hotel de Milán. En el hotel no pueden entrar ni niños ni perros.
 ....
 ....

4. Piero vive en un pueblecito de la India. En ese pueblo todavía no hay luz ni teléfono.
 ....
 ....

5. Francesca es profesora en una escuela, pero quiere dejar la enseñanza. En la escuela sólo hay veinte estudiantes.
 ....
 ....

- When the subject or object of a verb is a **subordinate** phrase with a conjugated verb, it is introduced by **que**:

  - *Tu hermana me ha dicho* **que** *viene el fin de semana.*
  - *He visto* **que** *te has comprado un coche nuevo.*
  - *La jefa quiere* **que** *trabajemos el sábado.*
  - *Me gusta* **que** *me rasquen la espalda.*
  - *Es importante* **que** *llevemos ropa de abrigo.*

  👁 **Que** is not used when the subordinate phrase is an **infinitive**:

  - *La jefa quiere* **trabajar** *el sábado.*
  - *Me gusta* **jugar** *con mi amigo Sebastián.*
  - *Es importante* **llevar** *ropa de abrigo.*

  ➲ 20. Non-personal forms

  ➲ 33. Indicativo or subjuntivo?

14 In which sentences do we need to put *que*? Mark with ↓ the place where it should go.

- ➲ No soporto llevar zapatos de tacón. Me duelen mucho los pies. (...✓....)
- ➲ No soporto↓leas el periódico en el desayuno. (..*que*.)
1. Quieren cenemos esta noche en un restaurante argentino. (........)
2. Quieren cenar en un restaurante argentino. (........)
3. ¿Es necesario llevar traje de etiqueta? (........)
4. ¿Es necesario lleve corbata? (........)
5. Le gusta le den masajes en los pies. (........)
6. Le gusta dar masajes en los pies. (........)
7. Últimamente no consigo dormir. Estoy muy nerviosa. (........)
8. Últimamente no consigo duerma. Está muy nerviosa. (........)

- We can use **como**, **donde** and **cuando** to refer to the manner, place or time at which an action happened:

Manner:

Como {
- *Prohibieron fumar en los bares* **como** *habían hecho en otros países.*
- *Voy a hacer la tortilla* **como** *me has dicho, sin cebolla y con ajo.*
- *Termina este trabajo* **como** *puedas, pero termínalo pronto.*

Place:

Donde {
- *Al abuelo lo enterramos* **donde** *nos había dicho.*
- *Mis gafas no están* **donde** *las he dejado. ¿Tú las has visto?*
- *Aparca* **donde** *encuentres un sitio, pero no en doble fila.*

Time:

Cuando {
- *Nos encontramos con Daniel* **cuando** *íbamos al instituto.*
- *Me pongo muy nerviosa* **cuando** *hay tormenta.*
- *Iremos a visitaros* **cuando** *tengamos unos días libres.*

➲ 33. Indicativo or subjuntivo?

15 ¿*Donde, como* or *cuando*?

➔ He colgado el cuadro

donde	me has dicho, con dos clavos finos.
como	me has dicho, al lado del espejo.
cuando	no había nadie en casa.

1. Marga hizo una cena

donde	sólo ella sabe hacerla: fantástica.
como	se fueron sus padres de viaje.
cuando	vive ahora, en casa de sus padres.

2. Hoy he comido

donde	he terminado de hacer cosas en el banco.
como	siempre, con prisa.
cuando	come Carlos, un restaurante estupendo.

3. En el concierto de ayer, Ravinof tocó el piano

donde	suele tocar los sábados, en el Auditorio General.
como	nadie se lo esperaba: ¡en la pausa!
cuando	suele tocar: fatal.

4. Me compré un traje

donde	el de tu madre, con cinturón, pero blanco y negro.
como	empezaron las rebajas.
cuando	se lo compró tu madre, en Zaza.

16 Carlota and Arnau are teenagers and always avoid answering their parents directly.
Link the questions with the answers and write in *donde*, *como* or *cuando* as appropriate.

➔ ¿Dónde vais de excursión?
1. ¿Cuándo pensáis volver?
2. ¿Dónde vais a dormir?
3. ¿Cómo vais a ir? ¿En coche?
4. ¿Cuándo tienes los exámenes del instituto?
5. ¿Cómo piensas aprobar si no estudias nada este fin de semana?

➔ ¿Cuándo vamos a conocer a tu novio?
6. ¿Y cómo se llama?
7. ¿Dónde vive el tal David?
8. ¿Cómo os conocisteis?
9. ¿Cuándo empezó a trabajar?

(➔) ...*Donde*... vamos siempre, al campo.
a. ( ) .... podamos, no sé, en autobús a lo mejor.
b. ( ) .... encontremos sitio, en una pensión o en un camping.
c. ( ) .... siempre. Ya estudiaré la semana que viene.
d. ( ) .... nos cansemos del campo, dentro de unos días.
e. ( ) .... acabe el curso, a finales de junio.

(➔) ...*Cuando*... él pueda. Es que tiene mucho trabajo ahora.
f. ( ) .... vivía la tía Lou, por allí cerca.
h. ( ) No sé, ... dejó el Instituto, supongo.
i. ( ) .... te he dicho mil veces, mamá: David.
j. ( ) Pues .... he conocido a todos mis novios: chateando, en la cola de un concierto, no me acuerdo.

E   Cuando, hasta que, en cuanto, mientras, siempre que, antes de (que), después de (que)

■ **Cuando** is used to indicate that two events are connected in time.
The two events may be simultaneous or one before the other:

Cuando	Simultaneous events	One event before and the other after

- *Jenaro canta ópera **cuando** se ducha.*
  [He sings and has a shower at the same time.]
- ***Cuando** llueve y hay sol, sale el arco iris.*
- *Siempre escuchaba música **cuando** estudiaba.*

  ➡ 33. Indicativo or subjuntivo?

- ***Cuando** terminó la película, nos acostamos.*
- *Esther se levanta de mal humor **cuando** duerme poco.*

- ***Cuando** nos acostamos, la película ya había terminado.*
  [Firstly, the film will finish. After this we will go to bed.]

17 Read the following sentences about Belén's habits, and then put the actions on the right into the correct order. Be careful, as some of the actions happen simultaneously.

A. Se levanta cuando suena el despertador.

B. Cuando sale de casa, apaga la tele.

C. Cuando se ha duchado, se viste.

D. Desayuna cuando está vestida.

E. Se ducha cuando se levanta.

F. Cuando termina el desayuno, sale de casa.

G. Ve la tele cuando desayuna.

➡ Primero ..*suena el despertador*.. ;

     después ..*se levanta*............. ;

1. después .... ;

2. luego .... ;

3. a continuación .... y

     .... ;

4. después .... ;

5. y, por último, ...

18 Match questions and answers, chose your own answer from the options and then check the results.

➡ Cuando no puedo dormir,

A. Cuando hace mucho calor,

B. Cuando mi novio/-a me deja,

C. Cuando estoy en un atasco,

I   a. salgo a buscar otro/-a inmediatamente.
    b. me retiro a un monasterio a meditar.
    c. me tomo una pastilla.

II   a. cuento ovejas.
    b. me levanto y como.
    c. me tomo una pastilla.

III   a. miro a las personas de los coches cercanos.
    b. me rasco la cabeza y me toco la nariz.
    c. me tomo una pastilla.

IV   a. meto la ropa interior en el frigorífico.
    b. me doy un baño en cubitos de hielo.
    c. me tomo una pastilla.

Mayoría de a: Eres una persona más o menos normal, no te preocupes.
Mayoría de b: Eres genial, sigue así.
Mayoría de c: Tienes un problema.

■ To connect two events in time, we can also use *en cuanto*, *siempre que*, *hasta que* or *mientras*:

➲ 33. Indicativo or subjuntivo?

En cuanto   One event happens immediately before another.

- **En cuanto** supo que su abuela estaba enferma, cogió un avión y se fue.
- Salimos corriendo de clase **en cuanto** suena el timbre.
- Dímelo **en cuanto** lo sepas, por favor, tengo mucha curiosidad.

- **En cuanto** suena el despertador, me levanto.

Desde que / Hasta que   One event marks the end in time of the other.

- Estuvo esperando **hasta que** lo llamé.
- Por las mañanas, **hasta que** me tomo un café, no puedo hacer nada.
- Por favor, **hasta que** yo te lo diga, no cuentes nada de nuestra relación.
- No he comido nada **desde que** desayuné.
- No he mirado a otra mujer **desde que** estoy contigo.
- No comeré nada **desde que** salga **hasta que** vuelva.

- No me levanto **desde que** me acuesto **hasta que** suena el despertador.

Siempre que   Every time one event happens, the other also happens.

- Antes íbamos al cine **siempre que** ponían algo interesante.
- **Siempre que** quedamos con mis padres, te pones enfermo.
- **Siempre que** vengas a Barcelona, ya sabes que puedes quedarte en casa.

- **Siempre que** paseo, escucho la radio.

Mientras   Two events happen at the same time.

- **Mientras** ella veía la tele nosotros jugábamos a las cartas.
- ¿Tú hablas con el móvil **mientras** conduces?
- No podrás comer verdura **mientras** tengas problemas de estómago.

- **Mientras** conduzco, canto.

19 Little Luis tells us about some of the things that happen to him, but he doesn't know how to speak properly yet. Help him by choosing the most appropriate option in each case.

➲ Juego con mis amigos en el parque en **cuanto/desde que/(hasta que)** mi madre me lleva a casa.

1. Pero no puedo ir al parque **mientras/siempre que/hasta que** quiero. Sólo una vez al día.

2. Me lavo las manos y la cara con jabón **en cuanto/mientras/hasta que** llego a casa, porque me ensucio mucho.

3. A veces lloro y lloro **desde que/ siempre que/hasta que** me compran un caramelo. ¡Es que me encantan los caramelos!

4. Mi madre me da la merienda **desde que/mientras/hasta que** vemos juntos la tele.

5. **Mientras/Siempre que/Hasta que** pego a otros niños, mi padre después se enfada y me castiga.

6. Por las mañanas, me quedo en casa de mis abuelos unas horas **en cuanto/mientras/hasta que** mis padres están trabajando.

7. Voy a la guardería **desde que/ mientras/hasta que** cumplí dos años. Pero no me gusta nada. Yo prefiero jugar en el parque.

Antes de (que) / Después de (que)	**One event comes before or after another**.

- *¿Por qué no limpiamos un poco **antes de que** lleguen los invitados?*
- *Tuvimos que limpiar un poco **antes de que** llegaran los invitados.*
- ***Antes de** apagar las velas, pide un deseo.*
- ***Después de que** se fueran los invitados, la casa estaba más sucia que **antes de** limpiar.*

- *Cenaré **después de** ducharme y saldré **antes de que** sean las diez.*

👁 With *Antes de (que)* and ***después de (que)*** we use either the subjunctive or the infinitive.

---

20 Paco Melena and Juan Pelón are talking about their experiences with baldness. Complete with *en cuanto, siempre que, desde que, hasta que, antes de (que)* or *después de (que)* as appropriate.

Paco Melena

➲ ....*En cuanto*.......... perdí el primer pelo, con 22 años, me puse en manos de un dermatólogo.

1. De hecho, ... yo naciera, mi padre ya estaba completamente calvo. Es cosa de familia.

2. Estuve haciendo el tratamiento veinticinco años: .... cumplí los 22 hasta los 47.

3. .... iba al peluquero, le pedía que me cortara mucho, para fortalecer el cabello.

4. Y .... no pasó el peligro, no probé ni una gota de alcohol.

5. .... terminar el tratamiento, no se me ha vuelto a caer ni un pelo. Ha sido un milagro.

Juan Pelón

6. No fui a un médico .... un niño me llamó calvo por la calle.

7. .... me quedé completamente calvo, me hice un peluquín, pero estaba muy feo, así que me compré una gorra.

8. .... perder el pelo, yo nunca llevaba gorra; pero ahora, si no me la pongo, me resfrío o se me quema la calva.

9. .... gastarme todo mi dinero en operaciones y trasplantes que no sirvieron de nada, decidí aceptarme como soy.

10. Además, ... mi novia me dijo que le gustan mucho más los hombres calvos, soy feliz.

237

F   Express conditions with *si*: *Si tienes tiempo, llámame*.

■ We use *si* to introduce a condition:

Si te casas conmigo, todo esto será tuyo, Vicky.

- *Podemos ir juntos al cine esta tarde, si os apetece.*
- *Si te compras un coche nuevo, ¿me dejarás conducirlo a mí?*
- *¿Vendréis a vernos en Semana Santa si encontráis un billete barato?*
- *Si llamara mi mujer, dígale que he salido.*

■ When we think that the condition could really happen (in the present or future), we use the **presente de indicativo** in the *si* clause:

- *Si me <u>suben</u> el sueldo, vamos a dar una fiesta para celebrarlo.*
- *Llámame por teléfono si <u>ves</u> algún problema.*
- *Si <u>tenéis</u> vacaciones en julio, ¿vendréis con nosotros de viaje?*

👁 We cannot use either the *Futuro* or the *Presente de subjuntivo* in the clause introduced by a conditional *si*:

El domingo, si ~~lloverá~~, nos quedaremos en casa.
lluEve

Si ~~quiera~~ venir con nosotros, la invitaremos.
quiere

➡ 33. Indicativo or subjuntivo?

21 Ramón Eurales is an elderly millionaire. He has made a will and has laid down certain conditions that his heirs will have to meet if they want to inherit. Complete the sentences with the verbs from the boxes.

➡ Mi hijo mayor, Juan, ...*será*....... director de la empresa si ...*termina*.... la carrera de Derecho. Mi hija Marta (1) .... con la casa de Santander si (2) .... de Ibiza y (3) .... con su novio. Mi mujer (4) .... 200.000 euros cada año pero sólo si no (5) .... a casar y no (6) .... más hijos. Mi sobrino Luis (7) .... la editorial Eurol si (8) .... de la cárcel y (9) .... la bebida. Mi hermano Pedro (10) .... vivir en la casa de la isla el resto de su vida si (11) .... a su amante y (12) .... con su mujer.

Ser	Terminar

Casarse	Volver
Quedarse	

Tener	Volverse
Recibir	

Dirigir	Dejar
Salir	

Volver	Poder
Abandonar	

■ When we think that the condition is impossible or improbable, we use the **imperfecto de subjuntivo** in the *si* clause:

Si algún día te divorciaras de tu mujer, a lo mejor podría casarme contigo.

- *Si <u>volviera</u> a nacer, me gustaría ser como tú.*
  [But I cannot be born again.]

- *Llámame por teléfono si <u>vieras</u> algún problema.*
  [But it is unlikely that there will be a problem.]

- *Si <u>tuviera</u> el dinero que me pides, te lo dejaría, pero no lo tengo.*

■ In the **clause that does not begin with** *si,* the form of the verb we use depends on what we want to say: a request, a statement, a supposition or a question etc:

- *Si vas a Barcelona el mes que viene,...*
  [I think it very likely that you will go.]

- *Si fueras a Barcelona el mes que viene,...*
  [I think it very unlikely that you will go.]

...<u>tienes</u> que ver a Montse.
...<u>llámame</u> por teléfono.
...<u>no olvides</u> traerme algo de vino.
...<u>conocerás</u> a Álex y a Lourdes.
...yo te <u>podría</u> acompañar.
...¿<u>visitarías</u> la Sagrada Familia?

---

22 Mark a ↓ where the *si* should go in each sentences, and then decide who was talking to Florentino Peláez: his boss (B), his wife (W) or his daughter (D).

➔ ↓no me **das** dinero, no **puedo** hacer la compra ..*W*...

1. **tendrá** que venir el sábado hoy no **pudiera** trabajar ....

2. te **vas** de viaje, **tráeme** una muñeca ....

3. **acabara** el informe antes de las dos, le **invito** a comer ....

4. ¿me **vas** a llevar de viaje contigo **saco** buenas notas? ....

5. **terminaras** pronto, **pasa** por el banco a sacar dinero ....

6. no me **podré** dormir no me **lees** un cuento ....

7. **dejamos** a la niña con mi madre, **podríamos** salir esta noche ....

8. **llámeme tuviera** algún problema el sábado en la oficina ....

---

23 Félix is always more optimistic than Tristán. Decide which of the two said the sentences below, and match them to the most appropriate ending.

➔ *Félix*....... Si mañana dejo de fumar,

　Tristán... Si mañana pudiera dejar de fumar,

1. .... Si estudiara un poco más cada día,

　............ Si estudio un poco más cada día,

2. .... Si Marta vuelve conmigo,

　............ Si Laura volviera conmigo,

3. .... Si gana este partido el Motril Fútbol Club,

　............ Si ganara este partido el Sexi Fútbol Club,

4. .... Si comiera menos bocadillos de calamares,

　............ Si como menos bocadillos de calamares,

5. .... Si adelgazo cinco kilos.

　............ Si adelgazara cinco kilos.

a. mi estómago me lo agradecía, seguro.

b. a lo mejor aprendo inglés en unos meses.

c. seguramente dejaría de toser y me sentiría mejor.

d. nos vamos todos a la playa a celebrarlo.

e. me gustaría ir con ella de vacaciones a Maldivas.

f. no tendría que comprarme ropa nueva
   para el verano.

239

24 Tristán has just inherited a fortune from his aunt Gloria and is making plans for the future. However, he feels that some things are possible, whereas others are not. Help him to form the *si* clauses correctly and then put them where they belong.

Piensa que es posible:

➲ Conseguir el amor de Laura

  Comprarles una casa a sus padres

  Mudarse a Madrid

  Dejar de trabajar un año

  Hacer muchos viajes a París

Piensa que es muy difícil:

➲ Tener cinco hijos

  Poder comprar todas las casas de su pueblo

  Vivir en Nueva York

  Dejar de trabajar para siempre

  Perder el miedo a los aviones

➲ *..Si.consigo.el.amor.de.Laura..................* , a lo mejor algún día nos casamos.

➲ *..Si.tuviéramos.cinco.hijos..................* , seríamos realmente felices juntos los siete.

1. .... , no pasa nada, ya trabajaré en el futuro.

2. .... , seguro que Laura se viene conmigo.

3. .... , podré aprender francés y hacer muchas compras.

4. .... , vivirán con más comodidad que ahora.

5. .... , en pocos años volvería a ser pobre.

6. .... , haría una urbanización de lujo.

7. .... , podría ir a Cuba, a Tailandia, a China...

8. .... , tendría un apartamento en la 5ª Avenida.

■ When the *si* clause concerns an impossible past, that cannot be true because something else happened, we use the **pluscuamperfecto de subjuntivo** in the *si* clause.

We use the **condicional compuesto** in the other part of the sentence to express a past hypothetical reality, and the **condicional simple** to express a hypothetical present or future:

- *Si <u>hubiera encendido</u> el cigarrillo, <u>habría estallado</u> el gas. Afortunadamente no encontró el mechero.*
- *Si <u>hubiera estudiado</u> más, <u>aprobaría</u> el examen de mañana. Seguro que suspendo.*

➲ 30. Condicional

➲ 31. Condicional compuesto

➲ 32. Forms of the subjuntivo

25 Complete the story with sentences from the box in the correct tenses. Add *si* when necessary.

Mi padre iba en un taxi. Hacía calor y abrió la ventanilla del taxi. Entró una abeja y le picó. Mi padre era alérgico a las picaduras de abeja y se puso muy enfermo. El taxista lo llevó al hospital. Mi padre se enamoró de la doctora que lo curó. Se casó con ella. Yo nací a los nueve meses. Por eso ahora estoy aquí y puedo contaros esta historia.

Era una tarde de verano, mi padre había cogido un taxi porque llegaba tarde al trabajo. ➲ *Si no hubiera hecho mucho calor* , (1) ....

.... la ventanilla del taxi. Si no hubiera abierto la ventanilla del taxi, (2) .... una abeja. (3) ....

.... a las picaduras de abeja, no (4) ....

muy enfermo. (5) .... muy enfermo, (6) el taxista

.... al hospital. (7) .... al hospital,

(8) .... de la doctora que lo curó. (9) ....

.... de la doctora que lo curó, (10) ....

.... con ella. Si (11) .... , yo

(12) .... Si yo (13) ....

nueve meses después, ahora (14) .... aquí y

(15) .... esta historia.

SECTION 7

Spelling

43. Letters and sounds

The Spanish alphabet is made up of the following letters:

A a *a*	**B b** *be*	**C c** *ce*	**Ch ch** *che*	**D d** *de*	**E e** *e*	**F f** *efe*	**G g** *ge*
H h *hache*	**I i** *i*	**J j** *jota*	**K k** *ka*	**L l** *ele*	**Ll ll** *elle*	**M m** *eme*	**N n** *ene*
Ñ ñ *eñe*	**O o** *o*	**P p** *pe*	**Q q** *cu*	**R r** *ere*	**RR rr** *erre*	**S s** *ese*	**T t** *te*
U u *u*	**V v** *uve*	**W w** *uve doble*	**X x** *equis*	**Y y** *i griega, ye*	**Z z** *zeta*		

The letters are feminine: • *Aquí tienes que poner **una** be, no **una** uve.*

In Spanish, there is generally a close correspondence between the way something is written and the way it is said.

👁 The letter *h* is silent.

A   Groups of letters that represent a single sound

■ The following combinations of letters represent a single sound:

ch [tʃ]	*ll* [ʎ]	*rr* [ʀ]

champú   chocolate
Chicago   hecho

ella   llave
lleno

perro   correr

■ The letter *q* **always** appears in combination with the u (the u is not pronounced). This combination is **always** followed by *e* or *i*:

qu [k]

👁 [͆uatro]   [͆uota]
      c   *c*

queso   quiero   aquí   que

❶ In Spanish there are many kinds of food with combinations of letters. Find out what they are by completing the words below.

➲ A mí me encanta el ..*ch*..ocolate. Pero engorda.

1. Es extraño, pero a Joaquín no le gusta ningún ......eso. Ni los frescos ni los curados.

2. La pae......a es un plato de mediodía. Los españoles nunca la pedimos para cenar.

3. ¡Qué buena está la torti......a de patatas!

4. En Madrid toman ......urros en el desayuno.

5. Estoy harto de comer po......o. ¿No podríamos comer una buena ......uleta un día de éstos?

6. Las ......irimoyas son una fruta de invierno, ¿verdad?

7. Prueba las alca......ofas con ......orizo de ese restaurante. Están buenísimas.

B Letters that can represent different sounds

LETTERS					SOUNDS

g → *a, o, u*

gato   apagar   amiga
gota   gorra   mago
gustar agua   antiguo

[g]

gu → *e, i*

guerra   juguete
guitarra conseguir

👁 There are some words (very few) where the u is pronounced. In these cases, the u is written with a dieresis or umlaut above it: ver*güe*nza, pin*güi*no.

g → *e, i*

gerundio ángel
gitano   frágil

[χ]

c → *a, o, u*

casa   escapar
comer   poco
cuñado   oscuro

[k]

c → *e, i*

cenar   hacer
cocina   encima

👁 In these cases, most Spanish speakers pronounce the [θ] sound as an [s]: *cenar* [senár]; *cocina* [cosína]...

[θ]

rr

Always comes between vowels and is **rolled**:

carro   perro   erre   hierro

r

Is **rolled** when it is the first letter of a word:

ropa   reír   río   Roma

and when it comes after *l, n* or *sub-*:

*En**r**ique   al**r**ededor*
*sub**r**ayar*

👁 [al~~r~~ededor] [En~~r~~ique]
      r   r

[R]

r

Is a **softer**, slightly rolled sound in all other cases:

caro   mejorar   empezar   ahora   transporte
crece   gracias   abrazo   salir   aprendo
señor   flor   pero   poder

[r]

y

As the first letter of a word or between vowels:

yo   yate   yegua
ayer   haya   leyendo

[ʎ]

y

As the last letter of a word or by itself:

hoy   hay   rey   Paraguay
detrás y delante

[i]

2 Guillermo Alfredo is a very studious parrot and wants to arrange these words according to their sounds. Help him.

a. Underline the letters with an [ɾ] sound and circle those that have the sound [R].

claro	cárro	risa	escribir	Roma	rosa	alrededor
rincón	roto	ratón	Sara	familiar	recibir	calor
sierra	raro	aparcar	caro	revolución	subrayar	toro

b. Underline the letters with an [k] sound and circle those that have the sound [θ] or [s].

cosa	cielo	cola	velocidad	conoces	práctico	felices
casco	acusar	costa	cerrar	cuscús	crema	casa
encerrar	canción	círculo	conciencia	oscuro	claro	

c. Underline the letters with an [g] sound and circle those that have the sound [χ].

guerra	gitano	antiguo	lengua	gesto	gente	ceguera
guapo	gris	dirigir	agenda	tragedia	generoso	gas
gato	guitarra	gorro	ágil	gracioso	cirugía	

d. Underline the letters with an [ʎ] sound and circle those that have the sound [i].

yo	ayer	haya	hay	y	ya	rey
reyes	jersey	playa	ley	leyes	hoy	trayendo

C   Different letters that can represent the same sound

LETTERS			SOUNDS
c { a	cama	poca	
o	correr	loco	
u	cubierto	oscuro	
qu { e	querer	quedar	[k]
i	quise	equipo	
k vocal	Alaska keroseno (o *queroseno*) kilo (o *quilo*) whisky (o *güisqui*) kurdo (o *curdo*)		
	👁 Very few words are written with *k*, Many of these can also be written with *c* or *qu*.		
c { e	cerrar	pertenece	
i	canción	encima	[θ]
	👁 In these cases, most Spanish speakers pronounce the [θ] sound as an [s]: *cerrar* [seRár]; *plaza* [plása] ...		
z { a	zapato	plaza	
o	zoo	zorro	
u	zumo	zurdo	
	👁 Very few words are written with *ze/zi*: *zeta, zigzag*...		
b	broma	Barcelona	[b]
	obtener	cambio	
v	vaso volver enviar		

g	}	e	gente mujer	
j		i	girar jirafa	[χ]

ll		llueve llamar pollo	
y		haya playa yo	[ʎ]

3 Complete the words that correspond to the following definitions. All of them have at least a *c* or a *z*.

➲ Una verdura que nos hace llorar. *C* e b o *l* *l* *A*

1. Género musical español parecido a la ópera. .... a r .... u e ....
2. Lugar donde podemos ver animales de sitios muy diferentes. .... o l ó g i ....
3. Parte del cuerpo donde tenemos el cerebro. .... a .... e .... a
4. Antiguo emperador de Rusia. .... a ....
5. Forma geométrica redonda. .... í .... u l ....
6. Persona que no puede ver. .... i e g ....
7. Número igual a nada. .... r o
8. Ciudad más importante de un país. .... p .... t l
9. Espectáculo con payasos y fieras. .... i r ....

4 Put the SMSes below into normal Spanish.

① ¿Ke tal estás? ¿Kómo va todo? ¿Te vienes a la disco esta tarde?

② Te kiero un montón. ¿Kedamos en kasa?

③ ¿Ké me dices? ¿Kieres venir o no?

④ Kalla, kalla, ke ayer konocí a un tipo guapísimo ;-)

⑤ Kuando vengas al kole, trae medio kilo de churros, ke tengo hambre. Hoy hemos komido fatal.

⑥ Viaje muy inkómodo. Demasiados kilómetros.

5 Help Guillermo Alfredo to get it right. Use a dictionary if necessary.

¿g or j?

masa....e	extran....ero	ener....ía	frá....il	pá....ina	mensa....e	condu....e	corri....ió
ló....ico	má....ico	....igante	vie....o	....irafa	gara....e	ur....ente	co....emos

¿b or v?

fa....uloso	....ino	cam....iamos	estu....o	....erde	o....tener	....er	ha....itación
posi....le	mó....il	a....razo	....om....a	ha....lar	....otella	....itamina	....oca....ulario
....oca	hier....a	....aso	....i....o	....uelo	sam....a	o....jeti....o	

¿ll or y?

....ueve	....o	....a	....evaron	a....er	....amar	pla....a	....eno
estre....a	....egarán	....orar	....egua	....oga	le....endo	be....a	bo....o

---

D   The ñ

■ The *ñ* is the most characteristic Spanish letter. In English, the special accent on this letter is sometimes referred to with the Spanish word "tilde", though in Spanish this word refers to written accents of all types:

> ñ [ɲ]   *español   niño   enseñar   bañera*

6 Many of the words below should be written with an ñ, not an n. Find and correct them.

> ⮕ En español tenemos muchas eñes, una letra típica de esta lengua.

1. Los suenos que no nos gustan se llaman pesadilllas.
2. Cuando echamos de menos algo, lo anoramos.
3. En otono, en el campo, cortamos mucha lena para poder encender la chimenea.
4. Cuando algo nos duele, decimos que nos hace mucho dano.
5. Tenemos nenes y nenas, pero también ninos y ninas.
6. Nos banamos en el mar y en baneras.
7. Ensenamos nuestra lengua a los que quieren aprenderla.
8. Y celebramos el ano nuevo comiendo doce uvas.

7 Letter soup: find the words that correspond to the definitions (they may be written horizontally or vertically).

> ⮕ Pronombre de primera persona singular.

1. Animal que tiene el cuello muy largo.
2. Animal que ladra.
3. Sirve para borrar.
4. Número entre el 3 y el 5.
5. Mucha gente lo toma por las mañana, sobre todo si es de naranja.
6. A los ratones les encanta comerlo.
7. Femenino de 'él'.
8. Gran corriente de agua que va al mar.
9. Lo usamos para lavarnos el pelo.
10. Lo contrario de 'barato'.
11. Última comida del día.
12. El día anterior a hoy.

Q	M	J	I	R	A	F	A	S	S
U	T	G	I	V	C	E	Y	O	C
E	H	X	Z	Z	H	C	E	N	A
S	B	O	C	U	A	T	R	O	R
O	F	C	Q	M	M	R	W	G	O
D	Ñ	R	Í	O	P	E	I	O	M
E	L	L	A	X	Ú	V	K	M	V
P	E	R	R	O	P	F	C	A	C

44. Accentuation

A   Word stress

■ Words are made up of syllables, which are groups of sounds that are said together, in a single breath:

ven	*ho-ja*	*plan-ta*	*co-ci-na*	*e-jem-plo*	*or-de-na-dor*	*im-pre-sio-nan-te*
[1 syllable]	[2 syllables]	[2 syllables]	[3 syllables]	[3 syllables]	[4 syllables]	[5 syllables]

■ In Spanish there are words made up of:

ONE SYLLABLE	TWO SYLLABLES	THREE OR MORE SYLLABLES
y, de, mi, pan, ten, col, sin, sal, ver, flor, luz...	*li-bro, me-sa, lá-piz, go-ma, co-che, dis-co...*	*sen-ci-llo, tran-qui-lo, bo-te-lla, te-le-vi-sor, im-pre-sio-nan-te, in-te-re-san-tí-si-mo...*

■ All words have a **stressed** syllable. One of the syllables is pronounced **louder** than the others. This is the **stressed syllable**:

yo	*e-llos*	*sá-ba-do*	*quí-ta-se-lo*
so-fá	*do-min-go*	*po-lí-ti-cos*	*re-ga-lán-do-se-las*
se-ma-nal	*con-tro-la-da*	*fri-go-rí-fi-co*	
re-pro-duc-tor	*ma-ra-vi-lla-dos*		
des-tor-ni-lla-dor			

Most words in Spanish have the following stress pattern: ··· ■ ■ ■ ■

■ There is only one written accent (or *tilde*): (´). which is always written over the vowel of the stressed syllable: *á, é, í, ó, ú* (*ca-fé, mó-vil, mé-di-co...*), taking into account the rhythm and the word ending:

If ending in a CONSONANT (except -*n* or -*s*): WITHOUT ACCENT	If ending in a VOWEL, -*n* or -*s*: WITH ACCENT	If ending in a VOWEL, -*n* or -*s*: WITHOUT ACCENT	If ending in a CONSONANT (except -*n* or -*s*): WITH ACCENT	ALWAYS WITH ACCENT	
can-tad	*so-fá*	*ma-pa*	*có-mic*	*mú-si-ca*	
re-loj	*es-quí*	*ma-pas*	*cés-ped*	*plá-ta-no*	
con-trol	*hin-dú*	*ha-bla*	*ár-bol*	*rá-pi-do*	
ha-blar	*jar-dín*	*ha-blas*	*fá-cil*	*sí-la-ba*	
sa-lir	*sa-lón*	*sa-len*	*ál-bum*	*mé-di-co*	
sa-lid	*sa-lí*	*sa-les*	*Ló-pez*	*plás-ti-co*	
ac-triz	*qui-zás*	*di-ce*	*cán-cer*	*cás-ca-ra*	
an-da-luz	*ja-rrón*	*ha-bían*	*dó-lar*	*fan-tás-ti-co*	
es-cri-tor	*de-trás*	*en-tra-da*	*lá-piz*	*gra-má-ti-ca*	
a-mis-tad	*fran-cés*	*can-ta-bas*	*a-zú-car*	*ki-ló-me-tros*	*pá-sa-me-lo*
pa-si-vi-dad	*can-ta-rás*	*fran-ce-sa*	*di-fí-cil*	*te-lé-fo-no*	*pí-de-se-las*
ro-tu-la-dor	*ca-ta-lán*	*es-cri-to-ra*	*por-tá-til*	*an-ti-pá-ti-cos*	*co-mén-ta-se-lo*
des-tor-ni-lla-dor	*co-mu-ni-ca-rán*	*de-mo-cra-cia*	*re-fe-rén-dum*	*de-mo-crá-ti-cos*	*to-mán-do-se-las*

■ Monosyllabic words are generally not written with an accent:

con, en, por...
pan, ser, sal, sol...
di, haz, pon, ten...

1 Jaime is teaching his parrot, Guillermo Alberto, how to write, but he's having problems with the written accents. Help him by putting in the written accents where necessary.

gustan, árbol, pajaro, llevamelo, menu, calor, cadaver, mejor,

coñac, abril, kilometro, examen, caracter, ademas, angel, hotel,

imbecil, ojala, agenda, haz, daselos, palabra, dormir, dormid,

sin, camisa, llamalo, fin, velocidad, saltatela, subir, suben,

descontrol, descontrolados, tomala, callad, callado, rayo, doctor,

tranquilidad, goma, sal, botella, bebetelos, primo, escribir, alegre,

inteligente, papel, papeles, salud, conductor, conductora.

2 The Herodes Academy has set an accents exam, but Rodrigo doesn't know the rules very well and hasn't written a single one. Write in the ten missing accents (not counting the example).

➜ La moneda española es el euro y la de Estados Unidos es el dólar.

1. Los Reyes Magos me van a traer un camion de madera y lo van a dejar en la cocina.

2. En el jardin de mis primos hay un arbol muy grande y siempre nos subimos.

3. Este verano voy a ir a Granada en tren y voy a pasar por un tunel.

4. Yo quiero tener un movil pero mis padres no me dejan.

5. Ayer tuve una discusion con mi hermano mayor porque no me llevaba de excursion.

6. Prefiero sentarme en el sofa y ver la television que hacer deberes.

7. Esto de poner acentos es muy dificil.

- When we add pronouns to an infinitive, a gerund or a positive imperative, the word stress stays on the same syllable. However, as the position of this stressed syllable within the word has changed, sometimes you have to write in an accent:

➜ 16. Position and combination

Pon + la → ponla	But:	*Pon + se + la → pónsela*
Pasar + lo → pasarlo		*Pasar + me lo → pasármelo*
		Entreguen + se las → entréguenselas
		Explicando + se lo → explicándoselo

➜ 34. Imperativo

- In the case of adverbs made up of an ADJECTIVE + -**mente**, if the base adjective is written with an accent, then the adverb will also be written with an accent:

claramente [cla-ra + men-te]	*fácilmente* [fá-cil + men-te]
igualmente [i-gual + men-te]	*cómodamente* [có-mo-da + men-te]

3 Write the following combinations of verbs and pronouns as single words, writing in the accent if necessary.

➜ comprando + se + la ...*comprándosela*...

1. escribid + nos + la ....

2. secar + lo ....

3. canta + la ....

4. pon + se + lo ....

5. mira + me + lo ....

6. haz + los ....

7. devolver + me + la ....

8. preparad + lo ....

9. resolviendo + lo ....

10. solucionar + la ....

11. pintando + nos + las ....

12. levantar + las ....

13. di + lo ....

14. haz + se + los ....

15. di + se + lo ....

4 Substitute the underlined part of the sentence for one of the adverbs in the box, writing in the accent if necessary.

| unicamente | seguramente | normalmente | estupidamente ✓ | tontamente | ultimamente |

➲ Se comportó <u>como un imbécil</u>. Empezó a dar gritos y a romper cosas y me marché.

...............*estúpidamente*...............

1. <u>Todas las noches</u> me tomo un vaso de leche antes de acostarme.

....

2. Ha engordado mucho <u>en estos tres meses</u>. Está mejor.

....

3. <u>Casi con toda probabilidad</u> tendrán que cambiar de casa. Van a tener trillizos.

....

4. Van a trabajar <u>sólo</u> con nosotras.

....

5. <u>De una forma absurda</u>, por culpa de un solo cigarro, volvió a fumar.

....

B Diphthongs

■ When a word has two vowels in a row, they can form two syllables or just one.
Two syllables are formed when the vowels *a, e* and *o* are combined:

| *a-é-re-o* *o-cé-a-no* *a-ho-ra* *ma-es-tro* *po-e-ta* *le-o* *te-a-tro* |

■ A single syllable is formed when an *a, e* and *o* are combined with an *i*, or a *u*, or when an *i* is combined
with a *u*. When vowels come together in this way in a single syllable they are called **diphthongs**:

-ai-, -au-:	*ai-re, au-la*	-ie-, -ue-:	*pien-so, rue-da*	-ia-, -ua-:	*pia-no, a-gua*
-io-, -uo-:	*sa-bio, cuo-ta*	-ei-, -eu-:	*pei-ne, eu-ro*		
-iu-, -ui-:	*ciu-dad, rui-do*	-oi-:	*oi-go*		

■ When the stressed syllable of a word contains a diphthong, the accent falls on the vowels *a, e, o,*
or on the second vowel of the combinations *-iu-* or *-ui-*:

sa-béis	*rue-da*	*cui-dan*	*cons-trui-do*
au-la	*bue-no*	*diur-no*	*viu-do*
biom-bo	*pia-no*		

■ There are some words where the stressed syllable does not fall on an *a, e,* or *o,* , but on an *i* or a *u*. In these
cases, the combination of vowels form two syllables and an accent is written over the *i* or the *u* to show
this:

| *Ma-rí-a* | *dí-a* | *rí-o* | *grú-a* | *a-hí* | *le-í-do* | *o-í-do* |

5 Guillermo Alberto is having problems with his diphthongs. Help him to write the accents where they are needed.

puerta viaje suavidad erais paella línea sauna diez pais
leon cuidala caida Ruiz raiz sabeis contais seis nueve
veintiseis infierno feo reuniamos devolvais soy buho Raul
cliente fiel confiabamos siguiendolos cruel diente sueño huir
ibais jerseis vais prohibo reisteis siguientes teorico feisimo
cien igual siesta duo via huevo guion ingenuo sabia sabia
sintiendo pie riesgo luego fuimos sepais hay

C Distinguishing between words by the accent: *te / té*

■ Some words are phonetically the same, but have different meanings.
When we write them, we have to distinguish between them by the use of accents:

MONOSYLLABIC WORDS

WITHOUT ACCENT

de [preposition]
el [article]
mi [possessive]
que [conjunction, relative]
se [pronoun]
te [pronoun]
si [conjunction: *Si quieres, voy.*]

WITH ACCENT

dé [*Presente de subjuntivo* of the verb *dar*]
él [pronoun]
mí [pronoun]
qué [interrogative or exclamation]
sé [*Presente de indicativo* of the verb *saber*]
té [noun: a drink]
sí [affirmative adverb: *Sí, ven.*]
sí [reflexive pronoun: *Se defendió a sí mismo.*]

OTHER WORDS

WITHOUT ACCENT

como [comparative, conjunction]
cuando [conjunction]
quien, quienes [relatives: *Es él quien viene.*]
este, esta, ... [demonstrative adjectives]
ese, esa, ... [demonstrative adjectives]
aquel, aquella, ... [demonstrative adjectives]
solo [adjective: *Estoy muy solo.*]

WITH ACCENT

cómo [interrogative]
cuándo [interrogative]
quién, quiénes [interrogatives: *¿Quién viene?*]
éste, ésta, ... [demonstrative pronouns]
ése, ésa, ... [demonstrative pronouns]
aquél, aquélla... [demonstrative pronouns]
sólo [adverb: *Ella sólo va conmigo.*]

⊛ 6. Demonstratives

6 Luisito is writing his first love letter, but is having difficulties with some of the accents. Help him by writing them in.

Querida Susana:

El otro día en casa de tu madre cuando ella tomaba el te y tu buscabas el .CD, te miré a los ojos y, buf, fue genial. Para mi eres la chica más estupenda que he visto en mi vida. No se, eres fantástica....

¿Vienes este domingo a patinar conmigo? Tengo unos patines nuevos. Aquellos que te gustaban tanto se rompieron. Si quieres venir, me mandas un sms. Pon solo una palabra: si. Y entonces yo estaré muy contento porque no pasaré la horrible tarde del domingo solo.

Luis

7 Susana is also having problems with the accents. This is what she has written in her diary.

Querido diario:

Hace muchos días que no te escribo. El domingo pasado salí con Luis y, bueno, fue un poco rollo. El no habló casi nada y como yo hablo tanto, no se qué pensar... ¿Se aburrió? ¿Se divirtió? No se.... Me escuchó, eso si, pero no se si me escuchó con ganas (yo a veces no escucho mucho si algo no me interesa mucho).

Ah, Luis tiene unos patines nuevos... Me gustan mucho más estos que los otros que tenía antes... Estos son mucho más chulos... Pero yo a aquellos les tenía cariño...

Y el final, fue horrible... Sobre todo cuando el me dijo: "Susana, tu a mi me gustas mucho. Y yo, ¿yo te gusto a ti?"

Y yo le dije: "¿Tu a mi?"

Y entonces me puse muy nerviosa, cogí mis patines y me fui.... Si le gusto, volverá.... ¿verdad que si?

Conjugated verbs

Conjugated verbs

A   Regular verbs

HABLAR   All regular verbs ending in -*ar* conjugate in the same way as *hablar*.

INDICATIVE

Presente	Pretérito pluscuamp.	Futuro perfecto
Hablo	Había hablado	Habré hablado
Hablas	Habías hablado	Habrás hablado
Habla	Había hablado	Habrá hablado
Hablamos	Habíamos hablado	Habremos hablado
Habláis	Habíais hablado	Habréis hablado
Hablan	Habían hablado	Habrán hablado

Pretérito perfecto	Pretérito indefinido	Condicional
He hablado	Hablé	Hablaría
Has hablado	Hablaste	Hablarías
Ha hablado	Habló	Hablaría
Hemos hablado	Hablamos	Hablaríamos
Habéis hablado	Hablasteis	Hablaríais
Han hablado	Hablaron	Hablarían

Pretérito imperfecto	Futuro	Cond. compuesto
Hablaba	Hablaré	Habría hablado
Hablabas	Hablarás	Habrías hablado
Hablaba	Hablará	Habría hablado
Hablábamos	Hablaremos	Habríamos hablado
Hablabais	Hablaréis	Habríais hablado
Hablaban	Hablarán	Habrían hablado

SUBJUNCTIVE

Presente	Pretérito pluscuamp.
Hable	Hubiera (-se) hablado
Hables	Hubieras (-ses) hablado
Hable	Hubiera (...) hablado
Hablemos	Hubiéramos hablado
Habléis	Hubierais hablado
Hablen	Hubieran hablado

Pretérito perfecto	GERUND
Haya hablado	Hablando
Hayas hablado	
Haya hablado	PAST PARTICIPLE
Hayamos hablado	Hablado
Hayáis hablado	
Hayan hablado	

Pretérito imperfecto	IMPERATIVE Affirmative/Negative
Hablara (-se)	
Hablaras (-ses)	Habla /No hables
Hablara (...)	Hable/ No hable
Habláramos	
Hablarais	Hablad /No habléis
Hablaran	Hablen /No hablen

COMER   All regular verbs ending in -*er* conjugate in the same way as *comer*.

INDICATIVE

Presente	Pretérito pluscuamp.	Futuro perfecto
Como	Había comido	Habré comido
Comes	Habías comido	Habrás comido
Come	Había comido	Habrá comido
Comemos	Habíamos comido	Habremos comido
Coméis	Habíais comido	Habréis comido
Comen	Habían comido	Habrán comido

Pretérito perfecto	Pretérito indefinido	Condicional
He comido	Comí	Comería
Has comido	Comiste	Comerías
Ha comido	Comió	Comería
Hemos comido	Comimos	Comeríamos
Habéis comido	Comisteis	Comeríais
Han comido	Comieron	Comerían

Pretérito imperfecto	Futuro	Cond. compuesto
Comía	Comeré	Habría comido
Comías	Comerás	Habrías comido
Comía	Comerá	Habría comido
Comíamos	Comeremos	Habríamos comido
Comíais	Comeréis	Habríais comido
Comían	Comerán	Habrían comido

SUBJUNCTIVE

Presente	Pretérito pluscuamp.
Coma	Hubiera (-se) comido
Comas	Hubieras (-ses) comido
Coma	Hubiera (...) comido
Comamos	Hubiéramos comido
Comáis	Hubierais comido
Coman	Hubieran comido

Pretérito perfecto	GERUND
Haya comido	Comiendo
Hayas comido	
Haya comido	PAST PARTICIPLE
Hayamos comido	Comido
Hayáis comido	
Hayan comido	

Pretérito imperfecto	IMPERATIVE Affirmative/Negative
Comiera (-se)	
Comieras (-ses)	Come / No comas
Comiera (...)	Comed / No comáis
Comiéramos	
Comierais	Coma / No coma
Comieran	Coman / No coman

VIVIR All regular verbs ending in *-ir* conjugate in the same way as *vivir*.

INDICATIVE

Presente	Pretérito pluscuamp.	Futuro perfecto
Vivo	Había vivido	Habré vivido
Vives	Habías vivido	Habrás vivido
Vive	Había vivido	Habrá vivido
Vivimos	Habíamos vivido	Habremos vivido
Vivís	Habíais vivido	Habréis vivido
Viven	Habían vivido	Habrán vivido

Pretérito perfecto	Pretérito indefinido	Condicional
He vivido	Viví	Viviría
Has vivido	Viviste	Vivirías
Ha vivido	Vivió	Viviría
Hemos vivido	Vivimos	Viviríamos
Habéis vivido	Vivisteis	Viviríais
Han vivido	Vivieron	Vivirían

Pretérito imperfecto	Futuro	Cond. compuesto
Vivía	Viviré	Habría vivido
Vivías	Vivirás	Habrías vivido
Vivía	Vivirá	Habría vivido
Vivíamos	Viviremos	Habríamos vivido
Vivíais	Viviréis	Habríais vivido
Vivían	Vivirán	Habrían vivido

SUBJUNCTIVE

Presente	Pretérito pluscuamp.
Viva	Hubiera (-se) vivido
Vivas	Hubieras (-ses) vivido
Viva	Hubiera (...) vivido
Vivamos	Hubiéramos vivido
Viváis	Hubierais vivido
Vivan	Hubieran vivido

Pretérito perfecto
Haya vivido
Hayas vivido
Haya vivido
Hayamos vivido
Hayáis vivido
Hayan vivido

Pretérito imperfecto
Viviera (-se)
Vivieras (-ses)
Viviera (...)
Viviéramos
Vivierais
Vivieran

GERUND

Viviendo

PAST PARTICIPLE

Vivido

IMPERATIVE

Affirmative/Negative

Vive / No vivas
Vivid / No viváis

Viva / No viva
Vivan / No vivan

B Verbs with two or more irregularities

ANDAR

INDICATIVE

Presente	Pretérito pluscuamp.	Futuro perfecto
Ando	Había andado	Habré andado
Andas	Habías andado	Habrás andado
Anda	Había andado	Habrá andado
Andamos	Habíamos andado	Habremos andado
Andáis	Habíais andado	Habréis andado
Andan	Habían andado	Habrán andado

Pretérito perfecto	Pretérito indefinido	Condicional
He andado	Anduve	Andaría
Has andado	Anduviste	Andarías
Ha andado	Anduvo	Andaría
Hemos andado	Anduvimos	Andaríamos
Habéis andado	Anduvisteis	Andaríais
Han andado	Anduvieron	Andarían

Pretérito imperfecto	Futuro	Cond. compuesto
Andaba	Andaré	Habría andado
Andabas	Andarás	Habrías andado
Andaba	Andará	Habría andado
Andábamos	Andaremos	Habríamos andado
Andabais	Andaréis	Habríais andado
Andaban	Andarán	Habrían andado

SUBJUNCTIVE

Presente	Pretérito pluscuamp.
Ande	Hubiera (-se) andado
Andes	Hubieras (-ses) andado
Ande	Hubiera (...) andado
Andemos	Hubiéramos andado
Andéis	Hubierais andado
Anden	Hubieran andado

Pretérito perfecto
Haya andado
Hayas andado
Haya andado
Hayamos andado
Hayáis andado
Hayan andado

Pretérito imperfecto
Anduviera (-se)
Anduvieras (-ses)
Anduviera (...)
Anduviéramos
Anduvierais
Anduvieran

GERUND

Andando

PAST PARTICIPLE

Andado

IMPERATIVE

Affirmative/Negative

Anda / No andes
Andad / No andéis

Ande / No ande
Anden / No anden

CABER

Presente	Pretérito pluscuamp.	Futuro perfecto
Quepo	Había cabido	Habré cabido
Cabes	Habías cabido	Habrás cabido
Cabe	Había cabido	Habrá cabido
Cabemos	Habíamos cabido	Habremos cabido
Cabéis	Habíais cabido	Habréis cabido
Caben	Habían cabido	Habrán cabido

Pretérito perfecto	Pretérito indefinido	Condicional
He cabido	Cupe	Cabría
Has cabido	Cupiste	Cabrías
Ha cabido	Cupo	Cabría
Hemos cabido	Cupimos	Cabríamos
Habéis cabido	Cupisteis	Cabríais
Han cabido	Cupieron	Cabrían

Pretérito imperfecto	Futuro	Cond. compuesto
Cabía	Cabré	Habría cabido
Cabías	Cabrás	Habrías cabido
Cabía	Cabrá	Habría cabido
Cabíamos	Cabremos	Habríamos cabido
Cabíais	Cabréis	Habríais cabido
Cabían	Cabrán	Habrían cabido

Presente	Pretérito pluscuamp.
Quepa	Hubiera (-se) cabido
Quepas	Hubieras (-ses) cabido
Quepa	Hubiera (...) cabido
Quepamos	Hubiéramos cabido
Quepáis	Hubierais cabido
Quepan	Hubieran cabido

Pretérito perfecto	GERUND
Haya cabido	Cabiendo
Hayas cabido	
Haya cabido	PAST PARTICIPLE
Hayamos cabido	Cabido
Hayáis cabido	
Hayan cabido	

Pretérito imperfecto	IMPERATIVE
Cupiera (-se)	Affirmative/Negative
Cupieras (-ses)	(Not used.)
Cupiera (...)	
Cupiéramos	
Cupierais	
Cupieran	

CAER

Presente	Pretérito pluscuamp.	Futuro perfecto
Caigo	Había caído	Habré caído
Caes	Habías caído	Habrás caído
Cae	Había caído	Habrá caído
Caemos	Habíamos caído	Habremos caído
Caéis	Habíais caído	Habréis caído
Caen	Habían caído	Habrán caído

Pretérito perfecto	Pretérito indefinido	Condicional
He caído	Caí	Caería
Has caído	Caíste	Caerías
Ha caído	Cayó	Caería
Hemos caído	Caímos	Caeríamos
Habéis caído	Caísteis	Caeríais
Han caído	Cayeron	Caerían

Pretérito imperfecto	Futuro	Cond. compuesto
Caía	Caeré	Habría caído
Caías	Caerás	Habrías caído
Caía	Caerá	Habría caído
Caíamos	Caeremos	Habríamos caído
Caíais	Caeréis	Habríais caído
Caían	Caerán	Habrían caído

Presente	Pretérito pluscuamp.
Caiga	Hubiera (-se) caído
Caigas	Hubieras (-ses) caído
Caiga	Hubiera (...) caído
Caigamos	Hubiéramos caído
Caigáis	Hubierais caído
Caigan	Hubieran caído

Pretérito perfecto	GERUND
Haya caído	Cayendo
Hayas caído	
Haya caído	PAST PARTICIPLE
Hayamos caído	Caído
Hayáis caído	
Hayan caído	

Pretérito imperfecto	IMPERATIVE
Cayera (-se)	Affirmative/Negative
Cayeras (-ses)	Cae / No caigas
Cayera (...)	Caed / No caigáis
Cayéramos	
Cayerais	Caiga / No caiga
Cayeran	Caigan / No caigan

■ Other verbs that conjugate like *caer*: *decaer* and *recaer*.

CONDUCIR

INDICATIVE

Presente	Pretérito pluscuamp.	Futuro perfecto
Conduzco	Había conducido	Habré conducido
Conduces	Habías conducido	Habrás conducido
Conduce	Había conducido	Habrá conducido
Conducimos	Habíamos conducido	Habremos conducido
Conducís	Habíais conducido	Habréis conducido
Conducen	Habían conducido	Habrán conducido

Pretérito perfecto	Pretérito indefinido	Condicional
He conducido	Conduje	Conduciría
Has conducido	Condujiste	Conducirías
Ha conducido	Condujo	Conduciría
Hemos conducido	Condujimos	Conduciríamos
Habéis conducido	Condujisteis	Conduciríais
Han conducido	Condujeron	Conducirían

Pretérito imperfecto	Futuro	Cond. compuesto
Conducía	Conduciré	Habría conducido
Conducías	Conducirás	Habrías conducido
Conducía	Conducirá	Habría conducido
Conducíamos	Conduciremos	Habríamos conducido
Conducíais	Conduciréis	Habríais conducido
Conducían	Conducirán	Habrían conducido

SUBJUNCTIVE

Presente	Pretérito pluscuamp.
Conduzca	Hubiera (-se) conducido
Conduzcas	Hubieras (-ses) conducido
Conduzca	Hubiera (...) conducido
Conduzcamos	Hubiéramos conducido
Conduzcáis	Hubierais conducido
Conduzcan	Hubieran conducido

Pretérito perfecto	GERUND
Haya conducido	Conduciendo
Hayas conducido	
Haya conducido	PAST PARTICIPLE
Hayamos conducido	Conducido
Hayáis conducido	
Hayan conducido	

IMPERATIVE

Pretérito imperfecto	Affirmative/Negative
Condujera (-se)	
Condujeras (-ses)	Conduce / No conduzcas
Condujera (...)	Conducid / No conduzcáis
Condujéramos	
Condujerais	Conduzca / No conduzca
Condujeran	Conduzcan / No conduzcan

■ Other verbs that conjugate like *conducir*: *introducir, producir, reducir, traducir...*

CONFIAR

INDICATIVE

Presente	Pretérito pluscuamp.	Futuro perfecto
Confío	Había confiado	Habré confiado
Confías	Habías confiado	Habrás confiado
Confía	Había confiado	Habrá confiado
Confiamos	Habíamos confiado	Habremos confiado
Confiáis	Habíais confiado	Habréis confiado
Confían	Habían confiado	Habrán confiado

Pretérito perfecto	Pretérito indefinido	Condicional
He confiado	Confié	Confiaría
Has confiado	Confiaste	Confiarías
Ha confiado	Confió	Confiaría
Hemos confiado	Confiamos	Confiaríamos
Habéis confiado	Confiasteis	Confiaríais
Han confiado	Confiaron	Confiarían

Pretérito imperfecto	Futuro	Cond. compuesto
Confiaba	Confiaré	Habría confiado
Confiabas	Confiarás	Habrías confiado
Confiaba	Confiará	Habría confiado
Confiábamos	Confiaremos	Habríamos confiado
Confiabais	Confiaréis	Habríais confiado
Confiaban	Confiarán	Habrían confiado

SUBJUNCTIVE

Presente	Pretérito pluscuamp.
Confíe	Hubiera (-se) confiado
Confíes	Hubieras (-ses) confiado
Confíe	Hubiera (...) confiado
Confiemos	Hubiéramos confiado
Confiéis	Hubierais confiado
Confíen	Hubieran confiado

Pretérito perfecto	GERUND
Haya confiado	Confiando
Hayas confiado	
Haya confiado	PAST PARTICIPLE
Hayamos confiado	Confiado
Hayáis confiado	
Hayan confiado	

IMPERATIVE

Pretérito imperfecto	Affirmative/Negative
Confiara (-se)	
Confiaras (-ses)	Confía / No confíes
Confiara (...)	Confiad / No confiéis
Confiáramos	
Confiarais	Confíe / No confíe
Confiaran	Confíen / No confíen

■ Other verbs that conjugate like *confiar*: *desconfiar, enfriar, enviar, esquiar, guiar, variar...*

CONOCER

Presente	Pretérito pluscuamp.	Futuro perfecto	Presente	Pretérito pluscuamp.
Conozco	Había conocido	Habré conocido	Conozca	Hubiera (-se) conocido
Conoces	Habías conocido	Habrás conocido	Conozcas	Hubieras (-ses) conocido
Conoce	Había conocido	Habrá conocido	Conozca	Hubiera (...) conocido
Conocemos	Habíamos conocido	Habremos conocido	Conozcamos	Hubiéramos conocido
Conocéis	Habíais conocido	Habréis conocido	Conozcáis	Hubierais conocido
Conocen	Habían conocido	Habrán conocido	Conozcan	Hubieran conocido

Pretérito perfecto	Pretérito indefinido	Condicional	Pretérito perfecto	GERUND
He conocido	Conocí	Conocería	Haya conocido	Conociendo
Has conocido	Conociste	Conocerías	Hayas conocido	
Ha conocido	Conoció	Conocería	Haya conocido	PAST PARTICIPLE
Hemos conocido	Conocimos	Conoceríamos	Hayamos conocido	Conocido
Habéis conocido	Conocisteis	Conoceríais	Hayáis conocido	
Han conocido	Conocieron	Conocerían	Hayan conocido	

				IMPERATIVE
Pretérito imperfecto	Futuro	Cond. compuesto	Pretérito imperfecto	Affirmative/Negative
Conocía	Conoceré	Habría conocido	Conociera (-se)	
Conocías	Conocerás	Habrías conocido	Conocieras (-ses)	Conoce / No conozcas
Conocía	Conocerá	Habría conocido	Conociera (...)	Conoced / No conozcáis
Conocíamos	Conoceremos	Habríamos conocido	Conociéramos	
Conocíais	Conoceréis	Habríais conocido	Conocierais	Conozca / No conozca
Conocían	Conocerán	Habrían conocido	Conocieran	Conozcan / No conozcan

■ Other verbs that conjugate like *conocer*: *desconocer, reconocer, aparecer, agradecer, apetecer, crecer, establecer...*

CONSTRUIR

Presente	Pretérito pluscuamp.	Futuro perfecto	Presente	Pretérito pluscuamp.
Construyo	Había construido	Habré construido	Construya	Hubiera (-se) construido
Construyes	Habías construido	Habrás construido	Construyas	Hubieras (-ses) construido
Construye	Había construido	Habrá construido	Construya	Hubiera (...) construido
Construimos	Habíamos construido	Habremos construido	Construyamos	Hubiéramos construido
Construís	Habíais construido	Habréis construido	Construyáis	Hubierais construido
Construyen	Habían construido	Habrán construido	Construyan	Hubieran construido

Pretérito perfecto	Pretérito indefinido	Condicional	Pretérito perfecto	GERUND
He construido	Construí	Construiría	Haya construido	Construyendo
Has construido	Construiste	Construirías	Hayas construido	
Ha construido	Construyó	Construiría	Haya construido	PAST PARTICIPLE
Hemos construido	Construimos	Construiríamos	Hayamos construido	Construido
Habéis construido	Construisteis	Construiríais	Hayáis construido	
Han construido	Construyeron	Construirían	Hayan construido	

				IMPERATIVE
Pretérito imperfecto	Futuro	Cond. compuesto	Pretérito imperfecto	Affirmative/Negative
Construía	Construiré	Habría construido	Construyera (-se)	
Construías	Construirás	Habrías construido	Construyeras (-ses)	Construye / No construyas
Construía	Construirá	Habría construido	Construyera (...)	Construid / No construyáis
Construíamos	Construiremos	Habríamos construido	Construyéramos	
Construíais	Construiréis	Habríais construido	Construyerais	Construya / No construya
Construían	Construirán	Habrían construido	Construyeran	Construyan / No construyan

■ Other verbs that conjugate like *construir*: *atribuir, concluir, constituir, contribuir, destruir, disminuir, distribuir, excluir, huir, incluir, influir, instruir, reconstruir, sustituir...*

CREER

INDICATIVE

Presente	Pretérito pluscuamp.	Futuro perfecto
Creo	Había creído	Habré creído
Crees	Habías creído	Habrás creído
Cree	Había creído	Habrá creído
Creemos	Habíamos creído	Habremos creído
Creéis	Habíais creído	Habréis creído
Creen	Habían creído	Habrán creído

Pretérito perfecto	Pretérito indefinido	Condicional
He creído	Creí	Creería
Has creído	Creíste	Creerías
Ha creído	Creyó	Creería
Hemos creído	Creímos	Creeríamos
Habéis creído	Creísteis	Creeríais
Han creído	Creyeron	Creerían

Pretérito imperfecto	Futuro	Cond. compuesto
Creía	Creeré	Habría creído
Creías	Creerás	Habrías creído
Creía	Creerá	Habría creído
Creíamos	Creeremos	Habríamos creído
Creíais	Creeréis	Habríais creído
Creían	Creerán	Habrían creído

SUBJUNCTIVE

Presente	Pretérito pluscuamp.
Crea	Hubiera (-se) creído
Creas	Hubieras (-ses) creído
Crea	Hubiera (...) creído
Creamos	Hubiéramos creído
Creáis	Hubierais creído
Crean	Hubieran creído

Pretérito perfecto	
Haya creído	
Hayas creído	
Haya creído	
Hayamos creído	
Hayáis creído	
Hayan creído	

GERUND

Creyendo

PAST PARTICIPLE

Creído

IMPERATIVE

Pretérito imperfecto	Affirmative/Negative
Creyera (-se)	
Creyeras (-ses)	Cree / No creas
Creyera (...)	Creed / No creáis
Creyéramos	
Creyerais	Crea / No crea
Creyeran	Crean / No crean

■ Other verbs that conjugate like *creer*: *leer*, *poseer*.

DAR

INDICATIVE

Presente	Pretérito pluscuamp.	Futuro perfecto
Doy	Había dado	Habré dado
Das	Habías dado	Habrás dado
Da	Había dado	Habrá dado
Damos	Habíamos dado	Habremos dado
Dais	Habíais dado	Habréis dado
Dan	Habían dado	Habrán dado

Pretérito perfecto	Pretérito indefinido	Condicional
He dado	Di	Daría
Has dado	Diste	Darías
Ha dado	Dio	Daría
Hemos dado	Dimos	Daríamos
Habéis dado	Disteis	Daríais
Han dado	Dieron	Darían

Pretérito imperfecto	Futuro	Cond. compuesto
Daba	Daré	Habría dado
Dabas	Darás	Habrías dado
Daba	Dará	Habría dado
Dábamos	Daremos	Habríamos dado
Dabais	Daréis	Habríais dado
Daban	Darán	Habrían dado

SUBJUNCTIVE

Presente	Pretérito pluscuamp.
Dé	Hubiera (-se) dado
Des	Hubieras (-ses) dado
Dé	Hubiera (...) dado
Demos	Hubiéramos dado
Deis	Hubierais dado
Den	Hubieran dado

Pretérito perfecto	
Haya dado	
Hayas dado	
Haya dado	
Hayamos dado	
Hayáis dado	
Hayan dado	

GERUND

Dando

PAST PARTICIPLE

Dado

IMPERATIVE

Pretérito imperfecto	Affirmative/Negative
Diera (-se)	
Dieras (-ses)	Da / No des
Diera (...)	Dad / No deis
Diéramos	
Dierais	Dé / No dé
Dieran	Den / No den

DECIR

Presente	Pretérito pluscuamp.	Futuro perfecto
Digo	Había dicho	Habré dicho
Dices	Habías dicho	Habrás dicho
Dice	Había dicho	Habrá dicho
Decimos	Habíamos dicho	Habremos dicho
Decís	Habíais dicho	Habréis dicho
Dicen	Habían dicho	Habrán dicho

Pretérito perfecto	Pretérito indefinido	Condicional
He dicho	Dije	Diría
Has dicho	Dijiste	Dirías
Ha dicho	Dijo	Diría
Hemos dicho	Dijimos	Diríamos
Habéis dicho	Dijisteis	Diríais
Han dicho	Dijeron	Dirían

Pretérito imperfecto	Futuro	Cond. compuesto
Decía	Diré	Habría dicho
Decías	Dirás	Habrías dicho
Decía	Dirá	Habría dicho
Decíamos	Diremos	Habríamos dicho
Decíais	Diréis	Habríais dicho
Decían	Dirán	Habrían dicho

SUBJUNCTIVE

Presente	Pretérito pluscuamp.
Diga	Hubiera (-se) dicho
Digas	Hubieras (-ses) dicho
Diga	Hubiera (...) dicho
Digamos	Hubiéramos dicho
Digáis	Hubierais dicho
Digan	Hubieran dicho

Pretérito perfecto	GERUND
Haya dicho	Diciendo
Hayas dicho	
Haya dicho	PAST PARTICIPLE
Hayamos dicho	Dicho
Hayáis dicho	
Hayan dicho	

IMPERATIVE — Affirmative/Negative

Pretérito imperfecto	
Dijera (-se)	
Dijeras (-ses)	Di / No digas
Dijera (...)	Decid / No digáis
Dijéramos	
Dijerais	Diga / No diga
Dijeran	Digan / No digan

■ Other verbs that conjugate like *decir*: *contradecir, predecir*...

DORMIR

INDICATIVE

Presente	Pretérito pluscuamp.	Futuro perfecto
Duermo	Había dormido	Habré dormido
Duermes	Habías dormido	Habrás dormido
Duerme	Había dormido	Habrá dormido
Dormimos	Habíamos dormido	Habremos dormido
Dormís	Habíais dormido	Habréis dormido
Duermen	Habían dormido	Habrán dormido

Pretérito perfecto	Pretérito indefinido	Condicional
He dormido	Dormí	Dormiría
Has dormido	Dormiste	Dormirías
Ha dormido	Durmió	Dormiría
Hemos dormido	Dormimos	Dormiríamos
Habéis dormido	Dormisteis	Dormiríais
Han dormido	Durmieron	Dormirían

Pretérito imperfecto	Futuro	Cond. compuesto
Dormía	Dormiré	Habría dormido
Dormías	Dormirás	Habrías dormido
Dormía	Dormirá	Habría dormido
Dormíamos	Dormiremos	Habríamos dormido
Dormíais	Dormiréis	Habríais dormido
Dormían	Dormirán	Habrían dormido

SUBJUNCTIVE

Presente	Pretérito pluscuamp.
Duerma	Hubiera (-se) dormido
Duermas	Hubieras (-ses) dormido
Duerma	Hubiera (...) dormido
Durmamos	Hubiéramos dormido
Durmáis	Hubierais dormido
Duerman	Hubieran dormido

Pretérito perfecto	GERUND
Haya dormido	Durmiendo
Hayas dormido	
Haya dormido	PAST PARTICIPLE
Hayamos dormido	Dormido
Hayáis dormido	
Hayan dormido	

IMPERATIVE — Affirmative/Negative

Pretérito imperfecto	
Durmiera (-se)	
Durmieras (-ses)	Duerme / No duermas
Durmiera (...)	Dormid / No durmáis
Durmiéramos	
Durmierais	Duerma / No duerma
Durmieran	Duerman / No duerman

ENTENDER

INDICATIVE

Presente	Pretérito pluscuamp.	Futuro perfecto
Entiendo	Había entendido	Habré entendido
Entiendes	Habías entendido	Habrás entendido
Entiende	Había entendido	Habrá entendido
Entendemos	Habíamos entendido	Habremos entendido
Entendéis	Habíais entendido	Habréis entendido
Entienden	Habían entendido	Habrár entendido

Pretérito perfecto	Pretérito indefinido	Condicional
He entendido	Entendí	Entendería
Has entendido	Entendiste	Entenderías
Ha entendido	Entendió	Entendería
Hemos entendido	Entendimos	Entenderíamos
Habéis entendido	Entendisteis	Entenderíais
Han entendido	Entendieron	Entenderían

Pretérito imperfecto	Futuro	Cond. compuesto
Entendía	Entenderé	Habría entendido
Entendías	Entenderás	Habrías entendido
Entendía	Entenderá	Habría entendido
Entendíamos	Entenderemos	Habríamos entendido
Entendíais	Entenderéis	Habríais entendido
Entendían	Entenderán	Habrían entendido

SUBJUNCTIVE

Presente	Pretérito pluscuamp.
Entienda	Hubiera (-se) entendido
Entiendas	Hubieras (-ses) entendido
Entienda	Hubiera(...) entendido
Entendamos	Hubiéramos entendido
Entendáis	Hubierais entendido
Entiendan	Hubieran entendido

Pretérito perfecto	GERUND
Haya entendido	Entendiendo
Hayas entendido	
Haya entendido	PAST PARTICIPLE
Hayamos entendido	Entendido
Hayáis entendido	
Hayan entendido	

Pretérito imperfecto	IMPERATIVE
	Affirmative/Negative
Entendiera (-se)	
Entendieras (-ses)	Entiende / No entiendas
Entendiera (...)	Entended / No entendáis
Entendiéramos	
Entendierais	Entienda / No entienda
Entendieran	Entiendan / No entiendan

■ Other verbs that conjugate like *entender*: *atender, defender, encender, extender, perder, tender, verter...*

ESTAR

INDICATIVE

Presente	Pretérito pluscuamp.	Futuro perfecto
Estoy	Había estado	Habré estado
Estás	Habías estado	Habrás estado
Está	Había estado	Habrá estado
Estamos	Habíamos estado	Habremos estado
Estáis	Habíais estado	Habréis estado
Están	Habían estado	Habrán estado

Pretérito perfecto	Pretérito indefinido	Condicional
He estado	Estuve	Estaría
Has estado	Estuviste	Estarías
Ha estado	Estuvo	Estaría
Hemos estado	Estuvimos	Estaríamos
Habéis estado	Estuvisteis	Estaríais
Han estado	Estuvieron	Estarían

Pretérito imperfecto	Futuro	Cond. compuesto
Estaba	Estaré	Habría estado
Estabas	Estarás	Habrías estado
Estaba	Estará	Habría estado
Estábamos	Estaremos	Habríamos estado
Estabais	Estaréis	Habríais estado
Estaban	Estarán	Habrían estado

SUBJUNCTIVE

Presente	Pretérito pluscuamp.
Esté	Hubiera (-se) estado
Estés	Hubieras (-ses) estado
Esté	Hubiera (...) estado
Estemos	Hubiéramos estado
Estéis	Hubierais estado
Estén	Hubieran estado

Pretérito perfecto	GERUND
Haya estado	Estando
Hayas estado	
Haya estado	PAST PARTICIPLE
Hayamos estado	Estado
Hayáis estado	
Hayan estado	

Pretérito imperfecto	IMPERATIVE
	Affirmative/Negative
Estuviera (-se)	
Estuvieras (-ses)	Está / No estés
Estuviera (...)	Estad / No estéis
Estuviéramos	
Estuvierais	Esté / No esté
Estuvieran	Estén / No estén

FREÍR

INDICATIVE			SUBJUNCTIVE	
Presente	**Pretérito pluscuamp.**	**Futuro perfecto**	**Presente**	**Pretérito pluscuamp.**
Frío	Había frito	Habré frito	Fría	Hubiera (-se) frito
Fríes	Habías frito	Habrás frito	Frías	Hubieras (-ses) frito
Fríe	Había frito	Habrá frito	Fría	Hubiera (...) frito
Freímos	Habíamos frito	Habremos frito	Friamos	Hubiéramos frito
Freís	Habíais frito	Habréis frito	Friáis	Hubierais frito
Fríen	Habían frito	Habrán frito	Frían	Hubieran frito

Pretérito perfecto	**Pretérito indefinido**	**Condicional**	**Pretérito perfecto**	**GERUND**
He frito	Freí	Freiría	Haya frito	Friendo
Has frito	Freíste	Freirías	Hayas frito	
Ha frito	Frió	Freiría	Haya frito	**PAST PARTICIPLE**
Hemos frito	Freímos	Freiríamos	Hayamos frito	Frito
Habéis frito	Freísteis	Freiríais	Hayáis frito	
Han frito	Frieron	Freirían	Hayan frito	

Pretérito imperfecto	**Futuro**	**Cond. compuesto**	**Pretérito imperfecto**	**IMPERATIVE**
Freía	Freiré	Habría frito	Friera (-se)	**Affirmative/Negative**
Freías	Freirás	Habrías frito	Frieras (-ses)	Fríe / No frías
Freía	Freirá	Habría frito	Friera (...)	Freíd / No friáis
Freíamos	Freiremos	Habríamos frito	Friéramos	
Freíais	Freiréis	Habríais frito	Frierais	Fría / No fría
Freían	Freirán	Habrían frito	Frieran	Frían / No frían

■ *Freír* has a regular past participle *freído* that is little used.

HABER

INDICATIVE			SUBJUNCTIVE	
Presente	**Pretérito pluscuamp.**	**Futuro perfecto**	**Presente**	**Pretérito pluscuamp.**
He	Había habido	Habré habido	Haya	Hubiera (-se) habido
Has	Habías habido	Habrás habido	Hayas	Hubieras (-ses) habido
Ha (Hay)	Había habido	Habrá habido	Haya	Hubiera (...) habido
Hemos	Habíamos habido	Habremos habido	Hayamos	Hubiéramos habido
Habéis	Habíais habido	Habréis habido	Hayáis	Hubierais habido
Han	Habían habido	Habrán habido	Hayan	Hubieran habido

Pretérito perfecto	**Pretérito indefinido**	**Condicional**	**Pretérito perfecto**	**GERUND**
He habido	Hube	Habría	Haya habido	Habiendo
Has habido	Hubiste	Habrías	Hayas habido	
Ha habido	Hubo	Habría	Haya habido	**PAST PARTICIPLE**
Hemos habido	Hubimos	Habríamos	Hayamos habido	Habido
Habéis habido	Hubisteis	Habríais	Hayáis habido	
Han habido	Hubieron	Habrían	Hayan habido	

Pretérito imperfecto	**Futuro**	**Cond. compuesto**	**Pretérito imperfecto**	**IMPERATIVE**
Había	Habré	Habría habido	Hubiera (-se)	**Affirmative/Negative**
Habías	Habrás	Habrías habido	Hubieras (-ses)	(Not used.)
Había	Habrá	Habría habido	Hubiera (...)	
Habíamos	Habremos	Habríamos habido	Hubiéramos	
Habíais	Habréis	Habríais habido	Hubierais	
Habían	Habrán	Habrían habido	Hubieran	

HACER

INDICATIVE

Presente	Pretérito pluscuamp.	Futuro perfecto
Hago	Había hecho	Habré hecho
Haces	Habías hecho	Habrás hecho
Hace	Había hecho	Habrá hecho
Hacemos	Habíamos hecho	Habremos hecho
Hacéis	Habíais hecho	Habréis hecho
Hacen	Habían hecho	Habrár hecho

Pretérito perfecto	Pretérito indefinido	Condicional
He hecho	Hice	Haría
Has hecho	Hiciste	Harías
Ha hecho	Hizo	Haría
Hemos hecho	Hicimos	Haríamos
Habéis hecho	Hicisteis	Haríais
Han hecho	Hicieron	Harían

Pretérito imperfecto	Futuro	Cond. compuesto
Hacía	Haré	Habría hecho
Hacías	Harás	Habrías hecho
Hacía	Hará	Habría hecho
Hacíamos	Haremos	Habríamos hecho
Hacíais	Haréis	Habríais hecho
Hacían	Harán	Habrían hecho

SUBJUNCTIVE

Presente	Pretérito pluscuamp.
Haga	Hubiera (-se) hecho
Hagas	Hubieras (-ses) hecho
Haga	Hubiera (...) hecho
Hagamos	Hubiéramos hecho
Hagáis	Hubierais hecho
Hagan	Hubieran hecho

Pretérito perfecto	GERUND
Haya hecho	Haciendo
Hayas hecho	
Haya hecho	PAST PARTICIPLE
Hayamos hecho	Hecho
Hayáis hecho	
Hayan hecho	

Pretérito imperfecto	IMPERATIVE Affirmative/Negative
Hiciera (-se)	
Hicieras (-ses)	Haz / No hagas
Hiciera (...)	Haced / No hagáis
Hiciéramos	
Hicierais	Haga / No haga
Hicieran	Hagan / No hagan

■ Other verbs that conjugate like *hacer*: *deshacer*, *rehacer*. *satisfacer*.

IR

INDICATIVE

Presente	Pretérito pluscuamp.	Futuro perfecto
Voy	Había ido	Habré ido
Vas	Habías ido	Habrás ido
Va	Había ido	Habrá ido
Vamos	Habíamos ido	Habremos ido
Vais	Habíais ido	Habréis ido
Van	Habían ido	Habrán ido

Pretérito perfecto	Pretérito indefinido	Condicional
He ido	Fui	Iría
Has ido	Fuiste	Irías
Ha ido	Fue	Iría
Hemos ido	Fuimos	Iríamos
Habéis ido	Fuisteis	Iríais
Han ido	Fueron	Irían

Pretérito imperfecto	Futuro	Cond. compuesto
Iba	Iré	Habría ido
Ibas	Irás	Habrías ido
Iba	Irá	Habría ido
Íbamos	Iremos	Habríamos ido
Ibais	Iréis	Habríais ido
Iban	Irán	Habrían ido

SUBJUNCTIVE

Presente	Pretérito pluscuamp.
Vaya	Hubiera (-se) ido
Vayas	Hubieras (-ses) ido
Vaya	Hubiera (...) ido
Vayamos	Hubiéramos ido
Vayáis	Hubierais ido
Vayan	Hubieran ido

Pretérito perfecto	GERUND
Haya ido	Yendo
Hayas ido	
Haya ido	PAST PARTICIPLE
Hayamos ido	Ido
Hayáis ido	
Hayan ido	

Pretérito imperfecto	IMPERATIVE Affirmative/Negative
Fuera (-se)	
Fueras (-ses)	Ve / No vayas
Fuera (...)	Id / No vayáis
Fuéramos	
Fuerais	Vaya / No vaya
Fueran	Vayan / No vayan

JUGAR

INDICATIVE

Presente	Pretérito pluscuamp.	Futuro perfecto
Juego	Había jugado	Habré jugado
Juegas	Habías jugado	Habrás jugado
Juega	Había jugado	Habrá jugado
Jugamos	Habíamos jugado	Habremos jugado
Jugáis	Habíais jugado	Habréis jugado
Juegan	Habían jugado	Habrán jugado

Pretérito perfecto	Pretérito indefinido	Condicional
He jugado	Jugué	Jugaría
Has jugado	Jugaste	Jugarías
Ha jugado	Jugó	Jugaría
Hemos jugado	Jugamos	Jugaríamos
Habéis jugado	Jugasteis	Jugaríais
Han jugado	Jugaron	Jugarían

Pretérito imperfecto	Futuro	Cond. compuesto
Jugaba	Jugaré	Habría jugado
Jugabas	Jugarás	Habrías jugado
Jugaba	Jugará	Habría jugado
Jugábamos	Jugaremos	Habríamos jugado
Jugabais	Jugaréis	Habríais jugado
Jugaban	Jugarán	Habrían jugado

SUBJUNCTIVE

Presente	Pretérito pluscuamp.
Juegue	Hubiera (-se) jugado
Juegues	Hubieras (-ses) jugado
Juegue	Hubiera (...) jugado
Juguemos	Hubiéramos jugado
Juguéis	Hubierais jugado
Jueguen	Hubieran jugado

Pretérito perfecto	GERUND
Haya jugado	Jugando
Hayas jugado	
Haya jugado	PAST PARTICIPLE
Hayamos jugado	Jugado
Hayáis jugado	
Hayan jugado	

Pretérito imperfecto	IMPERATIVE Affirmative/Negative
Jugara (-se)	
Jugaras (-ses)	Juega / No juegues
Jugara (...)	Jugad / No juguéis
Jugáramos	
Jugarais	Juegue / No juegue
Jugaran	Jueguen / No jueguen

■ The sound [g] is written **g** before the sounds [o] and [a] , and **gu** before the sound [e]

MORIR

INDICATIVE

Presente	Pretérito pluscuamp.	Futuro perfecto
Muero	Había muerto	Habré muerto
Mueres	Habías muerto	Habrás muerto
Muere	Había muerto	Habrá muerto
Morimos	Habíamos muerto	Habremos muerto
Morís	Habíais muerto	Habréis muerto
Mueren	Habían muerto	Habrán muerto

Pretérito perfecto	Pretérito indefinido	Condicional
He muerto	Morí	Moriría
Has muerto	Moriste	Morirías
Ha muerto	Murió	Moriría
Hemos muerto	Morimos	Moriríamos
Habéis muerto	Moristeis	Moriríais
Han muerto	Murieron	Morirían

Pretérito imperfecto	Futuro	Cond. compuesto
Moría	Moriré	Habría muerto
Morías	Morirás	Habrías muerto
Moría	Morirá	Habría muerto
Moríamos	Moriremos	Habríamos muerto
Moríais	Moriréis	Habríais muerto
Morían	Morirán	Habrían muerto

SUBJUNCTIVE

Presente	Pretérito pluscuamp.
Muera	Hubiera (-se) muerto
Mueras	Hubieras (-ses) muerto
Muera	Hubiera (...) muerto
Muramos	Hubiéramos muerto
Muráis	Hubierais muerto
Mueran	Hubieran muerto

Pretérito perfecto	GERUND
Haya muerto	Muriendo
Hayas muerto	
Haya muerto	PAST PARTICIPLE
Hayamos muerto	Muerto
Hayáis muerto	
Hayan muerto	

Pretérito imperfecto	IMPERATIVE Affirmative/Negative
Muriera (-se)	
Murieras (-ses)	Muere / No mueras
Muriera (...)	Morid / No muráis
Muriéramos	
Murierais	Muera / No muera
Murieran	Mueran / No mueran

MOVER

INDICATIVE

Presente	Pretérito pluscuamp.	Futuro perfecto
Muevo	Había movido	Habré movido
Mueves	Habías movido	Habrás movido
Mueve	Había movido	Habrá movido
Movemos	Habíamos movido	Habremos movido
Movéis	Habíais movido	Habréis movido
Mueven	Habían movido	Habrán movido

Pretérito perfecto	Pretérito indefinido	Condicional
He movido	Moví	Movería
Has movido	Moviste	Moverías
Ha movido	Movió	Movería
Hemos movido	Movimos	Moveríamos
Habéis movido	Movisteis	Moveríais
Han movido	Movieron	Moverían

Pretérito imperfecto	Futuro	Cond. compuesto
Movía	Moveré	Habría movido
Movías	Moverás	Habrías movido
Movía	Moverá	Habría movido
Movíamos	Moveremos	Habríamos movido
Movíais	Moveréis	Habríais movido
Movían	Moverán	Habrían movido

SUBJUNCTIVE

Presente	Pretérito pluscuamp.
Mueva	Hubiera (-se) movido
Muevas	Hubieras (-ses) movido
Mueva	Hubiera(...) movido
Movamos	Hubiéramos movido
Mováis	Hubierais movido
Muevan	Hubieran movido

Pretérito perfecto	GERUND
Haya movido	Moviendo
Hayas movido	
Haya movido	PAST PARTICIPLE
Hayamos movido	Movido
Hayáis movido	
Hayan movido	

Pretérito imperfecto	IMPERATIVE — Affirmative/Negative
Moviera (-se)	
Movieras (-ses)	Mueve / No muevas
Moviera (...)	Moved / No mováis
Moviéramos	
Movierais	Mueva / No mueva
Movieran	Muevan / No muevan

■ Other verbs that conjugate like *mover*: *cocer, conmover(se), doler, llover, oler* (with this verb, the forms with *-ue-* are written with *h-*: *huelo*)...

OÍR

INDICATIVE

Presente	Pretérito pluscuamp.	Futuro perfecto
Oigo	Había oído	Habré oído
Oyes	Habías oído	Habrás oído
Oye	Había oído	Habrá oído
Oímos	Habíamos oído	Habremos oído
Oís	Habíais oído	Habréis oído
Oyen	Habían oído	Habrán oído

Pretérito perfecto	Pretérito indefinido	Condicional
He oído	Oí	Oiría
Has oído	Oíste	Oirías
Ha oído	Oyó	Oiría
Hemos oído	Oímos	Oiríamos
Habéis oído	Oísteis	Oiríais
Han oído	Oyeron	Oirían

Pretérito imperfecto	Futuro	Cond. compuesto
Oía	Oiré	Habría oído
Oías	Oirás	Habrías oído
Oía	Oirá	Habría oído
Oíamos	Oiremos	Habríamos oído
Oíais	Oiréis	Habríais oído
Oían	Oirán	Habrían oído

SUBJUNCTIVE

Presente	Pretérito pluscuamp.
Oiga	Hubiera (-se) oído
Oigas	Hubieras (-ses) oído
Oiga	Hubiera (...) oído
Oigamos	Hubiéramos oído
Oigáis	Hubierais oído
Oigan	Hubieran oído

Pretérito perfecto	GERUND
Haya oído	Oyendo
Hayas oído	
Haya oído	PAST PARTICIPLE
Hayamos oído	Oído
Hayáis oído	
Hayan oído	

Pretérito imperfecto	IMPERATIVE — Affirmative/Negative
Oyera (-se)	
Oyeras (-ses)	Oye / No oigas
Oyera (...)	Oíd / No oigáis
Oyéramos	
Oyerais	Oiga / No oiga
Oyeran	Oigan / No oigan

■ Other verbs that conjugate like *oír*: *desoír.*

PEDIR

INDICATIVE

Presente	Pretérito pluscuamp.	Futuro perfecto
Pido	Había pedido	Habré pedido
Pides	Habías pedido	Habrás pedido
Pide	Había pedido	Habrá pedido
Pedimos	Habíamos pedido	Habremos pedido
Pedís	Habíais pedido	Habréis pedido
Piden	Habían pedido	Habrán pedido

Pretérito perfecto	Pretérito indefinido	Condicional
He pedido	Pedí	Pediría
Has pedido	Pediste	Pedirías
Ha pedido	Pidió	Pediría
Hemos pedido	Pedimos	Pediríamos
Habéis pedido	Pedisteis	Pediríais
Han pedido	Pidieron	Pedirían

Pretérito imperfecto	Futuro	Cond. compuesto
Pedía	Pediré	Habría pedido
Pedías	Pedirás	Habrías pedido
Pedía	Pedirá	Habría pedido
Pedíamos	Pediremos	Habríamos pedido
Pedíais	Pediréis	Habríais pedido
Pedían	Pedirán	Habrían pedido

SUBJUNCTIVE

Presente	Pretérito pluscuamp.
Pida	Hubiera (-se) pedido
Pidas	Hubieras (-ses) pedido
Pida	Hubiera (...) pedido
Pidamos	Hubiéramos pedido
Pidáis	Hubierais pedido
Pidan	Hubieran pedido

Pretérito perfecto	GERUND
Haya pedido	Pidiendo
Hayas pedido	
Haya pedido	PAST PARTICIPLE
Hayamos pedido	Pedido
Hayáis pedido	
Hayan pedido	

Pretérito imperfecto	IMPERATIVE Affirmative/Negative
Pidiera (-se)	
Pidieras (-ses)	Pide / No pidas
Pidiera (...)	Pedid / No pidáis
Pidiéramos	
Pidierais	Pida / No pida
Pidieran	Pidan / No pidan

■ Other verbs that conjugate like *pedir*: *corregir, elegir, reír, repetir, seguir, servir...*

PENSAR

INDICATIVE

Presente	Pretérito pluscuamp.	Futuro perfecto
Pienso	Había pensado	Habré pensado
Piensas	Habías pensado	Habrás pensado
Piensa	Había pensado	Habrá pensado
Pensamos	Habíamos pensado	Habremos pensado
Pensáis	Habíais pensado	Habréis pensado
Piensan	Habían pensado	Habrán pensado

Pretérito perfecto	Pretérito indefinido	Condicional
He pensado	Pensé	Pensaría
Has pensado	Pensaste	Pensarías
Ha pensado	Pensó	Pensaría
Hemos pensado	Pensamos	Pensaríamos
Habéis pensado	Pensasteis	Pensaríais
Han pensado	Pensaron	Pensarían

Pretérito imperfecto	Futuro	Cond. compuesto
Pensaba	Pensaré	Habría pensado
Pensabas	Pensarás	Habrías pensado
Pensaba	Pensará	Habría pensado
Pensábamos	Pensaremos	Habríamos pensado
Pensabais	Pensaréis	Habríais pensado
Pensaban	Pensarán	Habrían pensado

SUBJUNCTIVE

Presente	Pretérito pluscuamp.
Piense	Hubiera (-se) pensado
Pienses	Hubieras (-ses) pensado
Piense	Hubiera (...) pensado
Pensemos	Hubiéramos pensado
Penséis	Hubierais pensado
Piensen	Hubieran pensado

Pretérito perfecto	GERUND
Haya pensado	Pensando
Hayas pensado	
Haya pensado	PAST PARTICIPLE
Hayamos pensado	Pensado
Hayáis pensado	
Hayan pensado	

Pretérito imperfecto	IMPERATIVE Affirmative/Negative
Pensara (-se)	
Pensaras (-ses)	Piensa / No pienses
Pensara (...)	Pensad / No penséis
Pensáramos	
Pensarais	Piense / No piense
Pensaran	Piensen / No piensen

■ Other verbs that conjugate like *pensar*: *cerrar, comenzar, despertar(se), empezar, sentar(se)...*

PODER

Presente	Pretérito pluscuamp.	Futuro perfecto	Presente	Pretérito pluscuamp.
Puedo	Había podido	Habré podido	Pueda	Hubiera (-se) podido
Puedes	Habías podido	Habrás podido	Puedas	Hubieras (-ses) podido
Puede	Había podido	Habrá podido	Pueda	Hubiera (...) podido
Podemos	Habíamos podido	Habremos podido	Podamos	Hubiéramos podido
Podéis	Habíais podido	Habréis podido	Podáis	Hubierais podido
Pueden	Habían podido	Habrán podido	Puedan	Hubieran podido

SUBJUNCTIVE

Pretérito perfecto	Pretérito indefinido	Condicional	Pretérito perfecto	GERUND
He podido	Pude	Podría	Haya podido	Pudiendo
Has podido	Pudiste	Podrías	Hayas podido	
Ha podido	Pudo	Podría	Haya podido	PAST PARTICIPLE
Hemos podido	Pudimos	Podríamos	Hayamos podido	Podido
Habéis podido	Pudisteis	Podríais	Hayáis podido	
Han podido	Pudieron	Podrían	Hayan podido	

Pretérito imperfecto	Futuro	Cond. compuesto	Pretérito imperfecto	IMPERATIVE
Podía	Podré	Habría podido	Pudiera (-se)	Affirmative/Negative
Podías	Podrás	Habrías podido	Pudieras (-ses)	
Podía	Podrá	Habría podido	Pudiera (...)	(Not used.)
Podíamos	Podremos	Habríamos podido	Pudiéramos	
Podíais	Podréis	Habríais podido	Pudierais	
Podían	Podrán	Habrían podido	Pudieran	

PONER

INDICATIVE

Presente	Pretérito pluscuamp.	Futuro perfecto	Presente	Pretérito pluscuamp.
Pongo	Había puesto	Habré puesto	Ponga	Hubiera (-se) puesto
Pones	Habías puesto	Habrás puesto	Pongas	Hubieras (-ses) puesto
Pone	Había puesto	Habrá puesto	Ponga	Hubiera (...) puesto
Ponemos	Habíamos puesto	Habremos puesto	Pongamos	Hubiéramos puesto
Ponéis	Habíais puesto	Habréis puesto	Pongáis	Hubierais puesto
Ponen	Habían puesto	Habrán puesto	Pongan	Hubieran puesto

SUBJUNCTIVE

Pretérito perfecto	Pretérito indefinido	Condicional	Pretérito perfecto	GERUND
He puesto	Puse	Pondría	Haya puesto	Poniendo
Has puesto	Pusiste	Pondrías	Hayas puesto	
Ha puesto	Puso	Pondría	Haya puesto	PAST PARTICIPLE
Hemos puesto	Pusimos	Pondríamos	Hayamos puesto	Puesto
Habéis puesto	Pusisteis	Pondríais	Hayáis puesto	
Han puesto	Pusieron	Pondrían	Hayan puesto	

Pretérito imperfecto	Futuro	Cond. compuesto	Pretérito imperfecto	IMPERATIVE
Ponía	Pondré	Habría puesto	Pusiera (-se)	Affirmative/Negative
Ponías	Pondrás	Habrías puesto	Pusieras (-ses)	
Ponía	Pondrá	Habría puesto	Pusiera (...)	Pon / No pongas
Poníamos	Pondremos	Habríamos puesto	Pusiéramos	Poned / No pongáis
Poníais	Pondréis	Habríais puesto	Pusierais	Ponga / No ponga
Ponían	Pondrán	Habrían puesto	Pusieran	Pongan / No pongan

■ Other verbs that conjugate like *poner: componer, presuponer, proponer, suponer...*

PROHIBIR

Presente	Pretérito pluscuamp.	Futuro perfecto
Prohíbo	Había prohibido	Habré prohibido
Prohíbes	Habías prohibido	Habrás prohibido
Prohíbe	Había prohibido	Habrá prohibido
Prohibimos	Habíamos prohibido	Habremos prohibido
Prohibís	Habíais prohibido	Habréis prohibido
Prohíben	Habían prohibido	Habrán prohibido

Pretérito perfecto	Pretérito indefinido	Condicional
He prohibido	Prohibí	Prohibiría
Has prohibido	Prohibiste	Prohibirías
Ha prohibido	Prohibió	Prohibiría
Hemos prohibido	Prohibimos	Prohibiríamos
Habéis prohibido	Prohibisteis	Prohibiríais
Han prohibido	Prohibieron	Prohibirían

Pretérito imperfecto	Futuro	Cond. compuesto
Prohibía	Prohibiré	Habría prohibido
Prohibías	Prohibirás	Habrías prohibido
Prohibía	Prohibirá	Habría prohibido
Prohibíamos	Prohibiremos	Habríamos prohibido
Prohibíais	Prohibiréis	Habríais prohibido
Prohibían	Prohibirán	Habrían prohibido

Presente	Pretérito pluscuamp.
Prohíba	Hubiera (-se) prohibido
Prohíbas	Hubieras (-ses) prohibido
Prohíba	Hubiera (...) prohibido
Prohibamos	Hubiéramos prohibido
Prohibáis	Hubierais prohibido
Prohíban	Hubieran prohibido

Pretérito perfecto	GERUND
Haya prohibido	Prohibiendo
Hayas prohibido	
Haya prohibido	PAST PARTICIPLE
Hayamos prohibido	Prohibido
Hayáis prohibido	
Hayan prohibido	

Pretérito imperfecto	IMPERATIVE Affirmative/Negative
Prohibiera (-se)	
Prohibieras (-ses)	Prohíbe / No prohíbas
Prohibiera (...)	Prohibid / No prohibáis
Prohibiéramos	
Prohibierais	Prohíba / No prohíba
Prohibieran	Prohíban / No prohíban

■ Other verbs that conjugate like *prohibir*: reunir.

QUERER

Presente	Pretérito pluscuamp.	Futuro perfecto
Quiero	Había querido	Habré querido
Quieres	Habías querido	Habrás querido
Quiere	Había querido	Habrá querido
Queremos	Habíamos querido	Habremos querido
Queréis	Habíais querido	Habréis querido
Quieren	Habían querido	Habrán querido

Pretérito perfecto	Pretérito indefinido	Condicional
He querido	Quise	Querría
Has querido	Quisiste	Querrías
Ha querido	Quiso	Querría
Hemos querido	Quisimos	Querríamos
Habéis querido	Quisisteis	Querríais
Han querido	Quisieron	Querrían

Pretérito imperfecto	Futuro	Cond. compuesto
Quería	Querré	Habría querido
Querías	Querrás	Habrías querido
Quería	Querrá	Habría querido
Queríamos	Querremos	Habríamos querido
Queríais	Querréis	Habríais querido
Querían	Querrán	Habrían querido

Presente	Pretérito pluscuamp.
Quiera	Hubiera (-se) querido
Quieras	Hubieras (-ses) querido
Quiera	Hubiera (...) querido
Queramos	Hubiéramos querido
Queráis	Hubierais querido
Quieran	Hubieran querido

Pretérito perfecto	GERUND
Haya querido	Queriendo
Hayas querido	
Haya querido	PAST PARTICIPLE
Hayamos querido	Querido
Hayáis querido	
Hayan querido	

Pretérito imperfecto	IMPERATIVE Affirmative/Negative
Quisiera (-se)	
Quisieras (-ses)	Quiere / No quieras
Quisiera (...)	Quered / No queráis
Quisiéramos	
Quisierais	Quiera / No quiera
Quisieran	Quieran / No quieran

SABER

INDICATIVE

Presente	Pretérito pluscuamp.	Futuro perfecto
Sé	Había sabido	Habré sabido
Sabes	Habías sabido	Habrás sabido
Sabe	Había sabido	Habrá sabido
Sabemos	Habíamos sabido	Habremos sabido
Sabéis	Habíais sabido	Habréis sabido
Saben	Habían sabido	Habrán sabido

Pretérito perfecto	Pretérito indefinido	Condicional
He sabido	Supe	Sabría
Has sabido	Supiste	Sabrías
Ha sabido	Supo	Sabría
Hemos sabido	Supimos	Sabríamos
Habéis sabido	Supisteis	Sabríais
Han sabido	Supieron	Sabrían

Pretérito imperfecto	Futuro	Cond. compuesto
Sabía	Sabré	Habría sabido
Sabías	Sabrás	Habrías sabido
Sabía	Sabrá	Habría sabido
Sabíamos	Sabremos	Habríamos sabido
Sabíais	Sabréis	Habríais sabido
Sabían	Sabrán	Habrían sabido

SUBJUNCTIVE

Presente	Pretérito pluscuamp.
Sepa	Hubiera (-se) sabido
Sepas	Hubieras (-ses) sabido
Sepa	Hubiera (...) sabido
Sepamos	Hubiéramos sabido
Sepáis	Hubierais sabido
Sepan	Hubieran sabido

Pretérito perfecto	GERUND
Haya sabido	Sabiendo
Hayas sabido	
Haya sabido	PAST PARTICIPLE
Hayamos sabido	Sabido
Hayáis sabido	
Hayan sabido	

IMPERATIVE

Pretérito imperfecto	Affirmative/Negative
Supiera (-se)	
Supieras (-ses)	Sabe / No sepas
Supiera (...)	Sabed / No sepáis
Supiéramos	
Supierais	Sepa / No sepa
Supieran	Sepan / No sepan

SALIR

INDICATIVE

Presente	Pretérito pluscuamp.	Futuro perfecto
Salgo	Había salido	Habré salido
Sales	Habías salido	Habrás salido
Sale	Había salido	Habrá salido
Salimos	Habíamos salido	Habremos salido
Salís	Habíais salido	Habréis salido
Salen	Habían salido	Habrán salido

Pretérito perfecto	Pretérito indefinido	Condicional
He salido	Salí	Saldría
Has salido	Saliste	Saldrías
Ha salido	Salió	Saldría
Hemos salido	Salimos	Saldríamos
Habéis salido	Salisteis	Saldríais
Han salido	Salieron	Saldrían

Pretérito imperfecto	Futuro	Cond. compuesto
Salía	Saldré	Habría salido
Salías	Saldrás	Habrías salido
Salía	Saldrá	Habría salido
Salíamos	Saldremos	Habríamos salido
Salíais	Saldréis	Habríais salido
Salían	Saldrán	Habrían salido

SUBJUNCTIVE

Presente	Pretérito pluscuamp.
Salga	Hubiera (-se) salido
Salgas	Hubieras (-ses) salido
Salga	Hubiera (...) salido
Salgamos	Hubiéramos salido
Salgáis	Hubierais salido
Salgan	Hubieran salido

Pretérito perfecto	GERUND
Haya salido	Saliendo
Hayas salido	
Haya salido	PAST PARTICIPLE
Hayamos salido	Salido
Hayáis salido	
Hayan salido	

IMPERATIVE

Pretérito imperfecto	Affirmative/Negative
Saliera (-se)	
Salieras (-ses)	Sal / No salgas
Saliera (...)	Salid / No salgáis
Saliéramos	
Salierais	Salga / No salga
Salieran	Salgan / No salgan

■ Other verbs that conjugate like *salir*: *sobresalir*, *equivaler*, *valer* (with the endings of *-er* verbs).

Conjugated verbs

SENTIR

Presente	Pretérito pluscuamp.	Futuro perfecto
Siento	Había sentido	Habré sentido
Sientes	Habías sentido	Habrás sentido
Siente	Había sentido	Habrá sentido
Sentimos	Habíamos sentido	Habremos sentido
Sentís	Habíais sentido	Habréis sentido
Sienten	Habían sentido	Habrán sentido

Pretérito perfecto	Pretérito indefinido	Condicional
He sentido	Sentí	Sentiría
Has sentido	Sentiste	Sentirías
Ha sentido	Sintió	Sentiría
Hemos sentido	Sentimos	Sentiríamos
Habéis sentido	Sentisteis	Sentiríais
Han sentido	Sintieron	Sentirían

Pretérito imperfecto	Futuro	Cond. compuesto
Sentía	Sentiré	Habría sentido
Sentías	Sentirás	Habrías sentido
Sentía	Sentirá	Habría sentido
Sentíamos	Sentiremos	Habríamos sentido
Sentíais	Sentiréis	Habríais sentido
Sentían	Sentirán	Habrían sentido

SUBJUNCTIVE

Presente	Pretérito pluscuamp.
Sienta	Hubiera (-se) sentido
Sientas	Hubieras (-ses) sentido
Sienta	Hubiera (...) sentido
Sintamos	Hubiéramos sentido
Sintáis	Hubierais sentido
Sientan	Hubieran sentido

Pretérito perfecto	GERUND
Haya sentido	Sintiendo
Hayas sentido	
Haya sentido	PAST PARTICIPLE
Hayamos sentido	Sentido
Hayáis sentido	
Hayan sentido	

Pretérito imperfecto	IMPERATIVE
Sintiera (-se)	Affirmative/Negative
Sintieras (-ses)	Siente / No sientas
Sintiera (...)	Sentid / No sintáis
Sintiéramos	
Sintierais	Sienta / No sienta
Sintieran	Sientan / No sientan

■ Other verbs that conjugate like *sentir*: *divertir(se), mentir, preferir, presentir, sugerir...*

SER

Presente	Pretérito pluscuamp.	Futuro perfecto
Soy	Había sido	Habré sido
Eres	Habías sido	Habrás sido
Es	Había sido	Habrá sido
Somos	Habíamos sido	Habremos sido
Sois	Habíais sido	Habréis sido
Son	Habían sido	Habrán sido

Pretérito perfecto	Pretérito indefinido	Condicional
He sido	Fui	Sería
Has sido	Fuiste	Serías
Ha sido	Fue	Sería
Hemos sido	Fuimos	Seríamos
Habéis sido	Fuisteis	Seríais
Han sido	Fueron	Serían

Pretérito imperfecto	Futuro	Cond. compuesto
Era	Seré	Habría sido
Eras	Serás	Habrías sido
Era	Será	Habría sido
Éramos	Seremos	Habríamos sido
Erais	Seréis	Habríais sido
Eran	Serán	Habrían sido

SUBJUNCTIVE

Presente	Pretérito pluscuamp.
Sea	Hubiera (-se) sido
Seas	Hubieras (-ses) sido
Sea	Hubiera (...) sido
Seamos	Hubiéramos sido
Seáis	Hubierais sido
Sean	Hubieran sido

Pretérito perfecto	GERUND
Haya sido	Siendo
Hayas sido	
Haya sido	PAST PARTICIPLE
Hayamos sido	Sido
Hayáis sido	
Hayan sido	

Pretérito imperfecto	IMPERATIVE
Fuera (-se)	Affirmative/Negative
Fueras (-ses)	Sé / No seas
Fuera (...)	Sed / No seáis
Fuéramos	
Fuerais	Sea / No sea
Fueran	Sean / No sean

TENER

Presente	Pretérito pluscuamp.	Futuro perfecto
Tengo	Había tenido	Habré tenido
Tienes	Habías tenido	Habrás tenido
Tiene	Había tenido	Habrá tenido
Tenemos	Habíamos tenido	Habremos tenido
Tenéis	Habíais tenido	Habréis tenido
Tienen	Habían tenido	Habrán tenido

Pretérito perfecto	Pretérito indefinido	Condicional
He tenido	Tuve	Tendría
Has tenido	Tuviste	Tendrías
Ha tenido	Tuvo	Tendría
Hemos tenido	Tuvimos	Tendríamos
Habéis tenido	Tuvisteis	Tendríais
Han tenido	Tuvieron	Tendrían

Pretérito imperfecto	Futuro	Cond. compuesto
Tenía	Tendré	Habría tenido
Tenías	Tendrás	Habrías tenido
Tenía	Tendrá	Habría tenido
Teníamos	Tendremos	Habríamos tenido
Teníais	Tendréis	Habríais tenido
Tenían	Tendrán	Habrían tenido

SUBJUNCTIVE

Presente	Pretérito pluscuamp.
Tenga	Hubiera (-se) tenido
Tengas	Hubieras (-ses) tenido
Tenga	Hubiera (...) tenido
Tengamos	Hubiéramos tenido
Tengáis	Hubierais tenido
Tengan	Hubieran tenido

Pretérito perfecto	*GERUND*
Haya tenido	Teniendo
Hayas tenido	
Haya tenido	*PAST PARTICIPLE*
Hayamos tenido	Tenido
Hayáis tenido	
Hayan tenido	

Pretérito imperfecto	*IMPERATIVE* Affirmative/Negative
Tuviera (-se)	
Tuvieras (-ses)	Ten / No tengas
Tuviera (...)	Tened / No tengáis
Tuviéramos	
Tuvierais	Tenga / No tenga
Tuvieran	Tengan / No tengan

■ Other verbs that conjugate like *tener*: *contener, mantener, obtener...*

TRAER

Presente	Pretérito pluscuamp.	Futuro perfecto
Traigo	Había traído	Habré traído
Traes	Habías traído	Habrás traído
Trae	Había traído	Habrá traído
Traemos	Habíamos traído	Habremos traído
Traéis	Habíais traído	Habréis traído
Traen	Habían traído	Habrán traído

Pretérito perfecto	Pretérito indefinido	Condicional
He traído	Traje	Traería
Has traído	Trajiste	Traerías
Ha traído	Trajo	Traería
Hemos traído	Trajimos	Traeríamos
Habéis traído	Trajisteis	Traeríais
Han traído	Trajeron	Traerían

Pretérito imperfecto	Futuro	Cond. compuesto
Traía	Traeré	Habría traído
Traías	Traerás	Habrías traído
Traía	Traerá	Habría traído
Traíamos	Traeremos	Habríamos traído
Traíais	Traeréis	Habríais traído
Traían	Traerán	Habrían traído

SUBJUNCTIVE

Presente	Pretérito pluscuamp.
Traiga	Hubiera (-se) traído
Traigas	Hubieras (-ses) traído
Traiga	Hubiera (...) traído
Traigamos	Hubiéramos traído
Traigáis	Hubierais traído
Traigan	Hubieran traído

Pretérito perfecto	*GERUND*
Haya traído	Trayendo
Hayas traído	
Haya traído	*PAST PARTICIPLE*
Hayamos traído	Traído
Hayáis traído	
Hayan traído	

Pretérito imperfecto	*IMPERATIVE* Affirmative/Negative
Trajera (-se)	
Trajeras (-ses)	Trae / No traigas
Trajera (...)	Traed / No traigáis
Trajéramos	
Trajerais	Traiga / No traiga
Trajeran	Traigan / No traigan

■ Other verbs that conjugate like *traer*: *abstraer, atraer, distraer, extraer...*

VENIR

Presente	Pretérito pluscuamp.	Futuro perfecto
Vengo	Había venido	Habré venido
Vienes	Habías venido	Habrás venido
Viene	Había venido	Habrá venido
Venimos	Habíamos venido	Habremos venido
Venís	Habíais venido	Habréis venido
Vienen	Habían venido	Habrán venido

Pretérito perfecto	Pretérito indefinido	Condicional
He venido	Vine	Vendría
Has venido	Viniste	Vendrías
Ha venido	Vino	Vendría
Hemos venido	Vinimos	Vendríamos
Habéis venido	Vinisteis	Vendríais
Han venido	Vinieron	Vendrían

Pretérito imperfecto	Futuro	Cond. compuesto
Venía	Vendré	Habría venido
Venías	Vendrás	Habrías venido
Venía	Vendrá	Habría venido
Veníamos	Vendremos	Habríamos venido
Veníais	Vendréis	Habríais venido
Venían	Vendrán	Habrían venido

Presente	Pretérito pluscuamp.
Venga	Hubiera (-se) venido
Vengas	Hubieras (-ses) venido
Venga	Hubiera (...) venido
Vengamos	Hubiéramos venido
Vengáis	Hubierais venido
Vengan	Hubieran venido

Pretérito perfecto	GERUND
Haya venido	Viniendo
Hayas venido	
Haya venido	PAST PARTICIPLE
Hayamos venido	Venido
Hayáis venido	
Hayan venido	

Pretérito imperfecto	IMPERATIVE
	Affirmative/Negative
Viniera (-se)	
Vinieras (-ses)	Ven / No vengas
Viniera (...)	Venid / No vengáis
Viniéramos	
Vinierais	Venga / No venga
Vinieran	Vengan / No vengan

■ Other verbs that conjugate like *venir*: *convenir, provenir...*

VER

Presente	Pretérito pluscuamp.	Futuro perfecto
Veo	Había visto	Habré visto
Ves	Habías visto	Habrás visto
Ve	Había visto	Habrá visto
Vemos	Habíamos visto	Habremos visto
Veis	Habíais visto	Habréis visto
Ven	Habían visto	Habrán visto

Pretérito perfecto	Pretérito indefinido	Condicional
He visto	Vi	Vería
Has visto	Viste	Verías
Ha visto	Vio	Vería
Hemos visto	Vimos	Veríamos
Habéis visto	Visteis	Veríais
Han visto	Vieron	Verían

Pretérito imperfecto	Futuro	Cond. compuesto
Veía	Veré	Habría visto
Veías	Verás	Habrías visto
Veía	Verá	Habría visto
Veíamos	Veremos	Habríamos visto
Veíais	Veréis	Habríais visto
Veían	Verán	Habrían visto

Presente	Pretérito pluscuamp.
Vea	Hubiera (-se) visto
Veas	Hubieras (-ses) visto
Vea	Hubiera (...) visto
Veamos	Hubiéramos visto
Veáis	Hubierais visto
Vean	Hubieran visto

Pretérito perfecto	GERUND
Haya visto	Viendo
Hayas visto	
Haya visto	PAST PARTICIPLE
Hayamos visto	Visto
Hayáis visto	
Hayan visto	

Pretérito imperfecto	IMPERATIVE
	Affirmative/Negative
Viera (-se)	
Vieras (-ses)	Ve / No veas
Viera (...)	Ved / No veáis
Viéramos	
Vierais	Vea / No vea
Vieran	Vean / No vean

■ Other verbs that conjugate like *ver*: *prever.*

VOLAR

INDICATIVE			SUBJUNCTIVE	
Presente	**Pretérito pluscuamp.**	**Futuro perfecto**	**Presente**	**Pretérito pluscuamp.**
Vuelo	Había volado	Habré volado	Vuele	Hubiera (se) volado
Vuelas	Habías volado	Habrás volado	Vueles	Hubieras (-ses) volado
Vuela	Había volado	Habrá volado	Vuele	Hubiera (...) volado
Volamos	Habíamos volado	Habremos volado	Volemos	Hubiéramos volado
Voláis	Habíais volado	Habréis volado	Voléis	Hubierais volado
Vuelan	Habían volado	Habrán volado	Vuelen	Hubieran volado

Pretérito perfecto	**Pretérito indefinido**	**Condicional**	**Pretérito perfecto**	**GERUND**
He volado	Volé	Volaría	Haya volado	Volando
Has volado	Volaste	Volarías	Hayas volado	
Ha volado	Voló	Volaría	Haya volado	**PAST PARTICIPLE**
Hemos volado	Volamos	Volaríamos	Hayamos volado	Volado
Habéis volado	Volasteis	Volaríais	Hayáis volado	
Han volado	Volaron	Volarían	Hayan volado	

Pretérito imperfecto	**Futuro**	**Cond. compuesto**	**Pretérito imperfecto**	**Affirmative/Negative**
Volaba	Volaré	Habría volado	Volara (-se)	
Volabas	Volarás	Habrías volado	Volaras (-ses)	Vuela / No vueles
Volaba	Volará	Habría volado	Volara (...)	Volad / No voléis
Volábamos	Volaremos	Habríamos volado	Voláramos	
Volabais	Volaréis	Habríais volado	Volarais	Vuele / No vuele
Volaban	Volarán	Habrían volado	Volaran	Vuelen / No vuelen

■ Other verbs that conjugate like *volar*: *acostar(se), costar, probar, recordar, soñar...*

VOLVER

INDICATIVE			SUBJUNCTIVE	
Presente	**Pretérito pluscuamp.**	**Futuro perfecto**	**Presente**	**Pretérito pluscuamp.**
Vuelvo	Había vuelto	Habré vuelto	Vuelva	Hubiera (-se) vuelto
Vuelves	Habías vuelto	Habrás vuelto	Vuelvas	Hubieras (-ses) vuelto
Vuelve	Había vuelto	Habrá vuelto	Vuelva	Hubiera (...) vuelto
Volvemos	Habíamos vuelto	Habremos vuelto	Volvamos	Hubiéramos vuelto
Volvéis	Habíais vuelto	Habréis vuelto	Volváis	Hubierais vuelto
Vuelven	Habían vuelto	Habrán vuelto	Vuelvan	Hubieran vuelto

Pretérito perfecto	**Pretérito indefinido**	**Condicional**	**Pretérito perfecto**	**GERUND**
He vuelto	Volví	Volvería	Haya vuelto	Volviendo
Has vuelto	Volviste	Volverías	Hayas vuelto	
Ha vuelto	Volvió	Volvería	Haya vuelto	**PAST PARTICIPLE**
Hemos vuelto	Volvimos	Volveríamos	Hayamos vuelto	Vuelto
Habéis vuelto	Volvisteis	Volveríais	Hayáis vuelto	
Han vuelto	Volvieron	Volverían	Hayan vuelto	

Pretérito imperfecto	**Futuro**	**Cond. compuesto**	**Pretérito imperfecto**	**Affirmative/Negative**
Volvía	Volveré	Habría vuelto	Volviera (-se)	
Volvías	Volverás	Habrías vuelto	Volvieras (-ses)	Vuelve / No vuelvas
Volvía	Volverá	Habría vuelto	Volviera (...)	Volved / No volváis
Volvíamos	Volveremos	Habríamos vuelto	Volviéramos	
Volvíais	Volveréis	Habríais vuelto	Volvierais	Vuelva / No vuelva
Volvían	Volverán	Habrían vuelto	Volvieran	Vuelvan / No vuelvan

■ Other verbs that conjugate like *volver*: *devolver, envolver, resolver...*

C   Verbs with one irregularity

ABRIR
- Conjugates like *vivir*.
  Irregular past participle: a**bier**to.
  Other verbs that conjugate like *abrir*: *entreabrir, reabrir.*

CUBRIR
- Conjugates like *vivir*.
  Irregular past participle: cu**bier**to.
  Other verbs that conjugate like **cubrir**: *descubrir, encubrir, recubrir.*

ESCRIBIR
- Conjugates like vivir.
  Irregular past participle: es**cri**to.
  Other verbs that conjugate like *escribir*: *describir, inscribir, reescribir, suscribir...*

IMPRIMIR
- Conjugates like *vivir*.
  Two past participle forms, one regular
  and the other irregular: impri**mi**do, impre**s**o.

ROMPER
- Conjugates like *comer*.
  Irregular past participle: **ro**to.

D   List of irregular verbs

- The verbs in bold on the left conjugate like the model verbs that follow in italics to their right.
  The information in square brackets [ ] refers to how certain forms of the verb are written.
  The information in ordinary brackets ( ) refers to conjugational irregularities.
  Verbs marked with an asterisk * are only used in certain forms.

Abrir: 272
Abstraer: *traer,* 269
Acertar: *pensar,* 264
Acordar: *volar,* 271
Acostar: *volar,* 271
Adquirir: *sentir,* 268
Advertir: *sentir,* 268
Almorzar: *volar,* 271
  [pr. subj.: almuerce...;
  pret. indef.: almorcé;
  imp.: almuerce...]
Andar: 253
Ansiar: *confiar,* 255
Anteponer: *poner,* 265
Aparecer: *conocer,* 256
Apetecer: *conocer,* 256
Apretar: *pensar,* 264
Aprobar: *volar,* 271
Arrepentirse: *sentir,* 268
Ascender: *entender,* 259
Atender: *entender,* 259
Atraer: *traer,* 269
Atravesar: *pensar,* 264
Atribuir: *construir,* 256
Avergonzar: *volar,* 271

Bendecir: *decir,* 258
(past part.: bendecido;
  fut.: bendeciré...;
  cond.: bendeciría...)

Caber: 254
Caer: 254
Calentar: *pensar,* 264
Carecer: *conocer,* 256
Cerrar: *pensar,* 264
Cocer: *mover,* 263
  [pr. ind.: cuezo, cueces...;
  pr. subj.: cueza...;
  imp.: cuece, cueza...]
Colgar: *volar,* 271
  [pr. subj.: cuelgue...;
  pret. indef..: colgué;
  imp.: cuelgue...]
Comenzar: *pensar,* 264
  [pr. subj.: comience...;
  pret. indef..: comencé;
  imp.: comience...]
Compadecer: *conocer,* 256
Competir: *pedir,* 264
Complacer: *conocer,* 256
Componer: *poner,* 265
Comprobar: *volar,* 271
Concebir: *pedir,* 264
Concluir: *construir,* 256
Conducir: 255
Confesar: *pensar,* 264
Confiar: 255
Conmover: *mover,* 263
Conocer: 256
Conseguir: *pedir,* 264

[pr. ind.: consigo, consi-
  gues...; pr. subj.: consiga...;
  imp.: consigue, consiga...]
Consentir: *sentir,* 268
Consolar: *volar,* 271
Constituir: *construir,* 256
Construir: 256
Contar: *volar,* 271
Contener: *tener,* 269
Contradecir: *decir,* 258
Contraer: *traer,* 269
Contraponer: *poner,* 265
Contribuir: *construir,* 256
Convenir: *venir,* 270
Convertir: *sentir,* 268
Corregir: *pedir,* 264
  [pr. ind.: corrijo, corriges...;
  pr. subj.: corrija...;
  imp.: corrige, corrija...]
Costar: *volar,* 271
Crecer: *conocer,* 256
Creer: 257
Criar: *confiar,* 255
Cubrir: 272

Dar: 257
Decaer: *caer,* 254
Decir: 258
Deducir: *conducir,* 255
Defender: *entender,* 259

Demostrar: *volar,* 271
Desafiar: *confiar,* 255
Desaparecer: *conocer,* 256
Desaprobar: *volar,* 271
Desatender: *entender,* 259
Descender: *entender,* 259
Descolgar: *volar,* 271
  [pr. subj.: descuelgue...;
  imp.: descuelgue...]
Descomponer: *poner,* 265
Desconfiar: *confiar,* 255
Desconocer: *conocer,* 256
Describir: *vivir,* 253
  (past part.: descrito)
Desentenderse: *entender,* 259
Desenvolver: *volver,* 271
Deshacer: *hacer,* 261
Desliar: *confiar,* 255
Desmentir: *pedir,* 264
Desmerecer: *conocer,* 256
Desobedecer: *conocer,* 256
Desoír: *oír,* 263
Despedir: *pedir,* 264
Despertar: *pensar,* 264
Destituir: *construir,* 256
Desviar: *confiar,* 255
Descubrir: *vivir,* 253
  (past part.: descubierto)
Detener: *tener,* 269

Devolver: *volver*, 271
Digerir: *sentir*, 268
Diluir: *construir*, 256
Disentir: *sentir*, 268
Disminuir: *construir*, 256
Disolver: *volver*, 271
Disponer: *poner*, 265
Distraer: *traer*, 269
Distribuir: *construir*, 256
Divertir: *sentir*, 268
Doler: *mover*, 263
Dormir: 258

Elegir: *pedir*, 264
  [pr. ind.: elijo, eliges...;
  pr. subj.: elija...;
  imp.: elige, elija...]
Empezar: *pensar*, 264
  [pr. subj.: empiece...;
  pret. indef.: empecé;
  imp.: empiece...]
Encender: *entender*, 259
Encerrar: *pensar*, 264
Encontrar: *volar*, 271
Encubrir: *vivir*, 253
  (past part.: encubierto)
Enfriar: *confiar*, 255
Entender: 259
Entreabrir: *vivir*, 253
  (past part.: entreabierto)
Entretener: *tener*, 269
Enviar: *confiar*, 255
Envolver: *volver*, 271
Equivaler: *salir*, 267
  (pero con term. *-er*)
Escribir: 272
Espiar: *confiar*, 255
Esquiar: *confiar*, 255
Establecer: *conocer*, 256
Estar: 259
Excluir: *construir*, 256
Exponer: *poner*, 265
Extender: *entender*, 259
Extraer: *traer*, 269

Favorecer: *conocer*, 256
Florecer: *conocer*, 256
Fluir: *construir*, 256
Fregar: *pensar*, 264
Freír: 260

Gobernar: *pensar*, 264
Guiar: *confiar*, 255

Haber: 260
Hacer: 261
Herir: *sentir*, 268
Hervir: *sentir*, 268

Huir: *construir*, 256

Impedir: *pedir*, 264
Imponer: *poner*, 265
Imprimir: 272
Incluir: *construir*, 256
Influir: *construir*, 256
Ingerir: *sentir*, 268
Inscribir: *vivir*, 253
  (past part.: inscrito)
Instituir: *construir*, 256
Instruir: *construir*, 256
Interferir: *sentir*, 268
Intervenir: *venir*, 270
Introducir: *conducir*, 255
Invertir: *sentir*, 268
Ir: 261

Jugar: 262

Leer: *creer*, 257
Liar: *confiar*, 255

Llover*: *mover*, 263

Manifestar: *pensar*, 264
Mantener: *tener*, 269
Medir: *pedir*, 264
Mentir: *sentir*, 268
Merecer: *conocer*, 256
Merendar: *pensar*, 264
Moler: *mover*, 263
Morder: *mover*, 263
Morir: 262
Mostrar: *volar*, 271
Mover: 263

Nacer: *conocer*, 256
Negar: *pensar*, 264
Nevar*: *pensar*, 264

Obedecer: *conocer*, 256
Obtener: *tener*, 269
Ofrecer: *conocer*, 256
Oír: 263
Oler: *mover*, 263
  [pr. ind.: huelo, hueles,
  huele... huelen;
  pr. subj.: huela, huelas,
  huela... huelan;
  imp.: huele, huela...]
Oponer: *poner*, 265

Padecer: *conocer*, 256
Parecer: *conocer*, 256
Pedir: 264
Pensar: 264
Perder: *entender*, 259

Permanecer: *conocer*, 256
Perseguir: *sentir*, 268
Pertenecer: *conocer*, 256
Poder: 265
Poner: 265
Poseer: *creer*, 257
Posponer: *poner*, 265
Preconcebir: *pedir*, 264
Predecir: *decir*, 258
Predisponer: *poner*, 265
Preferir: *sentir*, 268
Presuponer: *poner*, 265
Prevenir: *venir*, 270
Prever: *ver*, 270
Probar: *volar*, 271
Producir: *conducir*, 255
Prohibir: 266
Promover: *mover*, 263
Proponer: *poner*, 265
Proveer: *creer*, 257
  (past part.: proveído,
  provisto)
Provenir: *venir*, 270

Quebrar: *pensar*, 264
Querer: 266

Reabrir: *vivir*, 253
  (past part.: reabierto)
Recaer: *caer*, 254
Recomendar: *pensar*, 264
Recomponer: *poner*, 265
Reconocer: *conocer*, 256
Reconstruir: *construir*, 256
Recordar: *volar*, 271
Recubrir: *vivir*, 253
  (past part.: recubierto)
Reducir: *conducir*, 255
Reescribir: *vivir*, 253
  (past part.: reescrito)
Referir: *sentir*, 268
Regar: *pensar*, 264
  [pr. subj.: riegue...;
  pret. indef.: regué;
  imp.: riegue...]
Rehacer: *hacer*, 261
Reír: *pedir*, 264
Remover: *mover*, 263
Renovar: *volar*, 271
Reñir: *pedir*, 264
Repetir: *pedir*, 264
Reprobar: *volar*, 271
Reproducir: *conducir*, 255
Restituir: *construir*, 256
Retener: *tener*, 269
Retraer: *traer*, 269
Retribuir: *construir*, 256
Reunir: *prohibir*, 266

Revolver: *volver*, 271
Romper: 272
Rogar: *volar*, 271
  [pr. subj.: ruegue...;
  pret. indef.: rogué;
  imp.: ruegue...]

Saber: 267
Salir: 267
Satisfacer: *hacer*, 261
Seducir: *conducir*, 255
Seguir: *pedir*, 264
Sembrar: *pensar*, 264
Sentar(se): *pensar*, 264
Sentir: 268
Ser: 268
Servir: *pedir*, 264
Sobrentender: *entender*, 259
Sobreponer: *poner*, 265
Sobresalir: *salir*, 267
Sobrevenir: *venir*, 270
Soler*: *mover*, 263
Soltar: *volar*, 271
Sonar: *volar*, 271
Sonreír: *pedir*, 264
Soñar: *volar*, 271
Sostener: *tener*, 269
Sugerir: *sentir*, 268
Superponer: *poner*, 265
Suponer: *poner*, 265
Suscribir: *vivir*, 253
  (past part.: suscrito)
Sustituir: *construir*, 256
Sustraer: *traer*, 269

Temblar: *pensar*, 264
Tender: *entender*, 259
Tener: 269
Tostar: *volar*, 271
Traducir: *conducir*, 255
Traer: 269
Transferir: *sentir*, 268
Tropezar: *pensar*, 264

Vaciar: *confiar*, 255
Valer: *salir*, 267
  (pero con term. *-er*)
Variar: *confiar*, 255
Venir: 270
Ver: 270
Verter: *entender*, 259
Vestir: *pedir*, 264
Volar: 271
Volcar: *volar*, 271
  [pr. subj.: vuelque...;
  pret. indef.: volqué;
  imp.: vuelque...]
Volver: 271

Answer key

1. Noun. The gender of things

Page 14

1   1. vaso 2. gafas 3. casa 4. floreros

2   1. bolígrafo, pluma 2. piso, casa 3. marido, regalo
4. familia.

Page 15

3   1. **brazo** es masculina y las otras son femeninas.
2. **impresora** es femenina y las otras son masculinas.
3. **crema** es femenina y las otras son masculinas.
4. **canción** es femenina y las otras son masculinas.
5. **garaje** es masculina y las otras son femeninas.

4   Masculino: El salón. El sobre. El taxi. El microondas.
El café. El pie. El árbol. El sol. El lavavajillas.
Femenino: La crisis. La luna. La tesis. La clase.
La tarde. La sal. La leche. La nariz. La carne.

Page 16

5   I. el garaje, el ordenador, la clase
II. El potaje, el microondas, el champú, el paraguas,
el jersey
III. Un problema, la moto, las llaves
IV. Un error, la traducción
V. El tema
VI. El sillón, una reunión, una parte, la tarde, el móvil

6   1. el 2. la 3. el 4. el 5. el 6. el 7. la 8. el 9. el
10. la 11. el 12. el 13. la, el 14. el 15. la 16. el
17. el 18. la 19. la 20. la 21. el 22. el 23. la
24. la 25. la 26. la

2. Noun. The gender of people and animals

Page 17

1   1. g, moderna 2. d, nervioso 3. h, fantástica
4. a, comprensivo 5. c, extraordinario 6. f, loca
7. e, un artista

2   1. abuela 2. primas 3. amigos 4. hermanos
5. hermanas 6. niña

Page 18

3   1. padre, padre/madre 2. madre, padre/madre
3. mujer, mujer 4. hermana, padre/madre 5. hija
6. hermano, padre/madre 7. padre, marido/mujer
8. madre, marido/mujer 9. hijo 10. hija 11. hijo

4   1. pianista 2. pianista 3. policía 4. taxista
5. profesora 6. periodista 7. cantante 8. actriz,

9. actor 10. veterinario 11. futbolista

Page 19

5   **Marca de masculino/femenino:** gato/gata,
cerdo/cerda, tigre/tigresa, gallo/gallina,
Una palabra diferente para cada sexo:
caballo/yegua
Invariable femenino: jirafa, tortuga, hormiga, gamba.
Invariable masculino: cocodrilo, dinosaurio,
calamar, caracol, mejillón

6   1. ¿esto es un **canguro macho** o un **canguro
hembra**?
2. ¿es un **ratón** o una **ratona**?
3. ¿un **camaleón macho** o un **camaleón hembra**?
4. ¿un **pato** o una **pata**?
5. ¿Es una **serpiente macho** o una **serpiente
hembra**?
6. ¿una **lechuza macho** o una **lechuza hembra**?

3. Noun. Number

Page 21

1   1. pec**es** 2. sof**ás** 3. rel**ojes** 4. boton**es** 5. jers**éis**

2   1. papeles 2. sartenes 3. tenedores 4. luces
5. lápices 6. boligrafos 7. rotuladores 8. árboles
9. bebés

3   1. paraguas 2. lavadora 3. abrebotellas 4. sofá
5. cuadro 6. cafetera 7. abrelatas 8. microondas

Page 22

4   1. ~~la luz~~ / las luces 2. agua / ~~aguas~~ 3. carne / ~~carnes~~
4. vino / ~~vinos~~ 5. té / ~~tes~~

5   1. e, aplaudi**eron** entusiasmad**os** 2. c, estaba**n** muy
interesad**as** 3. sali**ó** muy content**o** 4. b, espera**ba**
atent**a** el final del concierto

6   1. pastel 2. pez 3. jersey 4. luz 5. canapé

7   1. Dos relojes de pared 2. Dos abrelatas
3. Dos cortinas de baño 4. Dos bragas de algodón
5. Dos paraguas

4. Adjective

Page 24

1   1. cariñosa 2. vaga 3. guapa 4. superficial
5. dormilona 6. ecologista 7. tímido 8. alegre
9. trabajador 10. independiente 11. frágil

12. nerviosa 13. fuerte 14. optimista
15. inteligente 16. fea 17. pedante

2 1. italiano (es el único adjetivo de género variable).
2. contento (es el único adjetivo de género variable).
3. lista (es el único adjetivo de género variable).
4. hermosa (es el único adjetivo de género variable).
5. joven (es el único adjetivo de género invariable).

3 1. dos niñas cursis 2. dos personas felices 3. dos niños llorones 4. dos camisas grises 5. dos hombres habladores 6. dos mujeres interesantes

Page 25

4 1. estadounidense 2. italianas 3. colombiano
4. turcas 5. cubanos 6. japonesa 7. escocés
8. senegalés 9. suizos 10. finlandesa 11. españoles
12. franceses 13. china

5 1. a, elegante 2. a, pequeña y ruidosa
3. b, amplia y luminosa 4. d, lento e inseguro
5. a, grande y rápido 6. b, incómodos
7. a, impresionantes

6 1. ...son asturianos, pero yo nací en Madrid.
2. ...son maravillosos, aunque hace mucho frío.
3. ...son medios más objetivos que la televisión.
4. ...son más ecológicas. Los coches contaminan mucho.
5. ...son muy malos para la salud.
6. ...están mojados y te puedes caer.

Page 26

7 1. Hay un grifo abierto.
2. Ponte el jersey naranja.
3. Dame un cenicero vacío.
4. Trae la ropa sucia.
5. Mete la botella llena.
6. Es un coche familiar.
7. Vivo en una residencia universitaria.
8. Los vuelos internacionales.
9. Está en un sobre cerrado.

Page 27

8 1. destaca 2. distingue 3. distingue 4. destaca
5. destaca 6. distingue 7. destaca 8. distingue

9 1. ~~industrial~~ edificio: edificio **industrial**.
2. ~~redondo~~ objeto: objeto **redondo**.
3. ~~japonés~~ reloj: reloj **japonés**.
4. ~~oficial~~ coche: coche **oficial**.
5. ~~vacía~~ casa: casa **vacía**.

Page 28

10 1. **segundo** marido 2. costas **caribeñas**
3. **tercer** marido 4. carretera **secundaria**
5. **cuarto** marido 6. barbacoa **familiar**

7. **próximo/futuro** marido 8. **próximo/futuro** presidente 9. banco **suizo**

11 1. ~~primer~~: primera. 2. ~~mal~~: malos.
3. ~~tercer~~: tercera. 4. ~~mal~~: mala.
5. ~~bueno~~: buen. 6. ~~grande~~: gran.
7. ~~grande~~: gran. 8. ~~buen~~: buena.
9. ~~bueno~~: buen. 10. ~~bueno~~: buen.

5. Articles: *un, el, ø*

Page 30

1 1. unas, unos 2. un, unas 3. una, un 4. un, una
5. los, las 6. las, del 7. el, la 8. la, al

Page 31

2 1. un 2. la, última 3. las 4. un, horrorosa 5. el
6. las 7. la, misma 8. el 9. las

Page 32

3 1a. b 1b. a 2a. b 2b. a 3a. a 3b. b 4a. a 4b. b
5a. b 5b. a

4 1. el, una 2. la/una, un 3. el 4. unos, los 5. el, un, el

5 1. sí 2. no 3. no 4. no 5. no 6. sí 7. sí

Page 33

6 1. Ø/el, d 2. Ø/~~un~~, f 3. Ø/~~un~~, c 4. Ø/el, e 5. Ø/un, b
6. Ø/el, g 7. Ø/~~el~~, l 8. Ø/un, j 9. Ø/el, i 10. Ø/~~un~~, k
11. Ø/el, h

Page 34

7 1. huevos 2. agua 3. café 4. pilas 5. aspirinas 6. dinero

Page 35

8 1a. III, 1b. I, 1c. II 2a. I, 2b. III, 2c. II 3a. III, 3b. II,
3c. I 4a. I, 4b. III, 4c. II 5a. III, 5b. I, 5c. II

9 1. el abanico 2. los cajeros 3. mostaza 4. los helados 5. las hormigas 6. el/un té, el/un café / el/un café, el/un té 7. el/un ratón 8. el carrito 9. agua

10 1. Después de cazar bisontes, nos duelen mucho **las** piernas, pero **el** gran jefe Halcón Maltés nos da zumo de uvas y aspirinas.
2. **Los** indios quieren ser como **el** oso y **el** águila y respetan a **los** seres vivos. Sólo cazan animales para comer.
3. A **los** indios les gusta fumar hierba seca con **el** anciano más viejo de **la** tribu.
4. Para **los** indios **el** amor es **el** sentimiento más hermoso. **Los** indios aman **la** naturaleza y también **al** hombre blanco.

Answer key

5. **Los** indios hacen fuego y bailan **la** danza de **la** lluvia cuando llega **la** primavera.
6. Todas **las** primaveras **los** osos bajan de **las** montañas **al** río para pescar salmones. **Los** indios aprenden mucho de ellos.
7. **Los** hombres indios se pintan para **la** guerra. **Las** mujeres indias nunca se pintan. Les gusta **la** paz.

Page 36

11 1. unas ~~medias~~
2. los ~~sobres~~ amarillos, los ~~sobres~~ que están ahí
3. una ~~cerveza~~
4. un*o* ~~reloj~~ que tiene cronómetro
5. la ~~chica~~ de las gafas, la ~~chica~~ alta, la ~~chica~~ que está de pie
6. unos ~~amigos~~ que conocí en la discoteca
7. ¿El ~~libro~~ gordo? ¿El ~~libro~~ de física?
8. un*o* ~~café~~ solo, un*o* ~~café~~ con leche

12 1. lleva peluca 2. guantes largos
3. pistola 4. delgado 5. pañuelo de lunares
6. está cantando 7. guapísimas

6. Demonstratives: *este, ese, aquel... esto, eso...*

Page 38

1 1. estas 2. estos 3. esta 4. ese
5. esa 6. esas 7. esos 8. aquella
9. aquellos 10. aquellas 11. aquel

2 1. d 2. b 3. c

3 1. estos 2. esas 3. aquel 4. aquella 5. esos

Page 39

4 1. d 2. c 3. a 4. f 5. b

5 1. hombres 2. hoja 3. chico 4. papel
5. pendientes

Page 41

6 1. esto 2. esto 3. eso 4. eso 5. eso 6. aquello
7. aquello

7 1. f 2. c 3. g 4. b 5. d 6. e
No sabe el nombre: 1, 3
No importa el nombre: 5, 6
No es un objeto: 2, 4

Page 42

8 1. eso 2. eso 3. esto 4. aquello 5. eso

9 1. aquello 2. esa chica / eso 3. esa carta 4. ésa
5. ese señor 6. aquella chica 7. aquello

8. este mueble / esto 9. ése

7. Possessives: *mi, tu, su... mío, tuyo, suyo...*

Page 44

1 1. nuestra, nuestras, nuestros
2. tu, tu, tu, tus, tus
3. mi, mis, mis, mi, mis
4. vuestro, vuestras, vuestras
5. su, su, su, su, sus, sus

2 1. mis 2. tus 3. tus 4. mi
5. tu 6. tu 7. mis 8. mi
9. tu 10. tu 11. tu

Page 45

3 1. f/suyos 2. e/vuestro 3. c/míos 4. d/suyos
5. b/vuestros

4 1. ~~de ti~~ tuyo 2. ~~de vosotros~~ vuestro 3. ~~de ti~~ tuyo
4. ~~de nosotros~~ nuestro

Page 47

5 1. a 2. b 3. b 4. b 5. b 6. b 7. a

6 1. **mis** camisones de seda 2. **mi** dentadura postiza
3. **nuestras** dieciocho maletas 4. **nuestros** seis abrigos de pieles 5. **nuestros** gorros de dormir 6. **su** magnífica colección de pipas de marfil 7. **mi** esposa
8. **su** último cumpleaños 9. **tu** ordenador portátil
10. **tus** doce palos de golf preferidos 11. algunos objetos **suyos** 12. **su** ordenador 13. varios poemas **suyos** 14. algunas joyas **suyas** 15. **su** anillo 16.
Dos pipas **suyas** 17. **sus** doce palos de golf 18. dos camisones **suyos** 19. **una** maleta suya 20. **su** dentadura postiza 21. **tu** pijama

Pages 48 y 49

7 1. Me gusta más su dentista que **el nuestro**. Hace menos daño.
2. Mi móvil se ha quedado sin batería. ¿Me dejas **el tuyo**?
3. Éstas son mis toallas. **Las tuyas** están en el armario.
4. El barrio donde vivo no está mal, pero **el suyo** es más tranquilo.
5. Mi sueldo es más alto que **el vuestro**. Y eso que trabajo bastante menos.
6. Yo tengo una letra muy difícil de leer, pero **la tuya** no se entiende nada.
7. Entre la bicicleta de David y **la nuestra**, prefiero la de David.
8. Tenemos el mismo coche, pero **el suyo** tiene aire acondicionado.
9. Nunca te lo había dicho, pero prefiero su café **al tuyo**.

8 1. nuestro 2. suyo 3. mío 4. suyas 5. mías
6. mía 7. mío 8. suya 9. mía/nuestra 10. mía
11. nuestras 12. mías 13. vuestras 14. nuestros
15. nuestro 16. vuestros 17. nuestra

9 1. el 2. las 3. la 4. la 5. el 6. las 7. las 8. los 9. las
10. la 11. la 12. el   1. C 2. D 3. B

8. Indefinite articles: *todos, algunos, alguien...*

Page 51

1 1. algunas, ninguna, todas 2. algunas, ningunas,
Todas 3. algunos, ninguno, todos 4. algunos, ninguno, todos 5. Algunas, ninguna, todas 6. algunos,
Ninguno, Todos 7. algunos, ninguno, Todos
8. Algunas, ninguna, Todas

2 1. algunas 2. algunos 3. todos, ninguno
4. ningún 5. algún 6. ningún 7. todas
8. alguna 9. algún

3 1. Algunos 2. algunas 3. ninguna
4. algunas 5. todas 6. Algunos
7. ninguno 8. todos 9. Todas
10. todos 11. Algunos

Page 52

4 1. algo 2. Nadie 3. algo 4. nada 5. todo
6. nada 7. alguien 8. algo 9. nada 10. algo
11. nadie 12. nada 13. alguien 14. nadie
15. todo 16. algo 17. algo

5 1. perezosa 2. barato 3. oscuro 4. rojo 5. rápido

Page 53

6 1. alguien, nadie, alguno, algo 2. algo, nada, algo,
nada 3. algo, algunas 4. algunas, ninguna 5. alguien,
algún 6. algo, ningún, Ninguno, nada 7. algo, alguno,
algún, algún 8. Alguno/algunos, algo, nada, alguno /
algunos, alguna

Page 54

7 1. *correcto* 2. Bueno, yo esperaba tu ayuda, pero si
no puedes, **no** pasa nada. 3. *correcto* 4. Dicen que
Rosa y aquel chico se besaron, pero yo **no** vi nada.
5. Tiene cuatro gatos, pero **no** quiere regalarme ninguno. 6. No lo dudo, será tu hijo, pero **no** se parece
en nada a ti.

Page 55

8 1. b/otro 2. a/otra 3. d/otras 4. c/otros

9 1. otras 2. otros tres 3. otro
4. otras dos 5. otra 6. otras dos

10 1. (una, casa, otra) otra casa 2. (otra, la, parte) la otra
parte 3. (otra, su, hija) su otra hija 4. (hijos, otros,
dos) otros dos hijos 5. (ternero, un, otro) otro ternero 6. (tres, casas, otras) otras tres casas 7. (chico,
otro, aquel) aquel otro chico

11 1. *correcto*
2. ¿Por qué te fijas en unos otros si me tienes a mí?
3. Jerónimo, yo no miro unos otros ojos, no miro una
otra boca, no miro otras manos. Yo sólo te miro a ti.
4. Eso deseo yo, Alablanca. Porque tú eres mi única
luna y no hay en todo el mundo ninguna otra. Nunca
podrá haber una otra. Sólo te quiero a ti.

9. Cardinal numbers: *uno, dos, tres...*

Page 56

1 1. diez 2. dos 3. seis 4. doce 5. catorce 6. ocho
7. diez 8. seis 9. dos

2 1. dos, uno 2. una, tres 3. una, un 4. un, una
5. tres, dos, uno 6. dos, una, un

Page 57

3 quince - ocho = siete, nueve + cuatro = trece,
seis + tres = nueve, dos + nueve = once,
trece - siete = seis, diez + cuatro = catorce,
doce + tres = quince, siete + cinco = doce

4 1. treinta y nueve 2. treinta y uno
3. veintisiete 4. diecinueve 5. veintitrés
6. veinticinco 7. dieciséis

Page 58

5 1. setenta y una 2. sesenta y tres
3. ochenta y cuatro 4. tres 5. nueve
6. cincuenta y dos 7. cinco 8. dos

6 1. diecisiete 2. setenta y nueve 3. noventa y seis
4. treinta y tres 5. veintiuno 6. cuarenta y cinco
7. sesenta y uno 8. ochenta y dos 9. cincuenta y seis

7 **Cuaderno de Ana** (€): doscientos cincuenta (250),
ochocientos (800), setecientos dos (702),
novecientos veintidós (922)
Cuaderno de Julie (£): seiscientas doce (612),
quinientas treinta y una (531), setecientas (700),
cuatrocientas cincuenta (450)

Page 59

8 Electricidad: 281 euros, doscientos ochenta y uno
Móvil: 789 euros: setecientos ochenta y nueve
Teléfono: 411 euros: cuatrocientos once
Agua: 576 euros: quinientos setenta y seis
Droguería: 125 euros: ciento veinticinco

9   1. 4.179 cuatro mil ciento setenta y nueve
2. 95.167 noventa y cinco mil ciento sesenta y siete
3. 5.021 cinco mil veintiuno
4. 81.184 ochenta y un mil ciento ochenta y cuatro
5. 31.901 treinta y un mil novecientos uno
6. 27.432 veintisiete mil cuatrocientos treinta y dos

Page 60

10   1. ciento cuatro millones doscientos mil ciento sesenta y cinco habitantes
2. veinticinco millones doscientos ochenta y siete mil seiscientos setenta habitantes
3. catorce millones cuatrocientos cuarenta y siete mil cuatrocientos noventa y cuatro habitantes
4. seis millones ochenta y cuatro mil cuatrocientos noventa y un habitantes
5. catorce millones trescientos catorce mil setenta y nueve habitantes
6. cuarenta y un millones setenta y siete mil cien habitantes
7. dieciséis millones cuatrocientos noventa y ocho mil novecientos treinta habitantes

11   1. Cuarenta y dos mil ciento y cinco (42.105)
2. Tres millones y ochenta y ocho mil trescientos y cuarenta y seis (3.088.346)
3. Cuatrocientos y cinco mil sesenta y uno (405.071)
4. Cincuenta y nueve mil y once (59.011)
5. Noventa y dos mil trescientos y quince (92.315)
6. Ochocientos y cinco mil quinientos y ochenta (805.580)
7. Trescientos y veintiséis (326)
8. Setecientos y setenta mil (770.000)

12   Golandia tiene una superficie de seiscientos quince mil km² y un total de **dos millones quinientos sesenta y cinco mil** habitantes. La capital, Gola City, está situada al norte del país y tiene **ochocientos cuarenta y nueve mil trescientos** habitantes. La segunda ciudad importante de Golandia es Rúcola, con **trescientos siete mil** habitantes. El monte principal de la isla es El Golón con una altura de **cuatro mil cincuenta y ocho metros**, y tiene dos ríos principales: el Gologolo, de **cuatrocientos setenta y nueve** kilómetros y el Golín, de **doscientos treinta y cinco kilómetros**.

10. Ordinal numbers: *primero, segundo...*

Page 61

1   Carlos es el **tercero**, María es la **quinta**, Juan es el **sexto**, Francisco es el **cuarto**, Laura es la **segunda** y Ricardo es el **séptimo**.

2   1. Segundo 2. Noveno
3. Octavo 4. Tercer
5. Primera 6. Tercera 7. Primer

Page 62

3   1. Tercero 2. Quince 3. Décimo 4. Segunda
5. Trece

4   El primer día, la orquesta va a tocar el **segundo** concierto para piano de Brahms y la **cuarta** sinfonía de Bruckner. El **segundo** día, el **cuarto** concierto para violín de Mozart y la **octava** sinfonía de Mahler. Y el **tercer** día va a tocar el **quinto** concierto para piano de Beethoven y la **sexta** sinfonía de Tchaikovsky.

Page 63

5   Primero, se corta una rebanada de pan. **Segundo**, se unta con tomate. **Tercero**, se echa sal y aceite de oliva. **Cuarto**, se cubre con lonchas finas de jamón.

6   1. 69 2. 46 3. 91 4. 18 5. 11
6. 82 7. 76 8. 34 9. 50
10. 12 11. 99

7   1. cuadragésimo quinto 2. vigésimo sexto
3. décimo novena 4. trigésimo primera

11. Quantifiers: *demasiado, mucho...*

Page 64

1   1. Hay **mucha** agua y **pocos** cubitos.
2. Hay **bastante** agua y **bastantes** cubitos.
3. No hay **nada** de agua y **demasiados** cubitos.
4. Hay **demasiada** agua y **ningún** cubito.

Page 65

2   1. nada de 2. nada de 3. ninguna
4. ningún 5. nada de 6. ningún

3   1. Bonifacio 2. Dolores
3. Dolores 4. Bonifacio
5. Bonifacio 6. Dolores
7. Dolores

4   1. un poco de 2. poca 3. un poco de 4. poco
5. un poco de 6. poco 7. un poco de 8. un poco de
9. poco

Page 66

5   1. demasiadas 2. bastante
3. demasiados 4. muy
5. demasiado 6. Demasiado
7. poco 8. Demasiado
9. Muy 10. bastante

6   1. demasiado 2. bastante
3. poco 4. demasiados, poco
5. demasiadas

12. Personal pronouns. Introduction.

Page 69

1 1. Leonor 2. Paco 3. Dolores
    4. Elisabeth 5. Eduardo 6. María
    7. la casa 8. agua 9. el desayuno
    10. la compra 11. a los pequeños
    12. la ropa 13. al bebé
    14. la comida y la cena 15. a las plantas
    16. a sus hermanos pequeños 17. a todos

2 1. El secretario anota siempre: a/CD
    El secretario le anota sus citas: b/CI
    2. El profesor les enseña música jugando: b/CI
    El profesor enseña con juegos: a/CD
    3. El hijo les lava y les plancha la ropa: a/CI
    La lavadora lava y seca en dos horas: b/CD
    4. Paco pone en la mesa: a/CD
    Paco le pone la comida: b/CI

Page 70

3 1a. a 1b. b/reflexivo 2a. a/reflexivo 2b. b
    3a. b/reflexivo 3b. a

4 1a. la cabeza 1b. Alicia
    2a. unos helados 2b. Los niños
    3a. ese problema 3b. nosotros
    4a. Tu madre 4b. los niños
    5a. el ruido 5b. Los niños
    6a. Las chicas 6b. la música disco
    7a. La tele 7b. Tu madre

13. Subject pronouns: *yo, tú, él...*

Page 71

1 1. nosotras 2. nosotros 3. ellos 4. tú 5. él 6. ella
    7. ellas 8. vosotros 9. vosotras

2 1. tú, h 2. tú, b 3. usted, d 4. usted, a 5. tú, g
    6. usted, e 7. tú, f

Page 72

3 1. a, b 2. a, b 3. a, b 4. b, a 5. a, b

14. Pronouns with prepositions: *a mí, para ti...*

Page 73

1 1. vosotras, b, nosotras 2. usted, a, mí 3. tú, f, ti
    4. vosotros, d, nosotros 5. mí, ustedes, e, vosotros

Page 74

2 1. ti 2. ella 3. nosotras

---

    4. ella 5. contigo
    6. nosotras 7. él 8. ella

3 1. conmigo 2. contigo 3. para ellos 4. a ti
    5. entre tú y yo 6. sin nosotras 7. de mí
    8. hasta yo 9. de ti 10. según tú 11. por mí
    12. sobre ti

15. Object pronouns: *me, te, nos...*

Page 75

1 1. me 2. Nos 3. Nos 4. Os
    5. Te/Os 6. Te 7. nos 8. os, os

Page 77

2 1. las 2. lo 3. las 4. la 5. los 6. la 7. los

3 1. les 2. le 3. les 4. le 5. le

4 1. le 2. lo 3. le 4. la 5. les 6. les
    7. los 8. lo 9. la 10. los 11. las

Page 78

5 1. b (N) 2. b (N) 3. a (M) 4. b (N) 5. b (N)
    6. b (N) 7. a (M)

16. Position and combination of object...

Page 79

1 I. mayordomo (D)
    1. ¿Le reservo mesa en su restaurante
    de siempre?
    2. ¿Lo llevo a alguna parte?
    3. ¿Le preparo un baño caliente?
    II. pareja en el coche (C)
    4. ¿Te llevo a la peluquería?
    5. ¿Te pongo música?
    6. ¿Te enciendo el aire acondicionado?
    7. ¿Te abrocho el cinturón de seguridad?
    III. hablando con extraterrestres (A)
    8. ¿Os laváis los dientes?
    9. ¿Os acostáis temprano?
    10. ¿Os llevan al médico?
    11. ¿Os hacen regalos en Navidad?
    IV. grupo musical (B)
    12. Nos han aplaudido durante veinte minutos.
    13. Me han tirado ropa interior al escenario.
    14. Nos han pedido muchos autógrafos.
    15. Me han hecho miles de fotos.

Page 80

2 1. los 2. la 3. lo 4. me la 5. os los
    6. nos lo 7. te la

Answer key

Page 81

3   1. se lo 2. se lo 3. se los 4. se los, se los 5. se lo

4   1. se las he devuelto 2. te los limpio 3. os lo pongo
4. nos lo lees 5. se lo he dado 6. te la doy 7. os la
doy 8. nos las hemos lavado 9. se la he echado, se la
10. se lo he dado

Page 82

5   1a. moviéndolas, 1b. moviéndoselas
2a. doblándolas, 2b. doblándoselas
3a. girándola, 3b. girándosela
4a. moviéndolas, 4b. moviéndoselas
5a. subiéndola, 5b. subiéndosela
6a. moviéndolo, 6b. moviéndoselo

6   1. cógele 2. mírala 3. dile 4. despertaos
(despertados) 5. levantaos (levantados)
6. pruébale 7. cógele 8. ponle 9. tírale
10. dile

Page 83

7   1. déjame 2. **me** estás regañando / estás
regañándo**me** 3. **me** puedes dejar / puedes dejar**me**
4. cómprame, dime 5. **os** tenéis que decir / tenéis
que decir**os** 6. **nos** tenemos que decir / tenemos que
decir**nos** 7. mánda**le**, diciéndo**le**, llámala, decir**le**

8   1. **los** quieres recoger / quieres recoger**los**
2. **los** vas a recoger / vas a recoger**los**
3. **los** tienes que recoger / tienes que recoger**los**
4. **los** estoy recogiendo / estoy recogiéndo**los**
5. **te** vas a tomar / vas a tomar**te**
6. **me la** estoy tomando / estoy tomándo**mela**
7. apága**la**
8. **la** tienes que apagar / tienes que apagar**la**
9. **la** vas a apagar / vas a apagar**la**
10. **la** estoy apagando / estoy apagándo**la**

9   1. le 2. me los 3. Les 4. Le
5. Nos las 6. nos 7. os

17. Presence and redoubling of pronouns

Page 84

1   *Columna izquierda*:
1. lo 2. la 3. las 4. lo
Columna derecha:
1. le 2. se 3. les 4. le 5. se 6. se, se

Page 85

2   1. *correcto* 2. ~~Lo~~ han descolgado el teléfono. No
paraba de sonar. 3. *correcto* 4. *correcto* 5. *correcto*
6. *correcto* 7. ~~La~~ prepararé la ensaladilla y la meteré

enseguida en el frigorífico. 8. *correcto* 9. No ~~las~~ he
metido las sábanas en la secadora. Las he tendido.

Page 86

3   1.I-b, 1.II-a 2.I.a, 2.II-b 3.I-a, 3.II-b 4.I-a, 4.II-b
5.I-b, 5.II-a

4   1. te 2. me, os 3. nos 4. nos 5. os

5   1. no **me** miras (a mí)... 2. **Nos** pasa algo ~~a nosotros~~
3. Antes **nos** besábamos ~~a nosotros~~... 4. Yo **te** adoro
(a ti)... 5. Y yo también **te** quiero (a ti) mucho...
6. Pues si **nos** queremos tanto ~~a nosotros~~... 7. ¿por
qué no **nos** compramos ~~a nosotros~~...?

6   1. a. a él / d. a usted 2. b. a sus hijos / c. a ellas / e. a
ustedes 3. b. a Corina / c. a usted 4. a. a ella / b. a su
marido / c. a ustedes / d. a ellos / e. a sus amigas
5. a. a ustedes / c. a ellos 6. b. a ustedes / d. a ellas

18. Reflexive and opinion-expressing...

Page 87

1   1. No hay verbo reflexivo 2. te acuestas
3. No hay verbo reflexivo 4. se ha puesto
5. No hay verbo reflexivo 6. nos vestimos
7. No hay verbo reflexivo 8. No hay verbo reflexivo
9. os ponéis 10. No hay verbo reflexivo
11. se levantan

2   1a. b, 1b. a 2a. a, 2b. b 3a. b, 3b. a 4a. a, 4b. b

Page 88

3   1. ducha 2. acuestan 3. se duermen 4. nos 5. nos
levantamos 6. se 7. me levanto 8. me visto 9. se
afeita 10. se baña, se peina 11. te levantas

Page 89

4   1. se, las 2. se, las 3. se, el 4. se, los 5. se, los
6. se, los 7. se, el

5   1. f 2. g 3. a 4. c 5. h 6. b 7. e 8. c 9. d 10. h 11.
b 12. a 13. f 14. e 15. g

6   1. Nos 2. os 3. nos 4. os 5. nos 6. se enamoraron
7. se cayeron 8. se besaron 9. se entienden

Pages 91 y 92

7   1. *A mi madre* no *le* gusta**n los chicos** con pelo largo.
2. *A mis hermanas* **les** gusta **la ropa** y **salir** por la noche.
3. *A mí* **me** encanta sobre todo **viajar** y **dormir**.
4. *A todos nosotros* **nos** gusta mucho **el queso** francés.
5. *A todos nosotros* **nos** duele a menudo **la cabeza**.
6. ¿*A tus padres* **les** molesta **el tabaco**?

7. *¿A tus hermanos **les** interesa **la ecología**?*
8. *¿A vosotros **os** gusta**n la sangría y la paella**?*
9. *¿A vosotros **os** molesta**n los gatos**?*
10. *¿A tu hermana **le** gusta **esquiar**?*

8 1. me encanta, me gusta / c. les molesta
2. os fastidia, Os da vergüenza / a. nos molesta
3. nos molesta / e. me fastidia
4. te gusta / d. me encanta
6. me fastidia / j. les encanta
7. te molesta / i. me molesta, le importa
8. me encanta, Me relaja / h. me molesta
9. nos gustan / g. me gustan

9 1. Me da rabia... 2. Me alegran...
3. Me cae fatal... 4. Me apasionan... 5. Me resulta
espantoso... 6. Me dan alergia...
    A **Jerónimo le da rabia** ir de caza en invierno y
coser zapatillas. **Le alegran** la luna llena sobre las
montañas y mi sonrisa. **Le cae fatal** la nieta del jefe
Pluma Roja.
    A **Alablanca le apasionan** el olor a tierra moja-
da, pintarse la cara de colores y mi sonrisa. **Le resulta espantoso** lavar la ropa en el río y preparar tortas
de maíz. **Le dan alergia** el humo de la pipa de la paz
y los adornos de plumas.

---

19. Conjugation. The basic building blocks

Page 94

1 **Verbos en** *-ar*: entrar, llamar, levantarse, ocuparse,
cortarse, acostarse, ducharse
Verbos en *-er*: poner, ser, tener, poder, aprender,
haber, perderse, ponerse
Verbos en *-ir*: salir, conducir, oír, decir, reproducir,
partir, irse, vestirse

Page 95

2 **Verbos en** *-ar*: cocinar (cocina), estar (estás),
trabajar (trabajan), sentar (sentamos),
cantar (cantas)
Verbos en *-er*: aprender (aprenden), ver (vemos),
beber (bebe), traer (traen), comer (comemos),
leer (lee)
Verbos en *-ir*: salir (salís), escribir (escribimos),
pedir (pedís), dormir (dormís), vivir (vivimos),
sentir (sentimos)

3 Abrir, terminar, escribir, aprender, comer, desayunar,
poder, conducir, pedir, recibir, salir, querer, poner,
nacer, encantar, romper, prohibir, soñar, dormir,
pensar

Page 96

4 **yo:** creo **tú:** escribes, envías, sabes

él, ella, usted: sabe
nosotros/-as: salimos, tenemos, cantamos, sabemos,
saldremos
vosotros/-as: hacéis, comunicáis, venís
ellos, ellas, ustedes: llamarán, fueron, decían, tradu-
jeron, estaban

5 1. llegaremos 2. podrás, sales
3. cenan 4. llevamos 5. pueden
6. agradecerán 7. iréis

---

20. Non-personal forms: *hablar, hablando...*

Page 97

1 1. saltar 2. contar 3. rodar 4. salir 5. entrar 6. venir
7. vender 8. hacer 9. sentir 10. ir 11. amar
12. correr 13. volver 14. sudar

Page 98

2 1. ~~conduciendo motos~~ 2. ~~corriendo mañana~~
3. ~~acabo de comiendo~~ 4. ~~durmiendo sola~~
5. ~~durmiendo mucho~~

3 1. no girar a la derecha 2. no tocar el claxon
3. no adelantar 4. no comer 5. no hacer pipí
6. no besarse 7. no dormir

Page 99

4 1. yo 2. Cristina 3. yo 4. en general
5. tus amigos 6. la policía 7. Sra. López
8. en general 9. yo 10. vosotras
12. Antonio y Luis 13. en general

5 1. nadando 2. haciendo 3. poniendo
4. mordiendo

Page 100

6 2. repetir (irregular): repitiendo
3. dormir (irregular): durmiendo
4. reír (irregular): riendo
5. sufrir: sufriendo
6. oír (irregular): oyendo
7. decidir: decidiendo
8. ir (irregular): yendo
9. salir: saliendo
10. competir (irregular): compitiendo
11. seguir (irregular): siguiendo
12. producir: produciendo
13. mentir (irregular): mintiendo
14. compartir: compartiendo
15. sentir (irregular): sintiendo

7 1. ... cuando **estaba entrando** al cine
2. Ilsa **está estudiando** español...
3. Yo **estuve saliendo** con una chica francesa...

4. Yo ya me **estaba yendo**, cuando...
5. **Estuve trabajando** en esa empresa...

8 1. a 2. e 3. c 4. d 5. b

Page 101

9 1. ~~viniendo~~ venir
2. ~~Jugando~~ jugar 3. *correcto*
4. *correcto* 5. ~~buscando~~ buscar
6. *correcto* 7. ~~hablando~~ hablar
8. ~~estando~~ estar 9. *correcto*

Page 102

10 1. ha **escapado**: *correcto*, ha ~~volvido~~: **vuelto**, ha visto:
correcto, ha ~~morido~~: **muerto** 2. ha ~~ponido~~: **puesto**,
frito: *correcto*, he **comido**: *correcto* 3. he ~~rompido~~:
roto, han ido: *correcto*, han ~~descubrido~~: **descubierto**
4. he encontrado: *correcto*, he ~~abrido~~: **abierto**, ha
~~escribido~~: **escrito**

11 1. puesta 2. dicho 3. rotos 4. hechas
5. sorprendidos 6. resueltas 7. estudiada
(la mitad de...) / estudiados (los temas de...)

Page 103

12 1. Los científicos han **resuelto** bien el problema.
2. Elena no me había **convencido** con su explicación.
3. ¿Todavía no has **devuelto** los libros?
4. Pedro la habrá **asustado** con sus gritos.
5. Los economistas habían **previsto** una crisis.

13 1. rotas 2. rota 3. rotas 4. roto
5. abierta 6. abierto 7. abiertas
8. abierta 9. resuelto
10. resueltos 11. resuelto 12. resuelto

21. Presente de indicativo

Page 104

1 1. como, ceno: *yo* 2. puede, estudia, lee,
escribe, practica: *usted / el amigo de Hans*
3. vives, comes: *tú* 4. subes, llamas, abres, entras: *tú*
5. miráis: *vosotros tres* 6. cantan: *Lucía y
Sole / usted y su marido*, bailamos: *Elena y yo*
7. vivís: *vosotros tres*

2 1. toco, tocas, dejas 2. significa, levantas, significa,
madrugas 3. pasa 4. debo, esperan, bebemos
5. escuchas, significo 6. habláis, hablamos, practica-
mos 7. lleváis, vivís

Page 105

3 1. pierden 2. empiezo 3. pensamos
4. prefieren 5. cierras 6. entendéis

7. sentimos 8. duele 9. recordáis
10. mueren 11. jugamos 12. encuentro
13. duermes 14. cuesta 15. vuelves
16. volamos

Page 106

4 1. ríe, reímos 2. piden, pedimos
3. persigue, perseguimos 4. repiten, repetimos
5. compiten, competimos 6. mide, medimos

5 1. hablo, ~~sabo~~ sé 2. parece, ~~parezo~~ parezco
3. ~~conozo~~ conozco 4. ~~salo~~ salgo, ~~caio~~ caigo

Page 107

6 1. veo 2. doy 3. traigo
4. sé 5. conduzco
6. desaparezco 7. supongo
8. reconozco

7 1. digo, dices, decimos 2. tengo, tienes, tenemos
3. oigo, oyes, oimos 4. estoy, estás, estamos
5. vienes, estoy, digo, oyes, estás, tengo

Page 108

8 1. sois 2. voy, hemos, vamos
3. hay, hay 4. has, he
5. es, son 6. vais

Page 109

9 1. Es verdad 2. No lo sabemos 3. Es verdad
4. No lo sabemos 5. Es verdad

10 Tengo, vuelven, es, tengo, es, voy, tengo

Page 110

11 puede, tienen, ayuda, Pueden, Miden, Pesan,
alimentan, mantiene, ama, necesita, encanta, nada

12 1. P 2. F 3. F 4. P 5. G 6. F 7. F 8. G 9. F

13 1. c/piensa 2. a/siente 3. e/ahorra, gasta 4. b/se ríe
5. d/ve

22. Pretérito perfecto de indicativo

Page 111

1 1. Yo 2. Sus hermanos 3. Alejandro y tú
4. Su novia 5. Tú

2 1. He encendido (F) 2. has metido (H)
3. ha tenido (A) 4. has bebido (B)
5. Hemos ganado (G) 6. Ha salido (C)
7. hemos llegado (D)

Page 112

3 1. e 2. a 3. g 4. f 5. d 6. b

4 1. Han bailado toda la noche. 2. Han comido muchos dulces. 3. Ha ganado el gordo en la lotería. 4. Han ido a la playa. 5. Ha salido en televisión muchas veces.

Page 113

5 1. Pedro siempre (a) **ha conseguido buenos trabajos** hasta ahora. Ángel (b) **ha tenido trabajos** difíciles muchas veces.
2. Pedro (b) **ha ganado mucho dinero** en los últimos años. Ángel (a) **ha perdido mucho dinero** últimamente.
3. Pedro (b) **ha tenido muy buena salud** este año. Ángel (a) **se ha puesto enfermo tres veces** en los últimos meses.
4. Pedro (a) **ha conocido a una chica fantástica** esta semana. Ángel (b) **se ha separado de su mujer** esta semana.
5. Pedro (a) **ha encontrado una billetera** esta mañana. Ángel (b) **ha perdido su billetera** esta mañana.

Page 114

6 1. Pasado 2. Futuro 3. Pasado 4. Pasado 5. Futuro 6. Pasado 7. Futuro 8. Pasado

7 1. sí 2. no 3. no 4. sí 5. sí 6. no

23. Pretérito indefinido

Page 115

1 1. abriste 2. cerramos 3. bailó
4. canté 5. (indefinido) 6. oíste
7. hablé 8. huyeron 9. decidí
10. (indefinido) 11. invitaste
12. salió 13. comimos 14. (indefinido)
15. terminaron 16. vivimos 17. creyó
18. bebisteis 19. leyó 20. (indefinido)
21. encontraste 22. entraron
23. (indefinido) 24. construyeron
25. (indefinido) 26. estudiasteis
27. escondiste 28. decidisteis

Page 116

2 1. Presente 2. Indefinido
3. Indefinido 4. Presente
5. Presente 6. Indefinido
7. Indefinido 8. Presente

3 1. ~~veniste~~ **viniste**, ~~Hacimos~~ **hicimos**, bañamos
2. ~~condució~~ **conduje**, quise, ~~podí~~ **pude**, quitó
3. ~~dició~~ **dijo**, compraste, ~~teniste~~ **tuviste**

Page 117

4 1. introduje, produjo 2. dije, viniste, quisiste
3. tuvimos, conduje 4. traduje, pude 5. hubo, hice

5 1. (irr.) repitió, repitieron 2. (irr.) hirió, hirieron
3. (r.) discutió, discutieron 4. (irr.) oyó, oyeron
5. (irr.) impidió, impidieron 6. (irr.) midió, midieron
7. (r.) salió, salieron 8. (r.) repartió, repartieron
9. (irr.) mintió, mintieron 10. (r.) decidió, decidieron
11. (irr.) prefirió, prefirieron 12. (irr.) persiguió, persiguieron 13. (irr.) rió, rieron 14. (irr.) presintió, presintieron 15. (irr.) compitió, compitieron

Page 118

6 1. Fuimos, dio 2. fuimos, fuimos, fuimos
3. dimos, Fue

7 1. oí 2. tomé 3. llegó 4. Llamaste

8 1. Hablaste 2. comimos
3. influyeron 4. Oísteis
5. bebimos

24. Perfecto or indefinido? *Ha salido / Salió*

Page 120

1 1. b 2. a 3. b 4. a 5. a 6. b 7. b

2 1. has arreglado, he tenido 2. hemos pasado, fue
3. has ido, fui, he estado 4. has hecho, salí, casamos

Page 121

3 1. 'aquí' 2. 'aquí' 3. 'allí' 4. 'aquí'
5. 'aquí' 6. 'allí' 7. 'allí' 8. 'allí'
9. 'allí' 10. 'allí' 11. 'allí' 12. 'aquí'
13. 'allí' 14. 'allí' 15. 'aquí'

4 1. ha funcionado, dio 2. he dicho, has dicho, dijiste
3. pasaron, se casó, he pasado 4. hemos tenido, estuvimos, dijo 5. se enfadó, cambió

5 1. En los años 90 **ganamos** siete veces el campeonato de fútbol.
2. En los últimos diez años **hemos ganado** dos veces el concurso de levantar piedras.
3. En las fiestas del verano pasado **perdimos** la carrera de sacos.
4. Casi siempre en los últimos años **hemos perdido** el concurso de belleza masculina.
5. Siempre hasta ahora **hemos perdido** el tiro al plato de espaldas.
6. En el año 2004 **empatamos** en el concurso de paellas de marisco.
7. Últimamente, muchas veces, **hemos empatado** en el concurso de bandas de música.

Page 122

6 1. hemos traído 2. recordé 3. he olvidado 4. vi
5. ha empezado 6. has mojado 7. tapé 8. has cerrado 9. cerré 10. hemos tenido 11. encontré

25. Pretérito imperfecto de indicativo

Page 123

1 1. No le gustaba ir a los restaurantes. Nunca come
en casa. 2. Llevaba una ropa muy clásica. Viste muy
moderno. 3. No tenía amigos. Sale todas las noches
con sus amigos. 4. Quería tener muchos hijos. Tiene
tres perros.

Page 124

2 Cuando los padres de Blas llamaron a la puerta, él y
Silvia estaban bailando muy pegados. Casimiro, el
novio de Silvia, no **paraba** de mirar a Blas. **Había**
varias botellas de cerveza en la mesa y el cenicero
estaba lleno de colillas. La música **estaba** muy alta y
todo el mundo se **reía** sin parar. La hermana de
Silvia y el hermano de Blas **dormían** en el sofá, cogidos de la mano. La foto de los padres de Blas **tenía**
tres chicles pegados. En la cocina, cuatro chicos **estaban** tirándose aceitunas unos a otros.

3 1. Ella 2. Usted 3. Él 4. Ella 5. Yo 6. Él 7. Yo
8. Ella 9. Yo

Page 125

4 1. iba 2. era 3. erais
4. veía 5. eran 6. veíais
7. éramos 8. ibais

Page 126

5 1. Tenía, Había, Era 2. era, se parecía, iba, llevaba
3. Se llamaba, Tenía, gustaba, sabía 4. Era, Costaba,
llegaba, gastaba

6 1. cocinábamos, era, tenemos 2. podemos, veíamos
3. buscábamos, compramos 4. estamos, pasábamos,
hacíamos

Page 127

7 1. Estaba en la oficina. Estaba hablando con el jefe.
2. Estaba en casa. Estaba comiendo solo. 3. Estaba
en unos grandes almacenes. Estaba comprando ropa.
4. Estaba en el coche. Estaba besando a una chica.

8 1. Eran 2. Era 3. Hacía 4. había 5. cantaban
6. paseaba 7. corrían 8. estaba 9. miraba 10. era
11. conocía 12. parecía 13. bailaba 14. miraba
15. podía 16. Era 17. estaba 18. quería 19. gustaba

26. Imperfecto, Indefinido or Pretérito perfecto?

Page 129

1 1a. volvimos 1b. volvíamos 2a. llevamos
2b. llevábamos 3a. supe 3b. sabía 4a. pareció
4b. parecía 5a. escondían 5b. escondieron

Page 130

2 1. estuve, estaba 2. estuvo, estaba 3. estábamos,
estuvisteis, estuvimos 4. estabas, estaba, Estuve
5. estaba, estuve 6. estábamos, Estuvimos

Page 131

3 1. ¿Cómo **era** tu primera casa? 2. ¿Cómo **fue** el partido de fútbol? 3. ¿Cómo **era** el perrito que tenías?
4. ¿Cómo **era** la falda que llevaba Elena? 5. ¿Cómo
fue tu primer día de trabajo? 6. ¿Cómo **era** tu
hermana de pequeña? 7. ¿Cómo **era** el ladrón?
8. ¿Cómo **fue** la conferencia? 9. ¿Cómo **era** el hotel
donde dormiste? 10. ¿Cómo **fue** el viaje?
11. ¿Cómo **fue** el curso de alemán? 12. ¿Cómo **era**
el reloj que te regalaron?

4 1. era 2. Fue 3. estuvo 4. estaba 5. era 6. fue
7. se llamó 8. se llamaba

Page 132

5 1a. fui (hecho completo) 1b. iba (situación regular)
2a. estuvimos (hecho completo) 2b. estábamos
(situación regular) 3a. llamaron (hecho completo)
3b. llamaban (situación regular) 4a. llevaba (situación regular) 4b. llevó (hecho completo) 5a. fue
(hecho completo) 5b. eran (situación regular)

Page 133

6 Ayer yo **caminaba** tranquilamente por el bosque, porque **iba** a casa de Alablanca para llevarle pasteles y,
de pronto, en el camino, un lobo muy malo **salió** de
los árboles y se **puso** enfrente de mí, con la boca
abierta. Yo **estaba** muerto de miedo, pero **salí**
corriendo y, al final, **conseguí** escapar de él. **Podía**
hacer dos cosas: o **volvía** a mi casa o **intentaba** llegar
a casa de Alablanca, a pesar de todo. **Decidí** seguir
andando para visitarla. Cuando **entré** en la casa, ella
estaba acostada en la cama, pero **tenía** una cara muy
extraña con muchos pelos. Por eso yo, rápidamente,
dejé la comida al lado de su cama y **volví** a mi casa
corriendo. Yo **era** Jerónimo, no **era** Brus Güilis.

7 1a. llevábamos 1b. hemos llevado 2a. sabía
2b. he sabido 3a. ha parecido 3b. parecía

Page 134

8 1. ha estado, estaba 2. habéis estado, hemos estado,

estábamos 3. estabas, estaba, He estado

Page 135

9   1. he ido 2. era 3. he hablado 4. ha invitado
    5. quería 6. he ido 7. conocía 8. he dicho 9. era
    10. ha creído 11. ha sido 12. estaba 13. era
    14. he tenido 15. ha sido

10 1. trabajaba 2. era 3. tenía 4. preguntó 5. mentí
    6. estaba 7. dije 8. era 9. estaba 10. Era 11. tenía
    12. invitaba 13. contaba 14. fuimos 15. invitó
    16. sabía 17. gustaba 18. llamé 19. fuimos
    20. dije 21. era 22. puso 23. fue

27. Pluscuamperfecto de indicativo

Page 136

1   1. **habíais** dejado (b) 2. **había** ido (d) 3. **habían** que-
    dado (e) 4. **había** quedado (f) 5. **había** visto (a)

Page 137

2   1. habíais arreglado/habían arreglado 2. había pre-
    parado 3. había sido 4. había estudiado 5. había-
    mos dejado 6. había ido

Page 138

3   1. habían comprado 2. había contado
    3. había estudiado 4. había hecho 5. habían estado

4   1. correcto 2. ~~había viajado~~ **viajé** 3. ~~había echado~~
    echó 4. correcto 5. correcto 6. ~~había venido~~ **vino**
    7. correcto

28. Futuro

Page 139

1   1. P 2. F 3. P 4. F 5. F 6. P

Page 140

2   1. volverá 2. cambiaré 3. comeremos 4. dolerá
    5. invitarás 6. hablaré 7. Estaréis 8. estarán

3   1. ~~deciré~~ **diré**, ~~venirá~~ **vendrá**, quitará dará 2. volverá
    ~~ponerá~~ **pondrá** 3. ~~saliré~~ **saldré** jugaré 4. iré, ~~saberé~~
    sabré, ~~poderé~~ **podré** 5. traerán, ~~poneré~~ **pondré**
    recogeré, ~~quererá~~ **querrá**

Page 141

4   1. cabrá 2. tendrán 3. dirá 4. vendrá 5. saldrán
    6. hará 7. sabrá 8. valdrá 9. podré 10. habrá

5   1. a 2. e 3. h 4. i 5. b 6. f 7. c 8. d

Page 142

6   1. conocerás, sentirás 2. cambiará 3. abandonará
    4. Ganarás 5. querrá 6. Tendrás/Tendréis 7. morirás

7   1. Saldrá con otra. 2. Conocerá a otra persona más
    interesante que él. 3. Se arruinarán. 4. La próxima
    Navidad no estarán juntos. 5. Se separarán.

Page 143

8   1. Tendrá 2. sabrá 3. tendrá 4. gustarán 5. Vendrá
    6. Estará 7. querrá 8. sabrá 9. Tendrá

9   1. b 2. b 3. a 4. b 5. b 6. b 7. a

10 Si hablas con ella:
    1. tienes 2. eres 3. conoces 4. gusta 5. usas
    6. Sales 7. Quieres 8. das 9. importa
    Si hablas con tu amigo:
    1. tendrá 2. será 3. conocerá 4. gustará 5. usará
    6. Saldrá 7. Querrá 8. dará 9. importará

29. Futuro perfecto

Page 144

1   1. Habrás trabajado 2. habréis asustado
    3. Habremos tomado 4. habrá olvidado
    5. habrán perdido 6. Habrá salido

Page 145

2   1. (Lo sabe) 2. (Lo imagina) 3. (Lo imagina)
    4. (Lo imagina) 5. (Lo sabe) 6. (Lo sabe)

3   1. (sí) 2. (no) 3. (no) 4. (sí) 5. (no) 6. (sí)

30. Condicional

Page 146

1   1. ~~sabería~~ **sabría**, podría 2. ~~salería~~ **saldría**, pasearía,
    ~~hacería~~ **haría**, ~~venirías~~ **vendrías** 3. sería, daría, ~~deci-
    ría~~ **diría** 4. ~~querería~~ **querría**, ~~ponería~~ **pondría**, ~~habe-
    ría~~ **habría**, haría 5. reiría, ~~Poderías~~ **Podrías**

Page 147

2   1. sabría 2. estaría 3. tendría 4. apetecería

Page 148

3   1. Era 2. estaban 3. vería 4. Estaban 5. estaba
    6. Era 7. Querrían

4   1. gusta/~~gustaría~~ 2. ~~serás~~/serías 3. ~~llevaréis~~/llevaríais
    4. ~~casaré~~/casaría 5. ~~contrataré~~/contrataría

6. ~~será~~/sería 7. ~~gusta~~/gustaría 8. importa/importaría
9. Puedes/Podrías 10. debemos/deberíamos
11. encantaría/~~encanta~~ 12. Podríamos/Podemos

31. Condicional compuesto

Page 149

1 1. **habría** metido 2. **habrías** asustado 3. **habríais** asustado 4. **habría** tenido 5. **habrían** explicado

Page 150

2 1. habrían avisado 2. habría puesto 3. habría tenido
4. habría olvidado

3 1. ... habría escuchado con mucho gusto. 2. ... también se habría enfadado con él. 3. ... le habría preguntado a quién. 4. ... le habría dado otro a él. 5. ... lo habría consolado. 6. ... se habría sorprendido mucho, pero habría comprendido. 7. ... se habría sentido ofendida y las habría rechazado. 8. ... habría jurado también quererlo siempre.

32. Forms of the subjuntivo: *hablé*

Page 151

1 1. I, bebas 2. I, camine 3. I, perdone
4. I, rompa 5. I, viváis 6. I, miréis 7. limpias, S
8. I, cocine 9. cuida, S 10. caminas, S 11. corres, S
12. rompéis, S 13. I, limpiemos 14. miras, S
15. perdona, S 16. I, partamos 17. beben, S
18. I, corra 19. I, mejoren 20. saludamos, S

Page 152

2 1. sonreímos, sonriamos 2. amáis, sintáis
3. competimos, compitamos 4. preferís, prefiráis
5. dormimos, durmamos

Page 153

3 1. ~~ponamos~~ pongamos, traiga
2. ~~salamos~~ salgamos, ~~tena~~ tenga, ~~vena~~ venga
3. ~~conduza~~ conduzca, oiga

Page 154

4 1. veas 2. estés 3. vayas 4. seas 5. haya

Page 155

5 1. vivieron, viviera 2. probaron, probáramos
3. mintieron, mintiera 4. vinieron, viniéramos
5. eligieron, eligiéramos 6. rieron, riera
7. pudieron, pudieras 8. condujeron, condujera
9. quisieron, quisieras 10. escaparon, escapara

6 1. **tuvisteis**: es la única forma que no es subjuntivo
2. **vieron**: es la única forma que no es subjuntivo
3. **conduzca**: es la única forma que es presente de subjuntivo
4. **cayese**: es la única forma que es subjuntivo
5. **oyera**: es la única forma que es subjuntivo

Page 156

7 1. hayáis encontrado 2. haya llegado
3. hayas terminado 4. haya perdido
5. hayamos acertado

8 1. hubieras (-ses) cortado 2. hubiera (-se) ido
3. hubiera (-se) cambiado 4. hubiéramos (-semos) decidido

33. Indicativo or subjuntivo?

Page 158

1 1. no 2. sí 3. sí 4. sí 5. no 6. no 7. no 8. no
9. no 10. no

Page 159

2 **Columna izquierda:**
Me parece que..., Estamos seguros de que...,
Sé que..., Me han contado que..., Pensamos que...,
Todos imaginan que...
Columna derecha:
¿Me permite que...?, Es fundamental que...,
¿No preferís que...?, ¿Me recomiendas que...?,
¿Necesitas que...?, No me puedes pedir que

Page 160

3 1. Nosotros/-as 2. Tú 3. En general 4. Tú
5. Nosotros/-as 6. Vosotros/-as 7. Tú 8. Tú
9. Nosotros/-as

4 1. ver 2. que hable 3. que hable 4. que no piense
5. que llame 6. que llame 7. que piense
8. que podamos 9. que confiese 10. que espere
11. que sepa

5 1. hablar 2. no insistas 3. busques 4. cambie
5. no esté 6. confieses 7. esperes 8. no está
9. estés 10. ayudarte

Page 161

6 1. cumplas, *g* 2. tengas, *b* 3. diviertas, *a*
4. descanses, *c* 5. tengas, *f* 6. seáis, *d*

7 1. Que no te pelees con nadie.
2. Que te comas tu bocadillo entero.
3. Que vayas siempre cerca de la maestra.
4. Que no te ensucies la ropa.

Page 163

8 **Introducimos una afirmación:**
Es evidente que..., Te aseguro que...
Introducimos una suposición:
Suponen que..., A ellas les parece que... Sospecho que...
Consideramos una posibilidad:
Me parece probable que..., Es bastante posible que..., Es posible que...
Rechazamos una idea:
No es cierto que..., Es falso que...

Page 164

9 1. son, tienen 2. sean, tengan
3. aprenden, son, tienen 4. aprendan, sean, tengan
5. aprendan, sean, tengan 6. aprenden, sean, tengan

10 1. ...**llevan** su casa en la espalda. 2. ...**son** muy lentos.
3. ...**son** muy pacíficos. 4. ...**puedan** ver la comida a varios kilómetros de distancia. 5. ...**tengan** una inteligencia muy parecida a la humana. 6. ...se **suban** encima de la cabeza de las palomas.

Page 165

11 1. baile, baila 2. no quiere 3. no quiere
4. tenga 5. no diga 6. deje 7. parezco
8. soy 9. sea 10. puede 11. voy, vaya
12. coma, como

Page 167

12 **Columna izquierda:**
Me imagino que..., Su marido piensa que..., He oído que..., ¿Ana te ha contado que...?, Yo he visto que ..., Me parece que...

Columna derecha:
Es difícil que..., Es estupendo que..., Es verdaderamente extraño que..., ¿Crees que es importante que...?, No me importa que..., Odio que...

13 1. *Es curioso/...* que Groenlandia **suspenda** su festival de nieve por una ola de calor.
2. *Me parece preocupante/...* que dos ex ladrones **presenten** un programa de televisión sobre robos.
3. *Me parece muy justo/...* que más de la mitad de los ministros del gobierno español **sean** mujeres.
4. *Está muy bien/...* que los japoneses ya **puedan** pagar en los supermercados con la huella dactilar.
5. *Me parece ridículo que/...* que una conocida marca de helados **investigue** en la fabricación de un helado para perros.
6. *Me parece exagerado/...* que un juez **mande** a prisión a un hombre por hacer chistes sexistas.
7. *A mí me da igual/...* que un perro **espere** diez días en la puerta de la comisaría hasta que liberan a su amo.

8. *Yo pienso que es lógico/...* que el gobierno **pague** 500 euros mensuales por cada hijo menor de tres años.

Page 168

14 1. Tú 2. Ellos/-as/Ustedes 3. Yo 4. Usted 5. Yo
6. Ellos 7. Tú 8. En general 9. En general

Page 169

15 1. b 2. a 3. b 4. a 5. b

Page 170

16 1. a 2. c 3. c 4. c

17 1. estás / ~~estés~~ 2. dice / ~~diga~~ 3. ~~dice~~ / diga 4. dice / ~~diga~~ 5. ~~quieres~~ / quieras 6. ~~puede~~ / pueda 7. dice / ~~diga~~ 8. lleva / ~~lleve~~ 9. ~~puedo~~ / pueda

Page 171

18 1. P 2. H 3. H 4. H 5. F 6. H 7. F

19 1. H, puedo 2. P, podía 3. H, tomo 4. P, tomaba
5. F, tome 6. P, hacíamos 7. F, haga 8. H, hago

Page 172

20 1. callara/-se 2. encuentre 3. tenga 4. visitara/-se
5. hubiéramos/-semos comido 6. haya querido
7. hayan previsto 8. vayas 9. hubiera/-se quedado
10. pensaras/-ses

21 1. sea 2. haya ocultado 3. fuera/-se
4. inventara/-se 5. pueda 6. haya estado
7. haya sido

34. Imperativo

Page 173

1 1. Ruego 2. Orden 3. Instrucción 4. Dar permiso
5. Invitación 6. Consejo

Page 174

2 1. Enciende 2. Llora 3. Sube, baja 4. Bebe 5. Baila
6. Sé 7. Ven 8. Ve 9. Pon 10. Di 11. Sal 12. Haz
13. Propón

3 1. Id 2. Tomad 3. Seguid 4. Tened 5. Hablad
6. Haced 7. Sed 8. venid 9. Volved

Page 175

4 1. salga 2. traduzca 3. Hablen
4. Perdone 5. Tenga 6. Oiga 7. Hagan
8. Ponga 9. Vengan

5 1. fumes 2. salgas 3. bebas 4. conduzcas
5. pienses 6. tengas 7. creas

Page 176

6 1. fuméis 2. salgáis 3. bebáis 4. conduzcáis
5. penséis 6. tengáis 7. creáis

7 1. Escríbele, léeselas 2. Llámala 3. Díselo
4. Acompáñala 5. Perdónaselos 6. Házsela
7. Dúchate, ponte

8 Segunda columna:
No **se las deis** No **se las dé** No **se las den**
Tercera columna:
Piénsalo No **lo pienses** No **lo penséis** **Piénselo**
Piénsenlo
Cuarta columna:
Siéntate No **te sientes** **Sentaos** **Siéntese** No se
siente No **se sienten**
Quinta columna:
No **nos lo traigas** **Traédnoslo** No **nos lo traigáis**
Tráiganoslo No **nos lo traiga** **Tráigannoslo** No **nos
lo traigan**

35. *Ser* and *estar*

Page 177

1 Mis guantes son de lana. Son rojos.
Son pequeñísimos.
Mis gafas son de sol. Son muy oscuras.
Son cuadradas.
Mi móvil es rojo. Es Ricsson. Es un poco antiguo.

Page 178

2 1. están 2. están 3. está
4. estoy 5. Estoy 6. están
7. están 8. está

Page 179

3 1a. está 1b. (incorrecto)
2a. es 2b. (incorrecto)
3a. (incorrecto) 3b. es
4a. son 4b. (incorrecto)
5a. (incorrecto) 5b. es
6a. (incorrecto) 6b. está
7a. (incorrecto) 7b. están
8a. está 8b. (incorrecto)
9a. es 9b. (incorrecto)
10a. (incorrecto) 10b. está
11a. es 11b. (incorrecto)

4 **Juan** está contento. Está sentado. Es moreno.
Es mayor. Es alto. Es oficinista.
Pedro es un chico. Es joven. Es rubio. Es deportista.
Está triste. Es bajo.

5 1. Estábamos 2. era 3. soy 4. Tenía
5. estaba 6. es 7. está 8. es 9. están
10. son 11. Son 12. es 13. Era 14. está
15. está 16. es 17. es 18. estaba

36. *Haber* and *estar*

Page 181

1 1. hay (i) 2. ha (d) 3. hay (g) 4. Han (c)
5. Habéis (e) 6. hay (b) 7. hay (h) 8. hemos (f)

2 1. ~~habían~~ había coches, ~~hubieron~~ hubo muchos cambios 2. había silencio, ~~habían~~ había ruidos
3. había ordenadores 4. ~~han habido~~ ha habido unas
fiestas 5. ha habido más gente 6. correcto

Page 182

3 1. Vegetación: En Vepiturno hay árboles.
En Marsatón no hay árboles, pero hay plantas.
2. Geografía: En Vepiturno hay un río.
En Marsatón no hay ríos, pero hay dos mares.
3. Vivienda: En Vepiturno hay pueblos.
En Marsatón no hay pueblos, pero hay una ciudad.
4. Habitantes: En Vepiturno hay niños.
En Marsatón no hay niños, sólo hay jóvenes
o mayores.

Page 183

4 1. hay 2. están 3. hay 4. están
5. hay 6. hay 7. hay 8. hay 9. están
10. hay 11. hay 12. hay 13. está
14. está 15. hay 16. hay

Page 184

5 Queridos Reyes Magos: Este año hemos cambiado
de casa y quiero explicaros dónde ~~hay~~/**está** la nueva.
En Barcelona **hay**/~~está~~ una calle que se llama Vía
Layetana. En esta calle no ~~hay~~/**está** mi casa. Es una
calle muy larga que va al mar. En esta calle **hay**/~~están~~
muchos edificios bastante altos. A mitad de la calle,
hay/~~está~~ un trozo de las murallas romanas. Enfrente
de las murallas romanas **hay**/~~está~~ una callecita muy
estrecha y en la esquina ~~hay~~/**está** "La Colmena", que
es una pastelería muy buena. Bueno, pues al lado de
esa pastelería **hay**/~~está~~ un portal muy grande, de
madera. Ésa es la puerta de mi casa. Cuando entras,
hay/~~está~~ una puerta de hierro muy grande. Es la
puerta del ascensor. Tenéis que subir al quinto piso.
Al salir **hay**/~~están~~ dos puertas, una, a la derecha, y
otra, a la izquierda. La de la derecha es la de mi casa.
En mi casa **hay**/~~están~~ cuatro dormitorios. Mucho cuidado, mi dormitorio ~~hay~~/**está** al final del pasillo. En
la puerta **hay**/~~está~~ un cartel que pone "Anita". Yo soy
Anita. Traedme muchos regalos, que he sido muy
buena este año. Un beso para los tres. Anita.

37. Periphrastic verbs

Page 185

1 1. Va a suspender 2. Van a entrar 3. Va a nevar 4. Va a explotar 5. Va a saltar

2 1. vais a estudiar 2. vas a comer 3. vas a volver 4. vas a comprar 5. vais a ir

Page 186

3 1. iba a suspender 2. íbamos a entrar 3. iba a nevar 4. iba a explotar 5. iba a saltar

Page 187

4 1. **tienes que** / ~~hay que~~ 2. **tienes que** / **hay que** 3. **tienes que** / **hay que** 4. **tenía que** / ~~había que~~ 5. **ha tenido que** / ~~ha habido que~~ 6. **tienes que** / ~~no hay~~ 7. ~~Habéis tenido que~~ / **Ha habido que**

Page 188

5 1. Estamos aparcando, *e* 2. está sonriendo, *b* 3. están durmiendo, *d* 4. estoy planchando, *c*

Page 189

6 1. **dan** / ~~están dando~~ (d) **reciben** / ~~están recibiendo~~ 2. **hierve** / ~~está hirviendo~~ (f) 3. **está hirviendo** / ~~hierve~~ (a) 4. **Estamos dando** / ~~Damos~~ (e) 5. **dan** / ~~están dando~~ (g) **Me mareo** / ~~estoy mareando~~ 6. (c) **Estaba guardando** / ~~Guardaba~~ 7. **íbamos** / ~~estábamos yendo~~ (h) **Guardábamos** / ~~Estábamos guardando~~

7 1. parece 2. Estáis haciendo, tiene 3. estamos viendo, Es 4. estaba 5. estaba cortando, Estaba, llevaba 6. querías, estaba haciendo, sabía

Page 190

8 1. no 2. no 3. sí 4. no

9 1. Hicieron / ~~Estuvieron haciendo~~ 2. ~~estuvo naciendo~~ / nació 3. He estado leyendo / ~~He leído~~ 4. ~~había estado perdiendo~~ / había perdido 5. Estuve escribiendo / ~~Escribí~~

Page 193

38. Prepositions (1): *de, a, desde, hasta, en...*

1 1. de 2. al 3. en 4. de 5. al 6. de 7. a 8. de 9. de 10. a 11. de 12. a 13. del 14. de 15. al 16. de 17. de 18. de 19. a 20. a 21. A 22. en 23. en 24. de 25. a 26. a 27. a 28. de

29. de 30. de

2 1. correcto 2. Tengo un billete ~~a~~ **de** avión ~~con~~ **de** ida y vuelta 3. correcto 4. correcto 5. ¿Por qué estamos aquí? Me han traído ~~de~~ **a** la fuerza. 6. ¿Han venido ~~en~~ **a** Arábiga sólo a interrogarnos? 7. correcto 8. Perdone, inspector, ¿hay un teléfono cerca ~~a~~ **de** aquí? Tengo que hablar con mi mujer.

Page 194

3 1a. a 1b. b 2a. a 2b. b 3a. b 3b. a 4a. b 4b. a 5a. a 5b. b 6a. b 6b. a 7a. b 7b. a 8a. a 8b. b

4 1. b 2. b 3. b 4. a 5. a 6. b

Page 196

5 1. en, a 2. en, a 3. en 4. En, en 5. En, a, en 6. en, a 7. en

6 1. en *c*. entre 2. en *a*. en 3. en *b*. en 4. entre *f*. en 5. en *e*. en 6. en *d*. en, entre

7 1. incorrecta (~~A~~ **En** un bosque...) 2. correcta 3. incorrecta (~~Al~~ **En** el interior de...) 4. incorrecta (~~Al~~ **En** el centro de...) 5. incorrecta (~~Entre~~ **En** una palmera...) 6. correcta 7. incorrecta (Envuelto ~~a~~ **en** una...) 8. correcta

Page 197

8 1. por 2. por 3. por 4. por, por, por 5. Para 6. para 7. por 8. por 9. por 10. para 11. por 12. por

Page 198

9 1a. a 1b. b 2a. a 2b. b 3a. a 3b. b 4a. b 4b. a

10 1. correcto 2. correcto 3. correcto 4. correcto 5. correcto 6. correcto 7. incorrecto: por 8. incorrecto: por 9. incorrecto: para 10. correcto 11. incorrecto: por 12. incorrecto: por 13. incorrecto: por 14. correcto 15. correcto 16. correcto 17. correcto 18. correcto 19. correcto 20. correcto 21. correcto 22. correcto 23. correcto 24. correcto 25. incorrecto: para 26. incorrecto: por 27. correcto 28. incorrecto: por 29. incorrecto: por 30. correcto

Page 199

11 1. Todo lo ha descubierto **por**/~~para~~ los problemas con las preposiciones. 2. Los inocentes ya pueden volver ~~por~~/**para** sus casas. 3. Pero los culpables tienen que ir a la cárcel ~~por~~/**para** ser juzgados. 4. El juicio está previsto ~~por~~/**para** dentro de un mes. 5. La policía está muy agradecida **por**/~~para~~ tu trabajo y te van a nombrar policía de honor del reino de Chilab.

Answer key

Page 200

12 1. con, sin 2. con, con 3. con, sin, con, sin, con 4. sin 5. con, sin 6. con, sin 7. con, sin 8. con 9. con 10. con 11. con, con 12. sin 13. con

13 1. contra, hacia 2. Contra, hacia 3. Hacia, hacia, hacia 4. Hacia, hacia, hacia, hacia 5. Contra, hacia

39. Prepositions (II): *encima (de), debajo (de)...*

Page 202

1 1. delante 2. detrás 3. debajo 4. lejos 5. encima

2 1. al lado de/ a la derecha 2. debajo de 3. encima de 4. encima de 5. al lado de/ a la izquierda del 6. encima de 7. alrededor de 8. debajo de 9. debajo de 10. Encima de 11. encima de 12. encima de 13. encima de 14. detrás de 15. enfrente del/delante del

Page 203

3 1. detrás de Iván 2. enfrente del Banco Capital 3. enfrente de la vecina rubia 4. detrás del coche rojo 5. a la izquierda de la moto 6. delante de 7. enfrente de Colón 8. delante de 9. a la izquierda de, delante de 10. debajo de

4 1. al fondo 2. al otro lado 3. antes de 4. en el centro 5. después de 6. al final 7. Dentro 8. En medio 9. dentro del 10. después de 11. dentro de 12. fuera del 13. Al final del 14. dentro del

40. Questions and exclamations

Page 206

1 P.: Usted se llama Javier Rosales, ¿**verdad**?
J.: Sí, efectivamente.
P.: Trabaja en la universidad de verano de Laponia, ¿**no**?
J.: Sí, así es.
P.: Es evidente que usted conocía a la difunta Mercedes Clarín. **¿Eran amigos o algo más?**
J.: Éramos simplemente amigos.
P.: **¿Sabía que Mercedes Clarín salía con otro hombre?**
J.: No tenía ni idea. Tampoco me importa.
P.: **¿Estuvo en casa de Mercedes el viernes 28 de enero alrededor de las 22.30?**
J.: **¿Tengo que contestar a eso?** Es mi vida privada.
P.: Es mejor colaborar. Créame.
J.: De acuerdo, estaba en el bingo. Canté línea. Aquí tiene el cartón. Puedo irme ya, ¿**verdad**?

Page 207

2 1. Cuándo, *d* 2. Dónde, *e* 3. Cómo, *b* 4. Cuándo, *f* 5. Dónde, *a*

3 1. Cómo/Qué tal 2. Cómo 3. Qué tal 4. Cómo 5. Cómo/Qué tal 6. Qué tal 7. Qué tal

Page 208

4 1. Cuánto, *f* 2. Cuántas, *b* 3. Cuánta, *h* 4. Cuánto, *a* 5. Cuánto, *d* 6. Cuánta, *c* 7. Cuántas, *g*

5 1. Cuánto 2. Cuánta 3. Cuántos 4. Cuánto 5. Cuántas 6. Cuánto 7. Cuántos

Page 209

6 1. Por qué no, por qué no 2. Por qué no, porque 3. Por qué, porque 4. Por qué, porque 5. Por qué no, porque 6. Por qué no

7 1. ¿Dónde? 2. ¿Cómo? 3. ¿Cuándo? 4. Cuánto 5. ¿cuánto? 6. ¿Por qué?/¿Por qué no? 7. ¿Por qué?/¿Por qué no? 8. ¿Cómo?

Page 211

8 1. Qué, qué, cuál 2. Cuáles 3. Qué, cuál 4. Qué 5. Qué 6. qué, cuál, Cuál 7. Cuáles

Page 212

9 1. Qué 2. quién/cuál 3. quién 4. quién 5. Quiénes 6. quién 7. quiénes/cuáles 8. quién, cuál 9. Quién

10 1. Quiénes, *a* 2. Qué, *c* 3. Quién, *b* 4. Qué, *h* 5. Cuál, *g* 6. Cuáles, *f* 7. Qué, *e*

11 1. dónde 2. qué 3. Quién 4. cuántos 5. Cómo 6. Por qué 7. cómo/qué tal 8. qué

Page 213

12 1. I d, II c 2. I e, II f 3. I h, II g 4. I j, II i 5. I l, II k 6. I m, II n 7. I p, II o

Page 214

13 1. Qué 2. Cuál 3. Qué 4. Cuál 5. qué 6. Qué 7. Cuáles 8. Qué

14 1. De quiénes 2. Contra qué 3. Por cuál 4. De quiénes 5. Con qué 6. En quién 7. Con quién

15 1. **¿Con cuántos** pasajeros a bordo? 2. **¿Hasta cuándo** permanecerá en nuestra ciudad?

3. ¿**Adónde/Dónde** se trasladará ese mismo día?
4. ¿**Por cuántos millones** la ha comprado?
5. ¿**Desde cuándo** pertenece Intergas a Carlos Etéreo?

Page 215

16 1. qué 2. cuánto 3. dónde 4. si 5. cómo 6. cuál
7. qué 8. cuál 9. si 10. si 11. cuántos 12. cómo
13. cómo 14. si 15. qué 16. cuál 17. si 18. quién
19. cuáles 20. si

Page 216

17 1. d 2. c 3. b 4. h 5. f 6. e 7. g 8. k 9. j 10. l 11. i

Page 217

18 1. ¡Cuántos hijos tiene! 2. ¡Cuánto pesaba y fumaba antes y qué poco come ahora! 3. ¡Qué poco fuma ahora! 4. ¡Cuánto le gustan la música y el cine!
5. ¡Cuántos discos tiene! 6. ¡Cuánto sabe sobre actores, directores y películas! 7. ¡Qué poco va al cine!

19 1. ¡Cómo ha crecido Clara! 2. ¡Cómo ladra el perro!
3. ¡Cómo está la cocina! 4. ¡Cómo está el jardín!
5. ¡Cómo están los precios!

41. Comparisons

Page 218

1 1. ... menos ojos que los Lisus. 2. ... más altos que los Lisus. 3. ... menos inteligentes que los Rizus.
4. ... más temprano que los Rizus. 5. ... más tarde que los Lisus. 6. ... más alcohol que los Lisus. 7. ... menos que los Rizus.

Page 219

2 1. La vida era más tranquila que ahora. 2. Los trenes iban más despacio que ahora. 3. La gente se casaba más joven que ahora. 4. La fruta tenía más sabor que ahora. 5. Hay más igualdad entre hombres y mujeres que antes. 6. La gente se divorcia más que antes. 7. La gente vive más años que antes. 8. La gente viaja más que antes.

Page 220

3 1. Lola (Carmen) es tan alta como Carmen (Lola). / Lola (Carmen) es igual de alta que Carmen (Lola). / Lola y Carmen (Carmen y Lola) son igual de altas 2. Lola no es tan delgada como Carmen. / Lola no es igual de delgada que Carmen. / Lola y Carmen (Carmen y Lola) no son igual de delgadas. 3. Lola (Carmen) desayuna tan tarde como Carmen (Lola). / Lola (Carmen) desayuna igual de tarde que Carmen (Lola). / Lola y Carmen (Carmen y Lola) desayunan

igual de tarde. 4. Lola (Carmen) conduce tan rápido como Carmen (Lola). / Lola (Carmen) conduce igual de rápido que Carmen (Lola). / Lola y Carmen (Carmen y Lola) conducen igual de rápido.
5. Carmen no vive tan cerca del trabajo como Lola. / Carmen no vive igual de cerca del trabajo que Lola. / Carmen y Lola (Lola y Carmen) no viven igual de cerca del trabajo. 6. Lola no gana al año tanto como Carmen.

4 1. Carmen fuma tanto como Lola. / Carmen fuma igual que Lola. / Carmen fuma lo mismo que Lola. / Carmen y Lola fuman lo mismo. 2. Carmen habla igual que Lola. 3. Carmen bebe tanto como Lola. / Carmen bebe lo mismo que Lola. / Carmen y Lola beben lo mismo. 4. Carmen se pinta tanto como Lola. / Carmen se pinta lo mismo que Lola. / Carmen y Lola se pintan lo mismo. 5. Carmen duerme igual que Lola. 6. Carmen no desayuna tanto como Lola. / Carmen no desayuna lo mismo que Lola. / Carmen y Lola no desayunan lo mismo.

Page 222

5 1. la misma 2. el mismo 3. tanto, como, el mismo
4. pastillas, tantas 5. los mismos 6. amigas, las mismas 7. la misma, que

6 1. igual 2. igual de 3. el mismo 4. igual de
5. el mismo 6. las mismas 7. igual de
8. el mismo 9. el mismo 10. igual de 11. la misma

Page 223

7 1. c, e 2. e, a 3. b, f 4. f, c 5. a, d
6. k, h 7. j, g 8. h, j 9. g, k 10. i, i

Page 224

8 felicísimo/-a saladísimo simpatiquísimos
jovencísimo/-a interesantísimos/-as
antipatiquísimo amabilísimos/-as
facilísimo/-a sequísimas
agradabilísimo/-a divertidísimo

9 frágil tontos jóvenes grande
felices amable
blanco agradable

10 muchísimo recientísimamente lejísimos
poquísimo clarísimamente tardísimo
lentísimamente facilísimamente prontísimo
tranquilísimamente tempranísimo

11 1. cortísimo 2. rubísimo 3. larguísimo
4. altísimos 5. horrible 6. feísimo 7. espantoso
8. feísimo 9. larguísima 10. despeinadísimo
11. gastadísimos 12. normalísima 13. baratísima
14. magnífico 15. Guapísimo 16. elegantísimo
17. precioso 18. educadísimo 19. simpatiquísimo

Answer key

20. lejísimos 21. cerquísima

Primera pregunta: Mimín y Felix
Segunda pregunta: Alejandro

12 1. carísimo 2. creidísimo 3. feísimo 4. muy bonito
5. horrible

Page 225

13 1. mejor 2. peor 3. mejor 4. menor 5. mejores 6.
peores 7. mejores

14 1. ~~que a él~~, ~~que el suyo~~ 2. como él, ~~como~~ él 3. ~~que yo~~ 4. ~~como él~~ , ~~que él~~ 5. como yo 6. ~~que a él~~ 7. ~~que él~~, ~~que yo~~ 8. como yo, como a mí, ~~como yo~~, ~~que yo~~
9. ~~que a él~~, ~~que de ella~~

42. Joining sentences: *y, o, pero, sino, porque...*

Page 226

1 1. a 2. d 3. f 4. c 5. e 7. l 8. g
9. h 10. i 11. j 12. m

Page 227

2 1. 1 2. 1 3. 1 4. 0 5. 2 ó 2 6. 2 7. 2 ó 1 8. 1

3 1. y 2. o 3. o 4. ni 5. ni 6. o 7. ni 8. ni 9. y 10. y

4 1. y 2. y 3. ni, ni 4. ni 5. y 6. ni, ni
7. ni, ni 8. ni, ni 9. y

Page 228

5 1. pero, o, y 2. o, y, pero 3. o, y, pero 4. pero, o, y
5. o, pero, y

Page 229

6 1. Su marido no se llamaba Paco Frutales, sino
Antonio Frutales. 2. Su marido no la abandonó por
otra, sino que murió de un infarto. 3. Su primera
película no fue un gran éxito sino un fracaso. 4. No
fue la protagonista de "Historia de G" sino que tuvo
un papel secundario. 5. No tiene siete hijos, sino
tres. 6. Su hijo Julián no es director de cine sino que
trabaja en un circo. 7. No ganó un Óscar por la película "José y yo" sino el premio "Cuidad de Teruel".

7 1. No tiene casa en Hollywood, pero tiene casas en
París y en Roma. 2. Gregory Peck nunca la quiso,
pero tuvo romances con varios actores de
Hollywood. 3. Nunca ha tenido una buena crítica,
pero ha ganado mucho dinero en el cine.

8 1. ~~pero~~ sino 2. correcto 3. ~~pero~~ sino 4. correcto
5. ~~pero~~ sino 6. correcto 7. ~~pero~~ sino 8. ~~pero~~ sino

Page 230

9 *Como Catalina sabe latín,* le he pedido que me
ayude con la traducción. 2. Los niños no están en
casa *porque se han ido al parque con su madre.* 3.
Como el banco estaba cerrado, he tenido que pedirle
dinero a mi hermano. 4. No te he llamado por teléfono *porque me he quedado sin batería en el móvil.*
5. *Como ya teníamos las entradas para el concierto,*
no tuvimos que hacer cola. 6. Hemos puesto un
ejemplo más *porque necesitábamos ocho.*

Page 231

10 1. Es que no había huevos. 2. Sí, porque, si no, se va
a enfriar el pescado. 3. No, porque no hay mucho
que hacer en la oficina. 4. Es que no tengo cepillo.
5. Es que no tenemos a nadie con quien dejar al niño.
6. Es que mi madre es de Milán. 7. Porque ya estamos en junio y los días son más largos.

Page 232

11 1. que puede andar 2. que canta 3. que vi ayer en el
cine 4. que se enamora y se casa 5. que vive en un
país 6. que ha ganado el festival 7. que tiene nueve
años 8. que quiere comprarse

12 1. Un primo mío está casado con una japonesa *que
se llama Machiko.* 2. Mi madre es traductora en una
empresa *que está a 10 Km. de nuestra casa.* 3. Paola,
mi hermana, escribe novelas *que tienen mucho éxito.*
4. Ferdinando, mi hermano, tiene una cámara *que era
de mi abuelo* y se dedica a la fotografía. 5. Y yo
tengo un trabajo *que no me gusta nada,* pero también tengo tiempo para estudiar español.

13 1. Bianca es azafata en una compañía aérea *donde
gana mucho dinero* y también es bailarina. 2. Silvia
trabajaba antes en una editorial *donde yo trabajé
también,* pero ahora se dedica a escribir guías de
viaje. 3. Lucca vive todo el año en un hotel de Milán
donde no pueden entrar ni niños ni perros. 4. Piero
vive en un pueblecito de la India *donde todavía no
hay luz ni teléfono.* 5. Francesca es profesora en una
escuela *donde sólo hay veinte estudiantes,* pero quiere dejar la enseñanza.

Page 233

14 1. Quieren **que** cenemos esta noche en un restaurante argentino. 2. Correcto 3. correcto 4. ¿Es necesario **que** lleve corbata? 5. Le gusta **que** le den masajes en los pies. 6. Correcto 7. Correcto 8. Últimamente no consigo **que** duerma. Está muy nerviosa.

Page 234

15 1. ...donde vive ahora, en casa de sus padres. ...como
sólo ella sabe hacerla: fantástica. ...cuando se fueron

sus padres de viaje. 2. ...donde come Carlos, un restaurante estupendo. ...como siempre, con prisa. ...cuando he terminado de hacer las cosas en el banco. 3. ...donde suele tocar los sábados: en el Auditorio General. ...como suele tocar: fatal. ...cuando nadie se lo esperaba: en la pausa. 4. ...donde se lo compró tu madre, en Zaza. ...como el de tu madre, con cinturón, pero blanco y negro. ...cuando empezaron las rebajas.

16 1. (d) Cuando 2. (b) Donde 3. (a) Como
4. (e) Cuando 5. (c) Como 6. (i) Como
7. (f) Donde 8. (j) como 9. (h) cuando

Page 235

17 1. se ducha 2. se viste 3. desayuna, ve la tele
4. apaga la tele 5. sale de casa

18 A. IV B. I C. III

Page 237

19 1. siempre que 2. en cuanto 3. hasta que
4. mientras 5. siempre que 6. mientras
7. desde que

20 1. antes de que 2. desde que 3. Siempre que
4. hasta que 5. Después de 6. hasta que
7. En cuanto 8. Antes de 9. Después de
10. desde que

Page 238

21 1. se quedará 2. vuelve 3. se casa 4. recibirá
5. se vuelve 6. tiene 7. dirigirá 8. sale 9. deja
10. podrá 11. abandona 12. vuelve

Page 239

22 1. Tendrá que venir el sábado **si** hoy no pudiera trabajar. (B) 2. **Si** te vas de viaje, tráeme una muñeca. (D) 3. Si acabara el informe antes de las dos, le invito a comer. (B) 4. ¿Me vas a llevar de viaje contigo si saco buenas notas? (D) 5. **Si** terminaras pronto, pasa por el banco a sacar dinero. (W) 6. No me podré dormir **si** no me lees un cuento. (D) 7. **Si** dejamos a la niña con mi madre, podríamos salir esta noche. (W) 8. Llámeme **si** tuviera algún problema el sábado en la oficina. (B)

23 1. Tristán, Félix, b 2. Félix, Tristán, e
3. Félix, Tristán, d 4. Tristán, Félix, a
5. Félix, Tristán, f

Page 240

24 1. Si dejo el trabajo un año... 2. Si me mudo a Madrid... 3. Si hago muchos viajes a París... 4. Si les compro una casa a mis padres... 5. Si dejara/-se de

trabajar para siempre... 6. Si pudiera/-se comprar todas las casas de mi pueblo... 7. Si perdiera/-se el miedo a los aviones... 8. Si viviera/-se en Nueva York...

25 1. mi padre no habría abierto 2. no le habría picado 3. Si mi padre no hubiera / -se sido alérgico 4. se habría puesto 5. Si no se hubiera/-se puesto 6. no lo habría llevado 7. Si no lo hubiera/-se llevado 8. no se habría enamorado 9. Si no se hubiera/-se enamorado 10. no se habría casado 11. no se hubiera/-se casado con ella 12. no habría nacido a los nueve meses 13. no hubiera/-se nacido 14. no estaría 15. no podría contaros

43. Letters and sounds

Page 242

1 1. **qu**eso 2. paella 3. tortilla 4. **ch**urros
5. pollo, **ch**uleta 6. **ch**irimoyas
7. alca**ch**ofas, **ch**orizo

Page 244

2 a) r̲isa esc̲r̲ibir̲ R̲oma r̲osa alr̲ededor̲ r̲incón r̲oto r̲atón Sar̲a familiar̲ r̲ecibir̲ calor̲ sier̲r̲a r̲ar̲o apar̲car̲ car̲o r̲evolución subr̲ayar̲ tor̲o

b) c̲osa c̲ielo c̲ola veloc̲idad c̲onoc̲es prác̲tic̲o felic̲es c̲asc̲o ac̲usar c̲osta c̲errar c̲uscús c̲rema c̲asa enc̲errar c̲anc̲ión c̲írc̲ulo c̲onc̲iencia osc̲uro c̲laro

c) g̲uerra g̲itano antig̲uo leng̲ua g̲esto g̲ente ceg̲uera g̲uapo g̲ris diri̲g̲ir ag̲enda trag̲edia g̲eneroso g̲as g̲ato g̲uitarra g̲orro ág̲il g̲racioso ciru̲g̲ía

d) y̲o ay̲er hay̲a hay y̲ y̲a rey rey̲es jersey play̲a ley ley̲es hoy tray̲endo

Page 245

3 1. **z**arzuela 2. **z**oológico 3. ca**b**e**z**a 4. **z**ar
5. **c**írculo 6. **c**iega 7. **c**ero 8. **c**apital 9. **c**irco

4 1. ¿~~Ké~~ **Qué** tal estás? ¿~~Komo~~ **Cómo** va todo? ¿Te vienes a la disco esta tarde?
2. Te ~~kiero~~ **quiero** un montón. ¿~~Kedamos~~ **Quedamos** en ~~kasa~~ **casa**?
3. ¿~~Ké~~ **Qué** me dices? ¿~~Kieres~~ **Quieres** venir o no?
4. ~~Kalla~~, **Calla**, ~~kalla~~, **calla**, ~~ke~~ **que** ayer ~~konocí~~ **conocí** a un tipo guapísimo ,-)
5. ~~Kuando~~ **Cuando** vengas al ~~kole~~ **cole**, trae medio kilo de churros, ~~ke~~ **que** tengo hambre. Hoy hemos ~~komido~~ **comido** fatal.
6. Viaje muy ~~inkómodo~~ **incómodo**. Demasiados kilómetros.

293

Answer key

Page 246

5 ¿g o j?
masaje extranjero energía frágil
Page mensaje conduje corrigió
lógico mágico gigante viejo jirafa
garaje urgente cogemos

¿b o v?
fabuloso vino cambiamos estuvo verde obtener
ver habitación posible móvil abrazo bomba
hablar botella vitamina vocabulario boca hierba
vaso vivo vuelo samba objetivo

¿ll o y?
llueve yo ya llevaron ayer llamar playa lleno
estrella llegarán llorar yegua yoga leyendo bella
bollo

6 1. sueños 2. añoramos 3. otoño, leña 4. daño 5.
niños, niñas 6. bañamos, bañeras 7. enseñamos 8.
año

7 1. jirafa 2. perro 3. goma
4. cuatro 5. zumo 6. queso
7. ella 8. río 9. champú 10. caro
11. cena 12. ayer

44. Accentuation

Page 248

1 gustan, árbol, pájaro, llévamelo, menú, calor,
cadáver, mejor, coñac, abril, kilómetro, examen,
carácter, además, ángel, hotel, imbécil, ojalá, agenda,
haz, dáselos, palabra, dormir, dormid, sin, camisa,
llámalo, fin, velocidad, sáltatela, subir, suben,
descontrol, descontrolados, tómala, callad, callado,
rayo, doctor, tranquilidad, goma, sal, botella,
bébetelos, primo, escribir, alegre, inteligente, papel,
papeles, salud, conductor, conductora.

2 1. camión 2. jardín, árbol 3. túnel 4. móvil
5. discusión, excursión 6. sofá, televisión 7. difícil

3 1. escribídnosla 2. secarlo 3. cántala
4. pónselo 5. míramelo 6. hazlos
7. devolvérmela 8. preparadlo 9. resolviéndolo
10. solucionarla 11. pintándonoslas 12. levantarlas
13. dilo 14. házselos 15. díselo

Page 249

4 1. normalmente 2. últimamente 3. seguramente
4. únicamente 5. tontamente

5 <u>Puer</u>-ta, <u>via</u>-je, sua-vi-<u>dad</u>, e-<u>rais</u>, pa-<u>e</u>-lla (no es diptongo), <u>lí</u>-ne-a (no es diptongo), <u>sau</u>na, <u>diez</u>, pa-<u>ís</u>
(dos sílabas), le-<u>ón</u> (no es diptongo), <u>cuí</u>-da-la (tres
sílabas), ca-<u>í</u>-da (tres sílabas), <u>Ruiz</u>, ra-<u>íz</u> (dos sílabas),
sa-<u>béis</u>, con-<u>táis</u>, <u>seis</u>, <u>nue</u>-ve, vein-ti-<u>séis</u>, in-<u>fier</u>-no,
<u>fe</u>-o (no es diptongo), reu-<u>ní</u>-a-mos (cuatro sílabas),
de-vol-<u>váis</u>, <u>soy</u>, <u>bú</u>-ho (dos sílabas), Ra-<u>úl</u> (dos sílabas), <u>clien</u>-te, <u>fiel</u>, con-<u>fiá</u>-ba-mos, si-<u>guién</u>-do-los,
<u>cruel</u>, <u>dien</u>-te, <u>sue</u>-ño, <u>huir</u>, i-<u>bais</u>, jer-<u>séis</u>, <u>vais</u>, pro-
<u>hí</u>-bo (tres sílabas), re-<u>ís</u>-teis (tres sílabas), si-<u>guien</u>-
tes, te-<u>ó</u>-ri-co (no es diptongo), fe-<u>í</u>-si-mo (cuatro síla-
bas), <u>cien</u>, i-<u>gual</u>, <u>sies</u>-ta, <u>dú</u>-o (dos sílabas), <u>ví</u>-a (dos
sílabas), <u>hue</u>-vo, <u>guion</u> (también <u>guión</u>), in-ge-<u>nuo</u>, sa-
<u>bí</u>-a (tres sílabas, imperfecto de 'saber'), <u>sa</u>-bia (feme-
nino de 'sabio'), sin-<u>tien</u>-do, <u>pie</u>, <u>ries</u>-go, <u>lue</u>-go, <u>fui</u>-
mos, se-<u>páis</u>, <u>hay</u>.

Page 250

6 *Carta de Luisito*:
Querida Susana: El otro día en casa de tu madre
cuando ella tomaba el **té** y **tú** buscabas el CD, te
miré a los ojos y, buf, fue genial. Para **mí** eres la chica
más estupenda que he visto en mi vida. No **sé**, eres
fantástica... ¿Vienes este domingo a patinar conmigo? Tengo unos patines nuevos. **Aquéllos** que te gustaban tanto se rompieron. Si quieres venir, me mandas un sms. Pon **sólo** una palabra: **sí**. Y entonces yo
estaré muy contento porque no pasaré la horrible
tarde del domingo solo. Luis.

Diario de Susana:
Querido diario: Hace muchos días que no te escribo.
El domingo pasado salí con Luis y, bueno, fue un poco
rollo. **Él** no habló casi nada y como yo hablo tanto, no
sé qué pensar... ¿Se aburrió? ¿Se divirtió? No **sé**... Me
escuchó, eso sí, pero no **sé** si me escuchó con ganas
(yo a veces no escucho mucho si algo no me interesa
mucho). Ah, Luis tiene unos patines nuevos... Me gustan mucho más **éstos** que los otros que tenía antes...
Éstos son mucho más chulos... Pero yo a **aquéllos** les
tenía cariño... Y el final, fue horrible... Sobre todo
cuando **él** me dijo: "Susana, **tú** a **mí** me gustas mucho,
y yo, ¿yo te gusto a ti?"... Y yo le dije: "¿**Tú** a **mí**?" Y
entonces me puse muy nerviosa, cogí mis patines y
me fui... Si le gusto, volverá... ¿Verdad que **sí**?

Thematic index

A: 192, 195
contraction with the definite article (*al*): 30, 192
with a person as direct object (DO) : 68, 192
with an indirect object (IO): 68, 90, 192
with personal pronouns: 68, 70, 73, 85, 90
A la derecha / izquierda (de): 201
Accents:
on verb tenses:
Condicional simple: 146
Futuro: 139, 140
Imperativo: 174
Imperfecto de subjuntivo: 154
Presente de indicativo: 104, 105, 107
Presente de subjuntivo: 151, 152
Pretérito imperfecto de indicativo: 124, 125
Pretérito indefinido: 115, 116, 117
see also: written accents
tilde: 246
see also: written accents
Accusative (DO): 68
Adjective: 23-28
absolute superlative (-ísimo/-a...): 223
agreement with the noun: 25
gender: 23-24
ending in -*ista*: 23
ending in -or: 23
ending in consonant: 23
ending in stressed vowel + -n: 23
ending in vowel: 23
formation of the feminine: 23, 24
nationality or origin: 23, 24
single form for both genders: 23
mejor, peor, mayor, menor: 223
number: 24
forming the plural: 24
plural ending in -*es*: 24
plural ending in -*s*: 24

singular ending in consonant: 24
singular ending in vowel: 24
participle: 101, 102
position:
after a noun: 26, 45
before a noun: 26, 27, 62
possessives: 43, 45
shortened forms (gran, buen, primer, tercer...): 28, 63
uses: 23, 26, 27
after a noun: 26
before a noun: 26, 27
with quantifiers: 66
¿Adónde?: 214
Adverb:
absolute superlative (-ísimo/-a...): 223
ending in -*mente*: 223
gerund: 99
written accents on adverbs ending in -*mente*: 248
Agreement:
in comparisons with *el/la mismo/-a, tanto/-a...*: 210
In exclamations with *cuánto, cuánta...*: 216, 217
in questions with *cuál, cuáles...*: 210, 211, 213
in questions with *cuánto, cuánta...*: 208
in questions with *quién, quiénes...*: 210
of adjective: 25, 225
of articles: 30
of cardinal numbers: 56, 57, 58, 59
of demonstratives: 37, 39, 40
of indefinite articles: 50, 52, 54
of ordinal numbers: 62
of participles and adjectives with *ser* and *estar*: 102, 177, 178
of participles used as adjectives: 102
of participles with *tener*: 102
of possessives: 43, 45, 47
of quantifiers: 64, 65, 66
subject and verb, the infinitive as

subject: 97
In opinion-expressing constructions: 90
the subject of the infinitive: 98
the subject of the subordinate verb: 159, 168
with grammatical persons: 43, 96
with the noun:
Ahora (mismo): 188
Al final (de): 203
Al fondo (de): 203
Al lado (de): 201
Al principio (de): 203
Al: 30, 192
Algo: see indefinites: 52
Alguien: see indefinites: 52
Algún, alguno, see indefinites: 50
Alguna vez (algunas veces...): 113, 120, 126
Alphabet: 242
relation between writing and pronunciation: 242-245
Alrededor (de): 201
Antes de (que): 203, 236
Antes: 123, 137, 138
Aquel, aquello...: see demonstratives
Articles: 30-36
agreement with nouns: 30
special cases: 30
contraction (*al, del*): 30, 192
forms: 30
forms of the definite article (*él, la, los, las*): 30
forms of the indefinite article (*un, una, unos, unas, uno*): 30
uses: 31, 33, 34
Ø zero article with nouns, countable and uncountable nouns: 33
definite article instead of the possessive: 49, 88
in reflexive constructions: 88
with the indefinite articles *otro, otra...*: 54
with the verb *haber* (hay, había,

295